Arts & Crafts
for the classroom

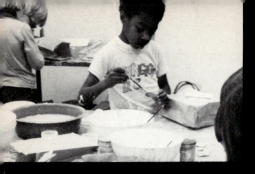

Arts &
for the

Earl W. Linderman
Marlene M. Linderman
Arizona State University

2nd edition

Crafts
classroom

Macmillan Publishing Company
New York

Collier Macmillan Publishers
London

*To the Artistic Spirit
in Each of Us*

Copyright © 1984, Macmillan Publishing Company, a division of
Macmillan, Inc.

Printed in the United States of America

Earlier edition (s), entitled Crafts for the Classroom
copyright © 1977
by Macmillan Publishing Co., Inc.

Macmillan Publishing Company
866 Third Avenue, New York, New York 10022

Collier Macmillan Canada, Inc.

Library of Congress Cataloging in Publication Data

Linderman, Earl W.
  Arts and crafts for the classroom.

  Rev. ed. of: Crafts for the classroom. c1977.
  Includes bibliographies and index.
  1. Handicraft—Study and teaching. I. Linderman,
Marlene M. II. Title.
TT150.L56 1984   372.5′044   83-698
ISBN 0-02-370860-3

Printing: 7 8   Year: 8 9 0 1 2

ISBN   0-02-370860-3

Preface

An artistic object is a combined product of the hand, the eye, and the mind. There is evidence of man's instinctive need to create and to form with his hands throughout the history of civilization. Early man was concerned with the utility of what he created. His art forms were used for dress, for cooking and eating implements, for shelter and tools, and for recreation and ritual practices.

Arts and crafts are a universal bond and language among all cultures. This book is for all those want to explore, discover, and grow through art. We hope that the book will assist classroom teachers who seek to guide and inspire the artistic spirit in the young.

Humans are the only creatures who have the unique abilities to create, express ideas, and thus reveal through a personal search their inner spirit. Arts and crafts help to uncover that spirit.

It is through intense perception and experience that we are able to enrich concepts for all natural and man-made forms. Teachers need to search actively for the most appropriate means by which children can learn an arts foundation. Through arts and crafts, we can make our perceptions, thoughts, and feelings communicate ideas in artistic form. The creative teacher should spark the student's curiosity and desire to search through to the fullest expansion of his or her imagination.

Through the examples of arts and crafts presented in the text, teachers can comprehend developmental stages and sequential objectives in a student's growth. They will also learn some of the skills needed for doing arts and crafts and how to evaluate the final results of their own and their students' efforts.

This second edition emphasizes the importance and expands the scope of the art curriculum. Creative development through art involves the total individual. This refers to development of artistic skills, awareness and appreciation of natural and man-made objects, and an awareness of our rich cultural heritage. It is to the formation of an aesthetically aware and expressive student that we dedicate this book along with the joy and satisfaction that is derived from art as a creative part of life.

The authors, as practicing artists and teachers, have researched the art concepts and skills discussed and have visited classrooms, art studios, and museums to obtain the best historical and contemporary illustrations available.

The text begins with the major objectives for arts and crafts. This includes perceptual, cultural, artistic, and creative experiences, and also communication, the place of art in the community, evaluation of art growth, and teacher strategies as objectives.

Chapter Two discusses the developmental stages and sequential objectives for the individual student at various growth levels. An important area discusses both the exceptional child and the physically, mentally, and emotionally handicapped child. This chapter also discusses integrating art with the other learning areas, as well as possible careers in art.

Chapter Three is an in-depth approach to the two-dimensional aspects of art: design, drawing, painting, and lettering. The subsequent chapters deal with paper, puppets, dyes, cloth, yarns, clay, sculpture, jewelry, printmaking, and photography. As before, we stress concepts and skills, always to be considered in relation to perception, growth levels, historical and contemporary cultures. The goal is for the student to heighten his ability to evaluate and form individual aesthetic judgments.

Arts and crafts are a timeless and unlimited aesthetic journey of discovery for the student and the instructor. Teachers can use this book to develop a unique, individualized curriculum. We encourage each of you to adapt the material presented within these pages to the personal approaches you feel are essential to classroom teaching. We are certain that your awareness, your enthusiasm, and your creative potential will emerge as you participate and interact with your classes in the joy of creating art.

The authors wish to thank the following individuals and organizations for their contribution to the first edition: Arizona State University Library; Bob Richardson; Carlagay; Dintenfass Gallery, New York; Dr. Edna Gilbert, Mesa Public Schools, Arizona; Dr. William E. Arnold; Eastman Kodak; Eric Pollitzer; Exxon Company; Gabriel Weisberg, The Cleveland Museum of Art, Department of Art History and Educa-

An artistic object is a combined product of the hand, the eye, and the mind. There is evidence of man's instinctive need to create and to form with his hands throughout the history of civilization. Early man was concerned with the utility of what he created. His art forms were used for dress, for cooking and eating implements, for shelter and tools, and for recreation and ritual practices.

Arts and crafts are a universal bond and language among all cultures. This book is for all those want to explore, discover, and grow through art. We hope that the book will assist classroom teachers who seek to guide and inspire the artistic spirit in the young.

Humans are the only creatures who have the unique abilities to create, express ideas, and thus reveal through a personal search their inner spirit. Arts and crafts help to uncover that spirit.

It is through intense perception and experience that we are able to enrich concepts for all natural and man-made forms. Teachers need to search actively for the most appropriate means by which children can learn an arts foundation. Through arts and crafts, we can make our perceptions, thoughts, and feelings communicate ideas in artistic form. The creative teacher should spark the student's curiousity and desire to search through to the fullest expansion of his or her imagination.

Through the examples of arts and crafts presented in the text, teachers can comprehend developmental stages and sequential objectives in a student's growth. They will also learn some of the skills needed for doing arts and crafts and how to evaluate the final results of their own and their students' efforts.

This second edition emphasizes the importance and expands the scope of the art curriculum. Creative development through art involves the total individual. This refers to development of artistic skills, awareness and appreciation of natural and man-made objects, and an awareness of our rich cultural heritage. It is to the formation of an aesthetically aware and expressive student that we dedicate this book along with the joy and satisfaction that is derived from art as a creative part of life.

The authors, as practicing artists and teachers, have researched the art concepts and skills discussed and have visited classrooms, art studios, and museums to obtain the best historical and contemporary illustrations available.

The text begins with the major objectives for arts and crafts. This includes perceptual, cultural, artistic, and creative experiences, and also communication, the place of art in the community, evaluation of art growth, and teacher strategies as objectives.

Chapter Two discusses the developmental stages and sequential objectives for the individual student at various growth levels. An important area discusses both the exceptional child and the physically, mentally, and emotionally handicapped child. This chapter also discusses integrating art with the other learning areas, as well as possible careers in art.

Chapter Three is an in-depth approach to the two-dimensional aspects of art: design, drawing, painting, and lettering. The subsequent chapters deal with paper, puppets, dyes, cloth, yarns, clay, sculpture, jewelry, printmaking, and photography. As before, we stress concepts and skills, always to be considered in relation to perception, growth levels, historical and contemporary cultures. The goal is for the student to heighten his ability to evaluate and form individual aesthetic judgments.

Arts and crafts are a timeless and unlimited aesthetic journey of discovery for the student and the instructor. Teachers can use this book to develop a unique, individualized curriculum. We encourage each of you to adapt the material presented within these pages to the personal approaches you feel are essential to classroom teaching. We are certain that your awareness, your enthusiasm, and your creative potential will emerge as you participate and interact with your classes in the joy of creating art.

The authors wish to thank the following individuals and organizations for their contribution to the first edition: Arizona State University Library; Bob Richardson; Carlagay; Dintenfass Gallery, New York; Dr. Edna Gilbert, Mesa Public Schools, Arizona; Dr. William E. Arnold; Eastman Kodak; Eric Pollitzer; Exxon Company; Gabriel Weisberg, The Cleveland Museum of Art, Department of Art History and Education; Helen Cordero; Jean Stange; Joan Bessom; KOOL TV, CBS, Phoenix; Kunsthistorisches Museum, Vienna; Lenore Davis; Linda Deck; Madelaine Shellaby, University Art Museum, University of California, Berkeley; Margaret Burton; Maurice Grossman; Nancy Hartner; Nancy and Renny Mitchell; Mary Lou Mathes; Patsy Lowry; Paulo Soleri; Ivan Pintar; Perry Wray; Pierre Matisse Gallery, New York; Robin Kline; Roger Buchanan; Rachel Ellis, Scottsdale Public Schools; The Art Institute of Chicago; The Brooklyn Museum; The Hand and the Spirit Gallery, Scottsdale; The Heard Museum, Phoenix; The Shop of Art, Tempe; Thomas Eckert; Yvonne Lange, Museum of New Mexico, Santa Fe. A special thank you is due to the many artists, teachers, and students who graciously gave of their talents and examples.

The authors wish to thank the following organizations and individuals who contributed to the second edition: Betsy Benjamin-Murray; Berkeley Museum of Art; Ralph Bethancourt; Pam Castano; Susan Coffrey and Norma Hand, Scottsdale Fine Arts Commission, Scottsdale; Molly Cowgill, Ken Goldstrom, Zella Harris, Julia Hill, Anne Pixley, Joanne Rapp, Phil Van Voost, Laura Wilensky of The Hand and The Spirit Crafts Gallery, Scottsdale; Nancy Robb Dunst; Carol Eckert; Fine Arts Gallery of San Diego; Barbara Herberholz; Suzanne Koltz-Reilly; Tom Moore; Louise Nevelson; Phoenix Art Museum; Phoenix Chamber of Commerce; Santa Barbara Museum of Art; Fritz Scholder, Marilyn Butler Fine Arts, Scottsdale; Scottsdale Center for the Arts; Jon Sharer, "Children's Art Workshop," Arizona State University; Robin Swanson; Victor Verbalitis. A very special thank you goes to our children, Bill, Mark, Heather, Gwen, and Cheryl.

E.W.L.
M.M.L.

Correction(s) for the Color Form Between Pages 266–267.

The page references given in the figure captions are incorrect. They should read as follows:

Figures 1–2: See pages 138–140.
Figure 3: See page 48.
Figure 4: See page 200.
Figure 5: See page 202.
Figure 6: See page 215.
Figure 7: See page 228.
Figure 8: See pages 251–252.
Figure 9: See page 261.
Figure 10: See page 327.
Figure 11: See page 338.
Figure 12: See page 375.
Figure 13: See page 401.
Figure 14: See pages 84–86.

Contents

3

*Design, Drawing, Painting,
and Lettering*   **61**

4

Creating with Paper   *121*

5

Puppets   *155*

Dyes, Tie-Dye, and Batik 183

7 *Yarns, Needles, and Cloth* 213

Dyes, Tie-Dye, and Batik   183

6

7

Yarns, Needles, and Cloth   213

Weaving and Macrame 257

8

Pottery and Modeling 309

9

10

Sculpture: Constructing, Carving, and Casting   *347*

Jewelry and Adornment 399

11

12   *Fundamentals of Printmaking* 447

Photography 481

13

1

Arts & Crafts as Aesthetic and Cultural Experience

In the face of mechanistic change in a technological age, man is losing his ability to perceive, feel, and create. However, personal identity and individual vision can be renewed by building sensory, artistic, and cultural awareness in students.

In both the self-contained and open classroom, arts and crafts experiences emphasize humanistic and aesthetic expression for all students, each at his or her own level of ability.

Crafts are close to the earth and to natural things. Art *as experience* vigorously inquires into the aesthetic nature of man. In this respect, art is bonded to human conditions and is a reflection of the cultural fiber of society. For example, clay pertains to containers and dishware, wood to furniture and architecture, fabrics to clothing and textiles, and metal to tools, jewelry, and adornment. These are traditional media which have been formed in countless ways throughout history. Today, numerous additional media are being utilized: papers, plastics, synthetic yarns, glass, and found materials from innumerable sources. In school curricula we are able to incorporate the traditional and newer arts media. In the broader sense, we can think of media for classrooms as any materials that can be manipulated by children ultimately to form an aesthetically pleasing product. Arts and crafts media need not be restricted to only traditional materials, where prohibitive costs often limit supply. Excellent programs can be conducted with scrap or natural articles that are available in the environment. These articles include pebbles, pieces of driftwood, leaves, twigs, and a variety of remnants from man-made products. When these materials are combined with whatever resources the school can offer and good teachers, a crafts program is born.

Students delight in opportunities to work creatively with various highly manipulative media. An involvement with arts and crafts enables children to invent, construct, and express ideas without hesitation over the type of media being used. Often, students who work *only* on flat surfaces with pencil, paint, or crayon will hesitate in their expression because of the discrepancy between intellect and skill in rendering their personal image, which is openly revealed when they draw or paint. As the student sees his own image revealed in his drawings, especially at the intermediate grade level and higher, he often tends to close down the creative thrust of this thinking. He simply cannot take the jolt of seeing his figurative expression, which seems so inferior to his intellectual level. On the other hand, experiences with papier-mâché, weaving, found sculpture, clay, metal work, and various other crafts processes tend to open up creative thinking because the personal image is not as apparent.

Art opportunities are also direct adventures in understand-

1–1 *Crafts are close to the earth. The Navajo women pictured here shear, spin, and dye their own wool. The upright loom, the designs, and the cultural traditions, all invented long ago, are practiced today as they have been for generations. (The top photo is courtesy of the Phoenix Chamber of Commerce.)*

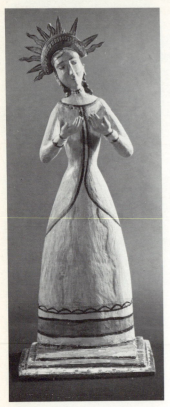

1–2 *Artifacts reveal our instinctive need to create with our hands. All cultures share the universal bond and language of crafts. "La Dolorosa" by Miguel Herrera from Arroyo Hondo, a carved polychromed wood santo, 1870. (Courtesy of Museum of New Mexico, Santa Fe, New Mexico.)*

ing visual and tactile forms, as the media used are both manipulative and three dimensional. With crafts media one can, if he or she chooses, start directly with the material by pushing and pulling it until inspiration comes. In this approach, design skills are awakened through the actual handling of the material. By starting directly with the media, the child can push, build, squeeze, cut, tie, glue, saw, carve, sand, weave, and otherwise shape ideas to come. Where drawing and painting deal with the illusion of reality on a flat surface, crafts is spatial reality from the start.

Another interesting aspect of art media for the classroom is that almost any material selected by an imaginative teacher or child can be transformed into an aesthetic product through thought, planning, and imagination.

Objectives for Arts and Crafts

Creating with art tools and materials, discussing what artists have created (historical and contemporary), and seeking aesthetic form in one's environment are means by which students can build aesthetic understanding.

The three major objectives of art teaching in the classroom are (1) perceptual experience, (2) cultural experience, and (3) artistic experience.

PERCEPTUAL EXPERIENCE

Perceptual experience is the increased awakening and use of all of our senses. Sharpening sensory awareness is the first stage in any discovery process. Our senses are the receptors that are fundamental to the eventual processes of thought, invention, imagination, and creative expression. A child who has a rich perception of his world will possess a detailed backlog of stored experiences that can be utilized in his art work. Building perceptual skills means seeking the detailed subtleties of every experience in taking in, through all of our senses, as many segments of data as possible without immediately categorizing and otherwise cutting off the flow of what we experience. To develop varied perceptions means that we must go beyond the recognition stage of discovering.

We can enrich our understanding of man and his culture by increasing our ability to perceive the many aspects of what is natural and what is man-made in our world. Sensory experience refers to visual sensitivity, or close observation, rather than merely to looking; tactile sensitivity is learning to discriminate through touch rather than merely touching; auditory sensitivity is sharpening our ability to listen rather

4

1–3 *Intense self-identification in experiencing art develops an appreciative eye. Crafts as art heritage offer opportunities to gather facts and to practice making discriminating art judgments. (Courtesy of Department of Art History and Education, the Cleveland Museum of Art.)*

than merely hearing; gustatory sensitivity is discovering differences in taste rather than merely eating; olfactory sensitivity is increasing one's sense of smell rather than merely being aware that something has an odor. Many oustanding classroom teachers constantly strive to improve their perceptual awareness in order to make their life an ongoing adventure in living and creating.

The following objectives will suggest possibilities for increasing perceptual and creative awareness:

1. Encourage individual directions and the development of personal imagery for each student.
2. Encourage openness, or the taking in of fresh ideas and imaginative approaches, whenever the opportunity is there. Emphasize invention, unusual and original possibilities, and enthusiasm for one's own efforts as well as those of others through the sharing of perceptions and artistic ideas.
3. Allow for experimentation, trial and error, and searching in both ideas and media. Encourage a continual interaction between students and their craftwork.

4. Invent perceptual games to awaken the students' potential to observe, feel, listen, taste, and smell. For example, in how many ways can an apple be expressed? (It can be expressed in media with clay, papier-mâché, cut paper, collage, drawing, painting, or printing. An apple can be presented as large as a wall; in a still life; in outline; in color; in black and white; cut open; on a tree; on a transparency; in a bin at a market; or with a bite taken from it.)

5. Challenge the child's mind so that he utilizes what he has perceived. Keep him thinking about creative possibilities, for art begins in the mind. Keep the flow of ideas coming through the continual experiencing of many aspects of the world. Encourage variations on each theme—new and fresh ways of seeing, feeling, and expressing.

CULTURAL EXPERIENCE

Cultural experience is the study and understanding of the art forms of cultures, both past and present. The study of arts and crafts as art heritage enables us to understand the nature of man. In most countries, past achievements have served as the derivative base for contemporary art forms. This is true of American culture. The American people are, after all, an

1–4 *Practice in creating enables the artist and student to improve their skills in specific art media. Helen Cordero, an Indian potter from Cochiti Pueblo, utilizes traditional concepts and processes with clay that date back to prehistoric times. (Courtesy of The Hand And The Spirit Crafts Gallery, Scottsdale, Arizona.)*

amalgamation of peoples from around the globe. With this immigration of people from many lands has come a great diversity of subcultures and craft forms. Until recently, the most visible art forms in the United States had been from European traditions, but presently the traditions of American Indians, Black Americans, Mexican Americans, and Asian Americans are being made visible.

Arts and crafts also provide excellent opportunities to study past cultures or aspects of them in depth. For example, in teaching stitchery as a craft form, one can discuss the creation of the Bayeux Tapestry. This tapestry, which is actually an embroidery that was misnamed, was created to commemorate the events surrounding the conquest of England by William the Conqueror of Normandy, in the historic Battle of Hastings in A.D. 1066. The embroidery is made from woolen threads sewn on a linen background; it is 231 feet in length (almost three fourths the length of a football field) and approximately 20 inches wide. What is remarkable about this fine art piece is that it has survived for more than nine hundred years and is still in excellent condition. It is the only surviving piece of fabric art of its kind and size from the Middle Ages. It reveals the expert craftsmanship that created exquisite pieces of embroidery and woven art during that period. What makes the piece so interesting, aside from its historical value, is the magnitude of the work itself. Sewn into the embroidery are 626 human figures, 190 horses or

1–5 *Art learning takes place through intense perceptual and cognitive means. After a crafts unit on Early American quilts, first-graders prepared individual panels with permanent felt-tip pens and the panels were then sewed together. (Courtesy of Arizona Republic, Phoenix, Arizona.)*

1–6 *Cultural awareness is the study of art forms of both past and present cultures. A detail of the Bayeux Tapestry. (Courtesy of Walter Curtin, Time-Life Picture Agency.)*

mules, 35 dogs, 506 other unnamed animals, 37 ships, 33 buildings, and 37 trees. (See Figure 1-6.)

Relating this sort of information to stitchery as craft helps to bring art in culture to life. It provides a frame of reference for the relationship of the artist to his culture. A logical next step pertaining to this period in history is to discover what crafts people in other countries were doing. In 1066, the approximate year of the Bayeux Tapestry, what was being created in Mexico, Africa, North America, and China? Asking questions that will uncover historical developments that ran parallel with artistic endeavors makes our art heritage meaningful and relevant to children and the curriculum.

Folk Art

Many ancient cultures utilized art to record and chronicle their achievements. Art was also a basic part of their religious and civil ceremonies and of other aspects relating to their society. Art from the past that has survived also reveals that man has always created beautiful forms for his fulfillment and enjoyment, apparently the result of a continuous aesthetic instinct. This need to express visually is evident in folk art, a universal form of craft expression.

Folk art is made up of art forms created by unschooled artists. Folk art is closely linked to crafts, for the materials used are available in the artist's locale: pinecones, leather, wood, bark, grass, metal, fruit, eggs, iron, bones, cloth, and manufactured parts. The folk artist is, thus, a resourceful and innovative person. Folk art includes dolls, toys, clothes, hats, masks, spoons, cooking utensils, religious symbols, furniture and shelter parts, personal items for adornment, and hundreds of other items.

Art made by folk artists is an international expression. These beautiful, crafted forms are a part of the religious, moral, musical, and recreational customs of the respective cultures in which they are made. They are both simple and complex and serve to foster traditions that identify the world's cultures.

Cultural awareness, then, can refer both to the study of arts and crafts as history and to appreciation through analysis or art judgment.

ARTISTIC EXPERIENCE

Artistic experience will increase our understanding and skill in using art media and in appreciating the work of other artists. Artistic experience deals with aesthetic content, media skills, and art judgment. It follows the data produced by perceptual experience.

Aesthetic content refers to our analysis of what other artists have created.

Media skills refers to an increase in our ability to perform in a medium such as paint, clay, wood, cardboard, paper, and so on.

Art judgment refers to our ability to make informed observations regarding the artisitic properties of a product.

In gaining artistic experience, we need to work toward developing our artistic eye, for the artist is our model in learning about art. We also need to develop the eye of the critic, for he is our model in making judgments about art. Artistic experience, then, is the combination of the creative eye and the cultured eye. When we teach students to develop skills and to comprehend what a pleasing art/craft form is, we have increased their artistic experience.

Arts and crafts enable each student to grasp the artistic elements of his experience. He does this by observing closely, touching, listening, creating, and evaluating. With arts and crafts as the base, the student can develop a vocabulary for discussing the arts of any historical period. He can study the work of professional artists and observe their role in society, both past and present. With his knowledge, he can discuss differences between pleasing artistic forms and what, in fact,

1–7 The visiting artist in the classroom can bring a new dimension of understanding to art growth. Lenore Davis says, "I have concerned myself with carefully constructing human figure ideas from childhood and adult observations; making soft (toy) objects of fabric and stuffing which invite touching, holding, wearing, and even thinking. The form and idea are the important thing; a cavity is sewn of dye-painted cloth, to be swelled to life with stuffing and perhaps embellished further." "Horse with 7 Riders," dye painting on velveteen, 28 inches. (Courtesy of The Hand And The Spirit Crafts Gallery, Scottsdale, Arizona.)

constitutes them. With practice in looking and analyzing, he learns to make informed art judgments.

Arts and crafts enable the student to perceive the beauty of his natural environment. Many of the craft materials used are organic. By working with and searching for pleasing visual and tactile forms in both nature and man-made objects, the student learns how to be more selective and reduce visual chaos.

Aesthetic Content

In every area of the arts, there have been artists who have excelled and thus made notable contributions to their particular field. In discussing and discovering the contributions of these artists, exemplary models are established for students. Innovators in the art fields should be studied just as the lives and works of presidents, statesmen, politicians, and figures in medicine, music, and sports are studied.

Like other subject areas, the arts has its own characteristic nomenclature. For centuries, artists and craftspeople have utilized the formal art *elements* of line, shape, form, texture, pattern, color, and space to distinguish an aesthetic form from a chaotic one. Creating an arts/crafts piece necessitates the correct, intuitive use of these formal elements. Artists and students alike incorporate the elements of art into their work by applying the *principles* of balance, harmony, rhythm, proportion, unity, and organization. Class discussion of art elements and principles, as well as the actual working and building with media, should include the language of arts and crafts. Teachers should regularly include the study of arts and crafts terms in the classroom curriculum. (See Chapter 3, "Design, Drawing, Painting, and Lettering.")

Further content for consideration should include:

The medium used
The function of the form (if any)
The culture within which it was produced
The subject or literary qualities

In responding to works of art, such as painting, pottery, modeling, or any other art product, you can plan your class discussion and participation around three basic aspects. They are a work's (1) *responsive attributes*, (2) *intellectual attributes*, and (3) *artistic attributes*.

1–8 *Traditional art forms in culture are integrated with religious and civil life. This painted wooden African mask from the Bobo tribe of Upper Volta is expressively articulated and suggests both mood and feeling. (Courtesy of the Art Institute of Chicago.)*

1. Responsive attributes deal with the *mood,* or *feeling,* of an art form. The questions to be asked in this category are: How do you like the mood of this work of art? How does it make you feel? What does it make you think of? Was the artist imaginative? Would you do it the same way? How would so and so do it? Is the creation a successful one? Do you like it? Why do you like it? An important point to remember is to encourage children to verbalize and

explain why they feel as they do. We want to move children to give reasons explaining why they have made specific comments. We need to help children crystallize their thinking by getting them to go beyond surface impressions when they respond. As adults, we are prone to make statements such as "Well, if I like it, that's all that matters," and expect the matter to be closed; at that point, so is the mind. Stimulate children to think by asking them why and encouraging them to dig deeper. This is the way to begin sensitizing children to beauty in art. We must look at and discuss art in order to grow.

2. Intellectual attributes are the content, ideas, subject, or the literary qualities of a piece of art. The questions to be asked here are: What was the artist trying to say? Is there a story here? What is it? Is this a realistic story? Is it an abstract form? What do we mean by mirror realism? What do we mean by abstraction? Has this artist said something with art materials that applies to you and me? How would you have solved it?

3. Artistic attributes are the compositional or design, or media aspects, of the work of art. The questions to be asked here are: How is it done? That is, what medium is used, how is it composed, and which artistic aspects of composition, technique, arrangement, working process, or other technical consideration are apparent? What, for example, is transparent watercolor? Who knows what acrylic is? Have you ever seen anything like this? Where did the artist begin his work? Could you improve on it? Is the work organized? How can you see that it is organized?

Do not ask these questions quickly, one after the other. Allow the students to consider each question asked carefully. Ask questions sequentially. Mix your questions with pieces of information that are geared carefully to lead the children to the point where they can learn and make a discovery (which is exactly your purpose here). Remember, when talking to children:

1. Challenge their imagination.
2. Challenge their intellect.
3. Challenge their artistic sense.

Media Skills

In order to grow in their appreciation of art, children need to learn the specific art skills required for each medium. Art skills in this sense refer to the process of making: how to contruct a loom, how to knot in macramé, how to hold and use tools for carving or modeling, or how to cut and glue. Each medium has definite procedures that must be learned in order to achieve success. Some media will require only minimum technical preparation or know-how, whereas others will be more complex, such as printmaking. To improve in a skill requires a good deal of practice. As in anything of value, one must give of himself wholeheartedly in order to achieve the success for which he strives. Each time art is practiced, new understanding is developed.

Art Judgment

Part of any arts program is the discussion by students and teachers of the arts and crafts done by themselves and others, including classwork. Opportunities to ask questions dealing with what makes form pleasing are needed. Students need to discuss the elements and principles of art in relation to their own efforts as well. They need to be able to critically assess, in a positive way, what they have made.

Encouraging children to be discriminating in their art judgments will enrich their artistic vision. Much of what we enjoy as adults has its roots in childhood experiences.

Criteria for Judging Arts and Crafts

In making art judgments, the following insights are helpful in getting started:

1. What medium has the artist used? What effect does the forming process have on the work?
2. What do you see and/or feel? This involves subject matter, an emotional reaction to a craft work, and a formal evaluation of the elements of art.
3. Does the artist express himself in a unique manner? How is this piece different from others you have seen? Compare this work with other work done in the same period.
4. Does the art product tell you when the artist lived? How does it give you this information?
5. What is the artist trying to say in his work? Does the artist suggest new ways of seeing something in the environment and/or new ways to understand other people or cultures?
6. How has the artist used his tools to form the piece?
7. Does this work of art have a place in history, or as a part of our heritage? Is there a cultural influence on the work?
8. Does the craft form function for a purpose?
9. What makes a work of art great?
10. What makes an artist great?

Arts and Crafts as Creative Experience

Arts and crafts learning can fire the imagination of students, for richness in thinking springs from practicing a continuously flowing stream of ideas. Seeking out and perceiving the subtle details of experiences provide data that can be transformed into original art products. Stretching the imagination stretches the mind. A willingness to try more unusual possibilities for ideas and materials often can push artistic discovery to new boundaries.

Arts and crafts encourage students to seek new ideas, to keep an endless input of possibilites germinating until an inspirational and unique result occurs. Encouraging students to become fluent in the language of art, open in their appreciation, and selective in their awareness of ideas for a project is basic to art growth.

Arts and crafts aid in developing originality of thought when the student expresses his thinking with the emphasis on the originality of his or her expression. Originality is one of the key areas of artistic growth. Do not use kits or stereotyped solutions; they stifle originality.

In the classroom, the teacher can encourage originality as well as feelings of worth and success by fostering a "let's try it" atmosphere that emphasizes search and inquiry and an attitude of adventure in imagining and inventing. Keep the achievement level of the students reachable. The achievement standards for a sixth-grader are far different than those for a first-grader. (See Chapter 2, "Developmental Stages and Objectives.")

Encourage the students to take creative risks without worrying about mistakes. This opens creative thinking and lets the student know that there is no fear of failure if he tries and experiments. Offer constructive criticism rather than being extremely critical. Teachers can encourage success and creativity by praising sincere effort and originality.

Arts and crafts teach students greater perception in that all of life's experiences become the fuel for creativity. This means that the eyes are utilized more fully for observing, the ears for listening, the fingers and bodies for feeling, the nose for smelling, and the mouth for tasting. Perceptual awareness is essential to creative growth and to experiencing a fuller, richer life-style.

1–9 *Crafts skills and experiences can be related to art forms from other cultures. Inspired by African masks and legends, these fifth-grade students created original masks and costumes and performed impromptu plays. (Courtesy of William E. Arnold.)*

Communication: A Visual and Tactile System

One of the greatest merits of art experiences is their value as nonverbal—that is, visual and tactile—communication. All language is not necessarily in spoken form. For example, when a child creates a product in crafts, he expresses an idea that he conceived. The product is an extension of himself. He looks at this work and says, "This is what I have done. This was my idea and creation." In examining his own efforts, he reinforces himself to continue to give out and express further ideas in visual media.

Art is also communication between the child and his teacher, the child and his parents, and the child and his classmates. The process and resulting product make possible searching, analysis, feedback, discussion, comparison, and evaluation. The entire class can discuss and share ideas pertaining to what is created in a particular medium. In sharing these ideas, communication takes place.

Community Vision

As a result of art experiences in seeing things perceptively and artistically, in building, in creating, and in forming, the student has a unique opportunity to translate his aesthetic vision to his community and its surroundings. The artistic sense that is nurtured can eventually crystallize in improved products for the society in which we live. An enlightened community can carry on educational programs that will consider the design of our homes, parks, shopping centers, and cities.

Units and models for "Redesigning Your Community" might be a starting point in a classroom program. These would include discussions and analyses of the design, function, and purpose of shelters, roadways, parks, and housing; environmental considerations; aesthetic needs and their justification; and study of several examples of architects of the past and present. (See Figure 1-10.)

Structure and Flow in the Curriculum

In planning for a curriculum in the classroom, establish specific objectives to be achieved (structure) and procedures (flow) to be followed.

1–10 *"Arcosanti Model" by Paolo Soleri. This hexahedron represents a future one-mile-high city environment. The model is made of lightweight plastic materials that can be assembled easily into architectural systems. (Photo by Ivan Pintar.)*

1. Present *sequentially* planned lessons to the class. Organize each lesson carefully, and seek to meet the goals you establish.
2. Discuss the aesthetic merits of original work in ceramics, weaving, macramé, sculpture, wood, painting, drawing, etc. Encourage students to evaluate and form judgments concerning their artwork as well as that of others. Students need to be able to communicate in verbal and nonverbal ways.
3. Develop a classroom center where children can bring in any objects they consider beautiful that they discover and want to share.
4. Provide an exhibit space where original work can be attractively displayed. Local galleries or friends can often lend examples. Other sources are exchange exhibits from other grades or from other schools and private collections.

1–11 *Visits to crafts centers, artists' studios, and museums are excellent sources for crafts learning. These children are watching a demonstration of weaving skills. Finished pieces are in the background.*

This project is an excellent opportunity to encourage a cultural awareness of folk and community art.

5. Invite guest artists to the classroom for demonstrations of their work. Encourage the students to ask questions about the art form as well as the expressive intent of the artist. The student wants to know who the artist is, what she or he produces, and how he or she makes a work of art. A class visit to an artist's studio is also a valuable experience. The art teacher is the model of the artist in the school.

6. Start a file collection of examples of beautiful and interesting things. Classifications might range from crafts in other cultures to crafts in American culture in various historical periods.

7. Encourage each child to make an arts-learning notebook. Information that the children learn can be added to the notebook. The sections of the notebook might be divided into media, art materials they have tried, artists they have learned about, art in history, and so on.

8. Encourage each child to be resourceful with materials and media.

EVALUATING GROWTH

Evaluating growth through arts and crafts experiences should be a basic part of any classroom program. A sequential program in crafts teaching will provide step-by-step opportunities for children to increase art skills and art knowledge. In measuring the crafts performance of a student, look for growth in the following areas:

1. Shows increased skill in handling craft tools and materials.
2. Knows the proper use and care of tools.
3. Uses imaginative solutions in expressing ideas, feelings, and experiences.
4. Pushes beyond ordinary or common solutions.
5. Comprehends the formal art elements and how they are part of a work. Develops an arts and crafts vocabulary.
6. Maintains a receptive attitude and is cooperative with others.
7. Completes assignments.
8. Shows improvement in art production.
9. Participates in discussions and exhibits.
10. Projects previously learned skills into future arts or crafts.
11. Is self-motivated, explores, and experiments.
12. Is able to make independent judgments, analyze, synthesize, and evaluate.
13. Participates in group efforts and inquires into various points of view.
14. Has a fundamental knowledge of historical and contemporary subject content.

15. Reaches both student- and teacher-established goals.
16. Evaluate notebooks, portfolios, and projects.
17. Include evaluation of student ideas and efforts through regularly scheduled conferences.

TEACHER STRATEGIES

As we reflect on the teaching of arts and crafts in the classroom, we should consider the following behaviors in establishing our objectives for improving teaching conditions.

The classroom teacher of arts and crafts should:

1. Be an inspiring, positive person.
2. Be informed on content and skills and demonstrate these with confidence and proficiency; be the artist model for the student.
3. Establish specific long-term and short-term objectives within the arts-and-crafts curriculum that can be attained by every child.
4. Have a knowledge of, and be able to meet, the varying needs of children and how they learn and grow and be able to provide facts, concepts, and skills at these various levels of child development.
5. Encourage conditions that stress questioning, good listening, interchange of ideas, and dialogues that are relevant to student interests and levels. Lead the student to the point where he makes his own discoveries.
6. Encourage experimental attitudes, uncommon responses, and self-initiated learning.
7. Encourage feelings of success, self-direction, responsibility, independence, individual ideas and research, varying interests, and various speeds of learning. Have a positive attitude, good rapport with students, and a good sense of humor.
8. Establish disciplinary measures with the students, so that each student realizes what is expected of him.
9. Plan and organize the lesson, be the leader, demonstrate the necessary procedures, integrate art learning to other classroom learning when possible, and relate the role of arts and crafts in past cultures and its appearance in careers today.
10. Establish a dynamic environment for arts and crafts growth that invites imaginative responses and reflects proper attitudes and interests: flexible space arrangements suited to different activity needs and displays related to art and studies in the school and community.
11. Have a broad knowledge of the related arts so that an arts and art-related vocabulary can be taught.
12. Exhibit each student's products at varying times.
13. Provide open-ended situations where a student can respond with his knowledge and skills.

14. Work with students in keeping materials and tools organized.
15. Review and evaluate past objectives and establish future objectives with students.
16. Keep individual folders for students' two-dimensional work and card files (and photos, if possible) of three-dimensional projects.
17. Plan meaningful individual conferences for personal evaluation and class critiques requiring group participation in constructive criticism.

In the following chapters, skills and procedures are presented that are suitable for all levels of the elementary classroom. Some skills will be better suited for primary grades and others for upper elementary grades. However, all arts and crafts can be adapted at all age levels if the creative teacher will present each to his or her class in terms that can challenge students.

Bibliography

ARNHEIM, RUDOLPH. *Visual Thinking.* London: Faber & Faber, Ltd., 1969

BARKAN, MANUEL. *Through Art to Creativity.* Boston: Allyn & Bacon, Inc. 1960.

———.*Foundations of Art Education.* New York: The Ronald Press Company, 1955.

BRITTAIN, W. LAMBERT. *Creativity, Art, and the Young Child.* New York: Macmillan Publishing Company, 1979.

CALIFORNIA STATE BOARD OF EDUCATION. *Art Education Framework: California Public Schools,* Sacramento, Calif., 1971.

COLE, NATALIE ROBINSON. *Children's Art from Deep Down Inside.* New York: the John Day Company, Inc., 1966.

———.*The Arts in the Classroom.* New York: The John Day Company, Inc., 1940.

CONANT, HOWARD. *Art in Education.* Peoria, Ill.: Charles A. Bennett Co., 1959.

———.*Seminar on Elementary and Secondary School: Education in the Visual Arts.* Cooperative Research Project no. V-003. New York: New York University Press, 1965.

———."Season of Decline." In *New Ideas in Art Education,* edited by Gregory Battcock. New York: E. P. Dutton & Co. Inc., 1973.

CONRAD, GEORGE. *The Process of Art Education in the Elementary School.* Englewood Cliffs, N.J.: Prentice-Hall, Inc., 1964.

DE FRANCESCO, ITALO L. *Art Education: Its Means and Ends.* New York: Harper and Row, Publishers, Inc. 1958.

DEWEY, JOHN. *Art As Experience.* New York: Minton, Balch & Co., 1934.

EISNER, ELLIOT. *The Educational Imagination.* New York: Macmillan Publishing Company, 1979.

————, AND DAVID ECKER. *Readings in Art Education.* Waltham, Mass.: Ginn Blaisdell, 1966.

ELSEN, ALBERT E. *Purposes of Art,* 4th ed. New York: Holt, Rinehart and Winston, 1981.

ERDT, MARGARET H. *Teaching Art in the Elementary School.* Rev. ed. New York: Holt, Rinehart and Winston, Inc., 1962.

FELDMAN, EDMUND B. *Becoming Human Through Art.* Englewood Cliffs, N.J.: Prentice-Hall, Inc., 1970.

GIRARD, ALEXANDER, H. *The Magic of a People.* New York: Viking Press, 1968.

GREENBERG, PEARL. *Art and Ideas for Young People.* New York: Van Nostrand Reinhold Co., 1969.

GRIGSBY, J. EUGENE. *Art and Ethics: Backgrounds for Teaching Youth in a Pluralistic Society.* Dubuque, Iowa: William C. Brown Company, Publishers, 1967.

Guidelines for Curriculum Development. St. Ann, Mo.: Cemrel, Inc., 1972.

HARDIMAN, GEORGE, AND THEODORE ZERNICH. *Art Activities for Children.* Englewood Cliffs, N.J.: Prentice-Hall, Inc. 1981.

HERBERHOLZ, DONALD, AND BARBARA HERBERHOLZ. *A Child's Pursuit of Art.* Dubuque, Iowa: William C. Brown Company, Publishers, 1967.

HERBERHOLZ, BARBARA. *Early Childhood Art.* Dubuque, Iowa: William C. Brown Company, Publishers, 1974.

HORN, GEORGE F. *Art for Today's Schools.* Worcester, Mass.: Davis Publications, Inc., 1967.

HUBBARD, GUY, AND MARY ROUSE. *Art 1–6: Meaning, Method, and Media.* Westchester, Ill.: Benefic press, 1973.

HURWITZ, AL, AND STANLEY MADEJA. *The Joyous Vision: A Source Book for Elementary Art Appreciation.* Englewood Cliffs, N.J.: Prentice-Hall, Inc., 1977.

JEFFERSON, BLANCHE. *Teaching Art to Children.* 2nd ed. Boston: Allyn & Bacon, Inc., 1963.

KAUFMAN, IRVING. *Art and Education in Contemporary Culture.* New York: Macmillan Publishing Co., Inc., 1966.

LANSING, KENNETH. *Arts, Artists, and Art Education.* New York: McGraw-Hill Book Company, 1971.

LICHTEN, FRANCIS. *Folk Art Motifs of Pennsylvania.* New York: Dover Publications, Inc. 1976.

LORD, PRISCILLA SAWYER, AND DANIEL J. FOLEY. *The Folk Arts and Crafts of New England.* Philadelphia: Chilton Book Co., 1972.

LINDERMAN, EARL W., AND DONALD W. HERBERHOLZ. *Developing Artistic and Perceptual Awareness: Art Practice in the Elementary Classroom.* 3rd ed. Dubuque, Iowa: William C. Brown Company, Publishers, 1974.

————. *Invitation to Vision.* Dubuque, Iowa: William C. Brown Company, Publishers, 1967.

LINDERMAN, MARLENE M. *Art in the Elementary School: Drawing, Painting, and Creating for the Classroom.* Dubuque, Iowa: William C. Brown Company, Publishers, 1974.

LOWENFELD, VIKTOR, AND W. LAMBERT BRITTAIN. *Creative and Mental Growth,* 7th ed., New York: Macmillan Publishing Co., Inc., 1975.

MCFEE, JUNE KING. *Preparation for Art.* Belmont, Calif.: Wadsworth Publishing Co., Inc., 1961.

MADEJA, STANLEY S. *All the Arts for Every Child.* New York: JDR 3rd Fund, 1973.

MATTIL, EDWARD L. *Meaning in Crafts.* 3rd ed. Englewood Cliffs, N.J.: Prentice Hall, Inc., 1971.

———, AND BETTY MARZAN. *Meaning in Children's Art.* Englewood Cliffs, N.J.: Prentice-Hall, Inc., 1982.

MOSELEY, SPENCER, PAULINE JOHNSON, AND HAZEL KOENING. *Crafts Design.* Belmont, Calif.: Wadsworth Publishing Co., Inc.

MONTGOMERY, CHANDLER. *Art for Teachers of Children.* Columbus, Ohio: Charles E. Merrill Publishers, 1968.

MORMAN, JEAN MARY. *Art: Of Wonder and a World.* Blauvelt, N. Y.: Art Education, Inc., 1971.

NATIONAL ART EDUCATION ASSOCIATION. *Art Education in the Elementary School.* Washington, D.C.: National Art Education Association, 1973.

PAZ, OCTAVIO, AND THE WORLD CRAFTS COUNCIL. *In Praise of Hands.* Greenwich, Conn.: New York Graphic Society, 1974.

PLUMMER, GORDON. *Children's Art Judgment.* Dubuque, Iowa: William C. Brown Company, Publishers, 1974.

READ, HERBERT. *Education Through Art.* New York: Pantheon Books, Inc., 1948.

RITSON, JOHN E., AND JAMES A. SMITH. *A Creative Teaching of Art in the Elementary School.* Boston: Allyn & Bacon, Inc., 1975.

RUESCHOFF, PHIL H., AND M. EVELYN SWARTZ. *Teaching Art in the Elementary School.* New York: The Ronald Press Company, 1969.

SAUNDERS, ROBERT J. *Teaching Through Art.* New York: American Book Company, 1973.

———. *Art and Humanities in the Classroom.* Dubuque, Iowa: William C. Brown Company, Publishers, 1977.

SCHWARTZ, FRED. *Structure and Potential in Art Education.* Lexington, Mass.: Xerox College, 1970.

TAYLOR, ANNE P., AND GEORGE VLASTOS. *School Zone.* New York: Van Nostrand Reinhold Company, 1975.

TEMKO, FLORENCE. *Folk Art for World Friendship.* Garden City, N.Y.: Doubleday & Co., Inc., 1976.

WACHOWIAK, FRANK, AND THEODORE RAMSAY. *Emphasis: Art.* 2nd ed. Scranton, Pa.: International Textbook Co., Inc., 1971.

WANKELMAN, WILLARD, PHILLIP WIGG, AND MARIETTA WIGG. *A Handbook of Arts and Crafts for Elementary and Junior High School Teachers.* 3rd ed. Dubuque, Iowa: William C. Brown Company, Publishers, 1974.

2

Developmental Stages and Sequential Objectives

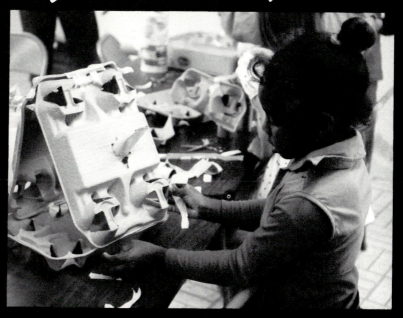

In this chapter an overview is presented of the developmental stages of children's art growth from preschool through elementary school. Development charts are included and provide a summary capsule following the chapter discussion. Objectives are suggested that provide a sequential curriculum that is in line with the developmental growth aspects of children.

Preschool–Kindergarten: Ages 3–5

IDENTIFYING CHARACTERISTICS

In a child's life, the visual and tactile world begins very early; nurturing this world requires rooting and developing. His world begins with himself as the center. Teachers and parents need to prompt a child's thinking as early as possible in order to encourage creative development. As soon as a child can hold a lump of clay or a ball of yarn in his hand, he is ready to discover the world of art. All children share similar developmental patterns. The first phase of growth is referred to as the scribbling stage. The scribbling stage has four main aspects that coincide with the child's developmental growth.

DISORGANIZED SCRIBBLING. This is the beginning of all art development. For most children, this phase starts when they seek to control their motions when using clay, crayon, or other art materials. We should not expect much from the child at this point. The fact that he can hold the clay and

2–1 Playing, pretending, and imagining are desirable directions for art growth, and media that reinforce these behaviors are meaningful. These two figures were done by our daughter Cheryl at ages four and seven. Note the remarkable similarity in content and expression. Collecting the work of a child over a period of time provides valuable longitudinal information pertinent to concept development.

pound it or make marks on a paper with a crayon signifies that he has a new relationship with his world. At this point, do not interfere, but encourage the child to continue to explore with the material.

CONTROLLED SCRIBBLING. After a period of time, which may be a week, a month, or longer (if art materials are made available), the child will discover that he can control his motions with clay, crayon, fingerpaint, or other manipulative materials. He may roll the clay into coils or attempt to join two pieces. He may pound the clay in an up-and-down motion. As scribbling is primarily kinetic, or concerned with the feeling for motion, the child will move his arm back and forth as he uses crayons on the paper. The fact that he can control his motions is a major step forward. Building with blocks of wood is a way for the child to join parts together and to build both upward and outward in space.

VARIABLE SCRIBBLING. As the child is provided with opportunities to manipulate media, he will soon learn to vary the manner in which he uses those media. As he experiences the material, he will make simple discoveries that will set the stage for more experiences. Children grow at different rates, and each one will proceed through these developmental levels at his or her own speed. Most children begin to vary their scribbling at around three years of age. In using clay, the child will join parts, change the size of a shape, and then repeat what he has done. It is through repetition of experiences that the child gains mastery over and confidence in his discoveries. Making circular motions with the crayon, or round forms with clay, is an outgrowth of controlled scribbling and reflects a greater control of his motions. From circular motions, repeated over a period of time, come the first beginnings of a head formation. Longitudinal (back and forth) motions become forerunner experiences for arms, legs, and body.

NAMING SCRIBBLING. This last phase of scribbling is significant, for the child now begins to "name" the forms that he puts together. When the child combines scribbles on paper or builds with blocks or clay he begins to tell stories about what he is doing. This means that the child is beginning to think in terms of images. Before this, only the motion was important, or the activity of doing. But now, the crystallization of image thinking takes over. Kinetic thinking is replaced by imagery. This is thought to be the point at which conscious memory begins for children.

SUITABLE MEDIA FOR AGES 3–5

assorted papers and sizes: manila, newsprint, colored papers, and cardboard

blocks in various sizes (scrap pieces from a lumberyard)
brushes: soft or stiff, round and flat, in various sizes from ¼ to
   1 inch
chalk for chalkboard or sidewalk
crayons of assorted colors and sizes
felt-tip pens in assorted colors
modeling materials: playdough, modeling clay, water-base
   clay, and modeling mixtures
poster paint (liquid or powder) and watercolor trays
spools, cardboard, cans, leather, fur, and other natural and
   scrap materials for arranging, joining, and stacking
yarns, cloth, and collected materials to arrange and manipulate

PERFORMANCE OBJECTIVES

Artistic and Perceptual Skills

Perceptual development in the child sets the foundation for all learning. Perceptual skills refers to the active use of the senses to bring in data through discovery, information that the mind can put to work for concept building. Teachers can guide children to the frontiers of their sensory awareness through carefully planned experiences that tap discovery through observing, touching, listening, smelling, and tasting. The more teachers can activate knowledge that a child has concerning natural and man-made forms, the more likely is the child to express ideas through materials and words. Children of preschool and kindergarten age need countless opportunities to seek and search out the forms of their world. They should also have many opportunities to develop artistic skills through continual practice with appropriate art media. At this stage, artistic skills can pertain to motor development in scribbling; arranging blocks, colors, or textures in cloth; or any other manipulative experience with art materials. It can be discovery in observing and finding shapes, lines, and textures in nature and in art forms. This is the time to acquaint children with pottery, leathercraft, jewelry, weaving, fabrics, and other crafts. Young children need opportunities to perceptualize flowers, butterflies, animals, birds, caterpillars, leaves, plants, bread, food, lumber, and such. They need also to visit floral shops, auto repair shops, airports, train depots, clock shops, taxidermist shops, candy shops, bakeries, and lumber mills.

Manipulative Skills

Provide many opportunities for young children to explore art media. They need time to scribble, arrange, discard, stack, put together, take apart, build, and handle. Provide a space in which the child can do these things. Encourage him to build with clay, draw with crayons, paint with a brush, or arrange and feel objects. Do not interfere with the child as he works or otherwise expresses himself through these early forms of inquiry. Always have discovery materials around (arts and craft materials) so that the child will learn the habit of seeking out and searching. Children have a natural curiosity and creative instinct. Teachers can nurture this natural drive by asking questions that *lead* the child to make *his own discoveries.*

Intellectual Skills

Intellectual development at the preschool-kindergarten stage is closely tied in with perception and motor development. The child should be encouraged to engage in activities that involve arranging, pounding, stacking, fitting, meeting, balancing, and marking. At the later end of this stage, each child will have formed concepts that will be continuously replaced through a search for what the world is like. Eventually, each child will arrive at a concept (schema) for every object experienced.

Primary (First and Second Grade): Ages 5–7

IDENTIFYING CHARACTERISTICS

The world of the primary child places him at the center of things. It is an ego-centered world in which the child is the dominant figure. There are no correct proportions, and realistic imagery as the adult knows it does not appear. Clay

2–2 *Each environment encountered offers new challenges in visual and tactile experiences. Space is limitless as the child extends her boundaries through the media of stick and earth.*

figures may be nothing more than coils of clay joined together, but to the child, they may represent daddy, mommy, or himself. The most significant characteristic of this stage is that the child has established a relationship between himself and the world. Every experience is a new one. In his craft products, the child includes parts that are important and meaningful to him. He omits the unimportant parts. There is little relationship between color selected and object represented. The child likes to play and pretend to use his imagination. He approaches crafts activities intuitively, and does not stop to analyze. Children at this stage are instinctive designers and creators; they are excited about everything.

All growth is sequential, implying that many stated objectives will overlap each level of growth. No particular child is typical of any defined skill level. There will be many individual differences depending on the temperament, intellect, environmental background, and maturity of the child.

In Figure 2–3 the figure on the right shows the basic body schema. The "king and queen" on the left repeat the body concept. Through repetition of forms, the child gains mastery of the concepts he has learned. This drawing emphasizes

2–3 *Identifying characteristics in this drawing by a seven-year-old indicate a variety of growth levels. The lower right figure form is geometric, and the left figures are schematic. The upper right figures (rabbit's feet) indicate three dimensions with shading.*

perceiving with greater realistic accuracy. The rabbit's feet in the background are significant, as they indicate shading of forms and the beginning of spatial depth. Interestingly enough, all parts of the drawing were completed at the same time.

SUITABLE MEDIA AND PROCEDURES FOR AGES 5–7: EMPHASIS ON DISCOVERY AND EXPERIMENTATION

Design:

Design is intuitive and spontaneously expressive. Direct involvement with colors, shapes, textures, patterns, and lines.

Paper:

Initial paper cutting experiences: scoring, curling, gluing, and constructing. Fold and dye, paper mosaic, tissue-paper pictures, stuffed paper creatures, paper environments, paper masks and costumes, introductory collage. Papier-mâché projects such as one large group effort, maracas, simple animals.

Puppets:

Paper bag puppets, paper cup or cereal box puppets, shadow puppets, finger and hand puppets, simplified ball and rod puppets, silhouette puppets, and pop-up surprise puppets.

Dyes, tie-dye, and batik:

Supervised dyeing experiences, tie-dyeing on a stick, crayon-resist tie-dye, initial binding techniques, painting on dyes, wax-resist eggs, substitute paste resist for batik, paper batiks.

Yarns, needles, and cloth:

Cloth collage "touch" pictures, easy burlap stitching, beginning stitches such as the running stitch, glued-on banners and flags, pillow pets and cloth dolls (glued closed), apple, corn husk, and yarn dolls, patchwork by glueing designs together on a backing, string or yarn pictures, yarn mobiles.

Weaving and macrame:

Cardboard and Styrofoam tray looms, weaving into cloth, paper weaving, fabric looms, spool and frame weaving, ojo de dios, introductory macrame knots and simple projects.

Pottery and modeling:

Nonhardening clay for spontaneous disposable projects; salt ceramic, baker's clay, playdough, water-base clay; beginning pinch, coil, and slab methods; edible modeling media such as bread sculpture dough, glass cookies, pretzels, candy, cookie, and vegetable art; candy castles; holiday villages.

Sculpture—constructing, carving, casting:

Paper and box constructions (large and small); wood shapes for constructing sculptures, Styrofoam sculpture, introductory model making, designing environmental spaces, wire, bone, and aluminum foil sculpture, mobiles and stabiles, toys such as optical spinners, tops, and kites, musical instruments, wood collage, stick or straw sculptures, and eggshell mosaics.

Jewelry:

Dip and dye, tissue paper, paper beads, corn husk, seed, string and yarn, found objects, aluminum, rings, clay and clay substitutes, wood, incised, shell, plastic, copper enameling, simple leather, button, beads, and spool jewelry.

Drawing, painting, and lettering:

Assorted papers to draw and paint on, crayons of various sizes and colors, charcoal, pencils, felt-tip pens that flow easily with intense colors, assorted paints such as poster and watercolor (brushes of assorted sizes and shapes), chalks, finger painting, words and pictures, words and messages, creative signatures, cartooning.

Printmaking:

Rubbings, rolling prints; plasticene, clay and stamping tools (stamped print); Styrofoam, soap block, plaster (relief print); cardboard on cardboard, glue on computer cards, cylinder, foam tape or foam sheeting (collage print); chalk, crayon, and paint stencil prints; monoprinting.

Photography:

Looking through the viewfinder, how to take photographs, simple camera parts, sun prints, photograms, blueprints, diazo or ozalid prints, painting on photographic paper, slide art, overhead light art, zoetrope art, drawing on film or filmstrips.

PERFORMANCE

Artistic and Perceptual Skills

Emphasis should be placed on investigation through observing, feeling, smelling, listening, and tasting by utilizing unusual approaches to discovery. Prisms, microscopes, telescopes, binoculars, magnifying glasses, and any other instruments or means that encourage new pathways for perception should be introduced in the classroom. Blindfold the children and have them identify things, or have them place paper over surfaces and rub them using a crayon. Provide opportunities to practice remembering through drawing what has been observed. Review such art elements as shape. Find basic shapes (rounds, squares, and triangles) in flowers, plants, animals, figures, birds, insects, and in man-made structures. Because children search for form concepts in all things

2–4 Clay, through its plastic properties, offers a wide range of perceptual exploration and conceptual challenges.

experienced, provide motivations that emphasize figurative subjects, including people, dogs, trees, stores, and so on. Make your own enthusiasm so contagious that students will catch the spirit. Always encourage children to be original, inventive, and always do their own work. Emphasize success, and minimize the effect of errors, for they are part of learning. Keep the children's welfare in mind always.

Arts and crafts making combines both tactile and visual experiences. Surfaces can be seen as well as touched. Children of primary age enjoy both visual and tactile experiences in creating art media. They are ready to learn many things about art. Most children of this age can identify such art qualities as the following:

straight, curved, or diagonal lines
lines that are long and short
lines and shapes that are thick, thin, and irregular
varieties of shapes (square, rectangle, circle, oval, triangle, and diamond)
spaces filled with various marks, dots, and lines to create designs and patterns
colors that are bright, dull, dark, and light
textural qualities (hard, soft, rough, or smooth)

Manipulative Skills

Select materials that will encourage a wide range of exploration in cutting, gluing, tearing, pasting, sewing, weaving, printing, sawing, painting, drawing, hammering, sanding, dipping, squeezing, pressing, and assembling. Some children of this age will have difficulty initially in learning the uses of tools, but patience will be rewarding for both the children and teacher. Discuss the manufacture of art tools: where they come from and what they are made of. Language is very important to children and aids them in analyzing art processes. (Don't forget to learn the "language" of each child.) Discuss also how tools are used in craft processes, as this is part of skill development. Provide time for repeated practice in learning to use tools and for discovering what can be done with materials. Children will grow

2–5 *Weavings by first-graders done on cardboard looms with only eight warps. Note the slits in the open weave, the wrapping, and the added beads.*

in their thinking if they have opportunities to utilize materials in many different ways. Through constant practice and "playing around" with materials, the children gain confidence and mastery in thinking and doing.

Intellectual Skills

Intellectual skills refers to the development of cognitive abilities, or the growth of concepts for all things experienced in the man-made and natural world. Intellectual growth can take place when children study about artists, art products, and the forms of subjects of their experiences. Intellectual growth concerns the reasoning aspects of art; it is the rational approach to things experienced. Arts become the means by which intellectually understood concepts can be strengthened. That is, in the making of a figure, such as in clay, the child has to rethink what he has experienced and knows about figures. This factual knowledge concerning people, animals, plants, and such helps the child to crystallize his thinking regarding what forms and things are like. For example, if the teacher would like the child to make a design of a bird, the child is unlikely to express a rich concept unless he has learned specific information dealing with the bird's body parts, feathers, and some careful observation of the bird in flight. This enrichment of concept can be stimulated and accomplished in the classroom by various means, such as bringing live subjects to class for a close-up study, using motion-picture films to present details through magnification and delayed-sequence photography that are not observable with the naked eye, and using illustrations from magazines and books.

Aesthetic Skill

Looking at and talking about art products and reproductions of pottery, metalwork, woodwork, leather, and the various crafts that relate to the child's interest will help develop his aesthetic sense. Primary-age children like just about everything, including subjects such as food, the circus, storytelling, shape and color relationships, themselves, family activities, makebelieve, television heroes, and inventing imaginative forms. Encourage the children to discuss art objects and to assist you in making class display arrangements.

Spend time each week discussing the forms that artists make. Have the children bring to class something from home that they consider to be a beautifully crafted form, such as utensils, bowls, salad servers, place mats, clothing, toys or anything made by hand or machine. In discussing art forms, encourage the children to give reasons why they feel or react a certain way about a specific art form. Children should be made to move beyond the surface impressions in their thinking about aesthetics.

Intermediate (Third and Fourth Grade): Ages 7–9

IDENTIFYING CHARACTERISTICS

Children at these ages are growing into the sociocentric stage; that is, they are moving out of their own preoccupation with self to discovering that others in the class are equally exciting to be with and to share ideas with. There is a desire to be in groups, or gangs. Children of this age are cooperative and enjoy sharing with each other. They are also proud of their new abilities to comprehend and create and they are full of ideas. They are willing to listen to opposing viewpoints, like to share in planning, and need to know the importance of finishing an assignment. They like to practice skills, desire to excel in something, and need their share of approval and attention. They are fully able to undertake assignments on their own, and they enjoy the sense of mastery in being independent. Their drawings and paintings may become less expressive, more rigid, and tighter because they perceive more details with increasing realistic accuracy. Art skills at this level are excellent means for keeping their creative spirit in full bloom. Many of the procedures—such as printmaking, sandcasting, papier-mâché, weaving, and macrame—require sequential steps in order to be completed.

**SUITABLE MEDIA AND PROCEDURES
FOR AGES 7–9**

Design (study the following):
   The design elements as found in the environment; art: two-dimensional objects as well as three-dimensional objects, art heritage, unifying relationships, design motifs, design exhibit areas.

Paper:
   Assorted weights for constructing, printing, papier mâché, collage, montage, masks, costumes, environments, mosaics, puppets and stuffed objects, fold and dye, message cards.

Puppets:
   Paper bags, cloth, hand, sock, finger, cereal box, paper cup, papier-mâché, vegetable and dough, apple head, rod puppets, shadow puppets, dancing puppets, simple marionettes (such as those made from Styrofoam or spools), pop-up surprise puppets, stage construction, integrating puppetry with script writing, expressive theater, math, social studies, literature, designing stage props, original music, production techniques.

Dyes, tie-dye, and batik:
   Gathering and extracting vegetable dyes, exploring various binding knots, designs through all dyeing techniques such

as block designs and bleach design, cloth, batiks, substitute paste-resist batik, wax-resist eggs, batiks for clothes, lamps, and so on.

Yarns, needles, and cloth:

Design with cloth; learn basic stitches, stitch and beading on clothing, collage touch pictures, beads on cloth, glued and sewn wall hangings, banners and flags; cloth-stuffed dolls, pillows, and pets; yarn, apple, and corn husk dolls; patchwork quilting (both glued and sewn), needlepoint, rug hooking, and cloth flowers; crocheting; yarn pictures and yarn and plastic mobiles.

Weaving and macrame:

Learning about textile materials, terms for weaving, various types of looms, including straw looms, frame looms, round looms, backstrap looms, free form weavings, flat circle looms; learn various weaving techniques, such as weave with beads, finger weaving, twining, braiding, spool weaving, frame weaving, ojo de dios, basket weaving, wrapping; combine for large wall hangings and sculptures, assortment of macrame cords and learn macrame knots, preplan designs or develop designs spontaneously once knots are mastered. Weave and macrame jewelry, clothing, belts, ties, lamps, handbags, and stuffed forms.

Pottery and modeling:

Continue experimenting; wedge, coil, slab construction, pinch, hand building techniques. Drape, texture, and combine ways of working. Build clay sculptures and larger forms. Learn glazing, tooling, and other decorating and finishing techniques; salt ceramic, baker's clay, sawdust modeling, use nonhardening clay inventively, playdough. Build sculptures with edible modeling media—bread sculpture, glass cookies, pretzels, candy castle, holiday villages.

Sculpture—constructing, carving, and casting:

Continue with previous procedures with added complexity; planning and building environments, design city and country spaces, architectural models, action toys, kites, musical instruments, tile mosaics, wood construction, carving, wood textures, stick and straw sculptures, mobiles, stabiles, carving wax, gourds, plaster, plastic, soap, sawdust, casting wax candles, and plaster sculptures.

Jewelry:

Continue with previously mentioned processes; learn basic construction methods, cutting, shaping, assembling, and joining techniques; produce all multifunctional jewelry including plastic methods, metal forming, stamping, painting and carving leather, and finishing procedures such as polishing and oxidizing metals. Cast, etch, and carve plastics.

Drawing, painting, and lettering:
Continue with all drawing and painting media. Experiment and learn techniques; design posters, murals, graphic design, layouts, matting, and exhibiting. Cartooning, advertising, calligraphy, moments in history, words and pictures, pictures in sequence, creative signatures, space designs, and lettering.

Printmaking:
All stamped prints, rubbings, roll prints, relief prints, collage prints, stencil prints, screen prints, and monoprinting.

Photography:
Viewfinder looking, taking pictures, the pinhole camera, take and develop a print, photograms, sun prints, negatives and sun prints; blueprints, diazo and ozalid prints, painting on photographic paper, painting on negatives; slide art, overhead light shows, moving pictures, the zoetrope. Drawing on film or filmstrips, film animation, planning films.

PERFORMANCE OBJECTIVES

Artistic and Perceptual Skills

This is the time for teaching overlapping, spatial concepts, varying viewpoints, subtlety of color, and value ranges and to give more concentrated attention to the specifics of designing. Teach children of this age details of line, shape, patterns, texture, and color. Stress the skillful handling of craft media, and demonstrate the beginning steps in a lesson. Encourage the class to search for information in books, films, and television as well as by listening to others and by constantly maintaining a "sharp" eye. In drawing and painting, discuss such spacial aspects as horizon line and ways to see space in perspective. Demonstrate how to shade. Discuss such principles of art as rhythm, proportion, repetition, and balance (see Chapter 3). Encourage awareness of the way things feel to the touch. Looking and feeling are the key words at this stage. Further the children's senstivity to the textural qualities of various surfaces such as earth, fur, brick, clay, sandpaper, eggs, and so on. Discuss their

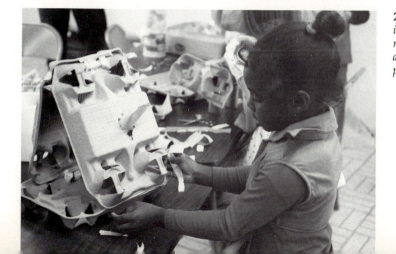

2–6 *Redefining materials into a fresh context can suggest new possibilities and beginnings and is part of the creative process.*

2–7 *Puppetry is cross-cultural and enjoyed by children throughout the world.*

differences and similarities. Discover how to create textures with various craft tools. Practice discovery through touching, pounding, squeezing, and grasping. Plan new and exciting sensory experiences involving touching as well as smelling, listening, and observing.

Manipulative Skills

Group activites are helpful at this stage: planning a city (have each group of children design and construct with wood and hammer, or cardboard, the parts to the city); making puppets (children can sew, cut, stuff, string, and get involved in a variety of manipulative skills that will challenge their growing sense of awareness); carving with soap; cutting linoleum prints; shaping clay; developing photographic prints; building a wooden frame loom; scoring paper; stringing beads; and constructing models. Activities such as macrame challenge children because of the dexterity and complexity involved. Provide manipulative activities that involve sanding, rubbing, gluing, pounding, pasting, twisting, knotting, weaving, and attaching.

Intellectual Skills

Teach children cognitive skills that deal with analysis, synthesis, and content, as well as the technical aspects of craft tools and media. In clay, study how glazes are achieved and what happens in the firing process. In photography, discuss the workings of the camera and how prints are made. Discuss how furniture is joined. Learn the various joints by name. Study the muscles and bones of the body. Discuss how they are necessary to the bending and operation of the body. Introduce such art terms as *aesthetic, form, function, abstraction,* and *surrealism.* The emphasis here is on the analysis and definition of terminology.

Aesthetic Skills

Now is the time to bring guest artists into the classroom for discussion and questioning. Trips to artists' studios and local galleries and museums are also in order. Cameras make good third eyes for students, for they open up vistas heretofore unfamiliar. Discuss with your class various ways in which artists make crafts. Discuss how the artist uses various media, such as a camera, a brush and paint, or a lump of clay to make a beautiful form. Discuss such concepts as originality, uniqueness, and personal statement with craft media. Start a collection of art prints for the classroom. Collect as many visuals as possible of natural and man-made forms, and also photographs of artists creating with media. Children need these reinforcing activities in order to build their art sense. Now is also the time to discuss what makes a craft product beautiful. Get children to verbalize their thoughts concerning art forms.

Upper Intermediate (Fifth and Sixth Grade): Ages 9–12

IDENTIFYING CHARACTERISTICS

During this period there is a maturing in the students' understanding of art. By now they should have a working art vocabulary and a foundation for analyzing, discussing, and appreciating various kinds of craft products. They are ready to study in more detail their art heritage and the relationships in art among and across cultures both past and present. Two types of student begin to emerge at this time. One is analytical, tending to visualize things and to mirror reality (the visual), whereas the other places an emphasis on feelings and inner direction regarding art forms and experiences (the haptic). Children enjoy working for longer periods of time on projects during this period. They also like their own feelings of independence. Children should be encouraged to pursue group as well as their individual interests. Students now experience social awareness: how bodies function, war, smoking, community responsibilities, personal grooming, family relationships, pollution, social structures, disease, and working toward the ·future. Now is also a good time to

2–8 *Pets are natural motivators that invite artistic expression. Bringing them into the classroom enables students to observe details at close range. The medium used here was charcoal.*

discuss the many and various careers that are possible in arts and crafts.

SUITABLE MEDIA AND PROCEDURES FOR AGES 9–12

Design:

The study of design (line, shape, surface, color, texture, size, space) as found in both organic and manmade objects; design study in clothing, furniture, houses, schools, personal spaces, city and town spaces; in arts and crafts objects, as part of our art heritage; using design to unify relationships and produce both two- and three-dimensional arts and crafts projects. Design cards, clothing, spaces, posters, exhibit areas, rooms for various uses (such as the library, laboratory, entries, landscapes). Design utilitarian objects and forms for fun.

Paper:

Assorted weights, textures, and patterned papers for painting and drawing, printing, papier-mâché, collage, montage, masks and costumes, building environments and spaces, mosiacs, puppets and stuffed sculptures, fold and dye, message cards, batiks, origami, kites, mobiles and stabiles, sculpture, toys, musical instruments, tissue paper pictures, jewelry, beads and found object jewelry, diazo, blueprint and photographic papers.

Puppets:

Paper bags (small for the hand, large to go over the body), cloth, socks, finger, cereal box, paper cup, papier-mâché, pop-up, Styrofoam ball, shadow puppets, vegetable and dough, apple head, marionettes (all kinds). Study and produce stage designs and construction. Integrate puppetry with speech and language, creative writing, expressive theater, math, social studies, music, literature, history, space studies, poetry, holidays, celebrations, television and other original productions.

Dyes, tie-dye, and batik:

Gather and extract vegetable dyes, dye yarns, and cloth. Explore various binding knots for tie-dye and other dyeing techniques such as block and bleach designs. Dye two or more colors, experiment with combining techniques. Produce batiks for clothing, banners, lamps, window shades, message card, wall hangings, jewelry, pillows.

Yarns, needles, and cloth:

Design "touch" collage pictures with cloth; do decoupage projects with cloth on both two- and three-dimensional surfaces such as round cannisters, shoe boxes, flower pots. Learn basic stitches and experiment with inventive stitches; stitch designs with yarns, threads, old jewelry, buttons, and beads on clothing, pillows, pillow pets, wall hangings, banners, flags. Design cloth stuffed dolls, yarn, apple, and

corn husk dolls; design clothes for dolls. Produce quilting and patchwork projects, needlepoint, rug hooking, cloth flowers, crochet, string and yarn pictures, mobiles; design hats, costumes, and inventive jewelry.

Weaving and macrame:

Gather yarns of various weights, textures, and colors. Study textiles, terms for weaving, looms. Design and build original looms. Weave on straws, frames, round and backstrap looms, free form, branches and trees, bicycle frames, cylinder, and other inventive looms. Learn and experiment with the various weaving techniques as described; weave with fingers, beads, twining, braiding, spool weaving, frame, ojo di dios, basket (rag and yarn), wrapping. Combine weavings to build large wall hangings and sculptures. Collect assortment of macrame materials (such as cotton, jute, heavy yarns); learn macrame knots; preplan designs or develop designs as you knot. Weave and macrame jewelry clothing, belts, bags, wall hangings, pot slings, ties, lamps, and sculpture forms.

Pottery and modeling:

Continue to learn and experiment with hand-building techniques such as wedge, coil, slab construction, pinch pots and sculpture. Learn clay terms. Drape, glaze, and texture clay. Experiment with finishing tools and decorative techniques. When possible, learn to "throw" or turn clay on a wheel. Build miniature environments and families with flat figures; animals and birds, flowers, butterflies, insects, and cars. Create inventive clay sculptures. Design clay mobiles, stabiles, hanging bell chimes, dishes, tiles, and jewelry. Design castles, buildings, and cities with clay. Help to fire the clay. Additional modeling media: salt and flour for sculptures, puppet heads, marionettes, dioramas; salt ceramic; baker's clay; sawdust; nonhardening clay. Bake edible sculptures from bread, cookie, and pretzel dough. Build candy castles, Eskimo villages, holiday villages, and fanciful animals using cookies and frosting.

Sculpture—constructing, carving, and casting:

Construct with boxes, papers, wood, plastic, foil, Styrofoam, metals, and clay. Plan and construct models as well as large environments, design city and country spaces. Redesign spaces such as home, school and city complexes. Build architectural models. Design action toys, kites, line design boards, spinners, tops, musical instruments, mosaics, wood collage, and constructions; carve with materials such as gourds, wax, soap, plaster, plastic, sawdust and cast plastic, plaster and wax.

Jewelry:

Continue with previously described processes. Experiment with design construction and joining such as cutting, shaping, and assembling. Learn jewelry terms. Design with paper, husk, seed, string, yarn, beads, found objects, foil, rings, clay, salt ceramic, baker's clay, wood, shell, plastic (by melting, carving, casting), metals, leather, and other jewelry materials as well as applying finishing procedures.

Drawing, painting, and lettering:

Experiment with and learn techniques using all drawing and painting media. Paint still lifes, mood pictures, surrealistic compositions (collage). Paint on rocks, with sand, and on other surfaces. Emphasize how art today is used as communication of ideas through advertising design, murals, posters, layout design, newspapers, magazines, calligraphy, cartooning, lettering, words and messages, space designs, television. Design creative signatures, pictures in sequence, moments in history, inventive alphabets.

Printmaking:

Use rubbings off surfaces, roll prints, stamp prints with variety of media, relief prints with all media, collage prints with all media. Stencil prints, screen printing, monoprinting, and linoleum printing.

Photography:

Design through the viewfinder; relate picture-taking to the expression of ideas and to other curriculum areas such as poetry, science. Learn photography terms. Construct a pinhole camera; learn parts of a camera. Discuss the importance of the camera today as well as the effect it has had on art in general and how it influenced history. Design a darkroom and develop prints. Make photographic images without a camera, such as with photograms, sun prints, negatives, copying machines, diazo prints, blueprints, painting on sensitized paper, painting on negatives. Learn how and where to mount them. Produce slide art, overhead light shows, moving picture procedures such as the zoetrope, drawing on film and filmstrips, and planning storyboards for film animation.

PERFORMANCE OBJECTIVES

Artistic and Perceptual Skills

Emphasize originality and uniqueness of thought in forming ideas and working with art media. Stress composing and designing art forms. Practice the interrelationship of the arts in the classroom: unite art, music, dance, drama, and writing with history, literature, and language curricula. Practice perceptual activities involving scents, sounds, colors, light, textures, touch, movement, and vision. Work lessons and activities that involve the student in perceptual activities. For example, blindfold students and have them feel many different objects; then have the students open their eyes and draw their impressions of what they felt, or have them redefine the images in clay or other modeling media. Another technique to use when dealing with the senses is to have the class make rubbings with crayons and paper over surfaces and then to combine the transferred images into a composition. Encourage the children to observe patterns and shapes in nature: flowers, trees, hills, and shadows; and in man-made things: fabrics, buildings, and furniture. Have them also create new patterns from their imaginations. Art growth occurs when one works at it.

Practice art concepts dealing with spatial visualization. Such concepts would include perspective, vanishing distances, objects and sculpture in the round, designing environments, architectural models, maps and city planning, and both realistic and abstract variations on space.

2–9 *The illusion of depth is a spatial art concept that challenges each student's realistic and abstract vision.*

Manipulative Skills

Students should learn how to proceed with a variety of art tools and materials: hammers, saws, chisels, watercolors, leather tools, clay, wood, papers, construction materials, and so forth. They also need many opportunities to practice their skills. Through continual practice in handling tools and materials in art experiences, the student is able to refine his sensitivity to aesthetic form. Developing positive lifelong attitudes about art and beauty sets the stage for the rest of one's life. Through practice with art media, greater understanding of techniques occurs, as well as the ability to express personal ideas aesthetically.

Intellectual Skills

Further enrich concepts for art terms, artists, art as heritage, folk art, art history, and art media in order to develop an art vocabulary that permits the student to converse on an intelligent level. Encourage students to give and develop reasons for the aesthetic choices that they make. Have students select an artist, or a period in art history, do detailed research into the background of their subjects, and then present a report on their research to the class. The emphasis here is on the student's investigative and analytical abilities.

Aesthetic Skills

Art appreciation can involve learning about artists, art works, tools, art vocabulary, and our art heritage through a study of art history and cultures. Students can learn to make value judgments concerning works of art. With this in mind, the class can develop an art center, where visual media can be maintained for use in discussing art forms as well as for motivating the formation of new ideas in arts and crafts media. At this level of his development, the student needs to be challenged extensively, for he is ready to learn about art as subject content as well as expressive activity.

Developmental Stages and
Sequential Objectives

Summary
Curriculum A—Preschool-Kindergarten, Ages 3–5: Developmental Characteristics and Sequential Objectives

IDENTIFYING CHARACTERISTICS	PERCEPTUAL	ARTISTIC	INTELLECTUAL
1. First time around experiences for all children. 2. All children begin art growth by scribbling. 3. Scribbling stage moves from uncontrolled to "naming" in four developmental steps. 4. Children in kindergarten move from scribbling into first representations for figure, house, tree, and the like. 5. Child is at the center of things where he is the dominant figure. 6. There are no correct proportions, and objects do not appear realistically in the child's artwork. 7. Children are open to all experiences and willing to try new things.	*Visual Skills:* 1. Incorporate experiences that involve the child in looking at natural and man-made forms. Emphasis on discovery through observation and noticing the details of things. Key words here are searching, pursuing, seeking, and discovering. 2. Constant encouragement of the child. Establishment of success-oriented experiences. *Tactile Skills:* 1. Emphasis on learning how things feel through touch. 2. Detecting differences in tactile discrimination through comparisons. 3. Discovering similarities in touch. *Listening Skills:* 1. Emphasis on discovery through listening to people, animals, and to natural and man-made sounds. 2. Flooding the child with continual opportunities to utilize his senses in order to take in data and to spark his learning receptors. Emphasis at this stage on the full awakening of one's potential through complete intellectual, sensory, and artistic stimulation through the fullest utilization of the senses. This builds the foundation for art.	*Manipulative Skills:* 1. Emphasis on tools that present uninterrupted movement such as felt-tip pens and crayons. Painting encourages large-muscle movements. 2. Encourage working with a variety of crafts involving sanding, rubbing, weaving, bending, modeling, shaping, pasting, and the like. *Production Skills:* 1. Experiences in making art forms that are unique to the child's expression and concepts. 2. Emphasis on a variety of subject matter and discovery experiences that lay the foundation for personal creative expression. 3. Opportunities to work in both two- and three-dimensional media. 4. Encourage the child to complete his work and to experiment as much as possible; do not interfere with the child as he works.	1. Emphasis on opportunities for the child to compare, relate, analyze, synthesize, and play around. 2. Learning the names of flowers, plants, trees, and mechanical things, people, clouds, vegetables, and the like. 3. Naming simple tools, learning colors, discovering craft media, putting things together, and taking things apart. 4. Inventing simple games on the spur of the moment to challenge the child and keep him at a state of alertness and primed for further discovery.

AESTHETIC	CREATIVE AND EXPRESSIVE	EVALUATIVE
Art Looking: 1. Experiences in looking at pictures and crafts of various types. 2. Combine looking with discussions at the child's level of thinking. 3. Subject matter should be of interest to the child, such as food, circus, work and play, self-image, body parts, make-believe, television, books, fantasy, and imagination. *Art Heritage Skills:* 1. Learning how various cultures contributed to America's growth. 2. Learning that art heritage begins with sharing one's own artwork. 3. Discussing art made in the past ("olden days"). *Art Judgment Skills:* 1. Emphasis on making aesthetic choices and telling why. 2. Choosing beautiful things in nature and of man and talking about it. Subjects can be clouds, machinery, stars, fruit, trees, cars, planes, pebbles, anything.	1. Continual encouragement to put down ideas with art media. One must scribble in order to grow. 2. Emphasis on an uninterrupted flow of scribbling experiences permits the child to gain fluidity and ease in controlling and varying his use of appropriate media. 3. Mastery of movement through repeated opportunities to model and make marks over and over. 4. Continuual giving out of information previously taken in.	*Perceptual Growth:* 1. Does the child scribble freely and without interruption? 2. Does the child cover the entire space? *Intellectual Growth:* 1. Does the work indicate richness of flow and detail? 2. Does the child concentrate? 3. Does the child talk about his work? *Artistic Growth:* 1. Is there a feeling for design? 2. Are the spaces well filled? 3. Are proportions intuitively felt? 4. Can the child handle the media? *Aesthetic Growth:* 1. Does the work show harmonious organization? 2. Does the child see value and color changes? *Creative and Expressive Growth:* 1. Is the work forceful? 2. Does the child say something unique in his work? 3. Is the child eager and enthusiastic?

Summary
Curriculum B—Primary, Ages 5–7: Developmental Characteristics and Sequential Objectives

IDENTIFYING CHARACTERISTICS	PERCEPTUAL	ARTISTIC	INTELLECTUAL
1. Open and spontaneous expression.	*Visual Skills:*	*Manipulative Skills:*	*Concept Skills:*
2. Perceptually aware and ready to learn.	1. Intense experiences through keen observation of all aspects of a form.	1. Develops skill in handling tools and materials: cutting, pasting, connecting, joining, folding and bending, constructing and modeling; discovering crayons, inks, pens, charcoal, pencils, paint, brushes, pastels.	1. Emphasis on experiences that encourage children to analyze, describe, identify, classify, and enrich concepts.
3. All experiences based on emotional aspects of reality.	2. Differentiating textures, colors, shapes, and lines of natural and man-made forms.		2. Enrich active knowledge for figure, animal, natural forms. Enrichment of concepts through working with clay, carving, drawing, and painting; craft experiences.
4. Searches for concepts for all things experienced.	3. Practicing recall of visual experiences through verbalization and craft making.	*Production Skills:*	
5. Representation of forms by geometric and linear symbols in child's art.	4. Detecting contrasts and similarities between forms observed.	1. Understands differences in size and shape of forms.	3. Emphasis on learning body parts of figures, animals, birds, and plants.
6. Repeats forms over and over to gain mastery.		2. Identifies shapes: square, rectangle, triangle, circle, irregular.	4. Study of natural forms such as trees, flowers, rocks, sky, sun, moon, and stars.
7. Searches for definitive ways to express concepts.	*Tactile Skills:*	3. Identifies colors: primary, secondary, variations.	5. Study in detail of man-made things including computers, typewriters, farm machinery, automobiles, and houses.
8. Exaggerates important parts and omits unimportant parts.	1. Differentiating between surfaces through touching, pounding, squeezing, and grasping.	4. Arranges: balancing, spacing, overlapping.	
9. Works intuitively without critical analysis.	2. Experiencing by touch and verbalizing the differences between soft, hard, furry, slippery, rough, smooth, sticky, and the like.	5. Uses contrasting values: bright-dull, light-dark, rough-smooth.	6. Building an active vocabulary for enrichment of concepts for all things experienced.
10. Is an instinctive designer and creator.	3. Reinforcing tactile discovery through craft making in clay, wood, fabric, paint, paper, leather, and plastic.	6. Discovers what line can do.	7. Developing rich concepts for use of art tools, art vocabulary including colors, shapes, and textures.
11. Enjoys pretending and using imagination.		7. Emphasis on following through to completion.	8. Identification with objects and their workings.
	Listening Skills:	8. Searching for ways to express one's ideas in an aesthetic manner.	9. Enrichment of spatial concepts such as base line, overlapping, X-ray pictures, and fold-over pictures.
	1. Differentiating sounds in nature: rain, ocean waves, wind in trees, birds singing.		10. Enrichment of concepts that refer to working with others as well as working individually.
	2. Differentiating sounds of man-made things: motors, machinery, whistles, telephones, radios.		
	3. Practicing sensory discovery through smell: apples, berries, citrus, peaches, hayfields, beaches, forests, leather, candy, bread.		

| | CREATIVE AND | |
| AESTHETIC | EXPRESSIVE | EVALUATIVE |

AESTHETIC

Art Looking Skills:
1. Recognizing expressive qualities in art forms.
2. Building a vocabulary of art looking terms.
3. Discussing art terms such as line, shape, color, shading, and the like.
4. Understanding different types of art forms such as sculpture, pottery, metalwork, and printmaking.
5. Discovering craft forms in the environment such as in appliances, furniture, clothing, and the like.
6. Searching for aesthetic forms in nature and in man-made things.

Art Heritage Skills:
1. Learning the crafted forms of past cultures, such as Greek pottery, Aztec jewelry, African weaving, and Eskimo carving.
2. Studying cultures as they relate to American heritage, including European backgrounds: Renaissance painting, Medieval cathedrals, French Impressionism; Mexican, American Indian, Oriental, and African ties to our past.

Art Judgment Skills:
1. Identifying aesthetic qualities in craftwork, including observations dealing with textures and surfaces, contrasts, and compositional aspects.
2. Verbalizing about craft products, explaining why one makes choices dealing with aesthetic judgment.

CREATIVE AND EXPRESSIVE

1. Developing originality in ones' craft expression.
2. Building personal expression.
3. Using expressive qualities such as happiness, sadness, mystery, and imagination.
4. Using a variety of subject matter.
5. Expressing ideas in multiple ways.
6. Practicing personal expression through constant performance in craft media.
7. Using materials in inventive ways.
8. Sharing creative thinking with others.
9. Opportunities to discuss, internalize, and examine one's creative efforts.

EVALUATIVE

Perceptual Growth:
1. Does the child know differences and similiarities in color, texture, line, shape, and form of craft products?
2. Does the child indicate visual and tactile evidence in his work?
3. Does the child use other than geometric forms?

Intellectual Growth:
1. Does the child's artwork show rich detail?
2. Is the work finished?
3. Can the child recall experiences in detail through verbalization?
4. Are the concepts for ideas expressed adequately?
5. Is there variety in the subject chosen?

Artistic Growth:
1. Are craft tools and materials used with dexterity?
2. Does the work show experimentation?
3. Is improvement in design concept indicated?

Aesthetic Growth:
1. Does the child use art terms to describe works of art?
2. Does the child know the names of artists and some of their works?
3. Does the child know some art of the past?

Creative and Expressive Growth:
1. Are the ideas original and imaginative?
2. Are personal feelings indicated?
3. Does the child work alone and with the group?

Summary
Curriculum C—Intermediate, Ages 7–9: Developmental Characteristics and Sequential Objectives

IDENTIFYING CHARACTERISTICS	PERCEPTUAL	ARTISTIC	INTELLECTUAL
1. Students growing out of egocentric into sociocentric stage.	*Visual Skills:* 1. Practice in distinguishing subtle differences and similarities in color changes, textures, and the refinement of positive and negative shapes.	*Manipulative Skills:* 1. Practice refinement in the use of craft tools and materials for weaving, stitching, knitting, appliqué techniques, printmaking, ceramics, jewelry, and leather.	1. Provide cognitive experiences in looking at objects. Study proportion, relationships of parts in creating designs, figures, animals and the like.
2. Able to work more independently with increasing attention span.	2. Practice in expressing visually one's increasing awareness of the natural and man-made world.	2. Practice in the development of individual techniques of mastering various craft tools.	2. Encourage spatial growth through study of horizon line, perspective, and points of view.
3. Interested in each other, helpful, cooperative.	3. Practice heightened visual perception through making increasingly acute distinctions between forms in terms of their aesthetic properties.	*Production Skills:* 1. Practice constructing in both two and three dimensions.	3. In clay, study how glazes are formulated and what happens during the firing process.
4. Full of ideas, interested in events around them.	4. Practice verbal recall of visual impressions.	2. Practice making aesthetic choices in the way parts are assembled.	4. In photography, study the principles of the camera and how prints are made.
5. Need their share of approval and attention, but willing to listen to opposing viewpoints.	*Tactile Skills:* 1. Looking and feeling are two ways to discover texture or the suface of things.	3. Work both independently and with the group.	5. Encourage subject study, such as learning and classifying the parts for insects, plants, animals, and man-made objects.
6. Like to practice skills, and to excel in something.	2. Practice textural discovery through texture walks and touch pictures.	4. Work toward creating effective results in color, value, surface, joining, and forming.	6. Practice skills in learning names of craftsmen and their artwork.
7. Like to share in the planning.	3. Further texture insights through discriminating between the tactile properties of brick walls, fabric, clay, earth, sandpaper.	5. Engage in group artistic activities that include murals, puppet shows, dramatic plays, costume making, mobiles, light shows, and group sculpture.	7. Learn the names of various art and craft tools.
8. Strongly social, with need for belonging and to be like their friends.	4. Discover how to create textures with various art tools such as pens, brushes, and clay tools.		8. Encourage "collecting" hobbies that allow for classifying, organizing, analyzing, arranging. This includes bottles, butterflies, stamps, coins, cards, and advertising items.

AESTHETIC	CREATIVE AND EXPRESSIVE	EVALUATIVE
Art Looking Skills: 1. Continued work on art vocabulary. 2. Understanding of the purposes of art. 3. Visits to art galleries, museums, artists' studios. 4. Identification of craftsmen in various fields including potters, weavers, sculptors, photographers, leather craftsmen, and industrial and graphic designers. *Art Heritage Skills:* 1. Learn the resource material for art history and appreciation including books, films, prints, and slides. 2. Learn the contributions of artists of various ethnic groups and their place in American culture. 3. Learn the place of artists in society and in one's community. *Art Judgment Skills:* 1. Practice perceiving and describing artistic forms in terms of techniques and expression. 2. Learn to define the meaning of art and the value of one work of art in comparison to another. 3. Compare works of art of various styles that deal with similar subjects. 4. Learn how knowledge of design and art principles aids one in making judgments of craft works.	1. Encourage individual art expression with emphasis on originality and uniqueness. 2. Learn a variety of crafts and how each requires its own expression. 3. Learn to express ideas in various ways. How many ways can one idea be expressed? 4. Practice expressing ideas from more than one point of view. See ideas in new contexts. 5. Relate crafts to other subject areas such as science, social studies, music, dance, and literature. 6. Provide a continuation of expressive objectives from primary level.	*Perceptual Growth:* 1. Is the child aware of the horizon line? 2. Does the child think in terms of proportions and size differences? 3. Does the child see differences between organic and man-made shapes? 4. Does the child create craftwork in a variety of ways? *Intellectual Growth:* 1. Does the child include many details in his work? 2. Is there evidence of artistic discovery, such as color composition and visual relationships? 3. Does the child use techniques to express specific ideas? *Artistic Growth:* 1. Is the work free from inhibition? 2. Is the work creative and original? 3. Does the work indicate artistic skill in using tools? 4. Can the child work independently? 5. Can the child discuss his work in artistic terms? *Aesthetic Growth:* 1. Does the child distribute the parts of his work harmoniously? 2. Is there a relationship between form and purpose? 3. Can the child express judgment preferences? 4. Does the child know various craft media and how they are used? *Creative and Expressive Growth:* 1. Is there a sequential growth development evident in the work? 2. Is the work uniquely personal? 3. Is the work said fully and well?

Summary

Curriculum D—Upper Intermediate, Ages 9–12: Developmental Characteristics and Sequential Objectives

IDENTIFYING CHARACTERISTICS	PERCEPTUAL	ARTISTIC	INTELLECTUAL
1. Some students are more analytical (visual thinkers).	1. Increasing level of visual discrimination in perceiving nuances of color, value, surfaces, and composition.	*Manipulative Skills:* 1. Increasing competency in the handling of one or more art media.	1. Emphasis on discussion that involves cognitive processes dealing with visual recall of paintings, sculpture, and craft objects.
2. Some students are more emotional (haptic thinkers).	2. Ability to compare and discuss three-dimensional with two-dimensional forms.	2. Knowledge of and ability to handle both craft and two-dimensional media well, including weaving, macrame, printmaking, papier-mâché.	2. Ability to discuss art movements of the past and present and to relate art to present culture.
3. Most fall between these two dominant trends.	3. Understanding of overlapping planes, varying points of view, position and size changes, and three-dimensional space.	*Production Skills:* 1. Emphasis on pursuit of various avenues of expression.	3. Study of form and function in relation to art designing.
4. Greater degree of concentration and working time expended.	4. Awareness of the look and feel of surfaces. Ability to discriminate between subtle nuances of texture as surface.	2. Understanding of art medium and how to use it to express ideas.	4. Enrichment of all art concepts dealing with art heritage and aesthetic judgment.
5. Student has greater social awareness, including how bodies function, drugs, war, smoking, community responsibility, personal grooming, family relationships, social structures, disease, and working toward the future.	5. Emphasis on the harmonious unity of perceiving, thinking, and feeling.	3. Development of personal approaches and a sense of understanding of how others work.	5. Explanation of new ideas about crafts to expand one's mental horizons.
6. Desire to learn more about how art relates to life, nature, and history.	6. Constant experiences in verbalizing, producing, evaluating, and judging one's work and that of others.	4. Learning to use both imaginative and observational skills in art media.	
7. Desire to express these ideas in art products.		5. Learning to draw on various sources for inspiration such as actual objects, places, books, and films.	
8. Interest in designing clothing, cars, planes, furniture, homes, and community spaces.		6. Explain or relate art skill to other subjects such as history, literature, and plays.	
9. Enjoys producing craft objects that are utilitarian.		7. Understanding of art elements of line, shape, color, texture, space.	
		8. Comprehension of composition and putting form together, using harmony, balance, space, and rhythm.	

AESTHETIC	CREATIVE AND EXPRESSIVE	EVALUATIVE
Art Looking Skills: 1. Knowing the difference between art forms, such as batik, weaving, tie-dye, woodblock print, silkscreen. 2. Discussion of classwork. 3. Development of collections of "discovered" craft forms in art and in all things. 4. Learning what to look for in art forms including surface, shape, color, unity, and harmony. *Art Heritage Skills:* 1. Understanding of major historical movements in our history: Renaissance, Baroque, Impressionism, Cubism. 2. Study of cultural backgrounds in arts and crafts including Mexican, African, European, Chinese, Japanese, American Indian. *Art Judgment Skills:* 1. Discussion of works of art, using contemporary terminology of art. 2. Learning to express adequate reasons for making comparisons of works of art, both written and oral. 3. Perceiving the beauty of forms in the natural and man-made world.	*Creative Skills:* 1. Expressing same ideas in many forms, including crafts, drama, music, literature, and history. 2. Organizing form thoughtfully in unique ways. 3. Expressing one's ideas in a unique way. 4. Completing assignments and working cooperatively. 5. Using materials flexibly. 6. Continually practicing one's art through working in expressive media.	*Perceptive Growth:* 1. Is the child usually observant? 2. Is the child perceptually sensitive? 3. Does he use his ears, eyes, and touch to perceive in detail? 4. Is the child continually seeking to discuss new ideas and things through searching? *Intellectual Growth:* 1. Is there a richness of concept for forms expressed? 2. Does the child have a solid grasp of such terms as *abstraction, expressionistic,* and *cubism?* *Artistic Growth:* 1. Are art tools handled with a measure of skill? 2. Is there evidence of improvement? 3. Is the child able to synthesize line, shape, and give texture, color, and form to his artwork? *Aesthetic Growth:* 1. Can the child name various craftsmen and artists both past and present? 2. Can the child discuss reasons for his decisions in creating his own artworks as well as those of others? 3. Is the child familiar with terminology for making works of art? *Creative and Expressive Growth:* 1. Does the child work openly and freely? 2. Does the child have unique ideas and approaches? 3. Does the child complete his work and follow through in art assignments? 4. Does the child state his ideas with original thought?

47

Arts and Crafts for the Exceptional Child

Craft experiences help the exceptional child to stay within the mainstream of classroom learning. The exceptional child, whether for intellectual, physical, or emotional reasons, does not receive the maximum advantage from the existing school curriculum. For this child, special programs must be planned to fit his specific needs.

In the following sections, the classroom teacher is aided in identifying the special child, and the more general forms of art expression that are typical of the exceptional child. Suggestions for motivating, and for suitable art material, also are made. The areas that follow have been randomly organized; all are equally significant. (See color Figure 3.)

THE PHYSICALLY AND MENTALLY HANDICAPPED

Almost all of the experiences and skills offered will need to be individually considered for the specific child with a physical handicap. Physical handicaps do not necessarily require special projects, but the individual child may need assistance with a particular project. The teacher can determine the child's needs.

As one teacher said, "The mentally handicapped child is the same as any other child, only he needs a little more time, patience, and understanding." The handicapped child develops in the same manner as typical students, but at a slower rate. Most children base their art expression on real-life experiences, but the child who has difficulty relating himself to the world in which he lives will have art ideas that deal with small, intimate events of personal involvement.

The handicapped child has had a great deal of frustrating, failure-oriented experiences. Many times he has not been encouraged to use his own initiative. Because of this, he develops feelings of inadequacy, has little patience and a short attention span, and often throws his art away. He is easily influenced by the ideas of others and very often would much rather copy a pattern than depend on his own art resources. He has little interest in academic studies and does not function well socially.

This child benefits greatly in a program planned for small groups that permit teaching on a one-to-one basis when possible. He is highly self-critical and requires constant supervision. He often can understand the initial steps in an art problem but loses interest and does not listen to the whole process. As a result, he tends to make mistakes and feels frustrated and unable to complete the project. Careful guidance is necessary. The child must be provided with opportunities to solve problems that he is capable of solving. The teacher should plan success-oriented projects, whose procedures are simple. These should include repetitive steps and processes that lead to a complete product. Because the child often experiences difficulty with manipulative skills, simple tools and materials should be used with adequate, clear explanations of procedures and expectations.

The most significant teaching strategy for dealing with mentally handicapped children is to build an attitude of success and self-confidence in helping them to achieve what they are capable of achieving. Success can come through patience, reinforcement of repetitive skills, and constant encouragement by peers and teacher.

Characteristics of Art Expression

The handicapped learner has a poor concept of his body. He has difficulty with size and in sorting and fitting things together. He may have difficulty with color, shapes, and textures. Some students have poor eye-hand coordination and motivations that encourage manipulation of materials can help their development. The handicapped child has difficulty with figure-ground discrimination. Art motivations that enable the child to distinguish foreground from background help develop other related performances such as sequence of letters, reading in place, locating places on a map, and locating objects. Many times his space and size relationships are broken and unrelated. Motivations that deal with relating the child to his space are important. Drawing two or more objects in relation to each other in space and relating these objects to oneself can help develop spatial awareness.

Motivations and Art Media

Crafts help develop eye-hand coordination. The same materials and tools are used as for the normal child, but more time is allowed and instruction is repeated if necessary. One-to-one guidance is given where possible. Through craft projects, work toward the following:

1. Motivations should deal with foreground-background discrimination.
2. Motivations should enable the student to distinguish objects in space and to relate these objects to himself.

3. Perceptual discrimination skills should be developed. These are developed by size relationships, sorting objects, and placing objects in sequential order.

4. Size relationships can be encouraged through constructing and building experiences, relating one object to another. This is developed by comparisons such as large, small, and middle.

5. Shape relationships can be encouraged through selecting and reproducing squares, circles, and triangles. Find these shapes in the child's environment in flowers, trees, and houses.

6. Sorting objects can be encouraged through selecting beads, rocks, and colors; relating textures (such as in cloth) develops perceptual discrimination.

7. Placing objects in sequential order is a very important learning skill. The crafts that develop this skill include weaving (over-and-under skill), beading (for a necklace), and sewing (placement of sequential stitches).

8. Spatial relationships should be developed—seeing two or more objects in relation to each other in space. These activities help develop good spatial relations: printmaking, pegboard designs, model building, and drawing relations of size, weight, and quantity. A student indicates his self-awareness of time and space in this example: He saw an airplane flying overhead and said "hello" to it. He was very disappointed because it didn't say "hello" back. He could not understand why.

9. Drawings, stories, and social situations should be talked about and interpreted. Details should be encouraged. Build up the student's ability to tell a story or draw a picture.

10. Crayons, felt-tip pens, colored chalk, paint, and scissors are important tools for manipulation. Provide instruction on how and where to mix paints or soon all the jars will have mixed colors. Cutting is important because it helps motor control—a given line must be followed.

11. Clay experiences, building with hammer and nails, and painting with finger paint are very good for releasing inner tensions.

12. Other excellent areas that will develop dexterity include puppets; papier-mâché; cardboard box construction; cardboard design construction; wood construction; the assembling of corks, spools, brightly colored pieces of burlap, felt, yarn, and scraps of cloth with blunt embroidery needles and plasticene.

Many craft skills are later incorporated into careers for these students; they will be using three-dimensional materials and related skills in making their living by using their hands.

THE EMOTIONALLY HANDICAPPED CHILD

When a child is emotionally handicapped, his relationship within and to his environment often is altered, depending on the degree of his handicap. Each child should be approached individually and encouraged to utilize as many materials and as many techniques as he can.

Two-dimensional experiences are highly important avenues to open doorways to the child's thoughts and feelings. Although the classroom teacher is not expertly trained to understand and interpret such drawings, he or she can learn to identify certain characteristics exhibited by emotionally disturbed children.

Drawings and paintings often contain indications of the events and/or people that are disturbing the emotionally upset child. The problems may be stated literally or in symbolic form. The child with the consistent upside-down mouth, the child who draws himself very small in the corner of the paper, and the child who paints with nothing but dark colors is identifying himself regarding his feelings and attitudes.

The omission of parts of the body indicates that the child has problems with body parts. Perhaps omitting hands indicates that the child feels helpless in effecting a change in his life. Omitting feet may also indicate that he cannot move or make change—again, a feeling of helplessness. We show our feelings about ourselves when we draw ourselves alone, by the details we include, by the parts that are exaggerated, and the parts that are left out. We also give clues to ourselves when we draw ourselves and our families, ourselves at home, and so on. Sharp, pointed trees and noses and other body parts may indicate anger and hostilities. Knowledge about how children use color is a somewhat more nebulous area, and research has not been done to explain how color indicates emotional preferences, other than that various colors (depending on the child) appear to indicate tension and levels of aggression.

Sensory experiences are important for these children. Textural opportunities and craft skills that deal with manipulation are helpful expressive experiences. Clay is a very good material, as the child can hit it, bang it, and pound it on the table to express his feelings toward it. Clay is easily manipulated, and he can show control over it by making it conform to his modeling.

Talking about his artwork helps the child to verbalize his feelings and attitudes. The teacher who listens very carefully can learn a great deal about such a child. Becoming socially involved with others in his peer group helps the emotionally handicapped child to learn cooperation and also to see how he is needed in the group.

Integrating Arts and Crafts with Other Learning Areas

Art can be integrated into other learning areas. In education, teachers process information, skills, materials, and learning experiences to the student with the hope that he will assimilate, internalize, and express his thinking in an individual way to build a new form or fresh insight. By integrating art thinking with other subject thinking, the classroom can be an adventure platform for all kinds of interdisciplinary learning. Art can serve as a catalyst for crystalizing thought in both conventional and imaginative realms. By integrating art with other areas of the school curriculum, visual thinking can expand traditional modes of instruction.

Goals that cross over learning areas would include finding relationships, building awareness, recall, improvisation, classification, logical thinking, organization, visual memory, visual discrimination, auditory memory and discrimination, expression, and kinesthetic responses.

1. *Language Arts.* In language arts the following arts and crafts procedures can be related: lettering, calligraphy, printing techniques, posters, constructing letters, collage messages, illustrating books and stories, using photographs to communicate ideas, learning crafts vocabulary and crafts terminology, and finding artistic lettering in newspapers, books, and on antiques. Design comic books and murals.
2. *Dramatics.* Puppetry, drama, storytelling (folklore), magic and pretending all make use of masks, costumes, stage scenery, and environmental spaces. Feelings can be expressed through drawing and painting as well as through acting.
3. *Music.* In music, one studies rhythm, pattern, texture, color, line, and composition; the history of music in cultures and times; historical musical instruments; and the construction of simple musical tools. Listening to moods in music can serve as a motivation to draw and paint. Musical titles can be used to motivate pictures, and listening to melodies and rhythms stimulates ideas for linear compositions.
4. *Dance*
   a. Expressive body movement is another nonverbal communication tool. The body-mind kinesthetically responds to rhythms. The music often tells us what to do; each participant influences the other's form and flow through space.

b. Movement can be a teaching tool such as in clapping, moving to words and poetry, or as counting beats.

c. Dance is also a release of creative energy when using such themes as floating, growing from a seed, magic, metamorphosis of a caterpillar; interpreting high-low, open-close, tiptoe, fast-slow, squatting, dynamic change, tempo variances, accents, breathing, wriggling, holding positions, and giant and tiny steps.

5. *Science*

a. Drawing and painting from natural objects are ways to focus on the study of growth and change in the movements of animals, flowers, and trees. One can identify and classify plants, animals, and insects and illustrate them. One also can study the terminology of the organization of plants, trees, animals, birds, and fish.

b. The differences between substances—such as soft, hard, smooth, and rough—and between organic and man-made objects can be studied. One can learn about the qualities of color and light through mixing colors and about the differences between prismatic, transparent, and opaque colors by building with materials such as stained glass. Materials such as woods, metals, and papers can be classified and their inherent qualities and differences can be noted. One can also learn to observe how substances change: clay becomes hard when heated; metal becomes liquid during heating. Different kinds of fibers and the ways they are used can be studied.

c. One also can study and use various kinds of tools to learn how they inflict change.

d. Imaginative topic motivations relate to science: reflections twirl gracefully around (go on a nature treasure hunt, or discover the mysteries of space); sparkling snowflakes are for touching with your hands and tongue (create your own storm or decorate the ceiling with stars and flying things); kites or gliders soar; shells ring as wind chimes. Take apart and draw mechanical objects.

e. Various kinds of natural materials can be used for sculpture, construction, carving, and casting.

f. Study our environment: where it comes from, how it is made, and how nature is affected by man-made products.

g. Learn about our bodies, body coverings, body parts, body functions, and joints.

h. Learn about our eyes, how they function and their similarities with a camera.

i. Learn how the camera functions; develop film; learn how photography aids in communication.

j. Study television and all the parts involved with its production. Use microscopes and magnifying lenses.

k. Study environmental space: how nature uses space and how we use our spaces.

l. Study how light affects what we see and atmosphere changes our feelings.

m. Learn how printing processes aid communication.

n. Study anthropology, geology, and botany as they are related to arts and crafts skills.

o. Study varieties of clay and the ways they are used; find and prepare clays.

6. *Social Studies.* Arts and crafts offer important ways to study cultural differences at all levels. This includes the study of the pottery, weaving, and jewelry of the American Indian, Inca, African, Mexican, and other cultures. The religious meaning and lore that adornment has had can be studied as well as the ancient practices of constructing utensils and coverings for the body.

a. Study the bases of our cultural heritage: how man has expressed his behavior through objects.

b. Learn how photography enhances communication for man. Television and film making as crafts also are avenues of social communication.

c. Study murals of the past and present. (For example, study the role of the mural during the Depression of the 1930s.)

d. Learn how printing processes and the printing press have influenced and changed the history of man.

e. Study architecture and how space units have changed in times and cultures.

f. Develop models designed for home, school, and community.

g. Learn how the Industrial Revolution brought about the change from handcrafted objects to industrially manufactured objects.

h. Learn the significance of the introduction of machinery and plastics to man's knowledge and performance.

i. Study the careers of celebrated artists and how art affects mankind: man's behavior, social concepts, and physical being.

j. Study religious themes and the history of traditional festivals and holidays. Craft procedures and objects are used at these times. There are symbols connected with religions, such as the Star of David, the menorah, the crucifix, and distinctive church architecture. Special celebrations provide us with costumes, folklore, ceremony, dances, processions, foods, and decorations that are descriptive of peoples throughout the world. Studying these traditions can excite the imagination to create related costumes, headdresses, banners, masks, shields, musical instruments, body paintings, foods, jewelry, plays, games, and poetry and stories. These activities can bring history to life for the student.

k. Ideas related to the immediate environment include making maps of all kinds: waterways in the state, transportation in the city, historic trails, farming in Georgia, and so on.

7. *Math*

a. Design puppets with features that have "eyes larger than noses"; hats that have specific shapes, such as a triangle; eyes and noses compose a specific unit of numbers.

b. Have students build model houses in order to learn measurements and proportions.

c. Weave God's eyes (Ojos de Dios) which require left-to-right and right-to-left movement, measurement, and over-and-under sequences.

d. Use macrame; but, before even beginning to teach macrame, students must measure their cords and plan designs. Most cords are cut four to eight times their finished length. Give the students a recipe for an 8- or 12-foot pot sling; usually, that is too big, so the student has to divide the recipe in order to make a 4-foot-length pot sling. Students utilize mathematics during the planning. They also learn quantities in macrame and weaving.

e. Quilting requires the study of various geometric shapes. One can draw hexagons and pentagons, and determine their measurements, using the compass and protractor. All geometric shapes can be made into quilts by fitting the shapes into a specific area.

f. Learn balance through mobiles, kites, and sculpture, both symmetrical and asymmetrical.

g. Invent puzzles, geoboards, measurement games, optical designs, line and string art, and modular patterns, which are problem-solving procedures that involve art thinking.

8. *Perceptual Games*

a. Design a two-dimensional game in which the student selects a photograph or word and places it under a correct listing—such as a smell, a taste, a sight, or a sound.

b. For color discrimination offer a variety of shades and sizes of a certain color (perhaps using brown felt). Have the student name and describe similarities and differences in brightness (lights and darks) for colors. Also match shades and values.

c. Sound discrimination requires the student to "match the sound." Fill two pairs of the same size cans with various materials such as marbles, rice, sugar, hairpins, cereal, and sand. The objective is to see if the student can match the cans that sound the same. The cans might have visual clues on the bottom for identification.

    d. Use matching games of all kinds: match textures, cloth patterns, artists, and paintings.

9. *Group Art.* Working together and cooperating on projects can be related to any learning area as well as art. Many stories, subjects, and themes contain multiple ideas, images, and objects so that each student can create an individual part that is added to complete the whole. Craft media for banners, panels, and murals can be stitchery, weavings, stuffed and quilted cloth, batik, constructions, clay, baker's clay (or bread dough), textured collage, woods, plastics, photographs, cut papers, and printing techniques. Themes can include: Secret Places, Pirates of the Sea, Harbors and Boats, Westward Ho, Aesop's Fables, Alice in Wonderland, The Land of Dreams, the Wizard of Oz, Planet of the Apes, Star Trek, Flower Gardens, Picture Verses, Favorite Fairy Tales, Folk Tales, Indian Lore, Mythology, The Pied Piper of Hamelin, Noah's Ark, Jungles, Clowns and Circus, Zoos, Heros, Parades, Car Shows, Antique Clothes, Colonial Towns, The Land From the Sky, Ivanhoe's Forest, Kidnapped, Giant Greeting Cards, Under the Microscope, Playgrounds, Happy Surprises, Insects, Sea Monsters, The State Fair, Holidays and Celebrations, Everything About Our Town, Favorite Questions, and Just Nonsense.

Career Possibilities in Arts and Crafts

Classroom teachers should discuss career possibilities in crafts with their students. It is never too early for a child to begin to think about a career. Most children think about what they will do when they grow up. If the classroom teachers can plant the seeds of art when children are young, they can be nurtured during the formative years. It is well to remember that the things we do as adults relate directly to the experiences we have had as children. In this respect, classroom teachers are in a good position to establish career ideas dealing with possibilities in arts and crafts occupations. In many of the art-related fields, as in any area of endeavor, it is the *interest* that motivates. If an interest can be developed and sustained in some form of art or crafts, this type of personal momentum can catapult one toward a future career. Many careers in crafts are in art-related fields that deal directly with community service and concern.

ARCHAEOLOGY	ARCHITECTURE	ART DIRECTOR
Photographer	Draftsman	Book and magazine
Illustrator	Designer	publishing
Historian	Architect	Television
		Advertising agency
		Newspaper

TEACHER	PHOTOGRAPHY	DESIGNER
Public school	Commercial	Film
College	Portrait	Fashion
University	Newspaper	Textile
Art school	Television	Graphic
Private school	Fine arts	Furniture
Hospitals	Film maker	Interior
Senior centers		Environmental
		Stage
		Costume

ARTISTS	INDUSTRIAL DESIGN	ILLUSTRATION
Ceramist	Automotive	Medical
Leathersmith	Record cover	Greeting cards
Metalsmith	Appliance	Book
Wrought iron	Machinery	Magazine
sculptor	Journalistic	Technical
Glassblower	Furniture	Calligrapher
Weaver	Packaging	Cartoon
Woodworker		Comic book
Jeweler		Court room
Sculptor		Television
Stone worker		Newspaper
Painter		
Illustrator		

MUSEUMS	HISTORIAN	PUBLISHING
Curator	Craft historian	Book author
Director	Historian for	Magazine reviewer
Educational	stage and	Art critic
director	film	Consultant
Historian	Search service	Art book dealer
Business	for art	Archivist
director	Antiques	
Administra-		
tive		
director		
Restorer		
Archaeologist		

SPECIAL FIELDS	COMMUNITY FIELDS	ART MARKETING
Occupational therapy	Art center teacher or director	Gallery director
		Artist's representative
		Model home art
Art therapy	Parks and recreation	Corporation art
Special education	Community arts	Lecturer
		Art in public places
Art alliance director	Civic club art teacher	
	Retirement center crafts teacher	

These are just a few of the many career opportunities that exist for youth today. Making the information available and discussing it with students in elementary classrooms are the best ways to encourage interest in craft fields. Classroom teachers might like to have children write to various companies that employ artists and ask to have literature pertaining to careers sent to them. Often, companies have their own public relations departments and will be happy to send helpful information, including photographs. Material of this sort can be posted and collected to be discussed whenever appropriate. It is also helpful for the teacher to invite locally available arts people to the classroom to discuss their specific careers directly with the children. Often parents can be invited to talk to the children about their work in art-related fields.

Bibliography

ALSCHULER, ROSE H., AND LA BERTA W. HATTWICK. *Painting and Personality: A Study of Young Children.* Chicago: University of Chicago Press, 1969.

ANDERSON, FRANCES, E. *Art for All the Children: A Creative Sourcebook for the Impaired Child,* 2nd ed. Springfield, Ill.: Charles C. Thomas, Publisher, 1978.

ANDERSON, WARREN H. *Art Learning Situations for Elementary Education.* Belmont, Calif.: Wadsworth Publishing Co., Inc., 1966.

BEITTEL, KENNETH R. *Alternatives for Art Education Research.* Dubuque, Iowa.: William C. Brown Company, Publishers, 1973.

BLAND, JANE C. *Creativity and Art Education.* Washington, D.C.: The National Art Education Association, 1964.

EISNER, ELLIOT. *Educating Artistic Vision.* New York: Macmillan Publishing Co., Inc., 1972.

FELDMAN, EDMUND. "Art and the Image of the Self," *Art Education,* Sept. 1976, Vol 29. No. 5, pp. 10–12.

GAITSKELL, CHARLES D., AND AL HURWITZ. *Children and Their Art,* 3rd ed. New York: Harcourt Brace Jovanovich, Inc., 1975.

HARRIS, D. B. *Children's Drawings as Measures of Intellectual Maturity.* New York: Harcourt Brace Jovanovich, Inc., 1963.

HOOVER, F. LOUIS. *Art Activities for the Very Young.* Worcester, Mass.: Davis Publications, Inc., 1961.

HURWITZ, AL. ED. *Programs of Promise: Art in the Schools.* New York: Harcourt Brace Jovanovich, Inc., 1972.

KELLOG, RHODA. *Analyzing Children's Art.* Palo Alto, Calif.: National Press Books, 1969.

KRAMER, EDITH. *Art As Therapy with Children.* New York: Schocken Books, Inc., 1974.

LINDERMAN, EARL W., AND DONALD W. HERBERHOLZ. *Developing Artistic and Perceptual Awareness,* 3rd ed. Dubuque, Iowa: William C. Brown Company, Publishers, 1974.

————. *Invitation to Vision.* Dubuque, Iowa: William C. Brown Company, Publishers, 1967.

————. *Teaching Secondary School Art.* Dubuque, Iowa: William C. Brown Company, 1971.

LINDERMAN, MARLENE. *Art in the Elementary School.* Dubuque, Iowa: William C. Brown Company, Publishers, 1974.

LOWENFELD, VIKTOR. *The Nature of Creative Activity.* rev. ed. New York: Harcourt Brace Jovanovich, Inc., 1952.

LUCA, MARK, AND ROBERT KENT. *Art Education: Strategies of Teaching.* Englewood Cliffs, N. J.: Prentice-Hall., 1968.

RUBIN, J. A. *Child Art Therapy.* New York: Van Nostrand Reinhold Co., 1978.

SMITH, RALPH A., ED. *Aesthetics and Curriculum in Art Education.* Chicago: Rand, McNally & Co., 1966.

TORRANCE, E. PAUL, AND R. E. MEYERS. *Creative Learning and Teaching.* New York: Dodd, Mead & Co., 1970.

UHLIN, DONALD C. *Art for Exceptional Children.* Dubuque, Iowa: William C. Brown Company, 1972.

3

Design,
Drawing, Painting,
and Lettering

Art making, whether it be pottery, jewelry, leathercraft, weaving, drawing, painting, sculpture, or any other craft, requires a solid grounding in the practice of good design concepts. In other words, the art maker, be he child or artist, should work at the challenge of understanding how to create aesthetic unities in order to arrive at a satisfying art work. This understanding of design applies to craftspeople as well as to painters; it is an essential part of every classroom crafts lesson. Understanding good design concepts generally means to develop skill in putting the art elements together into a pleasing artistic statement. The art elements of line, shape, color, pattern, texture, space, and volume are totally a part of all art works. They are the ingredients. When the artist practices composing and arranging these elements into interesting visual wholes, he arrives at a more pleasing and satisfying product. The following elements are essential ingredients in the understanding of arts and crafts expression for the classroom. Working both intuitively and intellectually with the organization of these elements will enable the student to arrive at a more successful art product.

Design can be *functional*—determined by the use of the object—or *decorative,* meaning the design that is added to the object to enhance its beauty and interest.

Elements of Art

LINE

There are no limitations on how linear techniques can be utilized in the building of a crafts product. Line can be a surface penetration or it can be integral to the construction and skeleton of the work itself, as it is in weaving. Line can indicate a compositional direction within or on the surface of the work. At all times it should be beautiful to contemplate, for it is part of the essence of the work. Lines indicate motion and flow through space. They can move in front of or behind a form. Lines that are repeated become patterns.

Linear properties are a natural part of all objects, although they are not always immediately visible. Line is what our eyes observe first, for it is the edges of objects that are most apparent. This order of observation is natural—to see in shorthand before one sees the details. The artist is aware of this phenomenon when he takes care to work at achieving a pleasing outline form in his work. In pottery, the outline edge is much in evidence. If we look at a piece of pottery, and if it has lumps in its form or any variation on the flow of the linear rhythm of the outside edge, we tend to notice it, and we may react against its visually upsetting properties. Of course,

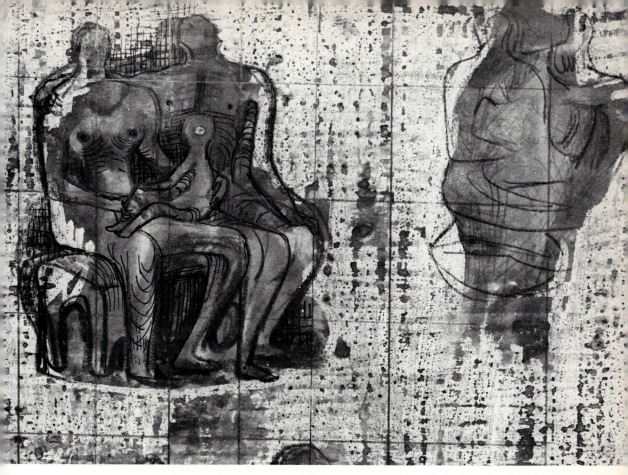

using line in art and discovering it in nature takes practice. Our artistic vision must be conditioned to increase our sensitivity to its potential.

Horizontal Lines

Lines that are horizontal in an art work suggest softly flowing movement or bodies at rest, as in sleep. Lines in the horizontal position suggest slow motion in their east-west rhythm.

Vertical Lines

Vertical lines suggest strength, for our past experience reminds us of the vertical positioning of building supports, poles, fences, and other structures. Here we have a north-south visual field, or up and down. Vertical lines may appear to move slowly up and down.

Diagonal Lines

Diagonal lines are the action lines of a form. They suggest rapid movement and sudden change. Our prior experience with diagonals comes from thinking of hills, running, diving, swooping, and speeding. It is difficult to look at a piece of pottery, a painting, or a weaving that has diagonal lines and not think of motion.

3-1 *"Studies for a Family Group," pen and ink drawing by Henry Moore. (Courtesy of the Fine Arts Gallery of San Diego, California.)*

Design, Drawing, Painting, and Lettering

63

3–2 *"Oiseau Solaire" by Joan Miró incorporates imaginative forms to express the artist's personal vision. Miró invented a form; another artist might choose the same idea but mirror reality. Plaster or soft woods can be sculpture media for classroom use. (Courtesy of Pierre Matisse Gallery, New York. Photograph by Eric Pollitzer.)*

Curved Lines

Curved lines, on the other hand, suggest grace of movement. Most of nature has curved forms, and we, therefore, think of natural forms as being graceful. Curved lines bring to mind dancers, flowers, and all things that are rhythmic and delicate. The elementary classroom student who works in crafts should understand these aspects of linear techniques (at his level) in order to control and organize his work.

In addition to the expressive qualities of the line, concern should also deal with aesthetic properties: how to make the line visually pleasing in itself. Art forms are like printed pages in that both transmit information back to the receiver. In art forms, it is possible for lines to become more than mere communication signals. Through practice in making a beautiful line, we develop that aesthetic property that extends the original message through the development of a more exquisite form.

SHAPE

When lines close on themselves, they form shapes. Shape is the outside form of the object. It may be considered the basic foundational appearance. The shape of an artistic piece in crafts is essential to its aesthetic properties. The shape may be the total unity of the form, or it may be a detail of the many other shapes that complete the work.

Shapes are essentially either *geometric* or *irregular*. By geometric is meant the basic forms of circle, square, rectangle, and triangle. Irregular shapes are amorphic, or not

3–3 *"Participation" is a stainless steel and aluminum sculpture by Jana Petersen, 6 feet × 8 feet high. It represents an abstraction of a semiconductor woofer and is installed at Motorola Corporation, Phoenix, Arizona. The artist originated the design by constructing a small 12 inch × 12 inch cardboard and wood model. (Courtesy of the Motorola Corporation, Phoenix, Arizona.)*

constant in their form. For example, a circle is always a circle (constant), whereas an irregular form is never dependable: the form, or shape, is always changing with no constant factor involved. We can create hundreds of irregular shapes and never repeat the same form. Circles, squares, rectangles, and triangles can change in color and size, but constant is the sameness of shape.

Deciding when the shape or shapes of your crafts form is satisfying is a personal decision that requires conditioning in the visual search for beautiful form through the practice of creating and the practice of observing. In fact, all artistic understanding is a conditioning process of sorts. To understand, one must *do* and *see*. Shapes, or forms, of objects tire the eye if they do not flow in the best possible way. When the proportion is off, or the balance is undecided, or there is a feeling of chaos in the flow of the line or shape, it can be

Design, Drawing, Painting, and Lettering

sensed by any child who has begun to learn the elements of art. In practicing one's craft or art, an awakening takes place in our aesthetic vision. We begin to learn a language that takes roots in our senses—in our vision and in our touch. This language is as much a form of communication as the spoken or written word. The more we utilize our senses, the further will we increase our feeling and our judgment for understanding aesthetic forms.

VALUE

Value is the degree of lightness or darkness in a tonal range. In making art, value should be considered within the design structure. All objects reflect light that changes in different atmospheres; they also cast shadows.

COLOR

Color is based on the transmission of light. As the light source changes, so does the color. In the absence of light, there is no color. The exciting thing about color is that each of us can respond to it with feeling. Some colors are attractive to us, while others repel. Each person develops his or her color palette early in life. That is, we have color preferences that affect our choices when we wear clothes, choose articles, and create art. Our color palette can be modified and expanded as we experience and work with it through art media.

Learning About Color

It is possible to learn about color in several ways:

1. We can observe it in our environment.
2. We can observe it in nature.
3. We can mix colors with paint.
4. We can mix colors with pastels or colored pencils when drawing.

When we mix one color with another, a new variation results. There are probably infinite color possibilities depending on the colors mixed. To lighten a color, add white. To darken it, add black.

We associate color with experiences. For example, we think of some colors as *warm*, such as yellow, red, and orange. These colors remind us of the sun, fire, fruit, and other forms which are bright and warm. Other colors are considered *cool*, such as blue, green, and purple. These colors remind us of water, sky, grass, and things which are cool to our eye.

Color can be studied in the classroom through mixing

paints together, combining pastels on a drawing surface, or grouping and overlapping printed color from paper samples, magazines, greeting cards, wallpaper, and so on.

Students can discover color in the environment by collecting specific colors. For example, a student may choose to find red. The assignment would be to collect as many reds as possible from magazines, advertisements, and other printed sources.

SURFACE AND PATTERN

A very important area of crafts technique is surface treatment, or the textural aspects of a work of art. Children need to understand that the surface properties are as essential as the basic form of a piece. Pattern is the treatment given to the surface. The surface can be purely textural, or it can be abstracted with subject matter images and forms that relate to the human and animal world.

For example, during Greece's golden era, artists decorated the surfaces of their pottery to express the stories and feelings

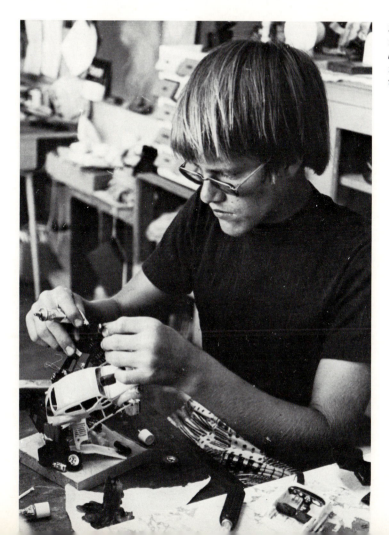

3–4 *This sixth-grader is totally involved in his assemblage sculpture made from model car parts glued together with airplane cement.*

of the age. Storytelling was entirely oral at that time, but the remains of their pottery tell us stories of their civilization.

In treating the surface of a crafts form abstractly, the child can employ geometric motifs in a repeated rhythm. Many ancient craftsmen used this technique and created subtle rhythms in visual movement. Geometric design configurations as an organic part of the surface treatment of art forms can be found in crafts from ancient as well as modern peoples from all over the world. The size of a crafted piece determines the repetition of forms around or along its surface to unify the feeling for the form. Art products have no limitation in size per se. For example, tapestries are as large as a wall surface will permit. A weaving can be as long as the weaver wishes. Jewelry can be as large as the body that will carry it. Often, the traditional view is that craft objects are small and suitable for table decoration. In the classroom, size can be whatever the child determines it to be.

In creating the surface of a craft form, the following suggestions are helpful:

1. Repeat a shape at regular or varied intervals.
2. Change the size of a shape and repeat it over and over.
3. Repeat a shape in a band that goes along or around a form.
4. Repeat a shape by using it in an over-all pattern.
5. Change the color of a shape while repeating it.
6. Have a dominant figure or shape, with subordinate figures or shapes around it.
7. Employ linear techniques as well as filled-in shapes and textures.
8. Make surfaces rough or smooth. Vary and mix contrasting surfaces.

TEXTURE

All materials have inherent properties that are both visual and tactile. The way an object feels influences its total appearance. Craft surfaces are to be felt, and combinations or similarities, as well as contrasts in texture, are important.

Texture, the surface look or feel of an art form, can be both seen and felt. In most cases, we see texture first. It can be expressed in a variety of forms. The student should try to add to the following list of texture possibilities:

rough	soft
smooth	rubbery
slippery	plastic
pebbly	spongy
grainy	sharp
sticky	rocky

gritty   furry
fuzzy   slimy
feathery   muddy

The following activities will get the student started in discovering textures:

1. Add water to dry clay to obtain various consistencies; then use various tools to make marks in the wet clay.
2. Create a collage with cloth.
3. Draw with art pastels or crayons and scratch through the surface.
4. Create rubbings from objects.

SPACE

The way in which forms are used together results in the spaces that are created. Therefore, think about positive spaces (the form) as well as negative spaces (around the form). Experiment with spacing materials to reveal their many possible forms and to indicate how simple changes will create an entirely new form. Craft objects occupy three-dimensional space, and therefore all design surfaces and spaces should be considered.

Size relationships are important in considering over-all design. It is interesting to have variety, but too much variety can be confusing. What we hope to arrive at in the creation of a craft product is an artistic ordering of each of the parts. In the process, we strive to reduce chaos.

3–5 *Example of positive space and negative space in design. The dancing, dark figures represent "positive" space; the background behind the figures is considered "negative" space.*

Design, Drawing, Painting, and Lettering

Principles of Composition

The *principles of composition* (or of *design*) refer to guidelines the artist uses to create good design. An art piece has *balance* when its forms appear to be in proportion to each other: when the distribution, weight, and appearance of a piece are equalized. Dark balances light; bright balances dull; soft balances sharp; and so on. All aspects of a craft form can be balanced: textures, shapes, lines, colors, and values. Balance provides *harmony*. There is *formal balance*, or symmetry, when one side is the same as the other. Or there is *informal balance*, or asymmetry, meaning that the design is unequal but it is a "felt" equilibrium.

Rhythm also is a basic aspect of harmony. In order to get rhythm in a piece, we need to feel the unison of one shape with another and one line with another. Rhythm provides unity and brings life into craft forms. Rhythm can be achieved through the repetition of lines, shapes, colors, textures, and surfaces. Rhythms can be dominant or secondary. Secondary rhythms echo primary rhythms. Rhythm is a regulated aesthetic flow of the elements that constitute a crafts piece. The interval of spaces within the designed form can contribute greatly to the rhythm.

Some other aspects of composition are:

Emphasis (or dominance) refers to the part that stands out or calls attention to itself. Often, emphasis is achieved with a "center of interest" or a "focal point."

3–6 *"Duckbill" by Alexander Calder, a standing mobile of sheet metal and steel wire, 26 × 35 inches. (Photo by Walter Rosenblum.)*

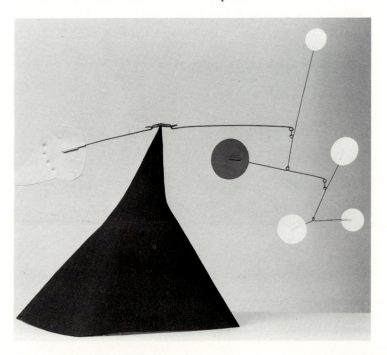

3-7 *Fish have endless design possibilities. In this collage, two stuffed fish have been placed in front of a background upon which first-grade students drew fish forms with felt pens.*

Proportion is the relationship of one part to another or to the whole.

Unity refers to the feeling and quality of oneness or wholeness.

Variety means having contrast or differences in the artwork.

Contrast refers to two opposing elements used together—for example, black and white, rough and smooth, or straight and curved.

Subjects for Art

The ideas discussed here are appropriate for the elementary classroom. The children can use them when designing or organizing their craft forms. These motifs are particularly suitable for stitchery, weaving, batik, leather, jewelry, and pottery.

IDEA LIST

Every item on the following list can become the subject for a drawing, painting, or craft form. Have the student choose a subject and bring in photographs or actual objects of the subject. They can serve as references for realistic or abstract interpretations.

Design, Drawing, Painting, and Lettering

71

Figurative Ideas
  Figures in motion
  Crowd scenes
  Seated figures
  Figure in repose
  Uniformed figure

The City
  Store fronts
  Bakery shop
  Candy counter
  Music store
  Supermarket
  Amusement centers
  Ocean liners
  Trains
  Sports car

Natural Forms
  Details of flowers
  Cactus
  Giant sequoias
  Venus flytrap

Birds and Tail Feathers
  Hawks
  Falcons
  Eagles
  Tropical birds
  Humorous birds

Animals, Alligators, and Fish
  Dogs
  Cats
  Frogs
  Lizards
  Turtles
  Snakes
  Dinosaurs

Sky, Land, and Sea Forms
  Clouds
  Fog and mist
  Sunlight and shadows
  Ocean waves
  Octopus
  Stingray
  Sunken treasure
  Pirate gold

Imagination Sparkers
  Television and movie
    themes
  Poems, plays, books,
    songs, music
  Social and holiday themes
  Real or imaginary trips
  Situations (family, com-
    munity, world)
  Feelings
  Circus
  Parades
  Special events
  Space
  Underwater fantasy
  The jungle

Birds

Bird forms are excellent subject possibilities. It is not necessary to draw specific birds, just the idea of birds. The design can show the bird flying, sitting, eating, pecking, scratching, or walking. The design can be a simple outline, a beautifully shaped piece, or an elaborately decorated surface, depending on the craft. Consider birds' combs, wattles, beaks, eyes, wings, feet, bodies, and feathers. Use parts of a bird around a dominant bird pattern. Use mother and father birds and baby birds; friendly birds (robins, doves, sparrows, and parrots); and birds of prey (eagles, hawks, gulls, vultures, and owls). All have visual properties that are conducive to interesting designs.

3–8 *Felt and trim are designed into aesthetic shapes to reconstruct the feeling for flight in these bird forms.*

3–9 *Childhood is the time to begin searching and discovering natural and man-made forms. The animal kingdom provides unlimited sources for artistic ideas. ("Charolais Bulls," photograph by Roger Buchanan.)*

Fish

The design possibilities from fish are endless. Tropical fish, for example, have a variety of forms and shapes. Encourage children to avoid stereotypes and to make their own carefully considered designs. Other forms from the sea also offer a great wealth of visual material. These include shells, starfish, and sea anemones. Peaceful fish include goldfish, bass, and trout, whereas aggressive fish include sharks, whales, and barracudas.

Animals

Animals come in every possible size, shape, color, texture, and form. They are hairy, smooth, fat, thin, tall, and squat. Domestic animals differ from wild game, and African animals differ from North American animals, and therein lie the possibilities for design. Some visually challenging varieties include tigers, lions, zebras, hippopotamuses, monkeys, snakes, crocodiles, deer, pigs, wolves, and panthers.

Insects

The tiny kingdom beneath the feet of man contains, as any child will tell you, a wealth of interesting creatures. Beetles, spiders, grasshoppers, and ants, so intricately designed themselves, lend themselves to interesting adaptive designs. Insects are transparent, opaque, round, elongated, textured, or camouflaged. Butterflies, in particular, are an amazing design source.

Flowers

Flowers, trees, and plants have been subjects for artists throughout the ages. Nature's forms are both subtle and variable. Flowers alone, for example, offer hundreds of variations on the circle. Examining natural forms can lead to beautiful discoveries that can be made relative to craft designing. There is very little chaos in nature. One of the

3–10 Magnification reveals the mysterious realm that surrounds us and provides a wealth of craft subject possibilities. Nature is the greatest designer, and we can draw our inspiration from it.

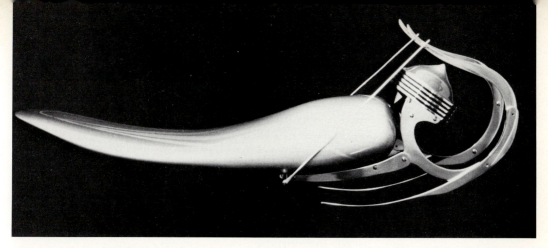

most significant discoveries that we can make by examining nature is the extraordinary order of things—the mystery, uniqueness, and relatedness of all the parts of nature's world.

ABSTRACT FORMS

Geometric and abstract forms make effective designs for crafts. Abstract design can be simplified, identifiable, or unrecognizable.

3–11 *"Stroke II" by Thomas Eckert. Metal, fiberglass, and paint. Note the similarity between this sculpture and the grasshopper in Figure 3–10. Although the materials used in this sculpture are polished steel and plastic, the artist, by utilizing his creative powers, was able to capture a feeling of both nature and man. (Courtesy of the artist.)*

Visual Spaces in the Classroom

Exhibit areas are very much a part of the visual and aesthetic aspects of the classroom environment. Areas for bulletin boards and other two-dimensional hanging areas, as well as areas for exhibiting three-dimensional work, should be carefully considered and planned for by both teacher and student. Even the most basic of rooms can be made visually attractive and be an improvement over just bare walls. If a classroom does not currently have a display board, one can be made from wallboard and installed at an eye level that fits the average height of the children in a particular grade. The material used as a display surface should be sturdy, but soft enough to receive thumbtacks, pins, and staples for pinning up lightweight materials. Displays should be arranged so that readability is effected. All lettering should be easily read. A general rule of thumb regarding lettering is to make it creative and attractive but simple enough to get the message across. Exhibits can be of any topic that will be of interest to the children: units they are studying or various subjects in the field of art. In displays that involve the subject of art, the following areas should be included.

Art history can be investigated by hanging reproductions or

Design, Drawing, Painting, and Lettering

original art. This could involve the work of one artist or of several artists. It might include great art of the past, such as ancient art, medieval art, Renaissance art, or contemporary art. Broadly treated topics could be presented, such as a survey of art from 1850 to 1973; or a detailed account of a specific point in art history could be displayed, such as "The Growth of the Gothic Cathedrals." A solo artist (or student) could be featured by a representative display of his work. Reproductions of the artist's work can be pinned to the display surfaces. The actual work could also be displayed on the wall areas or, if three-dimensional, on display tables set up for the purpose.

Art media procedures should be displayed. For example, "How to Use Drawing Tools" could be presented on a display wall. The tools could be attached and simple diagrams could show how to use each tool, as well as how to care for them.

Art concepts could be attractively presented to reinforce what the children have learned. "Designing a Picture" or "Composing in Fibers" could be presented as visual displays.

There are unlimited ideas for visual displays. One of the best displays is the work done by the class. Children love to see their own work, as well as the artwork of others. Some other broad categories for displays might deal with developing sense awareness: observing, feeling, listening, smelling, and tasting; or with intellectual awareness: observing animals, flowers, insects, plants, and trees. The artist, in order to make an interesting picture or work of art, has to be aware of his internal world and the world around him. In summary, visual displays in the classroom can center on areas such as:

Art history	Art skills
Art awareness	Art concepts
Artifacts	Art analysis

Displays should not be kept up so long that they become tiring or outdated. We all need variation in our daily diet of experiences. A change of displays once every week or two might be a useful rule. At no time should a display be kept up for the entire year.

In displaying material, consider the following:

1. Arrange all lettering in a readable fashion. The usual positioning is horizontal, but variations are up to the teacher.
2. Balance the material to be placed on the display surface. Let each item "breathe." Balance is formal when one side is geometrically the same weight as the other, or informal when a large picture on one side is balanced by three smaller pictures on the other side.

3–12 *Teachers need to plan many areas for educational displays as part of the crafts curriculum. Exhibit areas motivate individual and group discussions that relate to forming judgments and appreciation.*

3. Group material by topic, subject, or unit. Give the grouping a logical order and high visibility. Keep the display area free from objects in front of it. Do not let the area become a chaotic tack board of notes. An "idea" board, which could be a small posting area where any child in the class could tack up interesting sketches or ideas for other children to share or consider, may be provided in the room. Any child, or even the teacher, could use the idea display board to hatch or display ideas in progress, inventions, or discoveries. The emphasis on the idea board would be to push ideas by making them visible to the class. In this respect, it would be a team project, to post ideas that challenge others to work on, or to share. The idea board would be a visible bank from which good ideas are encouraged to flow. Any ideas, suggestions, thoughts, drawings, sketches, or discoveries could be included on this board.

4. A discovery display board area could also be provided in which the child can place whatever he brings in or "discovers" in the form of pictures, feathers, or objects. Discoveries can be tagged and information relative to them can be jotted down. Interesting things, found in the environment—objects, pictures, diagrams, and items from other countries—are suitable for an exhibit of this

Design, Drawing, Painting, and Lettering

THIS IS A DO-IT-YOURSELF KALEIDOSCOPE

3–13 *Our individual sensitivity to art in childhood determines what we will value as art in adulthood. This first-grader practices designing with interchangeable objects reflected in the mirror.*

sort. With this board one does not worry about formal aspects such as balance or readability, for that is not the purpose. If someone took a trip to a ghost town, old nails, lanterns, pottery, and other memorabilia from that town could be displayed. On discovery boards of this type, history, English, writing, ideas, art, and life can become intertwined, and relationships to living and experiencing can take place. Classrooms can become collection centers for art thinking and doing.

5. Carefully consider the planning of classroom display areas. But keep the learning environment in mind. Classrooms are for children. Rooms should look as though something is going on. Rooms that are always neat as pins suggest that nothing is going on. Classrooms are workrooms. Think of them as workshops, full of all sorts of visually interesting objects and tools to work with. Classrooms are environments that should be constantly changing and kept in tune with the changing experiences of the class. Classrooms should be places where children can pick up a flow for their thoughts; they should not be captive environments for the rigid dictation of information to be learned. Tables and chairs in a classroom should be portable, and the entire room can become thus a display-working area. Classrooms should be visual delights offering spaces for working creatively and observing aesthetic phenomena. Art is made up of all the things and ideas of life, including science, nature, mathematics, and literature. In other words, the artist gets his ideas from everywhere. Therefore, classrooms should have books and magazines on all subjects, and they should be available in the classroom. Children must be encouraged to read material that is challenging. This should include technical books with diagrams that are difficult to comprehend but that will suggest ideas for drawing or imagining.

6. Books that have elaborate architectural diagrams or technical details of space travel in rocketships might not be understandable in written form, but providing children in the third or fourth grade with an opportunity to examine drawings of rocketships could encourage their imagination and thinking far beyond what they are "expected" to learn. At times, the entire classroom becomes a display area, instead of the display area being an isolated wall surface over on the other side of the room. The total classroom becomes the display environment. And the environment can be continually changing and evolving in line with the development of the children in the class. "Islands of beauty" could be developed within the classroom environment.

7. Aesthetic display areas would contain visual beauty in the

78

form of paintings, sculptures, crafts, or beautiful things found in nature. Areas within the classroom environment might include a *building area,* with saws, hammers, and nails; an *ideas learning area,* with books, diagrams, and blueprints; an *art skill area;* an *art history area;* a *sensory area;* an *object involvement area,* where parts and pieces of the environment are brought in; and a *listening area* for music or any sounds that can be listened to or recorded. Cameras, phonographs, cassettes, recorders, films, tapes, and filmstrips would be included. All furniture would have to be lightweight and portable. Entire walls would have to be capable of having displays put on them or of having their shape changed by being covered with cardboard, cloth, or branches. At times, classrooms can be miniature airport hangars, space stations, antique shops, carpenter shops, scriptoriums, or whatever type of environment the learning situation calls for.

More than ever before, the classroom teacher must encourage the human aspects of living, of sharing, and of cooperating. Through art, in all of its ramifications, classroom teachers can show how creative art products provide a strand unbroken throughout the ages. The aesthetic form is a bridge between countries and generations. It is man's perpetuation

3–14 *(a) Louise Nevelson begins her sculptures with small models made from cardboard, wood, and other available materials. A much larger sculpture made of iron or steel is then formed. The shapes in this steel sculpture appear to change as the shadows move during the day in Scottsdale, Arizona. (b) After studying the sculpture of Nevelson, students created their own sculpture from found objects.*

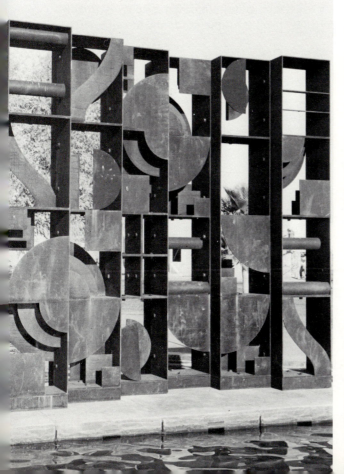

of his creative instinct. The classroom today is the grass roots of aesthetic vision. We have an unparalleled opportunity to educate for aesthetic vision, for the means of communication are there. If the teacher can develop his sensitivity to the aesthetic world, he can present this vision to the class.

Drawing and Painting

Drawing, painting, and lettering with tools that make marks on surfaces have their roots in prehistory. Clearly, man has always felt the instinctive need to record and express his ideas. Early man did so on the walls of caves and across the surfaces of rock.

These are two-dimensional experiences, in that a tool is used to record a flat image on a surface, which is the impression intended by the artist. Most people have probably at one time or another made drawings to visually express an idea, observation, or experience. Drawing, or recording on paper, stone, or any other flat surface, is actually instinctive in each of us.

Indeed, the difference between young children and their freedom to express ideas in any form is in contrast to the sense of risk that we develop toward creating word and picture forms as we grow older. It is our intention in this chapter to encourage teachers and students to regain that

3–15 *Acrylic painting on fur skin backs.*

freedom to express ideas and forms in two-dimensional terms through practicing art in specific media. Through art experiences in drawing and painting, we are able to keep our contact with the meaning of life and living, for art beckons to the creativity in each of us.

Drawing is a basic form of expression, for one must be concerned with visual and aesthetic arrangements. When drawing is done with a brush, it is called painting. Many aspects of, and approaches to, artistic vision have their foundation in the natural desire for the artist and the child to draw.

Drawing can be done on any surface. For example, artists who work with clay often inscribe their work as a surface decoration. A painting is often highly linear and is the result of drawing with the brush. Sculptors make careful preliminary drawings of their ideas.

To draw is a desire to clarify ideas by visually representing them. Putting ideas down helps to crystallize thinking and to record it for retrieval at a later time. There is, of course, the pure joy of drawing and painting that interacts with both the cognitive and affective domains.

Drawing and Painting Tools

One can draw with many tools. Some of the most familiar and easiest to obtain drawing tools are crayons, marking pens, charcoal, pastels (oil and chalk), pen and ink, and pencils. Each tool has its own characteristics and, thus, provides particular effects in accordance with the manner in which it is used. Drawing tools are linear in function, whereas paint is primarily a filling medium. Of course, there are times when the paintbrush is a drawing tool, and when the drawing tool, such as charcoal or pastel, is a filling medium.

CHARCOAL

Charcoal has blending properties that lend it to drawing in the elementary-school classroom. The two main types are vine and compressed. Vine charcoal is light in tone and erases very easily. Compressed charcoal is made from pulverized charcoal or carbon and is much blacker than vine. Both types of charcoal come in degrees of softness or hardness. The compressed type gives a very black line surface and does not erase easily. The vine type is nice at times because it can be erased with an eraser or cloth. Both types of charcoal also can be rubbed with the fingers or a

3–16 *First-hand experiences with the actual subject are the best way to observe all the details of a particular form. At other times, illustrations from books and magazines are utilized. Note that the drawings are exhibited on a board for discussion.*

cloth to modify the tones. The nice thing about charcoal is that it makes it possible to built up tonal surfaces or the feeling of dimension in a picture. It can be used at its point, or it can be held so that the side is the drawing tool. Charcoal is actually wood (willow, bass, or beech) that has been burned to dry carbon. Charcoal is an art tool that is appropriate to all grade levels.

PENCILS

Pencils are good linear and blending drawing tools. They come in many varieties and sizes, the most common being

3–17 *Charcoal is a fast, direct medium that is easily changed and blended with fingers, cloth, and a sponge eraser. In this lesson, facial proportions and features were discussed before portraits were drawn.*

charcoal pencils, graphite, and colored pencils. Pencils range in graphite hardness from 6B (softest) to 9H (hardest). Usually a 2B, HB, or even the regular school pencil will do the job. Pencil provides its own characteristic line. The softer pencils are probably the best to use, as light lines, dark lines, and shading are possible with them. Pencils are made by sheathing graphite or other material with wood. If you would like to know more about how pencils are made, write to a pencil company for printed matter explaining its manufacturing process. The company usually is happy to oblige.

PASTELS

Pastels come in many varieties and are essentially either a dry or an oil-base type. Both types of pastel can be blended easily and lend themselves to the making of colorful pictures

3–18 *"Snake Lady," a pastel by Earl Linderman, 17 inches × 14 inches.*

with a dry medium. Dry pastels are nice in that they can be blended by working two colors together or by using the fingers. Oil pastels are similar to crayons but have a much greater color range and are more permanent in nature. An infinite color range is possible by building up color, tone over tone. However, both dry pastels and charcoal must be sprayed with a fixative to keep them from fading. Hair spray often will substitute for commercially made lacquer fixatives.

MARKING PENS

Marking pens are especially suitable to the elementary-school classroom as the ink flows readily from the tube. The child does not have to work hard to produce a line. Children tire quickly from trying to cover a surface with crayons. This is not so with marking pens, which are available in either water-soluble or permanent colors. The water-soluble varieties are much cheaper and are only slightly more expensive than crayons. They offer greater color hues and large surfaces can be covered quickly. Keep the tops tightly on the pens.

PEN AND INK

Pen and ink also offer artistic possibilities in a wet medium. The pen is dipped and the drawing commences. Nonpermanent inks are more sensible for classroom use. Feathers can be made into quills, as can bamboo branches, and twigs can be dipped into ink to provide variations on what the pen can do. Brushes can also be used with ink. A good project with ink and brush or pen is calligraphy, or lettering. The Japanese and Chinese long ago mastered the art of drawing with brush, pen, and ink.

CRAYON TECHNIQUES

Crayons are the most available materials for the classroom. They come in a great variety of colors, including fluorescent. Varying sizes of crayons permit working on small as well as on large surfaces. Small hands can work with small crayons. Large mural papers are covered quickly with large crayons and free movements.

1. Peel the paper off the crayon and draw with the side of the crayon. Use a stack of newspaper under the drawing paper. Shade with the side of the crayon by applying different pressures.
2. *Rubbings.* Draw on paper placed over different kinds of

surfaces such as wood, cloth, sandpaper, cardboard, and bricks. Use the side of the crayon as well as the pointed end. Discover how many textures you can find using this technique. Coins, leaves, twigs, and screening offer more possibilities. Try using various papers as well.

3. *Wax-Resist.* This is the same procedure as number 3 in "Paint Ideas" (see page 89). Press heavily on the paper with the crayons. Brush paint, either tempera or watercolor, over the crayon-covered areas. The design will come through, like secret writing. Try brushing paint over some rubbings. Try wax-resist using crayon on dark paper and then brushing on lighter colored paint. (See Figure 12–3).

4. *Scratch Crayon.* Draw on a heavy coating of bright crayon areas; try patches, bars, or other color designs. Cover the whole crayoned paper with a dark crayon color. Use a pointed tool to scratch through the dark color to reveal a design in bright colors (See color Figure 14.)

5. *Encaustic.* Melt crayons in a muffin tin, placed over water in an electric fry pan. Or, hold crayons over a candle. Paint the crayon on heavy paper or cardboard. Use bristle brushes, sticks, or palette knives for painting. Clean brushes by placing them in a pot of boiling water, and then wash them in soapy water.

6. Scrape crayon shavings onto a piece of waxed paper. Place a second waxed sheet over the shavings. Cover the shavings with newspaper and press the sheets together with a warm (low heat) iron. The shavings will melt into the waxed paper as you iron to create beautiful, transparent designs. Cut out shapes and display them in front of

Design, Drawing, Painting, and Lettering

85

windows for light effects. Try this same idea using regular drawing or construction paper. Add linear details as a last step.

7. Refer to batik (Chapter 6) and crayon batik.

CHALK PAINTING

Chalks take on brilliant color and will not flake off when either of these methods is used.

1. Paint the paper with buttermilk, and then draw into the buttermilk.
2. Prepare a solution of 1 part of sugar to 3 parts of water; students can share the prepared mixture. Let the chalk soak in the solution for a few minutes. Then draw with the chalk, dipping it into the sugared water as needed.

TEMPERA

The best all-around paint for the elementary-school classroom is tempera, as it is relatively inexpensive and has several adaptable qualities. Tempera paint can be cleaned up easily, as it is mixed with water. If the budget permits, get the premixed paint; the consistency is much better. The formula for mixing powdered tempera paint with water is to mix them half and half. Milk cartons or lidded jars are good containers for mixing and storing powdered paint. The paint can be added to the container, along with an equal portion of water, and then mixed by shaking the container. Any container, such as a tin can, will also work, but you then have the problem of keeping the paint from drying out. Waxed paper or aluminum foil paper over the top, held with a rubber band, might do the trick. Most teachers will find it advantageous to mix up quart-sized proportions at the beginning of the school term, so that it will not be necessary to mix paint every time the class is to use it. Adding a small portion of soap flakes to the mixture will enable it to be removed from windows, clothes, and trays. For a thicker, creamier mixture, add liquid starch to the tempera paint. Let your eye tell you when it is thick enough. The starch will extend the life of the paint supply.

WATERCOLOR

Tempera paint can also be used as a watercolor. Just keep adding water until the paint's consistency is runny. A thinned tempera paint of this sort can also be used with a dip pen, quill, or mechanical drawing tool.

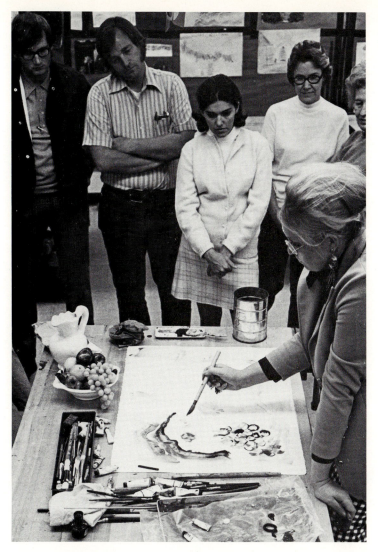

In order to keep any paint from souring, add a pinch of oil of cloves, evergreen, or peppermint.

Watercolor paints are available in boxes of eight to sixteen colors, in square or oval pans. Usually, the paint trays are plastic; they come with or without brushes. Refills can replace individual colors.

Watercolor brushes are available in both pointed or flat ends and in various sizes. They are made of hair, bristle, or nylon. Nylon brushes are best for acrylic paints. Make your own flat easel brushes with bristle brushes from the hardware store; cut them to size.

Watercolor paint is different from other paint because it is a transparent medium that is used with water. Transparent tones can be built up and the reflective quality of the underneath color is an inherent part of the technique. Paper,

Design, Drawing, Painting, and Lettering

87

wood, clay, plaster, and cloth can be painted on. Because of the see-through properties of the paint, the textures from underneath become part of the finished visual effect.

Watercolor is a highly fluid paint that responds to the needs of one's imagination and emotions, encouraging a free-flowing approach. It can be used boldly with vivid color, or subtly with soft, blended tones.

Drawing and Painting Techniques

WET INTO WET

1. Dampen a sheet of paper with a large sponge, brush, or cloth. Work on Formica tabletops or newspapers.
2. Brush into the wet surface; the color will spread and bleed into the wet areas.
3. Drip and dab color into the wet paper.
4. Tip the paper and move it around so that the colors combine.
5. Try loading one color on half the brush, another color on the other half, and then paint into the wet paper.
6. Draw with sticks, felt-tip pens, chalk, cotton swabs, brayers, and other inventive tools.

DRY PAINTING

1. Paint tones of one color. Let them dry. Paint over some of these same tones with deeper tones. See what color you can invent.
2. "Dry brush" means to wipe off excess water. Then heavily load the brush with paint. Wipe off any excess paint. Apply the paint to the paper. There should be a rough texture with the paper sparkling through the paint. Use the dry approach and dab paint on with a sponge, crumpled paper, or wadded cloth.
3. Paint linear detail.

WASHES

1. Load your brush with water and paint. Draw the brush across the paper from one edge to the next. Repeat this paint application again, letting the stroke touch the wet edge of the previous stroke.
2. Graduated washes are achieved by applying a streak of

paint across the paper and then loading the brush this time with water instead of paint. Touch the edge as in step 1, and the water and paint will blend to create lighter tones.

3–21 *"Adobe House," watercolor by Marlene Linderman, 48 inches × 36 inches.*

PAINT IDEAS

1. Drip paint onto half of a sheet of paper. Fold the paper in half and rub it flat with your hand. Open the paper and watch as interesting textures develop. Let the paint dry. Repeat the process by overlapping a new color. Draw over these with a felt-tip pen. Invent titles for these imaginative designs.

2. Load string with tempera paint. Drop the string into loops, and twist them on a piece of paper. Let the ends of the string extend beyond the edges of the paper. Place a second piece of paper over the first. Cover this with a piece of cardboard. Hold it tightly in place with one hand. With the other hand, take the end of the string and pull it out from between the papers. You will have two designs, one on each paper.

3. Draw with water-resist materials such as crayons, candles, candle drips, rubber cement, or white glue lines (let the glue dry first). Paint over these resist materials with

Design, Drawing, Painting, and Lettering

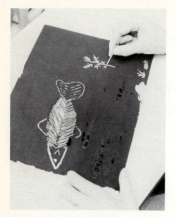

3–22 *Scratching through paint that has been applied to aluminum foil produces a light line on a dark surface.*

watercolors. The watercolor will run off the crayon, exposing the drawing.

4. Glue a piece of aluminum foil to a piece of cardboard. Smooth out any wrinkles. Add a few drops of liquid detergent to the tempera and paint over the foil. Etch a design through the paint with a nail or scissors. (See Figure 3–22).

5. Cover a piece of paper with a heavy coat of bright patches of crayon. Brush a contrasting tempera color over this. To make the paint stick to the crayon, swab a bar of soap with the brush in between applications of paint. After it is dry, scratch through the paint with a nail or scissors so that the crayon design is revealed. Or, dust crayon with talcum powder.

6. Paint a tempera design on paper using bright colors. Leave some unpainted areas. Let the paint dry thoroughly. Brush black waterproof India ink over the paper. Let the ink dry completely. Place the paper under a thin stream of running water. The water will cause the ink to run off where the paint is, leaving textures. The dark outlines around the color will give a stained-glass effect.

OTHER PAINTS

If you would like to make oil paint from the powder pigment, mix the pigment with linseed oil, varnish, or turpentine. To make white oil paint, mix zinc oxide with the linseed oil. If you want to make an inexpensive varnish, fill a jar with pieces of Styrofoam egg cartons and add about ⅓ paint thinner or turpentine. The Styrofoam pieces will dissolve, and the resulting mixture will be similar to varnish. It can be

3–23 *Artists paint subjects they know and like. This young horse lover paints from her memory with acrylic paints. Meat trays are disposable paint trays.*

3-24 *Working spaces are important in the classroom. This art room has large work tables grouped together. A mirror above ensures that all students can see the demonstrations. Paintings are exhibited on the ceiling as well as on the walls.*

painted on surfaces and will dry to a shine. To make an enamel paint, add clear shellac or varnish to the powder paint. You can use your homemade varnish mixture and add powder pigment to it.

WHERE TO PAINT

Painting can be done by the total class at one time, or by groups, or by an individual at an easel. It can be done indoors or outdoors. There is a good feeling that is contagious when an entire class paints at one time. Desk tops (if they are not screwed down) can become foundational surfaces, which can be placed together to form very large surfaces. Otherwise, tabletops or the floor work very well. To use the desk, table, or floor, simply spread newspaper down and divide the children into groups of five or six. By grouping them, they will have access to paint clusters: by placing three children on opposite sides of a carton of paint, with one water bucket for cleaning the brushes, all can paint with freedom. You can help to keep the paint containers from being tipped over by placing them in a grocery carton that has been cut 2 inches from its base. If your room is limited in size, you can move the desks or tables to the sides of the room. Another possibility is to use the hallway. For murals, butcher paper or kraft paper can be taped to the wall, or the paper can be unrolled and placed on the floor. The child can paint standing up or sitting down. However, it is probably better to have the paper flat rather than on a wall, as the paint has a tendency to run when it is added to paper that is on an easel. The drips really do not add to the quality of the child's ideas.

Design, Drawing, Painting, and Lettering

Brushes should always be cleaned out after use and stored with the brush end up in a container. Otherwise, the hairs will become bent out of shape by drying with their points down.

Painting surfaces can be papers, wood, walls, sidewalks, window shades, leather, clay, metal, plaster, plastics, cloth, old telephone and wallpaper books, cardboard, boxes, and animal skins.

STILL LIFE

Creating an art work by using a still-life arrangement as a model is a favorite art school method of encouraging the artist to practice his skill in drawing, painting, and observing. This is an excellent method for developing compositional, tool, and observational skills with children of any age. Even kindergarten children can draw or paint a still life. It is not the subject that matters, but the ability of the teacher to reach the children at the level of their frame of reference. Drawing or painting from a still life provides an excellent opportunity to observe closely the details of a subject and to record them. The still life emphasizes such art skills as *arrangement, line, shape, shading, design, texture,* and *value,* and the interrelation of each of the parts to form a new whole on the surface of the paper or canvas.

3–25 *Subjects for a still life can be arranged close to the work areas. The stacked shelves, upper left, hold wet paintings.*

First, select some highly interesting visual objects that you feel would look well together in an arrangement. Henri Matisse, a French artist, carefully arranged flowers, old books, pipes, horns, letters, vases, clocks, and other ornate but visually pleasing items. He positioned them on a table, so that the light could be focused precisely. In your travels as a teacher, you are bound to come across interesting things to draw. Other possibilities for still-life arrangements include fruit (apples, peaches, grapes, watermelons, lemons, and oranges) combined with plates, pitchers, and eating utensils. A floral arrangement also offers an inventive challenge for the searching eye. In this case, arrange flowers in season in a pitcher and you are ready to begin. Select an attractive piece of cloth for the table or other surface to brighten or enhance the arrangement. Keep the color selections sympathetic to the arrangement.

A still-life arrangement can be limited to a simple sphere and square block, or to any other basic geometric arrangement. Here the emphasis will be on the subtle relationships of volume, or shadows.

Artists of repute who have painted or drawn magnificent still lifes include Henri Matisse, Paul Cézanne, Georges Braque, William Harnett, and Charles W. Peale. Still lifes can be painted or drawn realistically, abstractly, or surrealistically.

THE STILL-LIFE LESSON

Procedure

1. Place visually appealing subjects in a still-life arrangement.
2. Arrange the objects on a small table in plain view of all. Any number of arrangements is possible, depending on what can be collected.
3. Collect a variety of forms, including rectangles, squares, circles, and elliptical or irregular shapes. Curved forms give softness to the arrangement.
4. Lightly draw the main lines of the objects to develop your composition. This is always an intuitive procedure. Your natural judgment will help you to decide where to place things.
5. Emphasize variety in your arrangement by keeping some forms larger than others.
6. Some interesting subject possibilities might include toys, model cars, dolls, hats, machinery, fruit, teapots, glassware, bottles, musical instruments, antique items, skulls, clocks, candles, and flowers.
7. Curves soften, diagonal lines suggest action, horizontal lines suggest rest, and vertical lines suggest strength and quiet. Do not overcomplicate your arrangement.

8. Let your mind do the talking, and coordinate it with your hand. Continue with any media, whether it be felt-tip pens, crayons, oil pastels, watercolors, or a combination of them. Discuss some possible design skills and arrangements with the students. Demonstrate two or more ways of beginning the drawing and ways of interpreting the still life.

9. If you decide to paint the still life, use a variety of strokes: broad, long, and short.

10. Draw with lines to define forms and shapes and to clarify edges.

11. Experiment with various ways to handle the brush: apply pressure, let up, use the point, and continue from there.

12. During the working time, and after completion, place the drawings on a wall for student examination. Discuss the many possible interpretations of the still life, and how we all "see" in various ways and with different emotions. Compliment students on the success of their drawings. In group discussions, ask what the students liked in the drawings of others. Discuss color combinations, shading, texture, line directions, patterns, and how the students used the picture space in arranging their designs. Teachers can point out at least one successful strength within each drawing. This can be a design element, compositional placement, emotional feeling, or any area that appears to reflect a personal statement by the

3–26 *Mood, shadow, and volume can be realistic or abstract. In this watercolor painting by Charles Burchfield, the lights glimmer in a fantasy forest. (Courtesy of Dintenfass Gallery, New York City.)*

student. If the subjects are interesting to the students, they may want to draw or paint them again, thereby gaining from the information absorbed during the discussion. Growth in art comes when we practice over and over, seeking new insights to crystallize understanding.

MOOD: SHADING AND SHADOWS

One of the fundamental skills in learning how to draw is how to shade to create volume, or three dimensions. Compressed charcoal is an excellent medium for creating tones and shading. It enables the artist or child not only to make black but also to get many variations of gray in between. A good picture can be done abstractly or realistically, at the option of the creator.

To motivate a class in shading, show the works of artists and point out examples of shading in their pictures. Two artists who come to mind are Rembrandt and Giorgio De Chirico. De Chirico used long, end-of-the-day shadows of buildings, anonymous figures in the distance, and, in general, a great deal of personal symbolism. Moods are created in a picture when darks and lights in tonal qualities and shadows are used. Shadows are part of every situation in which there is light. They are the contrast created when natural or artificial light sources are blocked.

SURREALISM

Surrealism can provide a wonderful springboard for the imagination and for thinking in other than humdrum terms.

3–27 *The world of dreams, the subconscious, and the imagination are inspirations for surrealistic paintings. These one-eyed creatures dance gracefully across the paper.*

Surrealism refers to *beyond* what is real, or beyond the realistic aspect of forms into the worlds of dreams, the subconscious, and the imagination. Thus, in surrealism we have the freedom to let our imaginations roam in search of unique images. Refer to the works of such surrealist masters as René Magritte, Giorgio De Chirico, and Salvador Dali to see that the usual and the unusual are often combined to create a statement. All of their works of art are very *un-ordinary*. They seek to startle us with arrangements of forms that do not usually go together. In a surrealistic picture, we can emphasize the following:

unusual size relationships or displacements—for example, roses the size of a room, a fish as large as a standing man
heavy objects that appear to float
transparent objects that are not usually transparent
mirrors that reflect something other than the object they mirror

Good subject matter for a surrealistic picture might include caskets, skulls, candles, spider webs, castles, strange light sources, and eerie shadows. After studying the paintings of Magritte, one class created surrealistic pictures that included elephants coming out of a mouse hole, a train on a tabletop, an alligator coming up a road, a fire in the ocean, and a brick wall in the sky. In other words, things were not represented as they ordinarily appear to be. The usual boundaries for subjects can be forgotten, and we can emphasize a more inventive exploration of visual relationships.

3–28 *This face-making machine is one way to arouse the imaginative curiosity of students. Four rollers carry the parts across the screen.*

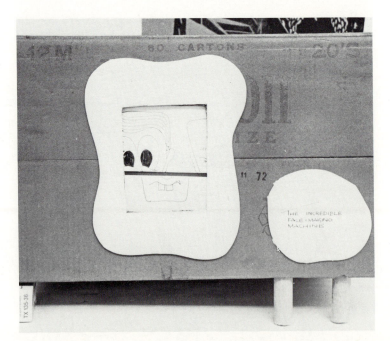

3–29 *Painting with acrylics. The subject is "Catching the Wind."*

Other imagination-sparking lessons can be initiated by simply brainstorming an idea or title. Here are some possible beginnings on which you can expand:

The Hidden Creatures Living Inside the Earth
The Dandelion Seed That Didn't Want to Grow
The Magic Garden
Secret Messages with Invisible Writing
I Wonder How a Motor Works
How We Built Our Spaceship to Saturn
How the Dot Grew into a Design
The Adventures of a Line
What We Think the Mona Lisa Is Smiling About
When I Walk into the Painting "Lady Before a Mirror" by Pablo Picasso
My Favorite . . .; I Wish I Were . . .; Back in 1880 . . .;
The Day the Clouds . . .; On My Flying Carpet We . . .;
Happiness Is . . .; Sadness Is . . .
If Abe Lincoln Hadn't Died
Do-Nothing Machines
A Poster That States: All About Me
Titles from Movies
Titles from Television Series
Swallowed by Me: My Adventures in My Stomach
Blow-ups of Machines, Eyes, Flowers, Hearts, Diamonds, Bird Legs, and so on
Our Visit with UFOs
If I Were a Wasp . . .; a Scorpion . . .; a Monster . . .; a Snake . . .; a Butterfly
If I Were President . . .; Cleopatra . . .; Paul Revere . . .; Benjamin Franklin . . .
Picture Yourself on a Sea Creature Traveling the Ocean
The Mysterious World Under the Water
The Sea—A Super-Giant Home for Sea Creatures
A "Creature Cage" for Wonderful Creatures
Ride the Clouds Over the World
Catch the Rain on Your Tongue
Catch the Wind in Your Hands
Reflection Pictures (look into metal, water, ice, and eyes)
Being Best Friends with Your Favorite Hero
If You Were Magic, You Could . . .

ROCK PAINTING

Begin your rock collection right now. Trips to parks, rivers, and mountains will reward you with rocks of many sizes, shapes, textures, and colors. It is fun to sort rocks into small boxes while considering their shapes as well as what you feel are your favorites. Learn the varieties of rocks that are commonly found in your area (in reference books, gem and mineral shops, and from rock collectors and clubs). Learning the names of rocks and where they are found is part of the fun. Observe how nature has stacked and placed rocks and boulders in their different environments.

Some rocks are so imaginately shaped they may even suggest "people you know." Other rocks can be built up to resemble animals and insects. Add decorative items after gluing the rocks together. Paint forms and details where desired with small brushes, toothpicks, or twigs.

Supplies Needed
rocks
masking tape
tissue paper
bric-a-brac
white (fast drying) and epoxy glue
paint (acrylic, enamel, or tempera)
clear finish (either acrylic, varnish spray, or clear enamel)
nail polish
brushes, toothpicks, or dried twigs
waxed paper

Procedure
1. Select a variety of rocks that you feel relate well enough to be combined in a three-dimensional sculpture. Consider texture, color, shape, and size.
2. Stack them as they will appear in their final form. Be sure to view the sculpture from all angles.
3. When you have found the most pleasing arrangement epoxy the bottom shape and build up from there.
4. Hold the rocks together with masking tape until the epoxy is dry.
5. Or tear tissue paper into various sizes and shapes. Glue the tissue pieces on a rock, overlapping and covering the rock completely with a coating of white glue. Place the rock on waxed paper to dry for about 24 hours. The glue finish will be glossy.
6. Paint a design or a scene of your choice on a rock, with small brushes or toothpicks dipped in enamel, acrylic, or tempera paint. Finish with a plastic spray or nail polish. Place on a small driftwood branch. Glue it to the branch with epoxy.

SAND PAINTING

Sand painting is a popular art form among the Navajo Indians. The shapes and symbols used have long had special meaning for them. For example, the Navajos will do a large

3–30 *A Navajo sand painting placed directly on the floor on a cloth surface (about 5 feet × 4 feet).*

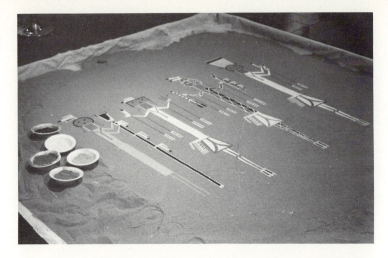

family painting with sand before a wedding takes place. Here is an easy formula for doing sand paintings in the classroom.

Supplies Needed

food coloring
heavy paper, cardboard, or sandpaper in assorted sizes
a pail, jar, or can of sand (cornmeal or rice can be substituted for sand)
white glue
spoon (optional)

Procedure

1. Mix vegetable food coloring, some water, and sand, cornmeal, or rice in jars or cans. (Or mix ordinary table salt along with some colored chalk shavings in a small jar.)
2. Shake to mix until the sand is evenly coated.
3. Lay the colored sand out on newspaper to dry overnight.
4. Paint a background color on the cardboard.
5. Draw a design on the background with a pencil.
6. Squeeze white glue onto the drawn lines (or brush on).
7. Dribble sand onto the glue either by using a spoon or a small jar with a perforated top, or with the fingers, as the Indians do. (The sand is in the palm, the thumb is placed over the middle of the first finger, and the flow of the sand is kept easy by the thumb.)
8. After one color has been used and the glue is dry, lift the backing and tap it lightly so the excess sand falls off.
9. Place the excess back in its container.
10. Add colors until the design is finished.
11. A variation can be done with colored rice. Outline the design with colored heavy yarn. Fill it in with rice of different colors. Sawdust also can be colored with dried tempera paint and sprinkled on a background.

3-31 *(a) The girl on the left is painting the glue on sandpaper to catch the colored sand that the girl on the right is sprinkling on. (b) She next carefully pats off extra sand and presses the rest into the wet glue.*

FINGER PAINTING

You have something no one else in the world has—your own special fingerprints. Children as well as artists enjoy finger painting. The fingers move smoothly over the surface, and swift, flowing, dynamic designs materialize almost immediately. The plasticity of the medium is such that the flow of ideas is continuous and spontaneous. Finger painting techniques permit a person's fullest range of expression.

Finger painting is one of the best ways to get started in drawing or painting. Abstract designs and rhythms—all sorts of harmonies—can be created. The really nice thing about finger painting is that visual effects can be achieved that are unobtainable from any other process.

The trick in making a successful finger painting picture is to draw the finger paint on a smooth surface, such as a linoleum-covered tabletop, desk top, cookie sheet, or other surface that is free of dirt.

Design, Drawing, Painting, and Lettering

Supplies Needed

sponge
absorbent paper
liquid starch
sticks and spoons
powdered tempera (silver, bronze, and gold powder,
  optional)
pinch of soap flakes
tabletop or desk top
glossy paper (desirable when finger painting directly on
  paper)

Procedure

1. Wash the table surface with a sponge.
2. Pour some liquid starch the size of a silver dollar on a
   tabletop. Add a small amount of dry finger paint (one or
   more colors) into the liquid starch. Mix.
3. By working directly on the tabletop, draw into the
   mixture with your fingers, fist, palm, or with tools such
   as sticks, spoons, and other assorted items. Try to
   achieve a variety of effects.
4. The freedom of drawing with the fingers and hands has
   an exhilarating effect. After experimenting for a few
   minutes, organize a design or a picture.
5. When the design is completed, you are ready to pull a
   print. Each finger paint image that you do ordinarily will
   permit only one print to be taken from the surface.
6. Lay the paper carefully on the surface of the image and
   press.
7. Lift the paper with clean hands. Your painting will be
   transferred to the paper.
8. Once you master the method, you will be able to put
   greater effort into the organization and composition of
   your finger painting.
9. Put a small amount of silver, bronze, or gold powdered
   tempera into the starch and powdered color to give a
   metallic effect.
10. Rice papers and other absorbent papers work best, but
    any kind of paper, including grocery store shelf paper,
    can be used when this tabletop method of working is
    employed.
11. Provide a space in the room in which to dry the
    fingerpaint prints. Exhibit them directly on bulletin
    boards, or hang them with clip clothespins on a portable
    clothesline.
12. Appoint monitors for each aspect of the lesson. Have
    monitors for brushes, paint containers, mixing, floor
    cleanup, storage, and for picture hanging, passing out,
    collecting, and so forth.

Checkpoints

1. Wear a smock or old shirt when finger painting.
2. Adding a pinch of soap flakes to the starch-paint mixture will make cleanup easier.
3. A variation of the preceding technique is to use chocolate pudding instead of starch and tempera. If the surface is clean, you can enjoy licking your fingers clean!

Graphic Communication

Communication is the word of the twentieth century. Through newspapers, magazines, and particularly television, we can be instantly aware of the events all over the world. The news of the day, the week, or the month is made more dynamic when the artist is asked to illustrate ideas in the various news and magazine stories. The artist can go beyond a single statement, such as "This is John Doe"—he can combine statements both realistic and imaginative in a single format.

Illustrating the courtroom drama is one example of how the artist enhances the media.

GREAT MOMENTS IN HISTORY

The objective of this art lesson is to push ideas by making a definitive, shorthand statement regarding some great event in our past or current history. All of the student's creative resources will be needed. Some suggestions of great events in the history of man follow:

3–32 *F. Lee Bailey questions a witness during a Phoenix trial. A courtroom artist must communicate graphically a shorthand statement and record images accurately for the reporter's story that is aired on television the same day. Drawing is 14 inches × 17 inches in mixed media and by Marlene Linderman.*

invention of the light bulb
invention of the steam engine
invention of electricity
invention of television
parting of the Red Sea
Custer's Last Stand
Greece's golden age
dropping the atomic bomb
invention of the computer
rockets to the moon
invention of the printing press
Paul Revere's ride
arrival at the North Pole
discovery of America
Battle of the Bulge

Students will be able to discover many more ideas that have shaped our civilization. They can stop to consider what the most effective way to symbolize a great event is. The picture can be approached humorously, satirically, abstractly, symbolically, or realistically. It can be a cartoon or it can contain words and messages.

Any techniques can be used: drawing, painting, and collage are examples. The point is to suggest an interpretation of the event by putting down visual cues in picture form.

PICTURES IN SEQUENCE

Here is a simple, but effective, art lesson that encourages both ideas and a sense of humor. The emphasis is on the free play of imagination to invent a situation (the before) and then to determine a solution (the after). The lesson consists of drawing two pictures. The first picture is the "before" situation; it establishes a subject and ideas. The second picture is the result, or what actually happens to the subject as a result of the first situation. The sequence, or "after" picture, can be expressed humorously, mysteriously, or in any manner the artist wishes.

First Sequence (Before)	Second Sequence (After)
man and fish swimming in the same direction	fish swimming after the man, who is swimming fast
boy waters a flower with a watering can	flower shoots up toward the sky
boy swats a fly with a fly swatter	boy turns around and a giant fly confronts him
girls throws a ball into the air	many balls rain down from the sky
woman puts money into a machine	machine pours out flowers of all sorts

3–33 *In this two-stage sequence, the girl (left) is about to drink the giant lemonade, and then (right) take a swim in the lemonade punchbowl.*

The following are examples of before and after sequences:
Marking pens are recommended for this lesson, for they move quickly over the paper. However, crayons, paints, or pencils will also serve the purpose. These pictures can be made in the form of a greeting card. The before sequence appears on the front fold, and the after sequence appears on the inside.

ILLUSION PICTURES

Supplies Needed
2 drawings or paintings of the same size
scissors
laminated or clear adhesive paper

3–34 *Students combine their drawings to complete a story. Tabs are inserted into slits in the drawings to provide movement. This group effort makes a clever book.*

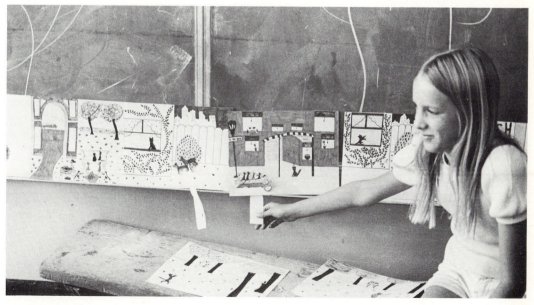

Procedure
1. Cut each picture into long strips.
2. Alternate the drawings, one strip from one, the next strip from the other.
3. Glue to a backing paper.
4. Laminate the picture or cover with clear adhesive paper.
5. Next, fold the completed picture in a V-shaped accordian fashion.
6. Tape or glue the V-shaped picture to a backing.

WORDS AND PICTURES

Throughout the curriculum, language and art play active roles in developing imagination. Words and pictures are a natural combination. In the following drawing projects, the objective is to stimulate and offer opportunities to develop a child's individual concept of an idea. Too often, we find that adult standards for drawings are presented for students to imitate. The following ideas are intended to motivate children to solve problems. The encounters can be interpreted for individual and class levels of development in accord with the specific needs and sequential objectives established within a specific program.

1. Develop your own classroom newspaper with stories and illustrations. Before the advent of the camera, staffs of artists always illustrated the news stories in newspapers.
2. Create original stories, books, and poems and illustrate them.
3. Create murals depicting various subjects and enhance them with word balloons and captions. These can be individually produced or developed as a group project.

4. Create classroom comic books. The comic strip develops ideas in sequential patterns and often relates words and pictures to complete the idea. Comic strips are exaggerations: the statement is brief, to the point, and often has a cause-and-effect structure. An important part of word structure is *sound*. Comic strips use many words that amplify and exaggerate sounds and sound effects. Ask students to make a list of sound words they can find. Such words would include ugh, slam, pow, yow, thud, socko, zam, zing, ouch, and wow. These are some ideas for comic strips.

   a. Imaginary trips, inventing, wishes and dreams, and pretending to be someone or something else.

   b. Mythology. Invent a superhero theme. Many of the ancient mythological characters are depicted with superhuman strength (such as Hercules). Our own "Superman" is based on this theme.

   c. Science fiction. These ideas are fantasy-based and relate to adventures and explorations.

   d. Invent an "anyone you want to" character (it could be your inner self, such as Charlie Brown, or your dog, such as Snoopy). Have the characters perform an activity that has a cause and effect, or illustrate an event that has an outcome. Exaggerate the features and the action.

5. Procedure for beginning a comic strip:

   a. Draw a three- or four-blank frame strip with blank captions. Or prepare the frames ahead of time, and pass them out to your students.

   b. Examine several comic strips, select your favorites, and study the characters, scenes, and plots. Next, cover the captions (so you can't see them) and look at the strip and action to see if you can figure out the plot without the words. Also examine comic book covers for condensed ideas. Study cartoonists in newspapers.

   c. Examine the words without the visuals to see if the ideas are clear. Study the sound and action words.

   d. Discuss the drawing techniques.

   e. Study the strip for various types of plots, sequence ideas, and exaggerations; discuss how the pictures and words describe each other, and how the student might complete a strip in his own way.

   f. Have the students select their ideas and plan a sequence of action to complete the ideas.

   g. Each frame should be sketched briefly in pencil.

   h. Complete each drawing and caption with ink outlines and color.

   i. When the strip is finished, exhibit it and share ideas.

   j. For variation, try completing an idea with three of the frames, and let your neighbor finish the fourth frame.

3–36 *Advertising and graphic design should be made relevant to the student. These greeting cards express different ideas.*

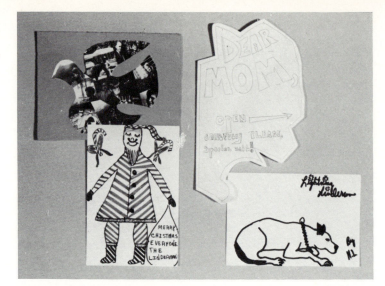

ADVERTISING DESIGN

Advertising subjects for graphic design projects should be as important and relevant as possible for the elementary student. They should grow from his past experiences and needs in his community, school, and home environment. To complete this project, the student should research his ideas, have knowledge of design concepts (such as line, color, texture, pattern, space, and shape), and have skills in lettering, illustration, and composition.

Design projects can include:

signs
calendars
boxes and packages

3–37 *A pen and ink drawing from a book of illustrations on knitting by Robin Swanson (11 inches × 14 inches).*

posters and murals that deal with school events, sports, social events, health programs, community events, and charitable organizations

record album covers, magazine covers

newspaper, magazine, and catalog advertisements

planning and designing television commercials

space display such as in store windows

message cards—special event cards with messages that are elaborately designed

story illustration

outdoor billboards

FANCY SIGNATURES

We write names thousands of times in the course of our lives. Our signatures are always written the same way. An interesting art lesson, which is a variation on the signature, teaches the child to embellish his name as elaborately as possible. The objective here is to emphasize each child's personality and, thus, enrich his self-concept. All children need success experiences, and there is no better way to begin in art than with one's name. The aim is to be as decorative and elaborate as possible, while keeping the signature legible. You can use several approaches to develop this lesson. The name can be written in the alphabet, or it can be

3–38 *Your own name can be as fancy and imaginative as you can make it.*

treated symbolically. A name can be written in the form of those things a person likes, such as music, in which musical instruments could be put together to form the letters of the name. The name could be written with pieces of fur or other tactile materials. Names can be constructed in a three-dimensional form so as to stand up. The supplies in this case are simple ones: cloth, marking pens, paper, and found materials. This project could serve as a lead-in to discovering decorative writing in the environment, such as on birthday cakes, neon signs, medieval manuscripts, the Declaration of Independence, and in calligraphy.

Lettering

Lettering is a form of writing, a relatively new means of communication for civilization. New, that is, if we consider civilization's development in terms of geologic time. Although man has been in a state of development for thousands of years or more, writing is only about five thousand years old.

One of the earliest forms of written language is attributed to the Sumerians, a people who lived some two thousand years before Christ in the area of the Middle East known as Mesopotamia. Sumerian writing, which was pressed into clay tablets by the use of wedge-shaped reeds, came to be known as *cuneiform* writing, a word whose roots are in the Latin *cuneus* (wedge) and *forma* (form). Another early form of writing existed in Egypt and is known as *hieroglyphic* writing. The development of writing proceeded rather slowly. The first writing surfaces were cave walls, structural walls, and clay or stone tablets. The earliest works were brief because they were inscribed on stone or clay. One either wrote on what he could carry or used a wall of some sort.

The discovery of a form of paper and pen changed the course of written language. The earliest known form of

3–39 *Such favorite sayings as "Snug as a bug in a rug," "He was as hungry as a horse," and "They were all ears" are illustrated by third-grade students. Earl Linderman stands in front.*

paper, papyrus, was developed by the Egyptians. Papyrus could be rolled, but even this prohibited lengthy manuscripts. Imagine how many rolls it took to write Homer's *Odyssey*. (The original Bible similarly was probably very bulky, as it was written on skins or leather, called vellum.) Papyrus was taken from a plant that grew near the Nile River. The plant was shredded and pounded into sheets and became the forerunner of paper (see Chapter 4, "Creating with Paper"). It made writing materials portable and writing available to many. These early writings were the forerunners of the magnificent manuscripts of the Middle Ages. The term *manuscript* itself means "handwritten."

The original pen, or quill, was a feather taken from various birds. Quills worked very well in combination with ink on parchment or vellum. The Latin word for feather (quill) is *penna* (pen). Parchment was sheep or goat skin; vellum was the premium quality skin obtainable from calf, kid, or lamb, sometimes before birth.

In Figure 3–40, we see the significance of drawing and lettering as a tool. In the earliest times, books were meticu-

3–40 *Devotional page from a French Book of Hours, A.D. 1492. (Courtesy of Special Collections, Library, Arizona State University.)*

lously written and illustrated by hand. As a result, the craftsperson's skill was revealed in the calligraphy of his handwriting, and in the marginal decorations that often accompanied the written or printed word. The advent of the printing press in Germany, in the midfifteenth century, began the period of incunabula, or books published prior to A.D.1500. Students can learn much of the beauty of lettering and the printed page by studying the early history of book development.

The first book printed with movable type in America was the "Bay Psalm Book," which was printed in 1640 by Stephen Daye at Cambridge, Massachusetts. Writing has been done on countless varieties of surfaces. In modern times, writing is done in neon on signs or by electronic impulses with computers.

CALLIGRAPHY

Calligraphy, which comes from the Greek word *kalligraphia,* is a beautiful form of handwriting. Lettering may be considered to be a derivative form of calligraphy. In school programs there are countless opportunities to utilize calligraphy and lettering on surfaces.

Many variations in the history of lettering were practiced over and again to arrive at the letter forms we know. There are three basic traditional groups—*roman, gothic,* and *script*—from which many variations are possible. Today, creative variations and derivations of letters are often used in the world around us.

LETTERING TOOLS

Many tools will produce visually pleasing lettering. They need not be expensive, and many can be made by hand.

Letters can be sawed, cut, or otherwise formed from wood, Styrofoam, clay, plastic, and other materials. Letters can be cut from newspapers, magazine photos, old ditto paper, tissue paper, corrugated paper, wrapping papers, wallpaper, telephone directories, as well as construction paper, tag board, and poster board. Letters can be cut from cloth, stitched, and stuffed. They can be stamped into clay, and they can be formed by being torn out of paper. The classroom teacher can obtain or make the following tools for lettering:

Pens
Ball-point, dip, and lettering pens are inexpensive.

Quills

Quills can be made by sharpening the point of a feather and making a slit up the middle from the point. Turkey or peacock feathers are preferable, but almost any other type that can be obtained will do. In early America, quills were a common writing tool. The Declaration of Independence undoubtedly was written with a quill pen.

Bamboo Pens

Bamboo pens are made by cutting a point in and slitting the end of a piece of bamboo stalk. This, and brushes, are favorite writing tools of Oriental people.

Brushes

Pointed brushes are good calligraphic tools. Sable brushes are the best, although any brush can be used.

Pencils

Many varieties of pencil are used for lettering: they range in hardness from 6B to 9H (H denotes hardness).

Unorthodox Tools

Fingers, cotton on a swab, cloth, twigs, and other instruments or articles can be dipped into paint or ink and then used to form letters.

Scissors

Letters can be cut from paper.

WORDS AND MESSAGES

Written words are a form of speech in graphic form. They have the capacity to excite and stir us with both their message

Design, Drawing, Painting, and Lettering

113

and their visual style. Indeed, it is the uniqueness of artistically made messages that attracts our attention. Much commercial advertising today depends on unusual and inventive ways of presenting language in visual terms. Even the way in which we sign our names advances a personal style that is individual to each of us.

ALPHABETS FOR ELEMENTARY CLASSROOMS

Consider how many ways there are to create letters. For example, instead of printing in either upper- or lower-case letters, with a pen or pencil, on a paper surface, try some of these approaches.

Cut Letters

Letters can be cut from any lightweight paper with scissors. Block letters (gothic) are the easiest to do, as there is no variation in the thickness of a letter. One need only consider the spacing of the letters after they have been cut.

Do not limit children to cutting simple block forms. Let them cut and embellish letters in any manner they invent. As a result of this approach, letters will have squiggles, wiggles, wriggles, curves, bumps, lumps, and humps; they will be perforated, fringed, and decorated. Even after cutting, such surface treatments as gluing can be used. Letters can be furry, shiny, reflective, transparent, soft-edged, textured, or otherwise altered. Letters can be cut from cardboard so that they will stand. Try cutting letters in Styrofoam or making them from cotton. Cut letters from cloth and glue them to paper.

3–42 Words can carry messages by the manner in which they are designed. Sixth-graders gave visual impact to word messages with an emphasis on original interpretations.

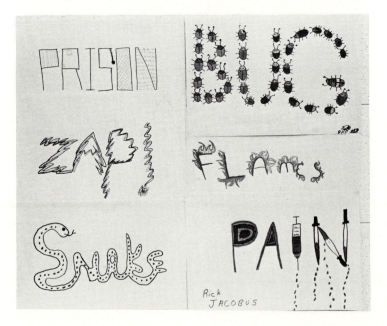

Drawn Letters

Letters can be drawn with a variety of tools: pens and ink, marking pens, pencils, feathers, twigs, droppers—almost anything that will mark a surface. Needless to say, drawn letters can be embellished in countless ways. It would be very boring to always make letters the same way. By just observing all of the signs in our environment, we can see the premium that is placed on designing letters well. Of course, letters form words in order to get messages across. Therefore, we must be able to read the message. Usually, when drawing a message our trained eye enables us to space the letters well enough so that the word or words can be read. We need to remember not to crowd letters and words together, but to permit them to breathe—although there may come a time when, for the sake of a creative idea, we sacrifice easy interpretation for artistic expression, in which the words become part of a larger whole.

Observe some manuscript pages from books that were created during the Middle Ages for good ideas for embellishing drawn letters. Most libraries will have many reference sources. The books listed at the end of this chapter can serve as a starting point for discovering interesting possibilities for lettering. This type of lettering ties in very nicely with units on history when, for example, actual documents representing our country's early years are studied.

Letters in Clay or Modeling Material

The earliest written forms of language appeared on clay tablets; the language was pressed into wet clay and then permitted to dry. Try writing by using a similar method. A Popsicle stick makes a good instrument for pressing letter forms into a flattened slab of clay.

Try reproducing letters from the ancient Sumerian alphabet and embedding them into a clay tablet. After pressing the message very carefully into the clay, having given every consideration to placement and readability, the clay tablets can be fired. Any modeling material that will permit an impression to be made can be used. To keep the clay from breaking, press it into a shallow cardboard box or the lid of a cottage cheese carton.

Carved Letters

Ancient peoples also carved messages in words and pictures into stone, on wood, on walls, and on other hard surfaces. They used any sharp instrument that was available. Children can use linoleum and a wood-cutting knife, a chisel and a flat board, a stick and a piece of copper foil, or even a nail and a flat stone that is soft enough to be gouged. Other variations on this method include making letters in sand and pouring plaster into forms that are created. (Figure 3–43).

3–43 *A variety of carved wooden letters from an old press. Invent letters in baker's clay, batik or tie-dye, cloth, stuffed designs, patchwork, Styrofoam, sponges, sandpaper, various papers, leather, papier-mâché, stitchery, yarn, weavings, foils, prints, or plaster.*

Letters from Various Materials

Other ways to create word messages include forming letters in pliable wire; with stones, pasta, sticks, cloth, buttons, seeds, and other small, found objects; with a modeling mixture; and with glue (also in combination with glitter and other tinsel materials).

Letters from Stencils

It is also possible to make letters from stencils. Stencils can be purchased, or they can be created by students. Draw the letters of the alphabet on a lightweight cardboard such as oak tag and then carefully cut them out with a knife. Using this method, the entire alphabet is cut into one sheet and the letters can be stenciled to another surface.

Rub-Off, or Transfer, Letters

Transfer letters can be purchased from art or stationery stores, and are preprinted on sheets of paper. When placed on a surface and rubbed with a pencil, they are rubbed off or caused to adhere to that surface.

Checkpoints

1. Use lightly ruled guidelines on paper.
2. Sketch letters on a background first to be certain that the spaces between, and the shapes of, the letters are correct.
3. Use rulers, T-squares, or other straightedges to measure and draw lines. Do not become overly dependent on mechanical means.
4. Use the whole arm when drawing, rather than let the wrist be locked to the table and thus restrict movement.
5. Gothic, or block, letters are the easiest to learn, as they are uniform in height and width. Also, they do not contain *serifs*, or variations on the ends of letter forms.
6. Intersections of letters that are horizontal can be above the middle or below the middle. This can be individually determined by the teacher.
7. Use the eye to judge spacing. It is preferable to using a rigid system of measurement for each letter to make them equidistant. (Each letter of the alphabet is visually different and the space around it has to fit this difference.)
8. Words read better when the spaces between the letters are smaller than the space occupied by the letters themselves.
9. Mix drawings and photographs with letters to put ideas across.
10. Design letters to interpret the words they express. For example, the word *ice* can be made of blocks of ice; *rain* of rain drops; and *glue* of sticky letters.

Design Bibliography

ANDERSON, DONALD M. *Elements of Design*. New York: Holt, Rinehart and Winston, Inc., 1961.

BATES, KENNETH F. *Basic Design: Principles and Practice*. New York: World Publishing Company, 1960.

BALLINGER, LOUISE B., AND THOMAS F. VROMAN. *Design: Sources and Resources*. New York: Van Nostrand Reinhold Company, 1965.

BEVLIN, MARJORIE ELLIOTT. *Design Through Discovery*. New York: Holt, Rinehart and Winston, 1977.

BEITTLER, ETHEL J., AND BILL LOCKHART. *Design for You*. New York: John Wiley & Sons, Inc., 1961.

BLOSSFELDT, KARL. *Art Forms in Nature*. London: Zwemmer, 1936.

CAPON, ROBIN. *Introducing Design Techniques*. New York: Watson-Guptill Publications, 1972.

CHEVREUL, M.E. *Principles of Harmony and Contrast of Colors*. New York: Van Nostrand Reinhold Co., 1982.

COLLIER, GRAHAM. *Form, Space, and Vision*. Rev. ed. Englewood Cliffs, N.J.: Prentice-Hall, Inc., 1972.

ELLINGER, RICHARD G. *Color Structure and Design*. New York: Van Nostrand Reinhold Co., 1981.

EMERSON, SYBIL *Design: A Creative Approach*. Scranton, Pa.: International Textbook Company, Inc. 1953.

GARRETT, LILLIAN. *Visual Design: A Problem Solving Approach*. New York: Van Nostrand Reinhold Company, 1966.

HILLIER, BEVIS. *The World of Art Deco*. New York: E. P. Dutton and Co., Inc. 1971.

HURWITZ, ELIZABETH A. *Design: A Search for Essentials*. Scranton, Pa.: International Textbook Company, Inc., 1964.

ITTEN, JOHANNES. *The Elements of Color*. New York: Van Nostrand Reinhold Co., 1980.

KEPES, GYORGY. *The Language of Vision*. Chicago: Paul Theobald, 1945.

KNOBLER, NATHAN. *The Visual Dialogue*, 3rd ed. New York: Holt, Rinehart, and Winston, 1980.

LACEY, JEANNETTE, F. *Young Art: Nature and Seeing*. New York: Van Nostrand Reinhold Company, 1971.

MACGILLAVRY, CAROLINE H. *Fantasy and Symmetry: The Periodic Drawings of M. C. Escher*. New York: Harry N. Abrams, Inc., Publishers, 1976.

MCILHANYL, STERLING. *Art As Design: Design As Art*. New York: Van Nostrand Reinhold Company, 1970.

MOHOLY-NAGY, LASZLO. *Vision in Motion*. Chicago: Paul Theobald, 1947.

PALMER, DENNIS. *Introducing Pattern*. New York: Watson-Guptill Publications, 1972.

PROCTOR, RICHARD M. *The Principles of Pattern*. New York: Van Nostrand Reinhold Company, 1969.

PYE, DAVID. *The Nature of Design*. New York: Van Nostrand Reinhold Company, 1964.

RANDALL, REINO, AND EDWARD C. HAINES. *Bulletin Boards and Display*. Worcester, Mass.: Davis Publications, Inc., 1961.

SAUSMAREZ, DE MAURICE. *Basic Design: The Dynamics of Visual Form*. New York: Van Nostrand Reinhold Co., 1981.

Drawing, Painting, and Lettering Bibliography

ALBERT, C., AND D. SECKLER. *Figure Drawing Comes to Life.* New York: Van Nostrand Reinhold Company, 1957.

BALLINGER, RAYMOND A. *Lettering Art in Modern Use.* New York: Van Nostrand Reinhold Company, 1970.

BETTI, CLAUDIA, AND TEEL SALE. *Drawing: A Contemporary Approach.* New York: Holt, Rinehart, and Winston, 1980.

CATALDO, JOHN W. *Lettering: A Guide for Teachers.* Worcester, Mass.: Davis Publications, Inc., 1966.

CHAET, BERNARD. *The Art of Drawing.* New York: Holt, Rinehart and Winston Inc., 1970.

CHOMICKY, YAR. *Watercolor Painting.* Englewood Cliffs, N.J.: Prentice-Hall, Inc., 1968.

DAVIDSON, MORRIS. *Painting with a Purpose.* Englewood Cliffs, N.J.: Prentice-Hall, Inc., 1969.

DOUGLASS, RALPH. *Calligraphic Lettering,* 3rd ed. New York: Watson-Guptill Publications, 1971.

GOLDSTEIN, NATHAN. *Figure Drawing: The Structure, Anatomy and Expressive Design of Human Form,* 2nd ed. Englwood Cliffs, N.J.: Prentice-Hall, Inc., 1981.

GRAY, BILL. *Lettering Tips.* New York: Van Nostrand Rinehold Co., 1980.

HAYES, COLIN. *Grammar of Drawing.* New York: Van Nostrand Reinhold Company, 1969.

HERBERHOLZ, BARBARA. "Lettering" filmstrip distributed by Barr Films, Pasadena, Ca.

HORNUNG, CLARENCE P. *Lettering From A to Z.* New York: William Penn, 1954.

HUTTER, HERBERT. *Drawing: History and Technique.* New York: McGraw-Hill Book Company, 1968.

JAMES, JANE H. *Perspective Drawing.* Englewood Cliffs, N.J.: Prentice-Hall, Inc., 1981.

KAMPMAN, LOTHAR. *Creating with Crayons.* New York: Van Nostrand Reinhold Company, 1967.

KAUPELIS, ROBERT. *Learning to Draw.* New York: Watson-Guptill Publications, 1966.

LAIDMAN, HUGH. *The Complete Book of Drawing and Painting.* New York: The Viking Press, Inc., 1974.

LALIBERTE, NORMAN, AND ALEX MOGELON. *Drawing with Pencils.* New York: Van Nostrand Reinhold Company, 1969.

————. *Painting with Crayons.* New York: Van Nostrand Reinhold Company, 1967.

MUSE, KEN. *Secrets of Professional Cartooning.* Englewood Cliffs, N.J.: Prentice-Hall, Inc., 1981.

NICOLAIDES, KIMON. *The Natural Way to Draw.* Boston: Houghton Mifflin Company, 1941.

PITZ, HENRY C. *Ink Drawing Techniques.* New York: Watson-Guptill Publications, 1957.

ROSEN, BEN. *Type and Typography.* New York: Van Nostrand Rinehold Co., 1981.

ROTTGER, ERNST, AND DIETER KLANTE. *Creative Drawing: Point and Line.* New York: Van Nostrand Reinhold Company, 1963.

SPROUL, ADELAIDE. *With a Free Hand.* New York: Van Nostrand Reinhold Company, 1968.

WATROUS, JAMES. *The Craft of Old Master Drawings.* Madison: The University of Wisconsin Press, 1957.

WATSON, ERNEST W. *Gallery of Pencil Techniques.* New York: Van Nostrand Reinhold Company, 1956.

————. *How to Use Creative Perspective.* New York: Van Nostrand Reinhold Company, 1965.

WEISS, HARVEY. *Pencil, Pen and Brush.* New York: William R. Scott, 1961.

WOODY, RUSSELL. *Painting with Synthetic Media.* New York: Van Nostrand Reinhold Company, 1964.

4

Creating with Paper

No one knows exactly when paper was invented, but the earliest records indicate that the first paper may have originated in China in approximately A.D. 100. Not until centuries later did the formula for its manufacture spread across the trade routes to Europe. The word *paper* is presumably derived from *papyrus*, a material of Egyptian origin that was used extensively in the Greco-Roman civilization. The original use of paper was for writing and printing. As the refinement processes in its manufacture developed over centuries, the utility of paper expanded in infinite directions.

Today, paper is used in every way imaginable, for it is one of our most inexpensive products relative to its purpose. Paper bags, for example, have an extensive variety of uses other than as containers. It is interesting to note that paper bags were unknown in the United States until the early nineteenth century when grocers and merchants made them by hand from jute paper. The first paper bag machine was invented by Francis Wolle in Bethlehem, Pennsylvania, in 1850. As he is considered the father of the industry, this was truly his "bag."

4–1 *Pieces of hand-cast paper are combined for a wall sculpture. (Courtesy Anne Flaten Pixley, The Hand and The Spirit Crafts Gallery, Scottsdale, Arizona.)*

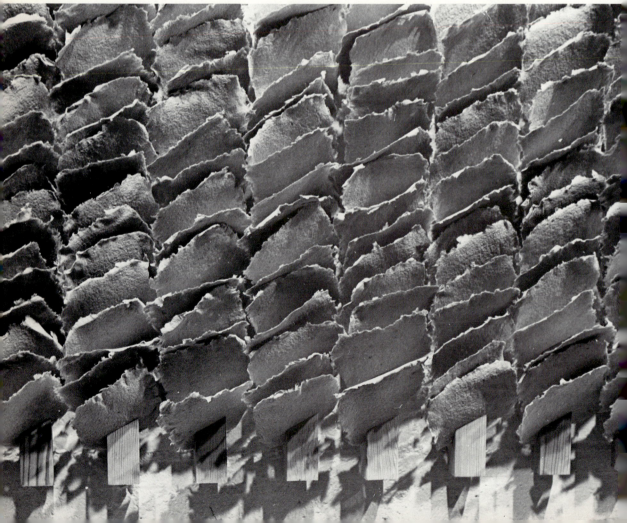

Several countries have been responsible for the creative development of paper as an artistic medium: China, Japan, Mexico, and Poland. Both peasant and professional artists have pushed the boundaries of what can be done with paper into visually exciting realms. Classroom teachers are in a unique position to utilize the wealth of background information that is available on paper and with imagination they can make paper a most versatile medium for children's use. Although many papers of the handmade variety are expensive, others are less expensive and available. If the school program has a reasonable budget, construction paper, poster paper, and butcher paper can be purchased. If no budget is available, it may be possible to supplement school supplies with papers that can be obtained from sources in the city: the newspaper plant (ask for roll ends), department stores, printing shops, and other areas in which paper products are used as containers and wrappers. Stores that sell furniture usually throw their packing and crating cardboards away. Rug stores are good sources for cardboard tubing of various thicknesses. Gift wrapping departments sometimes have throwaways of gift papers, ribbons, and tissues. Ice cream stores often have circular containers available. Grocery stores have many types of cardboard boxes. Many merchants would probably be happy to save things if they knew they were for classroom use. Often, children can bring in egg cartons, cheese cartons, meat trays, and other containers used at home. Papers and cardboards can be collected until there is enough for a specific project. Send a note home with children for parents to be on the lookout for supplies.

Making Paper

Perhaps the ancient Chinese learned paper making from watching wasps. It is the wasp that chews fibers and weeds into a paste. He then spits it out to form the walls and units of his hive. When the paste is dry, it is firm and becomes a three-dimensional house.

Paper today is made from various fibers such as weeds, bark, sawdust, wood shavings, dry leaves, wood pulp, corn husks, and rags. The fibers are mashed and reduced to a pulp by pounding or boiling. In paper factories, large vats containing the fibers are mixed together with water until it is a pulp mixture. The pulp mixture is called slurry.

To make your own paper in the classroom, tear up a sheet of newspaper into small pieces. Place the cut paper in a dishpan of water and let it soak for a few hours. Make a

4–2 *Above: Making paper with classroom materials. Below: Finished hand-cast paper made by fifth-grade students.*

screen that is smaller than the dishpan by stapling some window screen to a wooden frame. Place the screen in and under the slurry. Bring the screen up slowly (with the slurry on it) and let the slurry drain; be sure to squeeze out as much moisture as possible. Press the slurry and let it dry. The paper will lift off the screen when it is dry.

Experimenting with Paper

We can all enjoy finding common and unusual ways to work and build with paper. It is fun to experiment, from

124

creating the very smallest paper folding to the largest paper murals, working both flat and three dimensionally. Projects can be simple or complex, depending on the imagination and skill of the creator. We exist in three-dimensional space, and developing ideas into three dimensions with two-dimensional material presents a challenge and requires judgment. The qualities and types of paper used will influence the activity and accomplishment.

First, *experiment* with paper. Children become familiar with paper as one of their earliest experiences. Although they may never have thought of its use in the fine arts or as a sculptural material, children will quickly learn that various kinds of papers will produce different products. Working with paper can be a truly exciting adventure when the work is tackled with ingenuity. The many and varied uses of paper indicate its practically limitless potential. Essentially, paper can be transformed by being:

4–3 *Basically a flat material, paper can be made three dimensional by scoring, curling, bending, folding, fringing, and perforating it. This piñata witch from Mexico is made of rolled-up newspaper decorated with cut crepe paper and tissue.*

crushed	perforated
curled	rolled
cut into strips	scored
folded	scratched
fringed	singed on the edges
glued	slit
interlocked	stapled
overlapped	torn into shapes
papier-mâchéd	wadded
pasted	woven

The varieties of papers are almost endless. Some of the better known ones include:

aluminum foil	newsprint
art papers	oak tag
butcher paper	paper bags
cellophane paper	paper handkerchiefs
cardboard	paper napkins
charcoal paper	paper plates
confetti	paper toweling
construction paper	pastel paper
corrugated paper and	poster paper
cardboard	railroad board
drawing paper	rice paper
flocked papers	tissue paper
gift wrap papers	wallpapers
kraft paper	watercolor paper
magazine paper	waxed paper
metallic foil papers	

Creating with Paper

Several basic forms can be used to begin to create with paper and cardboard:

circles	rectangles
cones	squares
cylinders	strips
irregular shapes	

Paper can be used as an artistic medium in the classroom in many ways. Some of these are described in the following paragraphs.

CUTTING PAPER

Lightweight paper that can be cut easily can be used as a flat piece, or the paper can be folded one or more times before being cut. Sometimes paper can be folded into tiny squares, and then intricate designs and shapes can be cut from the folded edges. When the paper is unfolded, many detailed patterns are revealed. There are many variations to this approach.

4–4 *Large and simple shapes interestingly cut assume dramatic aesthetic forms when suspended freely. Being lightweight, they move gracefully in the air.*

The paper cutting can be pasted over a contrasting color, which permits the cut openings to show. Another method in paper cutting is to perforate the surface of a flat piece of paper. This can be done by folding and then cutting along the edges, or by inserting the point of the scissors into the paper and cutting openings into the paper that can then be folded upward. Varying surfaces that have a visual texture can be created in this manner.

Another method of cutting paper is to cut it into various lengths and strips. By this method, individual strips can be overlapped, folded together, curved into a circle, and stapled or glued. Paper also can be folded and attached to form a three-dimensional structure.

PERFORATING SURFACES FOR TEXTURE

Flat sheets of paper can be cut into at repeated intervals to create a visually textured surface form. Either curved or straight cuts can be made in an all-over pattern to change the surface form of the paper sheet. After the flat sheet has been perforated with a pleasing design pattern, the sheet can be rolled into a cone or folded to create a three-dimensional structure. Developing surface textures of this nature is similar to what an architect does when he designs the surface of a

4–5 *Cut paper designs are whimsical and delicate message cards. The flower cards are "windows" that hold in the flowers with acetate or clear adhesive paper.*

wall. Repeating the cut form in an interval pattern creates a textural rhythm on the flat surface. The repeated cuts can be done freehand with the scissors, or a light pencil design on the paper will ensure that all the cuts are uniform. Often it is more pleasing to let each cut vary somewhat in its repetition to achieve visual variation. In place of scissors, an art knife can be used to make the cuts. However, safety plays a factor here, and one has to be careful not to cut into the work surface. The use of a cardboard working surface would protect a tabletop in such an instance. But certainly at the primary level scissors are more suitable.

CURLING PAPER STRIPS

Paper cut into strips of various sizes and widths can be curled by being wrapped around a pencil or cylindrical form. Another method is to open scissors and press and drag a strip of paper against one blade for the length of the strip. Light paper will curl easily.

SCORING PAPER

Scoring is an excellent means for folding or creasing heavy papers. To score a flat sheet of paper, place a ruler along its surface and then lightly cut into it with the point of a scissors, being careful not to go through the paper. The crease, or fold, can then be executed with ease. To score curved lines, simply draw the curved line with a pencil and then follow along it lightly with a knife.

Craft Ideas with Paper

ORIGAMI HAT VARIATION

Origami, which means "folding paper," is an ancient Japanese folkcraft that is taught by Japanese grandmothers to young children. The process itself varies with each predesigned origami form but is essentially one of folding a piece of paper many times in order to arrive at a generalized version of a subject. Subjects generally include fish, birds, animals, hats, and costumes. The following method of origami uses a hat form as the foundation from which imaginative discovery can be explored:

Supplies Needed

one full page from a standard newspaper

transparent tape

oak tag or stiff paper for a hatband

scissors, paste, or stapler

assorted colored papers: construction, tissue, and gift wrap
  paper

Procedure

1. To make the origami hat foundation, begin by using a
   double page of newspaper folded to one page with the
   fold at the top and the opening facing you.
2. Bring the top two corners down to meet each other at the
   middle.
3. Fold the remaining portion of the top sheet up to meet
   the corners.

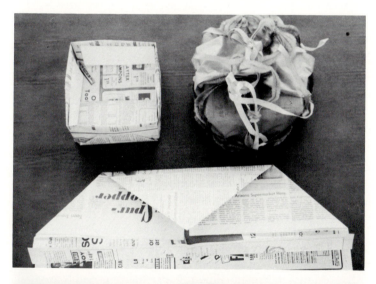

4–6 *The ancient art of
origami, or Japanese paper
folding, becomes the foundation
for these dress-up hats.*

Creating with Paper

4. Bring the point down to the fold and tuck it under.
5. Turn the paper over.
6. Fold both ends toward the middle by beginning the folds where each end changes direction.
7. Fold the bottom flap up so that it is even with the one underneath.
8. Open the folded paper at the bottom slit and press it flat.
9. With the slit horizontal to you, fold the top and bottom points to the middle and tuck them under the folds at the middle.
10. Open the slit and pinch the corners and base to make a square hat foundation.
11. Build imaginative forms from this foundation to create an original hat.

Uses for the Origami Hat Variation in the Classroom
1. Create a story based on the hat that you create.
2. Create a hat based on some character in history.
3. Create a hat as part of a play or theatrical production.
4. Create a hat based on a story.
5. Create a hat for a party, for a celebration, or for a holiday. Let your hat tell the story.

FOLD AND DYE

The Japanese art of paper folding and dyeing is an ancient one. Each paper creation is unique and the designs possible are endless. It is a captivating discovery process, because the design is unknown until the moment of surprise when the folds are opened and the magic of the colors can be seen.

The process is simple, and not much preparation is needed. The teacher may want to discuss color consciousness with students as well as illustrate the many possible ways of folding before beginning the project. But paper folding can and should be experimental to find exciting ways to form patterns.

Large-sized paper and large folds will create larger designs, and the opposite is true of working with small pieces of paper. A good beginning size is 9 × 12 inches.

4–7 The magic of color blending is enhanced in paper folding and dyeing.

Simple grocery store vegetable coloring can be used. Place the colors in muffin tins, cans, or cartons for easy dipping. New color combinations will appear when dipping and spreading paper. Also, by diluting colors (such as blue), different values happen, such as light blues and deep blues. Liquid vegetable dyes also can be mixed together for new hues before dipping.

Supplies Needed
facial tissue
newspaper
newsprint
rice paper
paper toweling
typing paper, tissue paper (Some papers are highly absorbent and have to be pulled from the dye quickly; other papers absorb more slowly.)
dropper (Apply dye colors to wet paper with a dropper.)
iron
muffin tins or small cans
paints (acrylic) and plastic spray
scissors
vegetable coloring or thinned tempera paint

Procedure (See Figure 4–7.)
1. After folding, dip a point of the paper into a color. The color will soak up slightly into the paper.
2. Remove the paper and blot the excess color out between sheets of newspaper.
3. Dip the paper into the next color, blot, and continue in this manner.
4. Be sure to dip both points and side edges into various colors.
5. Leave some spots undyed for variation.
6. Also, use the tops of the dye bottles or droppers to press point the paper (making sure the color goes through all of the paper) for strong color spots.
7. When the color dipping is finished, dry out the paper and then iron it flat.
8. Papers can be sprayed with a plastic finish, covered with an acrylic medium (vegetable dyes do run), or covered with plastic crystals and baked in the oven. Small 4-inch square designs can be used as jewelry pieces or as Christmas tree decorations.
9. Folded and dipped rice paper can be used to wrap special gifts. The designed papers are treasures to keep, share, and exhibit. They can be used also as greeting cards; carton, box, can, or book covers; notebook covers; bookmarks; and program covers.
10. For variation, try this: place lots of newspaper on the

table and a small amount of household bleach in a small pie tin. With a cotton swab, draw with the bleach on some colored tissue or construction paper for some unique effects.

PAPER MOSAIC

Historically, the mosaic has its roots in the early years of Christianity. It was used as an art form to both educate and adorn the walls of churches and palaces. By definition, a mosaic is a painting or image created by embedding small pieces of colored stone or glass or other material into the surface of a wall or ceiling. Each piece is fixed in close proximity to the next piece. For classroom mosaics, many rich and varied effects can be created by using visually interesting papers, mirrors, stones, woods, tissues, and foils and other reflective or shiny papers.

Supplies Needed
variety of papers with shiny, dark, and light values: bright, dull, opaque, and transparent colors; rough and smooth textures; varying thicknesses
colored paper scraps, gift wrapping, and lightweight cardboards
colorful magazines and heavier weight papers
colored tissue papers, foils, and construction papers
rubber cement, paste, or glue
scissors
a cardboard or paper surface

Procedure
1. Plan a light sketch on a backing surface.
2. The teacher should be certain that sufficient motivation has provided the class with interesting subject ideas. Mosaics can relate to either contemporary or historical themes. What an excellent opportunity to study the mosaics of the medieval world!
3. After all the papers have been selected, sorted, and cut into squares of varying size or into other small shapes, the pasting of the squares is started.
4. Give attention to all the qualities of good design in composing an arrangement. This would include light and dark, repetition, harmony, spacing, distribution of colors, and the student's intuitive sense of good design. (See Chapter 3, "Design, Drawing, Painting, and Lettering.")
5. Leave a small amount of space between the pasted pieces. This is what gives the effect of a mosaic.
6. Fill in the surface with colored papers until the mosaic is completed.

COLORED TISSUE PAPER PICTURE

Pieces of colored tissue paper glued to a backing make an extraordinary picture. The brilliant colors of the paper and the transparent quality of tissue as it is overlapped make this project an excellent vehicle for studying color, arrangement, and composition. It is an excellent experience at any grade level. Since the tissue paper color runs when wet, a variety of third colors will develop as two colors are overlapped during application with the glue. Color blending and crumpled textures will add new dimension to the tissue paper picture.

4–9 *Can you guess where this humorous-hatted character is strutting to? Transparent tissue paper forms are torn and cut, and then brushed with thinned glue to a backing.*

Creating with Paper

Supplies Needed
colored tissue papers
foils, cellophanes, and gift wraps
scissors
medium-sized brush
a mounting surface such as poster board, oak tag, cardboard or any heavyweight cardboard painted white, or a glass or plastic bottle
white glue that can be thinned

Procedure
1. Cut or tear tissue paper into interesting shapes.
2. Put an arrangement together spontaneously. This project can be handled in an imaginary way with an emphasis on inventiveness. Teachers should always keep in mind that original thinking and inventive ideas are two consistent objectives in art thinking. A second approach is to plan an arrangement ahead of time by sketching out a basic idea (such as a landscape or still life) and work out many of the compositional challenges before gluing the tissue paper into position.
3. When the material is assembled, the gluing process can begin. Paint the surface first with slightly thinned white glue, press the tissue into place one piece at a time, and then carefully paint the white glue over the placed pieces of tissue.
4. Continue the process until the entire picture is completed. Keep in mind that overlapping the tissue pieces will create new color relationships through the transparent combinations of mixing by overlapping.
5. As an added technique, the tissue paper picture can be combined with pen-and-ink drawing on the surface.
6. This project enables the teacher to discuss various design fundamentals: color mixing, intensity, and value; repetition; and arrangement on a two-dimensional surface.

STUFFED PAPER CREATURES

Brown wrapping paper or white butcher paper make an excellent material for creating instant large animals, people, and other creatures that can be stuffed and closed. One objective in this project is to increase manipulative ability. It is also a direct way to make a large figure and understand body proportions and placement.

Supplies Needed
brown wrapping, white butcher, or colored wrapping paper
newspaper
paint, brush, colored tissues, and marking tools
scissors
stapler or needle and yarn

Procedure

1. Draw the shape of a fanciful creature or animal on a flat piece of wrapping paper, or have the student lie down on the floor while a helper draws around him. (Remember that the paper has to be sturdy enough to contain the wadded newspaper.)
2. When the outside shape is completed, cut it out and place it on a second identical sheet of paper. Cut the second shape.
3. Pin the sides together, or staple them, but leave an opening into which the newspaper can be inserted as stuffing. (Small torn pieces make a good stuffing.)
4. Before the animal, bird, figure, or fish is stuffed, the student may want to decorate the surface. Paint, draw with felt-tip pens, paste cloth or papers on, or use any imaginative means. A student completing a self-image should be encouraged to examine and include all body details. Close the body by stapling or sewing.
5. Colored tissue papers cut into strips and curled make good appendages.
6. Buttons can be used for eyes and straw for hair. Shredded newspaper makes good furry parts.
7. Good sources for inspiration include the piñatas and other stuffed paper products that are made in Mexico.

See Figure 4–10. Loosely tied, the joints permit movability if you wish to suspend them from the ceiling or use them with string for marionettes.

4–10 *All kinds of paper shapes can be easily stuffed with bits of newspaper to become creepy creatures and imaginative sculptures. These crepe paper examples have added paper details. Loose joints permit mobility for marionettes.*

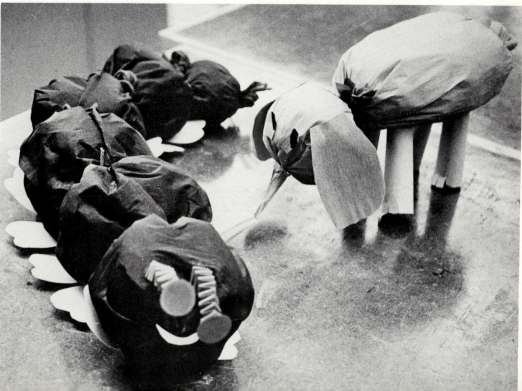

4–11 *Paper and cardboard can rapidly transform the environment. Learning units are enhanced with imaginative cut-paper murals.*

PAPER ENVIRONMENTS

Decorating with cardboard and paper is an amazingly rapid way to transform the classroom into a completely different space. Large cardboard boxes can be obtained from furniture stores or other places that use containers. Cardboard works well as an environment changer, as it quickly covers large spaces. Heavyweight cardboards can be slit and fit together to build forms up and around. Papier-mâché can be combined with cardboard to round out edges and provide additional covering.

Students can collectively participate in constructing such

4–12 *Fairy-tale castle made from combining found materials. Architectural models can be realistic or imaginative. Salt ceramic figures appear at the door.*

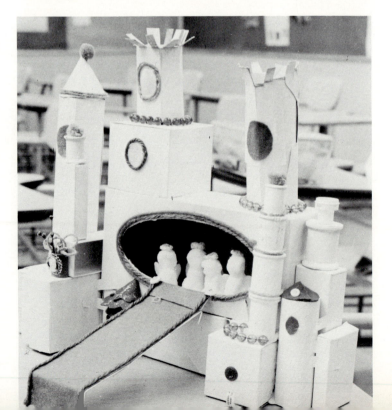

space structures. Themes can relate to theater sets, historical places, stories, paintings or photographs, spatial concepts, and imaginative ideas.

Supplies Needed
clear plastic sheeting
large, flat pieces of cardboard and boxes of all sorts
scissors and dull knives
paint and brushes
papers of all sorts
wire that bends easily

Procedure
The interior shape of the classroom can be changed by hanging interesting shapes cut from cardboard or plastic from wires. This can be done by stringing wire through a card-

4–14 *A paper family enjoys its cardboard furniture in a shoe box lid. Such simplified environments are in scale with the child and stimulate role playing and imagination.*

board and attaching the wire to the sides of the walls. Individual wires can also be attached to each cardboard shape and hung from light fixtures or from any other hooklike spots in the room.

Stand-up cutouts can be made by attaching a cutout to a base made from wood or cardboard. Slit the base and insert the cutout at right angles to the base. Butcher paper can be unrolled, decorated, and hung on a wire to make an effective screen. Clear plastic can be painted or doubled, filled with air, and sealed with heat from an iron to become giant floating shapes.

PAPER MASKS AND COSTUMES

Children delight in creating illusions with masks, hats, oversized glasses, and costumes and, thus, in instantly changing and freeing their image and personality. Magic, masks, and costumes have always been part of the mystery of rituals and ceremonies of societies throughout the world. In primitive times, masks and costumes were thought to provide contact with the spiritual world. As in ancient times, they were thought to help the wearer to ward off evil spirits, bring rain, drive away disease, tell stories, aid harvests and protect against the unknown. The artistic ceremonial masks made by Asians, Eskimo, and North American Indians are still in use today. Masks and costumes relate to disguises, theater, religion, battle, comedy, folk tales, and mythology. Plan to study these historical masks, as they help bridge cultures from different times and places.

Masks and costumes can transport one into the world of

make believe. Dramatically become a monster, a clown or a king on command, whether for a play, a party, or just for fun. The mask, costume, and role-playing will spark many adventures in imagining.

MASKS

Supplies Needed
brown wrapping, colored wrapping, or white butcher paper
colored construction or oak tag paper
brushes
paint
paper bags, cardboard
paper plates
papers
scissors
stapler
decorative yarns, buttons, scrap cloth
examples of masks

4–15 *Masks as disguises or new identities can be invented by perforating, rolling, fringing, and curling sheets of paper.*

Procedure
1. Masks can be constructed out of paper bags, paper plates, construction paper, oak tag, or cardboard. Exaggerate the features when designing unique, clever masks.
2. Space for the eyes is determined by holding the plate, cardboard, or paper up to the face and feeling for the distances between the eyes, nose, and mouth. Mark them. Provide for large enough holes to be able to see well, breathe, and speak easily. (Or, build a partial mask such as Super Sunglasses.)
3. When paper bags are being used, the eyes, nose, and mouth are cut from a wide side of the bag. When cardboard is used, fold it down the center as in a "V" shape. Cut out the spaces for the eyes and mouth. Put your imagination to work as you invent and decorate this special character.
4. Imaginative appendages can be added, such as a nose flap, crown, beard, or eyelashes that have been cut from fringed paper. (See Figure 4–15.)

Alternate Procedures
1. Masks can also be made over balloons or newspaper armatures with papier-mâché. Or a model can be made in plasticene relief and then covered with papier-mâché. (See pages 148–149.)
2. Large balloons are blown up (these masks will later fit over the head). Prop the balloon in a plastic bucket or small cardboard box so that the balloon stands upright. Do not papier-mâché around the base of the balloon; this part

Creating with Paper

4–16 *Inventive African masks designed after a unit on African folklore. Felt pens on oaktag paper, covered with clear plastic and mounted on a stick. From the classes of Ralph Bethancourt.*

stays open and will go over your head. Use paper strips and apply the papier-mâché. Leave the balloons propped up in containers until they are air dry (in a few days). Paint them.

3. The plasticene form is made flat against a cardboard, bas-relief style. The facial features are built up in relief to form the mask shape.

4. Grease the plasticene before using it so that the mask can be removed from the model. Do not grease the balloon.

5. This plasticene model can be used for many successive masks. For example, after it has been greased, papier mâché is used or plaster can be dripped over the plasticene to cover it. This is the plaster of Paris technique.

6. Paper toweling makes a very effective paper for masks of this sort in papier mâché. Tear the toweling in thin strips or small pieces; the papier-mâché forms well over the smaller details.

7. Finish the masks by painting inventive designs and gluing on decorative elements such as straw hair. Remove your mask from its propped-up position. Wear it and scare your friends. (See color Figures 1 and 2.)

COSTUMES

Procedure

1. Measure off a sheet of kraft or butcher paper from a large roll and cut it double the size of the child.

2. Fold it and cut a half-moon or half circle into the center of the folded portion. (This is where the child's head goes through. Be sure to allow enough room.)

3. Sew or staple closed the sides of the paper.

4. Remember to leave openings for the arms.

5. Paint and decorate the surface of the costume and paste on pieces of brightly colored cloth, papers, or yarn.

6. Attach fringed paper or paper strips, shapes, or other cut forms.

7. Make costumes also from old shirts, old sheeting, dresses, pants, or coats.
8. Cut interesting shapes and forms from scrap material and sew them onto old clothes to change them into exciting costumes.
9. Large-sized paper bags are good foundations for instant small folk costumes. These can be easily decorated and painted.

Designing Surfaces with Collage and Decoupage

Surface decoration is a very old craft. It is thought to have originated in Venice, Italy, in the seventeenth century when Venice led all European cities in printing. These prints were adhered to permanent surfaces. The art soon spread to France, England, Germany, and other countries.

COLLAGE

Collage originally began as a folk art many years ago. People would cut various kinds of papers into designs and add them to message cards. Other items were also used, such as cloth scraps, velvet, a piece of lace, an unusual button, bright yarn—anything that could be glued down. Today, if you visit an antique shop, you may discover a scrapbook from the past filled with delightful odds and ends, precious savings from another age. These have been randomly pasted into the book and create a handsome visual combination.

Collage has also been a favorite form among fine artists. Pablo Picasso and Georges Braque are well known for adding paper, cloth, and various objects to their painting. This was quite an innovation for the artist of fifty years ago. Henri

Creating with Paper

141

Matisse carried the art even further during the twilight years of his life; when his fingers were too crippled with arthritis to hold his brush, he cut out large, colorful paper shapes and made beautiful cut-paper murals.

The collage principle is challenging for any age group. It requires one to be resourceful in saving mementos and searching for and collecting collage materials. Introduction to the experience includes discussing tactile and textural qualities and color relationships, plus organizing one's designs. Discuss such words and their meanings as *furry, coarse, hard,* and *delicate.* How can materials be placed together to express a mood? Can you be selective and experiment to organize a pleasing design? Can a collage stimulate the eye? Think of how wallpaper, feathers, shells, sandpaper, candy wrappers, tickets, magazine pictures, and your photographs can create unique collage pictures.

Surface decorations can be applied to paper, cardboard, boxes, trays, lamps, shades, or furniture. Decorations can be glued on or held on with a self-adhesive, clear vinyl paper. (See Figure 4–5.)

In collage, small pieces of material, including papers, buttons, pins, sticks, and seeds, are arranged on a surface to create a pleasing composition that can be either pure design or contain subject imagery. Emphasis in a problem of this nature is on developing one's design experience and gaining insight into compositional arrangement, two of the fortes of the artist. We would all like to know the secrets of putting a "picture" together. This problem provides practice in composing the design elements of line, shape, texture, color, and space.

Supplies Needed

a mounting surface such as grocery cardboard or any heavy-weight paper

magazines, newspapers, old photos, calendars, postcards, tickets, stamps, papers of all kinds

pieces of cloth, buttons, seeds, metals, foils, grasses, flowers, nuts, feathers, furs, and sand

rubber cement, paste, or clear vinyl paper

scissors

Procedure

Interesting shapes can be cut or torn from paper and arranged on the mounting surface. In addition to papers of all sorts, the other materials mentioned can be combined with the paper to create the collage. Methods for making collages include overlapping, spatial arrangement, repetition, and using textures of various sorts.

1. Find interesting visual images in magazine photographs, and so on. Any printed image will work.
2. While looking for potential subject matter, consider possible relationships for combining apparently unrelated images.
3. One might emphasize a current social theme and present a message. For example, some are suggested here: The Energy Crisis, Patriotism, Pollution, Smoking, Lines in Space, *A Space Odyssey*, Letters Can Be Fun, Super Race Cars, Food and Health, Circus Delights, Summer Adventures, Our Loving Pet, Happy Hours, Optical Inventions, Our Trip to the Antarctic, and Inside the Earth.

Develop a surrealistic theme for variation. Surrealistic artists, such as Salvador Dali, René Magritte, Marcel Duchamp, and Yves Tanguy, tried to present superreal images, or images that related more to dreams, fantasies, and the unconscious. In this context, things could go together that normally would never go together. This problem is best approached if we consider the following: (1) distortion of the normal to exaggerate an idea; (2) images out of their usual context; and (3) unusual size relationships.

Other themes that would work well in this type of problem could deal with mysteries, adventures, takeoffs on commercials, special events, feelings, trips, exaggerations of television programs, or political variations. This problem is ideal for encouraging visual awareness, idea pushing, and putting unusual relationships together, all of which are fundamental to thinking about art. (For further ideas dealing with surrealism, refer to pages 95–98.)

Another variation on collage is the personality collage. Each child stands in the pathway of the light from a projector so that his image is projected against a wall. A partner draws around his silhouette on a large piece of kraft or butcher paper. This becomes the mounting surface. The teacher then encourages the children to search in magazines for both words and images that best express the idea, "Who am I?" The student selects all the printed words that he feels he is, or would like to be. "The Real You" or "The Future Me" could be titles for the personality collage. These collages often reveal hidden feelings concerning the student. (See Figure 4–18.)

4–18 *"The Real You" collage reveals your innermost wishes and dreams with magazine words and images. Head silhouettes as well as large dancing figures can be made by the student standing between the paper and a light source.*

DECOUPAGE

Many students enjoy keeping paper mementos of past events and special occasions: restaurant menus, circus tickets, candy wrappers, train tickets, and favorite photographs and drawings. Doing decoupage on a board with a collection of nostalgic items enables one to keep such mementos intact.

Supplies Needed
mementos: papers, photographs, and drawings
clear vinyl, liquid plastic (clear gloss), varnish, or thinned white glue
scrap wood pieces (lumberyards are good sources) and old boxes
brushes
wood stain (coffee or tea stains work)
rags

Procedure
1. Select an interesting piece of wood.
2. Brush over it with a thin coat of tempera. The paint will accent the grain of the wood. Rub off excess paint while it is still wet.
3. Cut or tear the edges of your papers for an interesting effect. With proper supervision, paper edges can be held over a candle and gently burned to make them look very old.
4. Arrange the papers on the wood in a well-composed design.
5. Brush the selected decoupage mixture on the wood—the vinyl, the polymer, or the glue.
6. Brush the papers with the mixture as they are placed on the wood. Press the papers from the center out to make them lie flat.
7. Cover the entire surface again with a coat of the working liquid.
8. Let it dry.
9. For an antique look after the photographs or other papers have been glued down, cover their surface with either a wood stain or a wash of coffee or tea.
10. Apply the final coating.
11. To hang the decoupage, place a soda pop can ring on the back of the wood with a thumbtack through the metal.

Papier-Mâché

Papier-mâché is an exciting medium that is used frequently today by artists, teachers, craftspeople, and students. It is an art method that builds a form in three dimensions or in low relief (flat). The term is French, and means "paper pulp." It was especially popular in France during the seventeenth century. The material itself is inexpensive and readily avail-

able for classroom use. In addition to the French, the Chinese, Japanese, and Mexicans use papier-mâché consistently for festival masks, ritual animals, and related holiday themes. Many commercial products from these countries also utilize this favorite form of art expression. Tiny figures as well as larger-than-life creations are made for religious festivals and special holidays.

For classroom use, both individual and group projects can offer challenging and versatile ideas. Papier-mâché is an excellent discovery material that is suitable for *any* grade level. Each teacher must plan for an art project that can be understood at a specific level. (See Figures 4–19 to 4–26.)

PIÑATAS

Many classrooms celebrate festivals and holidays with various kinds of papier-mâché piñatas. The original piñata is said to have originated in Italy during the Renaissance when it was used for entertainment at masquerade balls. The custom spread from Italy to Spain and from there to Mexico. The Mexican piñatas are fanciful creatures, sometimes traditional in design but often imaginative and humorous to delight children during the holidays.

The piñata is a container filled with candies or gifts and covered with papier-mâché and fringed colored paper, usually tissue paper. The papier mâché is shaped into animals, balls, stars, and original shapes. The tissue paper is fringed and glued on in layers to cover the shape. The piñata is hung from the ceiling; the children are blindfolded and take turns

Creating with Paper

trying to break the piñata with a stick. Often, someone holds the rope attaching the piñata and pulls it up and down through a pulley device so it is more difficult to hit. There is much laughing and anticipation as the piñata breaks and everyone scrambles for the candies that fall to the floor.

The last piñata of the season is broken on Christmas Eve in Mexico as a way of saying *noche buena*, or ''good night,'' at the party after the Midnight Mass and traditional feast.

PAPIER-MÂCHÉ PROCEDURES

Supplies needed
newspapers, including white paper toweling for the final coat armatures

wallpaper (wheat paste) paste thinned to a smooth consistency; paste substitutes include flour and water (about 1 cup of water to ¼ cup flour), liquid starch used full strength, or one part white glue to one part water mixed well (if using flour and water, add 1 tablespoon of salt to the mixture to prevent spoilage)

shallow bowls

finishing paints (tempera or acrylic) and felt-tip pens

large brush for surfaces and small pointed brush for details

clear varnish, shellac, or plastic spray

scrap and found materials: yarn, lace, braid, feathers, cloth, and old jewelry parts for accessories and finishing

Types of Armatures
Armatures can be made by crumpling paper into a ball or other bulky forms to suggest a basic body shape for an animal, human, or insect. Newspapers can be rolled into tight coils and taped together. By inserting coat hangers or

4–20 *This teacher is holding a figure built over a chicken-wire armature. The person at the right is using an old bucket as a base for a planter.*

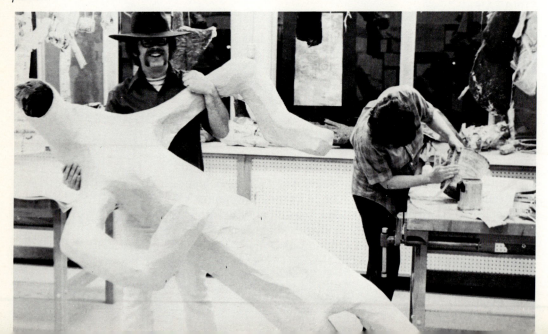

other *pliable* wire inside the paper coils, the coils can be bent and will hold their shape. In the absence of wire, string can be brought taut and tied around the legs or head of construction to keep the forms in position for applying papier-mâché. Bulk forms can be tied on or taped together with dampened paper kraft tape.

At the primary levels, in particular, papier-mâché can be begun more successfully by using bottles or other preformed shapes for support. The following armatures are suggested for all levels.

1. Utilize a liquid detergent bottle for a figure shape. Plastic bottles provide a ready base for figures and permit a supporting weight for balance. Add a small amount of earth inside the bottle to stabilize it.
2. Use a bowl for a bowl form or plastic plant pot for a basket form.
3. Ice cream containers and different-sized cans also make solid supports and are light enough to leave inside the construction. Styrofoam forms can also be cut and glued.
4. Small balloons blown to not more than 5 inches in diameter can be utilized as an armature, but be certain that the scale does not get out of hand, or completion of the project will require too much class time.
5. Aluminum foil can be bunched easily and retains its shape. An excellent mask base is heavy-duty aluminum foil. Work in pairs and carefully mold the foil over the head, under the chin, and back to the ears. Locate nose and punch holes for breathing. Capture the individual contours of the face. Bunch extra foil on the outside edges, which will help provide support and can be trimmed later. Place crushed newspaper under the foil, which helps give support while working. Gently apply strips of masking tape all over the foil to which the mâché paper strips can be attached.
6. Paper milk cartons, Styrofoam balls, and the end rolls from paper towels are good foundation supports.
7. Small jars and cans can be taped together and built high as a foundation for larger candleholders. Papier-mâché holds firm when dry. Add lace and cardboard designs during the paste process.
8. Musical maracas are built over burned-out light bulbs, cans, or gourds. Papier-mâché over the forms and let them dry. When dry, hit the bulb maraca against the floor to break the glass bulb that is inside. You will hear the broken glass when you shake the newly formed maraca. Or fill a juice can with some beans or rice and papier-mâché over it.
9. Laminated papers are pasted together while flat (layer upon layer). About four layers work well. Cut out outside

4–21 *Bottles become fanciful friends in a variety of sizes and shapes when combined with papier-mâché and paint.*

shapes and form three-dimensional designs while the mixture is wet. Use waxed paper under laminated forms for protection from sticking.

10. Finger puppets can be made by binding dampened sticky brown tape (sticky side facing out) around your finger to form the core. Add bulky crumpled paper right to the sticky core. Secure it with tape or string. Proceed as before for finishing.

11. Asbestos pulp or sawdust mixed with wheat paste for a thick mixture works well for modeling small figures and details. The mixture may also be used as a final coating over a base shape. Use a wet finger to smooth the final texture.

12. Yarn, cloth, and lace can be dipped into paste or starch (or plaster) and draped over bulky three-dimensional forms. Use waxed paper underneath and allow to dry.

4–22 *Masks, globes, or sculptures can be made by placing papier-mâché over balloons. Note the stamped-leather necklace.*

Procedure

1. Tear newspapers into narrow strips, about ½ inch wide, and pull them through a shallow dish containing a mixture of wallpaper (wheat) paste and water. (The mix is sifted into water until a smooth paste forms that is not too thick. Water may need to be added during process as paste has a tendency to dry out during use. Keep the mix the consistency of cream.) Coat the paper with the paste, and wipe off the excess with fingers.

2. Carefully wrap the strips around a supporting armature or foundation, selected from those mentioned here.

3. The underlying foundation will determine the final shape.

4. A substitute paste may be made from a dry starch and water mixed to a thick consistency. A thick starch paste will dry rock hard. Liquid starch is often used. Or use 1 part white glue to 1 part water.

5. Apply approximately three layers of paper. The layers of paper can be counted when different types of paper are used for each layer. Newspaper and toweling are two

types of paper that are commonly used. Apply strip layers in various directions for added strength. Toweling is best for the final layer.

6. Permit the paper to dry thoroughly in the air for several days. Prop the armatures up on bottles, buckets, and boxes; then the air can get underneath and inside. Propping also keeps the shapes from rolling about.

7. Remove the object. Sandpaper the surface where a smooth texture is desired.

8. If large balloons are used, they may fit over the head. Find where the eyes and nose go and insert holes, or cut the balloons in half vertically. Each student uses half a balloon for a face mask. If forming an Easter crèche, cut an opening in the egg shape.

9. If the papier-mâché construction is to be a puppet, insert all the hanging wires or dowel rods during the wet stage.

10. Be certain to smooth all cracks and loose edges on the final paper coat.

11. After the paste is dry, cover the papier-mâché with a single coat of white paint, thinned plaster, or regular white acrylic-based wall paint. Gesso is another good base coat, and a gesso substitute is made from spackle (a plaster patch for walls) mixed with water to the consistency of paint. Then decorate the shape with painted designs. If tempera paints are used, add some starch or white glue for permanence. Acrylic paints are permanent. If plain tempera is used, finish with a spray plastic, shellac, or varnish coat.

12. Allow the paints to dry thoroughly and decorate the shape very carefully with a brush. Many good results are often smeared by rushing to get finished. Patience and care should be stressed at all times, in order to ensure a satisfying, well-organized result.

13. Do not let the papier-mâché get so large that it takes forever to do it, unless two or more students are working on the same form—such as on a globe or a large animal.

14. Do not mix the paste too thin, or it will puddle up the form and will not hold.

15. Add a touch of liquid detergent to tempera to make cleaning up easier.

4–23   *Papier-mâché mask.*

4–24   *Papier-mâché giant.*

PAPIER-MÂCHÉ PULP

The ingredients here are the same as for mâché, but the mixture is worked wet. The technique is good for small sculptures or adding details to larger forms.

Procedure

1. Tear paper into ½-inch pieces or smaller.

2. Place the pieces of paper in containers and cover them with water.
3. Add 1 teaspoon of salt to each quart of pulp to prevent the pulp from spoiling.
4. Let the mixture stand overnight or longer.
5. Squeeze out any excess water from the paper pulp and add wallpaper paste (1 cup of paste [flour or plaster] to 5 cups of well-mixed pulp). Blend well. (Add tempera paint for desired colors.) Plaster dries quickly. Or add starch.
6. Model with the pulp to create the desired form. This process is recommended for facial details and small, sculptured forms.

LOW RELIEF FORMS (FLAT)

For those times when you want to build a three-dimensional design from a flat surface, use this procedure. It is excellent for building around box shapes, for creating wall plaques, for building small mobiles and jewelry, for making notebook covers, and for designing permanent messages for cards.

Procedure
1. Cut bird forms, leaves, and flowers from several layers (about eight) of newspaper, or cut out cardboard or Styrofoam shapes. (See Figure 4–25.)
2. Saturate each shape with mâché paste.
3. Lay the shapes flat together one on top of another, to create "steps" for a three-dimensional effect and wrap a last coating of paper toweling strips over all the layers.

4–25 *Signs and messages become hard in papier-mâché. This one, nestling in an old picture frame, is made with Styrofoam (meat tray) letters and shapes under paper-toweling mâché on a cardboard base.*

4. Let dry for a few days.
5. Use as mobiles or jewelry, or glue the forms to a flat cardboard box surface and paint them as shown.
6. Insert a wire in the back for hanging.
7. Add papier-mâché forms to three-dimensional objects such as old toys, pots and pans, buckets, mirrors, and frames.

PROJECTS WITH PAPIER-MÂCHÉ

The following are some suggestions for workable projects in papier-mâché:

1. Masks of all sorts (Halloween or party): papier-mâché is a good, basic, inexpensive form especially suited for young children.
2. Puppet heads: balloons are good starters (covered with 5-inch-long paper strips), as are light bulbs or Styrofoam balls.
3. Figures.
4. Farm or jungle animals.
5. Storybook characters.
6. Candleholders, wall decorations, and ring stands.
7. Insects, animals, birds, and flowers, all related to study units.
8. Globes and backgrounds for dioramas.
9. Mobiles.
10. Mexican piñatas are favorites. Instead of painting the final form, cover it with glue and pieces of brightly colored, curled tissue paper. Piñatas can be used in

4–26 *During a papier-mâché workshop, students surprised the teacher with a look-alike life-sized figure in stuffed clothing surrounded by friends.*

celebrations at any time of the year, especially at Christmas.
11. Easter egg crèche.
12. Christmas decorations.
13. Jewelry designs to be worn.

Checkpoints

Organize the lesson carefully. Plan sufficient supplies (newspapers); provide about 2 hours to complete the armature and papier-mâché.

1. Newspaper has a grain therefore, try ripping paper from the fold down. The paper should tear easily and in straight strips.
2. Keep projects light in weight if they are to be hung or carried (such as puppets), but heavier if they are to stand.
3. Helpers (older students) can assist the class members with armatures and aid with cleanup.
4. Secure the legs or appendages to the body of the construction with tape or string, so they will not pull apart.
5. Apply paste-saturated strips to the armature firmly, but avoid getting the form sopping.
6. Allow enough time for thorough drying so that the paint will not crack after it dries. Papier-mâché dries in a couple of days.
7. Heads and other round shapes dry out well when placed over the top of a bottle or when the shape sits in a box or bucket.
8. Use white toweling or plain newsprint for the last coat. White glue thinned with water and torn colored tissue make a good finish coat also.
9. Keep the paint thick enough to cover the finished papier-mâché form. A small amount of white glue added to the tempera paint will prevent cracking.
10. White water-based wall paint (in gallon cans) makes a good thick foundation paint to use after the papier-mâché has dried and before the final decorative paints. Normally, it dries in an hour.

Bibliography

AGEE, KATE KEFFER. "Newspaper Art." *Arts and Activities Magazine,* **68** (Jan. 1971), p. 38.

Argiro, Larry. *Mosaic Art Today*. Scranton, Pa.: International Textbook Company, Inc., 1961.

Barkley, Fred A. "A Torn Tissue Becomes Tradition." *School Arts Magazine*, **70** (Dec. 1970), 19–21.

Berg, Paul. "Twentieth Century Masks," *School Arts Magazine*, **69** (Feb. 1970).

Cizek, Franz. *Children's Colored Paper Work*. New York: G. E. Stechert and Co., 1927.

Clements, Claire. "Photo-Montage Murals." *School Arts Magazine*, **66** (Oct. 1966).

Curtis, Annabelle, and Judy Hindley. *The Know How Book of Paper Fun*. New York: Sterling Publishing Co., 1975.

Farnsworth, Warren. "Aspects of Collage." *Arts and Activities Magazine*, **71** (Feb. 1972), 36–39.

Farrer, Beverly J. "Tissue Paper Animals." *Arts Activities Magazine*, **70** (Oct. 1971), 42.

Granzow, Suzanne, "Papier-Mâché Bowls and Boxes." *School Arts Magazine*, **71** (March, 1972).

Green, Morris D. "Extra Fine Papier-Mâché Mix." *School Arts Magazine*, **71** (Nov. 1971).

Guthrie, Rita R. "Cardboard City—Mixed Media." *School Arts Magazine*, **68** (Sept. 1968).

Heath, Judy. "Paper-Bag Figures." *School Arts Magazine*, **71** (April 1972), 48.

Heller, Jules. *Papermaking*. New York: Watson-Guptill Publications, 1978.

Henkes, Robert. "Paper Mosaic." *Arts and Activities Magazine*, **72** (Jan. 1973), 30–31.

Hill, Wanda. "Texas-Size Mâché." *Arts and Activities Magazine*, **70** (Jan. 1972), 22–23.

Hobson, A. F. *Paper Sculpture*. Leicester, England: Dryad, Ltd., 1956.

Horacek, Connie R. "Boxes." *Arts and Activities Magazine*, **72** (Oct. 1972), 37.

Jablonski, Ramona. *The Paper Cut-Out Design Book*. New York: Stemmer House Pub. Inc., 1976.

Jacomo, Edward M. "Boxed in Creativity." *School Arts Magazine*, **68** (March 1969), 32–34.

Jambro, Thomas A. "Collage." *School Arts Magazine*, **68** (March 1969).

Johnson, Pauline. *Creating with Paper; Basic Forms and Variations*. Seattle: University of Washington Press, 1958.

Kenney, John B., and Carla Kenney. *The Art of Papier Mâché*. Philadelphia: Chilton Book Co., 1969.

Lidstone, John. *Building with Cardboard*. New York: Van Nostrand Reinhold Company, 1968.

Lorrimar, Betty. *Creative Papier-Mâché*. Cincinnati, Ohio: Watson-Guptill Publications, 1972.

Lyons, Michael Thomas. "Papier Mâché—The Art of Personal Adornment." *School Arts Magazine*, **68** (Sept. 1968).

———. *Paper Sculpture—Its Construction and Uses for Display and Decoration*. New York: Hastings House, Publishers, Inc., 1944.

Madsen, Edna. "Add Action to Your Papier-Mâché." *School Arts Magazine*, **70** (Oct. 1970.)

Mathews, Barbara. "Papier-Mâché Puppets." *School Arts Magazine,* **68** (Oct. 1968), 27.

Moseley, Spencer, Pauline Johnson, and Hazel Keonig. *Crafts Design.* Belmont, Calif.: Wadsworth Publishing Co. Inc., 1962.

Muente, Grace. "Something New in Papier Mâché." *Arts and Activities Magazine,* **72** (Dec. 1972), 36.

Murphy, Michael. "Bas-Relief Paper Sculpture." *School Arts Magazine,* **70** (Sept. 1970), 12–13.

Murray, William D., and Francis J. Rigney. *Paper Folding for Beginners.* New York: Dover Pub., Inc. 1960.

Museum of Contemporary Crafts. "Face Coverings." *School Arts Magazine,* **70** (June 1971).

Norton, E. Loise. "Papier-Mâché Book Characters." *School Arts Magazine,* **68** (Nov. 1968).

Oettel, Betty G. "Mask Making for Minors." *School Arts Magazine,* **68** (Nov. 1968).

Ogawa, Hiroshi. *Forms of Paper.* New York: Van Nostrand Reinhold Company, 1972.

Rainey, Sarita. "Disguising the Paper Bag for Puppetry." *School Arts Magazine,* **67** (Nov. 1967), 10–11.

Rottger, Ernst. *Creative Paper Design.* New York: Van Nostrand Reinhold Company, 1961.

Sadler, Arthur. *Paper Sculpture.* London: Blanford Press, Ltd., 1955.

Severs, Susan B. "From Classroom Grocery Store to Imaginary Zoo." *School Arts Magazine,* **70** (Sept. 1970), 8–10.

Sheehand, Marjorie J. "Papier-Mâché Project." *Schools Arts Magazine,* **67** (Dec. 1967), 16–17.

Stevens, Sylvia G. "Masks." *School Arts Magazine,* **69** (June 1970), 6–7.

Whitesel, Lita. "Cardboard Furniture for the Classroom." *Arts and Activities Magazine,* **71** (May 1972), 26–27.

———. "Designing Cardboard Play Equipment." *School Arts Magazine,* **70** (March 1971).

5

Puppets

Play-acting puppets are like fantasy little friends. They look and pretend they are alive. Puppets, as expressive theater, invite children to act through, identify with, become like, invent, animate, and imitate dynamic characters as well as act out real or make-believe situations. In this special, personal world, the child has complete control over what the puppet becomes, does, and says. Puppets have fresh new charm and appeal for all. Identifying with the invented life of the puppet and the performance of the puppeteer is fun for everyone.

Often, puppets are expressions of our innermost selves, of our desires, and reflect our dreams and wishes through natural and exaggerated action. When we watch children perform, we are catching a rare glimpse of their true feelings as they project and reveal their personalities through puppets in unique ways. Even the quietest students, the students with speech difficulties or special problems, come alive through the puppet and his world. During play dramas, we are sometimes surprised at the attitudes, expressions, interchanges and social resolving that takes place. We, as teachers, should provide such "pretending" opportunities for all students.

The production of a performance requires planning and coordination. Beginning with the concept, writing the original story and script, inventing and constructing the puppet, making the parts movable, designing the stage environments

5–1 *Wajavg puppets from Java. (Collection of the Santa Barbara Museum of Art, Alice B. Schott Doll Collection.)*

and props, to practicing the disguised voices required, makes this an exciting and memorable experience.

Puppets are one of the initial art experiences in our workshops and we provide a portable stage available for use all of the time. Everyone invents and performs with his puppet individually as well as in a group. Whenever there is time, students are encouraged to quietly participate in puppet producing. As an audience is desirable for puppet theater, students can reverse their roles. At times they are actors and other times they are audience. In both places, a great deal of artistic, emotional, and social learning takes place. Opportunities for spontaneous as well as rehearsed plays are always there.

History of Puppets

The history and development of puppets are fascinating. Throughout civilization, puppets have been a favorite form of entertainment and communication. The term *puppet* is derived from the Latin *pupa,* which means "doll." Puppets have been found in ancient Egyptian tombs. Greek literature as early as 300 B.C. speaks about "string puplers," perhaps puppeteers. In children's graves in Greece and Italy (circa A.D. 100) small jointed dolls with a wire attached to the head have been found. After the fall of the Roman Empire, the puppet theater kept the traditions of the empire alive.

As for the earliest site or origin of the puppet or puppetry, authorities are still unclear about the ancient past. In the Western world, such as Greece, they take on the form of entertainment, but in the Eastern world they are considered a traditional classic ritual and even today retain many of the original ancient mystical qualities. In China, as far back as the Han dynasty (about 12 B.C.), there were charming tales of departed beloved spirits visiting grieving emperors by appearing to them as shadows on screens that separated them. The Chinese call it "Screen of Death," the Javanese "Fog and Clouds," the Turkish the "Curtain of the Departing," the Arabs the "Screen of Dreams, Veil of Omnipotent Secret." It is the screen that becomes the mystical world of dreams, spirits, shadows, and death. The good and evil tales involve demons, gods, giants, heroes, and nobility in dramatic combat. The puppet used is a flat rod puppet operated from below. It is made from hide, pigment, and hair, with movable joints and elaborately pierced designs.

In Japan, the earliest recorded popular dramatic performances using puppets rather than live actors is as old as the Heian period, or A.D. 894–1185. Some authorities differ, saying it was the Kamakura period, between 1185 and 1333. At any rate, it was the second half of the sixteenth century before the Japanese puppet theater took on its specific characteristics. These included the continuous musical accompaniment with the three-stringed samisen and the continuous narration of the performance, including songs and chants.

The common term for Japanese puppet theater is the *Bunraku*, and it is still the name of a puppet troupe in Japan today. The first puppets were often carved wooden figures. They were about 2 feet high, and were held and manipulated by one person standing on a platform stage. By the end of the sixteenth century, the puppets had grown to 3½ feet and were operated on stage by three people. This is still the form often used today. The chief puppeteer operates the puppet's head with the left hand and the puppet's right hand with his own. A man on the left operates the doll's left hand and a third man the doll's feet. The puppeteers are sometimes hidden, working in a concealed area below the level of the stage.

The early movable parts of the puppet included the eyebrows, mouth, and eyes. Some puppets have movable ears and revolving noses. The parts are operated with strings and levers attached to the hollow head and arms. The heads were originally made of baked clay and were treasures handed down from one generation to another. The puppets wore wigs to change characters and elaborate costumes.

As with all the elements of traditional Japanese culture, historical continuity is strong, especially in the theater arts.

Usually, the play deals with the world of the townsmen, and the plots involve conflicting loyalties and responsibilities.

Various parts of Europe had puppet heroes who acted and performed like the people of the area. Many countries had touring puppet theaters, and towns were noted for puppet types. For instance, in Barcelona, Spain, the hand puppet was favored. In Cologne, Germany, the rod puppet was popular. Voltaire, the French philosopher and playwright, assisted with private puppet theaters in the castles and palaces. The German poet Goethe was inspired by a puppet theater gift on his twelfth birthday to write his own plays for it. Perhaps it was this gift at this time in his life that motivated his love of writing poetry. It is said that Lewis Carroll and Hans Christian Andersen were creators of toy puppet theaters and small hand puppets.

The puppet *Polcinello* came to France from Renaissance Italy in about 1640, and his name was changed to Polichinelle. He performed in England in 1660. It was there he became known as Punch. In 1928, a play about Punch and Judy was published in England and was illustrated by the artist George Cruikshank. The famous story line of Punch and Judy shows Punch fighting with his opponents and knocking them out. The conclusion of the show has Punch either victorious over the devil or being swallowed by a kind of crocodile character. This "moral" story has enchanted children of all ages for centuries.

In America, it is said that the Indians used puppets before the coming of Columbus. Puppets have long been a favorite form of entertainment. At the turn of the century, puppets were popular in circuses and fairs, schools and townhouses, and in parks and street shows. Condensed versions and interpretations of old-fashioned dramas were presented. Gradually, greater skill and artistry were incorporated; artists and writers used the puppet theater as an introductory form of their works of art. The professional puppet theaters of today are extensions of this form of artistry.

Perhaps our most well-known puppets today are those that appear in television productions such as "Mr. Rogers' Neighborhood" and "Sesame Street." There are other names to be remembered in the American history of small puppet theater. These include the Chicago Little Theater (1915); the string puppets of Ellen Van Volkenburg and of Tony Sarg, New York (1916); Remo Bufano, New York; Forman Brown and Harry Burnett and their "Turnabout Theater" in Los Angeles; Burt Tillstrom's "Kukla, Fran and Ollie"; Buffalo Bob Smith's "Howdy Doody"; Shari Lewis' "Lambchop"; Paul Winchell's "Jerry Mahoney"; Jim Henson's "Muppets"; and Edgar Bergen's "Charlie McCarthy." Puppet theater is great fun as well as fine artistry. It is worthwhile to note to students that they are carrying on an age-old traditional craft.

5–3 *A simple square of cloth stuffed with facial tissue and tied with a rubber band is transformed into a ghostlike character.*

Puppets

159

Objectives of Puppetry

Puppets can be integrated into the classroom art curriculum in many ways. The subsequent instructions for puppet construction and use will provide both students and teachers with an adventure that is full of surprises, excitement, and artistry. They can be any shape or size. Some are three-dimensional; others are flat and are used as silhouettes or shadows. They can be manipulated by hand or with strings or rods. When they come to life, they are as real as the person pulling the strings.

Puppet making has many educational objectives:

1. Puppets encourage inventive, open, and spontaneous communication.
2. Puppets enable the acting out of social situations and cultural differences.
3. A fourth-grade teacher has students select "careers" (what they would like to be when they grow up) and dress themselves in clothes that are appropriate to those professions. The students research a profession and then communicate the "whys and hows" of that profession with puppet talk.
4. A child can work out family and sibling relationships through puppet theater. Puppets encourage the expression of personal feelings, including anger, love, hope, and secret wishes. Puppets also can be used as an instructional tool to answer questions the children might have in specific subject areas.
5. A puppet can become a friend that goes everywhere with a child.
6. Inventing poems and stories to be told by the puppet is an important experience for children, as is creative writing and performing original as well as traditional plays.
7. Puppets help in the use of small-muscle and hand-eye coordination.
8. Puppets encourage the building of self-confidence through the expression of ideas.
9. Puppets provide opportunities to practice art learning: designing, modeling, painting, sewing costumes, and building puppets and stages.
10. Puppetry art can be studied as part of cultural history.
11. The acting out of study areas—such as language, reading skills, book reports, events in history, and characters from books or paintings—is fun with puppets as characters. Favorite characters from television, movies, and fairy tales can be assumed.
12. Puppets can be used as a tool for improving speech and

verbal skills. (Children who stutter usually do not stutter when speaking through a puppet character.)

13. Puppets can be adventurers who dare to do what the children wish they could.
14. Puppets are an introduction for the child to the theatrical arts and to new ideas.
15. Puppets can dance and move to musical forms.
16. Puppets provide for group participation and social interaction. Puppets add to holiday celebrations.

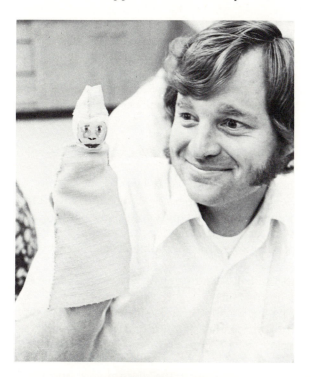

5–4, 5–5, and 5–6 *Puppets encourage imaginative thinking and spontaneous communication. Notice that teachers as well as children project their body images in their puppets. Figure 5–4 has an eggshell face; Figure 5–5 has a papier-mâché head; Figure 5–6 is a Styrofoam cup hand puppet.*

Puppets

A "TREASURE CHEST" FOR INVENTING PUPPETS

There are many ways to construct puppets, and you will want to build all of them and discover how they perform to meet your needs. Because of differences in classes, various grade developmental levels, and student performance, you will want to select an appropriate method of construction. The materials and tools needed are similar for most construction methods. Provide an available assortment of cloth, buttons, fringes, and so on to stimulate the children's imaginations. Sometimes it is difficult to decide which materials to choose when an exciting selection is at hand. Sharing odds and ends extends scraps for eyes and other features. One second-grade girl used poodle fur scraps for a puppet's beard, eyebrows, and hair. Puppets are such a good teaching tool that you will want to make several kinds during the year.

Supplies Needed
cardboard tubing, boxes, and paper cups
paper plates, egg cartons, paper toweling, and gift wrap
glue, rubber cement, paste, staples, pins, and clips
all kinds of cloth of varied colors, patterns, and textures
Popsicle sticks, tongue depressors, pipe cleaners, and wood
    dowels
old gloves, socks, baby clothes, baby blankets, yarns and
    thread, old tennis balls
tissue paper, paper bags, stockings, fringes, felt, and lace
rickrack, Styrofoam, sequins, cotton balls, and tassels
fake fur, salt clay, blown eggs, buttons, pins, and spools
containers, plastics, bells, old bows, and braiding
feathers, string, balloon, fruit, raffia, corn husks, and reeds
cards, food containers, cans, seed pods, ribbons, and felt-tip
    markers
paper, cellophane, oak tag, and rice and construction papers
scissors, tape, wooden spoons, doll clothes, and an old
    sewing machine

Procedure
1. Discuss how facial features and expressions change with our moods, such as happiness, grouchiness, or surprise. Faces also change with age.
2. How and what will project out from the head? What kind of costume does your puppet need? Will it be a clown, monster, or animal?
3. If possible, have several good examples to illustrate your ideas. Decide on the type of construction and have adequate materials and tools for use.

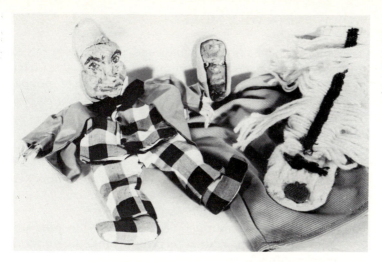

5–7 *The heads of these puppets are made from paper pulp modeled over tubing. The puppet at the left has an open back seam into which the hand fits to work the arms or walk the legs. The puppet on the right is a sock puppet.*

4. Have each student decide what his or her puppet is going to do and how it will be constructed.
5. Explore and select interesting materials that are fun to work with, good to feel, easily available, and suitable for your class.
6. Keep the design and construction simple and direct.
7. Study ways that peoples' and animals' body parts go together. Start with a general paper pattern for overall forms. If making a hand puppet, make it large enough to fit your hand.
8. When cutting cloth, it is helpful to cut the sides and large shapes for younger students after they select their materials. The teacher can use electric scissors or use a paper cutter with much caution (students must not go near it). This gets the puppet under way quickly.
9. If a sewing machine is available, it can be used to sew seams for younger students.
10. Old socks (chenille cloth feels good) make easy hand-puppet bodies for beginning puppeteers.
11. If one wants a puppet with a stiff mouth, cardboard or pellon can be sewn inside the part of the head designated for the mouth.
12. For fast construction, glue the seams. At hard-to-get-at places, squeeze the glue in and hold the area in tightly with straight pins or paper clips until it dries. On the second day, it is helpful to have the students reglue seams that were missed or did not take. White glue is a strong adhesive and serves the purpose well.
13. Explore the kinds of theatrical equipment that are available: stages, tape recorders, lights, phonographs, scenery, and props.

WHICH PARTS WILL MOVE?

Because we have only two hands and ten fingers, we need to decide which parts of the puppet we will want to have move. This, in turn, will determine the type of puppet construction we will select.

1. Does the mouth move?
2. Do the hands, arms, or ears move?
3. Do you want finger puppets?
4. Does the whole puppet move, as with a rod puppet or marionette?
5. Do the legs move to walk and dance?
6. Do you want a body puppet? (This puppet is life-sized and is held on your lap. Your arms protrude into the puppet's armholes, thus permitting mobility.)
7. Do you want a shadow puppet?

Much of the thrill and surprise in puppet making is in the creation and discovery of what will take place. It is difficult to decide which activity is more fun, inventing the character or operating and manipulating it. The children realize that the puppet is just a cloth or paper plate until it comes alive in a performance.

To keep the spontaneity, the design construction should be uncomplicated—able to be completed quickly at the student's performance level, whether it is preschool or eighth grade. For instance, paper plates and potato-head puppets are easily made and are quick to take on vitality. Marionettes and papier-mâché puppets are more durable and more difficult to construct (upper elementary grades may enjoy the challenge). Both perform with sparkle for the inventor and all are visually delightful.

Basic Puppet Construction: Hand Puppets

One of the most popular types of puppet construction is the hand puppet, a favorite of television as well as in the classroom. There are several variations of the hand puppet, which refers to any puppet that goes over the hand. Usually the head, arms, or mouth move; sometimes the legs and feet swing freely from the body. The puppet is worked from below the stage, which is usually a table, draped cloth, or enclosed stage. From then on, start gathering materials and you will soon have an exciting selection with which to begin. For young people, easily worked materials are a must.

5–8 *Firm Styrofoam covered with spackle and painted is the base for these hand puppets. The kindergarten teacher uses the puppets to teach vowel sounds.*

SOCK PUPPETS

Procedure

1. Find an interesting old sock—one that has an unusual texture, pattern, or color. Chenille socks are a good basic material. (See Figure 5–7.)
2. Have the child place his hand into the sock. The fingers go into the toe and the thumb is placed into the heel. As the child makes a fist with the hand, the puppet will come to life.
3. Add a piece of felt at the end of the sock, for a circular mouth, teeth, a tongue, or other facial feature.
4. Facial features and hair can be represented by buttons, beads, embroidered designs, felt scraps, rug scraps, fake fur, yarn, braid, lace, or rickrack.
5. Try tying off the sock with rubber bands where you might want the nose, ears, or cheeks.
6. Add body parts such as arms, hands, and legs by attaching felt or stuffed socks.
7. Construct clothing with a rectangular piece of felt with a cutout circle for the head, cloth scraps, or old doll clothes.
8. For variation, you can use the sock vertically; just cut a slit for the mouth and add an oval-shaped piece of felt.
9. Sew the clothing seams inside out, or use white glue. Sock puppets are a good project for first and second graders.

CLOTH HAND PUPPETS

Procedure

1. Design a puppet pattern by drawing around your hand on a piece of paper. (Visualize the size of the puppet body to fit an individual's hand.)

Puppets

165

2. Leave 2 inches all around to allow for seams and a comfortable hand fit.
3. Cut out the paper patterns and place them on cloth. Cut out cloth.
4. Demonstrate and cut out the round pattern for the mouth and show how the cloth mouth will fit into the two sides.
5. Sew or glue the two sides together along with the mouthpiece. White glue works well. Use straight pins to hold glued areas until dry.
6. If some seams open during drying, add more glue and pin the sides together with straight pins or paper clips.

Alternate Procedure
1. The head and body can be all made from one piece of felt or cloth.
2. If the head is made separately, then the cloth body is added.
3. The head can be made from papier-mâché, old tennis balls, cardboard tubing and construction paper (add faces and hair), Styrofoam balls with cloth features glued or pinned on, wooden spools with painted faces (felt-tip pens work well), potato heads with vegetable features pinned on, salt ceramic clay over a cardboard tube, blown eggs, or egg carton sections fastened together.
4. Decorative elements such as lace, buttons, bows, rickrack, stuffed fabric shapes, felt, cloth, and yarn should be used to decorate the puppet's head and body.

Another good idea, if the head is to be kept separate from the body, is to make the parts interchangeable. For instance, if you make several heads (one for teaching reading, one for teaching mathematics, and so on), then you can use the same body for each head. Separate felt heads can be made and their top areas stuffed and made stiff in the neck with cardboard tubing. Old doll clothes will fit over the body forms and the arms can be kept movable. Even a simple square of fabric can be turned into a costume. If you are making imaginative insects and animals, add tails and decorated backs.

PAPIER-MÂCHÉ HEAD

The papier-mâché head is a continuation of the hand puppet. The head is built up from wadded newspapers, rags, or tissues, or mâché over a small Styrofoam ball. (See Chapter 4 for the art of papier mâché.)

Procedure
1. Place the head material on top of a small length of cardboard tubing.

2. Tape the head to the tubing. (Fingers are to be placed inside the tubing.)
3. Cover the head form and tubing with paper strips that have been dipped into mâché. Papier-mâché pulp can be used, too.
4. Add projected features from paper pulp.
5. Build up the head with about three layers. The last paper layer should be white paper.
6. To dry, place the puppet head on a pencil and stick the pencil into an inverted egg carton (or paper cup) or place it on a plastic bottle and let it dry for a few days.
7. When the papier-mâché has dried, finish it by first coating it with a base coat of white paint. (Ordinary water-base house paint will work, or gesso.)
8. Paint over this with tempera or acrylic paints.
9. Add details with felt-tip pens.
10. Cover the head with a plastic spray coating. (Clear vinyl will work and so will shellac.)
11. Attach scrap materials for hair and ears, and add a cloth body and clothes. (See Figure 5–7.)

PAPER BAG PUPPETS

Paper bags come in all sizes and colors. A long-time favorite, paper bags are usually lunch size and can be purchased at supermarkets. Paper bag puppets are a direct expression and can be as simple or as complicated as you like. The bag can be used in two ways: the base end has a flap that becomes the mouth (for a fish or bird), or the flattened end of the bag is folded over and the face is drawn on the flat bottom

5–9 *Paper bag puppets of all sizes and shapes are created through various paper-cutting techniques.*

of the bag. The edge of the folded bag bottom becomes the mouth. Decorate the bag with pens, crayons, papers, paints, and all kinds of scraps. Do not forget to add arms, legs, backs, and costumes. Bag puppets are easy and inexpensive to make, and they are adaptable.

PAPER CUP OR CEREAL BOX PUPPETS

Procedure
1. Slit a Styrofoam cup or paper cup lengthwise. Cut a mouth from construction paper or from cloth.
2. Staple, tape, or glue the paper to both inside halves of the cup.
3. Add a body and facial features.
4. Using a cereal box, slit the front and two long sides along the horizontal center; fold over on the fourth side.
5. Decorate.
6. Insert your fingers in the top opening and your thumb below to make the puppet talk.

FINGER PUPPETS

Finger puppets are appropriate for the tiniest hands and fingers. Old cloth or rubber gloves can provide the basic structure for the finger puppet; they can be constructed from felt or other fabric; or they can be knitted. (See Figures 5–10 and 5–11.) Sew or glue on features.

Supplies Needed
Yarn	scraps
cloth	old glove (optional)
egg cartons	glue
scissors	accessories

5–10 *The library teacher uses gloved fingers as puppets to illustrate many of the stories she presents to students.*

Procedure

1. Draw a paper pattern of a puppet, to be sure it will be wide enough to go around a finger.
2. Pin the pattern to a piece of cloth (felt works well here).
3. Glue the sides and top together to make a finger tube.
4. Add features for rabbits, cats, or monsters.

Alternate Procedure

1. For this basic form of finger puppet, cut the fingers from gloves.
2. Draw on facial features.
3. Add some hair.

Finger puppets also can be made from knitted forms, cardboard tubing and cut paper, or salt clay over a paper tube.

Create as many finger characters as you can think of. Entire puppet families can be used to perform, with ten characters on two hands.

Puppets

169

Alternate Procedure

1. Egg cartons with tall projections can be used for finger puppets.
2. Each animal or person is made from two sections: one for the head, the other for the neck.
3. Remove the sections from the body of the carton.
4. Push the top of the neck part into the bottom side of the first section.
5. Cut a piece of colored construction paper to fit the back cover and glue it on.
6. Cut ears and other parts from the carton.
7. Add details with felt-tip pens, yarn, pipe cleaners, and string dipped in glue.

One third-grade teacher had an ingenious idea to accompany a science unit. She stuffed the hand and finger sections of a glove, cut off and stuffed three fingers from a second glove, and sewed them to the stuffed glove. (She left room in the glove to place her hand.) This puppet became "Oscar the Octopus."

Stick or Rod Puppets

5–12 Rod puppets made from decorated tubing and a stocking over a clothes hanger. Can you think of things to add?

A rod puppet is extended on a stick and worked from below. Rods can be made from Popsicle sticks, tongue depressors, wooden spoons, dowels, tree sticks, wire rods, construction paper tubes, broomsticks, cardboard rods, or coat hangers. All ages enjoy this puppet and building one can be as simple or as complicated as desired.

Heads for stick puppets can be made from any of the supplies listed for puppets on page 162. Body, legs, and arms are cut from cardboard. Joints should be left loose and can be held together with string or fasteners that permit movement. (See Figures 5–11 and 5–12.)

To make the arms move, attach a string to the ends of each of the puppet's hands. Bring the strings toward the center—where the heart would be. Run both strings through a plastic ring. Continue the strings together down to the bottom of the puppet where they can be manipulated from below without being seen. Operate the mouth from the inside with one hand and pull on the string from below to make the arms move.

POP-UP SURPRISE PUPPET

Supplies Needed

juice can or paper cup	rod
old sock	rubber band

Procedure

1. Place the rod into the end of the sock.
2. Stuff the sock loosely to form a head and close it around the rod with a rubber band.
3. Cut out both ends of the can or cup.
4. Place the sock over the can so that the rod extends from the bottom.
5. Move the head down into the can to conceal it.
6. Add dangling arms, tails, and legs.

The pop-up surprise occurs as the rod is moved up and down.

STYROFOAM BALL OR OLD TENNIS BALL ROD PUPPETS

Supplies Needed

cotton balls	papier-mâché
fabric (felt)	pins
feathers	pipe cleaners
glue	rod
paint	Styrofoam ball or old tennis ball

Procedure

1. Cover a Styrofoam ball with felt, cloth, or papier-mâché.
2. With a tennis ball, cut a small hole underneath for the dowel.
3. Pin cloth to the ball to form a costume.
4. Draw features on ball with felt-tip pens or crayons.

5–13 *This student is ready to try out her sock puppet and rod puppet. The rod puppet is made from a Styrofoam ball on a dowel. Bottle puppets rest on the counter. Try potato heads as rod puppets.*

5. Glue or pin on details and features from feathers, pipe cleaners, cotton balls and other decorative materials.
6. Insert a long dowel into the ball for about ¼ inch.

DANCING PUPPETS

For a dancing puppet, stuff the upper torso of a cloth puppet until it is stiff. An opening in the back of the puppet will allow the puppeteer to place a finger in each leg. The fingers do the dancing.

This same idea can be used with a paper index card.

Alternate Procedure
1. Fold one fourth of the index card up from the bottom.
2. On the remaining three fourths of the card, draw a head and torso.

5–14 *Old tennis rackets make great rod puppets. (Courtesy of Edna Gilbert, Mesa Public Schools, Mesa, Arizona.)*

3. Add dangles, arms, or hair.
4. On the bottom fourth of the rectangle, place two holes, one for each finger.

This puppet walks and dances.

Construction paper works well, too. Children in lower grades can do this one.

Alternate Procedure
1. Fold the construction paper in half vertically (9″ × 12″).
2. Staple the top and long side closed, leaving one short end opened.
3. Starting at the closed end, fold the paper under one third of the length of the rectangle. The hand goes in through the bottom end and the top, folded third becomes the head.
4. This third of the rectangle encloses the puppeteer's fingers.
5. Draw and add on features and appendages.
6. Dress the body using pens, paint, paper, or crayons.

SHADOW PUPPETS

Shadow puppets are figure or animal forms that are hinged, flat cutouts fastened to rods or sticks and controlled from below. The Chinese are famous for this form of puppetry and used it as early as the eleventh century. For a background, a cloth is stretched tightly, sometimes with a painted scene; the light is placed behind the cloth and figure; and a silhouette is created for the audience.

Marionettes

Marionettes are worked from above, usually on a stage. Many puppeteers transform the stage into a miniature theater. Marionettes can be constructed from any of the previously mentioned materials; just be sure the keep the body joints loosely hinged to permit flexible movement.

Supplies Needed
Popsicle sticks or tongue depressors
string
socks
paper
glue
felt

felt-tip pens
needle and thread
block of wood
cloth
doll clothes and shoes
marbles
yarn
stapler
scissors

Procedure

1. Cut the heel out of a sock. Sew closed.
2. Tie one end of the sock closed and stuff it with cloth for the head.
3. Tie the sock off and stuff the body.
4. Slit another sock up the middle for legs and sew up the sides. Cut arms in the same manner.
5. Place a marble or pebble in the top of each leg for a joint and tie the marble off above and below.
6. Stuff each leg with paper to the knee and put another marble in each leg to form a knee joint.
7. Stuff the legs to the feet. Stuff and tie the arms also.
8. Sew doll shoes onto the feet. Sew arms and legs to the body.
9. Attach strings to those joints you want to move. Knees, wrists, and head are the common joints. Heavier cord is best as it will not twist as easily.
10. Attach the strings to wooden Popsicle sticks and staple the cross sticks to the main stick. (Normally, two wrist strings are attached to one stick. Two knee strings go on another stick; optional. And the head string and bottom string go on the main stick. See Figure 5–15.)
11. Moving a marionette takes lots of practice, but the puppet is very flexible and can be made to dance and do stunt movements.
12. Bodies for marionettes can also be made from cardboard, plastic, or thread spools that are attached with thin, short leather strips, string, or pipe cleaners.
13. Another popular marionette is made out of stuffed paper bags. The bags are joined loosely with strings and their movements are controlled from above. The puppets' faces and bodies can then be painted, decorated, and clothed.

5–15 *Marionettes are more complex string puppets but provide plenty of movement and action. The crossbar here is approximately 5 by 7 inches. The front cord is attached to the head; the arm cords are tied to both ends of the crossbar. The back cord is attached to the seat of the puppet. A fifth-grade teacher uses this marionette to teach about traditional Navajo Indian customs.*

Puppet Stages

Any structure that will cover the puppeteers as they perform is a puppet stage. The simplest stage is a curtain stretched across a corner of a room or doorway that is tall enough for the puppeteer to stand behind. A sofa, table, or even a cardboard box can also serve the same purpose. Cloths can be stitched with appliquéd scenery. Large paper scenes are easy to make and are flexible. Some suggestions for stages follow:

1. Cut off the fourth side of a large cardboard carton or wooden box and open two of its sides. Cut the stage from the front side.
2. Hang a cloth in front of a long table and have the students sit under the table. This is a good stage for hand or rod puppets.
3. Use a long dowel or stick (a broomstick). Staple a cloth to it horizontally. The stick can rest on the shoulders of two students. The performers stand behind the cloth.
4. Cut three large panels from pegboards or wood. Cut a shape out for a stage. Wire or hinge the ends together for mobility. This structure is very durable.
5. Use a doorway with a curtain extended across it.
6. Assemble three cardboard rectangles. The stage is cut from the front piece. The ends are slit so that panels slip into slots. This structure is taken down easily and stored.
7. Turn a long table on its side. Decorate the front. The puppeteers perform behind the tabletop holding the puppets above the edge of the table.
8. Use the students' desks for impromptu stages.
9. Drop cloths with drawn-on backgrounds are simple and easily stored scenery environments.

Checkpoints

1. If a puppet is to be used frequently over a period of time, use construction materials that will be long-lasting.
2. Let the skill and grade level of students determine whether the puppets are to be simple or complicated in design. For young puppeteers, select simple procedures, such as the hand or pop-up puppet.
3. Keep materials inexpensive so that frequent and spontaneous use and creation can be encouraged.
4. Keep the puppets and plays child-oriented. Puppets should look as if they were made by children.
5. Plan lots of action in plays.
6. If a lot of handstitching is necessary, try to use a sewing machine for durability.
7. Use bright, sparkling colors and materials for the best visibility from a distance. Exciting textural materials— fake furs and old blankets—are favorites.

5–16 *More ideas for your puppet productions. Starting at the left, a surprise pop-up puppet; puppet made from popsicle sticks; a pencil-in-a-spool puppet; a witch over a small cup; a paper bag (safety officer) puppet; and paper plates with a face on each side.*

8. Send letters to the students' homes asking for scraps. You will be amazed at the variety you receive from the response. Even kitchen and household items become magical creatures and stimulate diverse creations.

9. For cloth puppets, and where much cutting is necessary, use electric scissors to cut out the basic shapes. It is fast and simple for the student to draw the pattern on the cloth and for one teacher to cut it out. A paper cutter also can be used to cut shapes.

10. Store puppets on bulletin boards, shelves, and other places that are easily seen and available to children.

11. Be sure to have the audience sit close to the stage, and have puppeteers speak "way out." Loud, noisy puppets are fun.

Presenting Puppets in Action

With eager children and cleverly made, irresistible puppets, you are ready to begin. As improvisations are the challenge, inventing plays will provide unique interpretations, personal solutions, imaginative performances, and exciting results. A student's level of creative powers, his interests, and his past experiences should be considered for plays, portrayals, and character roles. Because of the endless productive flow of the child's imagination, performances may require set time limits. Include a great deal of action when planning plays.

5–17 *Left to right: a felt finger puppet (over a popsicle stick); a shell doll; a mouse finger puppet out of salt ceramic; a pop-up surprise puppet from a wood clothespin, wood dowel, felt, and trim; a nurse on a straw; a corn husk and cloth lady; a yarn girl on a straw; and yarn dolls.*

The search for unique presentations can be met with individual monologues and group plays. Puppet fantasies provide children with a special freedom for endless role possibilities. Always be prepared to capture the creative spark and do not let the opportune moment pass by waiting for a more "convenient" time to perform. Interest may be lost and fascinating ideas may slip by, so take advantage of every possibility for meaningful involvement.

Allow small groups of students a few minutes to invent a plot for a play and to decide on who their characters will be. Certain dual characterizations are very successful: happy-sad, silly-serious, cowardly-brave, kind-selfish, evil-loving, foolish-clever—whatever needs are dictated by the roles—and the needs can change instantly. The Cookie Monster (a hand puppet) gobbling up every cookie (every puppet) he can find (which means gobbling up most of the cast, which he would have trouble doing) makes children roar (the throat seam is left open so things can be swallowed). The Cookie Monster soon becomes a favorite popular character. You may find that one character will spark another and many new puppet creations will suddenly appear and take on new dimensions. One successful teacher provides time for students to present play ideas for the first few minutes of each day.

5–18 *To make life-sized paper puppets, students trace their own body shapes on paper, then add clothing and facial details with felt-tip pens. Duplicate cutting permits forms that can be stuffed and then sewn or stapled.*

OTHER PUPPET THEMES

1. Imitate television and radio programs such as "Mystery Theater," "The Lone Ranger," or "Welcome Back Kotter."
2. Create a trip to a fantastic planet. Students can assume character parts of the shipmates, such as navigator, captain, cook, passengers, and stewardess.
3. Work out a story line in preparation for a trip.
4. Recreate a school dance or a magic ball. Imagine the scenario for "Michelangelo and Me."
5. Discuss aspects of social problems, such as economic conditions.
6. Recreate parts of popular movies, television shows, or advertisements. Interview television shows are fun.
7. Treat a school situation, such as how to organize and build areas of study. Puppets can represent the teacher, a parent, several students, the principal, and the school nurse.
8. Do a takeoff on a familiar play, such as *Little Red Riding Hood*, but invent new situations and happenings. The wolf could be a good character and Red could be a "hood."
9. Explore holiday themes.
10. Resolve family situations. Try role playing.
11. Invent puppets to accompany learning areas, such as mathematics and science units.

178

MAKING PUPPETS TALK: VENTRILOQUISM

All of us marvel at the wonderful puppeteers we see on television. The talent today seems to get better and better. After making puppets, we may ask how to make them come alive. Here are a few hints for making puppets talk.

1. Make a hard smile and keep it taut.
2. Grit your teeth together. Be sure there is air space at the sides of your mouth and between teeth.
3. Start talking without moving your lips. Say, "Hello, my name is Harry."
4. The problem sounds are *p, m, n,* and *b.*
5. In order to make these difficult sounds, place your tongue against the upper teeth, and do a lot of practicing.
6. Try talking in a high register and then in a low register. Become different characters through the use of different voices.

HOW TEACHERS INTEGRATE PUPPETS

1. "I'm a librarian, and my Mr. Bookworm puppet helps teach how to take care of and use books."
2. "In kindergarten, I have the community helpers, such as the policeman and fireman, explain their duties."
3. "My Navajo Indian puppet demonstrates the customs, jewelry, weaving, and clothes she wears as well as the functions performed by Navajo women."
4. "For home economics classes, we prepare amusing puppets that the students can take with them when they baby-sit to entertain their charges."
5. "I teach slow learners, and each student has his own

Puppets

179

puppet on his hand. The puppet helps him to read. For some reason, the child does better and has more confidence with the puppet for help."

6. "The first day of school, I introduce my Intelligent Bruce Puppet, who introduces the art materials and the areas of the art room. Bruce constantly corrects my mistakes and gets very angry when I forget to wash out my brush."

7. "In music class, the puppets bounce and dance around my head and really make the class sing louder. They encourage some very merry singing."

8. "It is very effective to have new vocabulary words for reading introduced by Mr. Frog. The children seem to retain the sight word much better than they did when I introduced a word."

9. "My puppet has created an enormous amount of interest in my seventh-grade class. The boys particularly seem to feel freer from inhibitions through the use of the puppet. Kevin decided he would kiss all the girls with the puppet and soon he had all the boys waiting their turn for the puppet. I used the puppet to give a spelling test and the students sat wreathed in smiles as they wrote the answers."

10. "We decided to use the puppets in reading class to make oral book reports. The students have three options: (a) They can make a report using my puppet Juan by speaking through him; (b) they can make their own puppet to represent a character from a book; or (c) they can go together, in groups of three, to make their own puppets and write a skit illustrating the book."

11. "I use my sock puppet with my class at the end of the day to discuss what we did during the day. They've named him Banana Fanana. Banana Fanana talks to them and helps them remember and asks them what their favorite activity is."

12. "I got the idea for my marionette form from the Indonesian shadow puppets. It is manipulated from the bottom instead of the top and can be used behind a sheet with lanterns forming a shadow. We also used it in social studies when learning about Indonesia."

13. "The girls and boys in the first grade love Egbert and Florabella. They teach them all kinds of things: math concepts, seasons of the year, and, especially, good manners and courtesy. Egbert and Florabella are always looking for children who use good manners."

14. "This puppet is used to teach short and long vowel sounds. I made one large puppet and five small ones. The large one represents the teacher; the small ones the students. The small ones represent the letters, *a, e, i, o,* and *u.* Soon children are making their own vowel finger puppets from cut-off glove fingers."

Anna	"A"	"What do you say?"	$aaaa$
Eddie	"E"	"Speak to me!"	$eeee$
Izzie	"I"	"What do you go by?"	$iiii$
Olive	"O"	"O what do you know?"	$oooo$
Ulna	"U"	"Let's hear from you, too!"	$uuuu$

MOTIVATING STUDENTS WITH PUPPETS

Here is how a puppet motivation might take place. Place a puppet on each hand:

"Hi. My name is Snooty Toot! I'm here to say that you boys and girls are going to make the tootiest puppets that ever were!"

"Oh, no, they're not. My name is Goofy Growl, and my goofiness says they can't make any tooty happy puppets."

"Oh, yes, they can and will. These boys and girls have great ideas, and they can invent the best creatures that have ever been. They can use ideas from comic characters, television, plays, poems, funny jokes, and many other areas that are especially important to them. They can see how beautiful I am. And I'm wonderful, too. And some people say I'm nonsensical!"

"Look at me. I'm the goofiest puppet you'll ever know. That's why I'm called Goofy and I'm always very angry! And I say that these boys and girls can't make the greatest puppets that ever were."

"Oh, yes, they can!"

"No, they can't. (And at this point the puppets playfully grab at each other and fight. Naturally, Toot wins, and Goofy falls over gently.)

"Oh boy, I win and now you can have fun making the most wonderful puppets, I know."

Bibliography

ALKEMA, CHESTER JAY. *Puppet-Making.* New York: Sterling Publishing Co., 1972.

BAIRD, BILL. *The Art of the Puppet.* New York: Macmillan Publishing Co., Inc., 1966.

BATCHELDER, MARJORIE. *The Puppet Theatre Handbook.* New York: Harper and Row, Publishers, Inc., 1947.

BENYON, HELEN. *Puppetry Today.* London: Studio Vista, 1965.

BUFANO, REMO. *Book of Puppetry.* New York: Macmillan Publishing Co. Inc., 1950.

FRASER, PETER. *Puppet Circus.* Boston: Plays, Inc., 1971.

HOPPER, GRIZELLA H. *Puppetmaking Throughout the Grades.* Worcester, Mass.: Davis Publications, Inc., 1966.

HOWARD, VERNON. *Puppet and Pantomine Plays*. New York: Sterling
Publishing Co., 1971.

JENKINS, PENNY DAVISON. *Magic of Puppetry*. Englewood Cliffs, N.J.:
Prentice-Hall, Inc., 1980.

KAMPMANN, ROBERT. *Creating with Puppets*. New York: Van Nostrand
Reinhold Company, 1972.

LANCHESTER, WALDO. *Hand Puppets and String Puppets*. Peoria, Ill.:
Charles A. Bennet Co., Inc., 1953.

MERTON, GEORGE. *The Hand Puppets*. New York: Thomas Nelson
Inc., 1957.

REINIGER, LOTTE. *Shadow Theatres and Shadow Films*. New York:
Watson-Guptill Publications, 1973.

ROBINSON, STUART, AND PATRICIA ROBINSON. *Exploring Puppetry*.
New York: Taplinger Publishing Co., 1967.

6

Dyes, Tie-Dye, and Batik

Techniques for creating colored dyes were known as early as 300 B.C.. During the eighteenth century, the French discovered chemically based dyes for commercial and industrial use. These dyes proved so popular that natural dyes began to disappear from the textile industry. The new chemical dyes (aniline and others) were easier to use and were economically feasible because they did not lose their intensities as the natural dyes did (in storage) and less time was required to extract colors from the raw materials. Many Africans and Indians of North and South America continued to use natural dyes until the nineteenth century, and even today many still prefer natural dye colors. Contemporary craftspeople, in a modern revival, have reintroduced natural dyeing to the textile crafts.

The fun of natural dyes is in going on trips to the woods and fields to find plants, making the dyes, and discovering what colors will be extracted. Natural dyes produce one-of-a-kind colors; no two dyes from plants are identical and each has subtle differences as a result of impurities in a particular plant. The secrets and beauty of natural dyeing bring us a special awareness of, and closeness to, our environment. Dyeing from plants provides a unique and fascinating opportunity to discover color and its properties. Commercial dyes are available in a multitude of colors.

6–1 *Hand dye-painted silk kimono. (Julia Hill, The Hand and The Spirit Crafts Gallery, Scottsdale, Arizona.)*

Natural Dyes and Dyeing Techniques

Color and dyeing facts can be discovered through trial and error. Exact colors are often unpredictable and there is excitement in that uncertainty. Try mixing dye colors and invent new names for special colors such as "dynamite purple" or "perceptual pink." These word games are as much fun as looking through the dye colors in glass jars and thinking up the color recipes.

Variations in color result from different growing conditions, growing areas, and soil quality; the manner of drying the plant; the time of year in which the plant was collected; hard or soft water; temperature of the dye bath; and the mordants. The longer the yarn is boiled in the dye, the deeper will be the color produced. Sometimes the color is not changed entirely. Overnight dye baths deepen and brighten colors. A mordant is a substance used to bind dyestuffs to fibers through chemical action. It controls the color as well as the colorfastness of the yarn. Not all plants need a mordant for dyeing. But, for others, the dye plant has a mordant close at hand, either another plant or a mineral. Proper amounts of mordant must be used. Cotton and other vegetable fibers do not absorb mordants as readily as wool. That is why wool is commonly used for natural dyeing. Cotton, like most vegetable fibers, takes dye better when it is soaked rather than boiled.

Supplies Needed
cheesecloth to strain dyes
clothesline for drying yarns in the shade

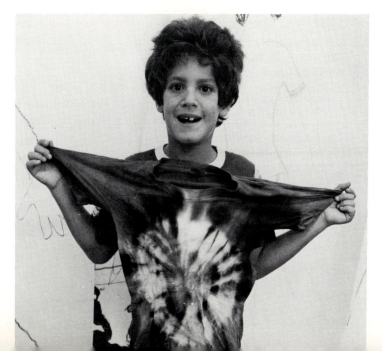

6–2 *Excitement is generated in tie-dyeing as forms and patterns are created quickly with splashes of color. This design was made with a rosette knot for a sunburst effect.*

Dyes, Tie-Dye, and Batik

enamel or copper kettles, large enough to immerse fabric

dyestuffs: plants, blossoms, berries, nut hulls, nut shells, barks, roots, grasses, and leaves

heating plates

measuring equipment: gallon, peck, and quart measures; tablespoons and dippers

neutral soap in which to wash yarns before dyeing; any starch, sizing, spots, and stain-resist dyestuffs can cause uneven dyeing

rubber gloves for hand protection with dyes and chemicals

sticks for stirring and turning materials

yarns and fibers: wool, cotton, silk, raffia, grasses, and jute

General Procedure

1. From 2½ to 3 gallons of dye bath is enough liquid to dye a pound of yarn. Additional water added to the dye bath will lighten the dye colors.
2. Recipes for dyeing are based on 1 pound of wool or cotton yarn.
3. The bath should be lukewarm when the yarns are put into it and should completely cover the material.
4. For basic dye colors, collect objects from the environment: plants, moss, herbs, berries, blossoms, roots, and nuts.
5. Chop them or put them through a meat grinder.
6. Place the chopped materials in an appropriate container and cover them with water.
7. Let the materials stand overnight unless otherwise directed.
8. Drain off the water and save it for stock.
9. Add more water to the pulp and simmer it for 30 minutes in an enamel or copper kettle.
10. Drain the water and add it to the stock.
11. Immerse the fabric in the stock and add enough water to cover it (at least 3 gallons).
12. Let the kettle simmer for 1 or 2 hours. Longer simmering will produce deeper colors.
13. After the dyeing process, let the fabric cool in the water.
14. Rinse the fabric and hang it to dry in the shade.
15. To make dyes permanent, refer to the mordanting processes and recipes described in many dyeing books. The following examples do not need a mordant:
    brown: walnut shells
    red-brown: onion skin, tree bark, or tea leaves
    purple: grapes, blueberries, or dandelion roots
    yellow: dandelion blossoms or mustard or peach leaves, sumac berries, or coffee beans
    green: beet greens or lichen or mint leaves
    black: oak bark or black walnut shells
    orange: finely grated carrots

How to Extract Vegetable Dyes

Natural dyes give a warmth and softness of color not achieved with commercial dyes.

BARK AND ROOTS

Collect bark and roots in late spring and winter when the sap is up, as the color has more substance at those times.

Procedure
1. Scrape and peel off the bark.
2. Dry it in the air, one layer deep in a well-ventilated place.
3. When the bark is dry, label it and place it in bags or containers.
4. When you are ready to use the bark, soak it in water for 24 to 72 hours, or allow it to ferment for 1 week.
5. Do not boil the bark.
6. Strain the liquid and reserve it.

LEAVES, GRASSES, AND VINES

Collect leaves, grasses, and vines late in the summer when the plant part is still in good condition. Do so before the first frost.

Procedure
1. Chop and shred the leaves and dry them in a well-ventilated area in a single layer.
2. Tie grasses and vines in bundles, label them, and hang them from the ceiling to dry.
3. When dried, they, too, should be shredded.
4. When you are ready to use them, cover the shredded material with cold water and boil it gently for 1 hour or more (depending on the color you want).
5. Strain the colored water and reserve it. Some leaves require soaking, shredded, in water for 24 hours in place of boiling. Sometimes, better results are obtained by leaving the plant to ferment for a week or more.

FLOWERS

Procedure
1. Blossoms can be dried in a slow, warm oven, or in single layers in a well-ventilated area, or use them freshly picked.

2. When dry, label them and place them in porous containers such as paper or cloth bags and store them in a dry place.
3. Blossoms sometimes lose their color in drying.
4. Blossoms cannot be frozen. (Dandelions and goldenrod, for example, must be used freshly picked.)
5. Boil blossoms for about ½ hour, strain them, and reserve the liquid. Dandelion roots will produce a purple color; the whole plant will produce a magenta color. Mint leaves will produce a green color.

BERRIES AND FLESHY FRUITS

Procedure

Berries and some fruits (such as grapes) can be frozen in plastic bags with little or no loss of color, or they can be used freshly picked. They often change or lose color if dried. Crush the berries and soak them overnight. Boil for 1 hour, strain them, and reserve the liquid.

WALNUT AND PECAN HULLS

Procedure

1. One pound of wool dyed in ¾ peck of walnut or pecan hulls will color the wool brown.
2. Break up the hulls from the nuts and boil them in water for 15 minutes.
3. Strain out the hulls and add cold water to make a 3-gallon dye bath.
4. Immerse the wool in the stock and simmer it for about 1 hour.
5. Rinse and dry the wool. The green outer husks of the black walnut shells will produce a dark brown to black color.

SUMAC BERRIES

Procedure

1. Four pounds of ripe sumac berries will dye 1 pound of yarn a light orange-brown color.
2. Grind the sumac berries between two stones.
3. Soak the berries in 3 gallons of lukewarm water for 1 day or until sufficient fermentation has taken place so the color of the fruit has passed into the dye water.
4. Strain and squeeze the pulp through and discard it.
5. Add *wet* yarn to the stock.
6. Let the stock and yarn stand in a warm place to ferment.
7. Rub the dye water into the yarn.
8. Rinse the yarn and hang it outside to dry.

RUSSIAN THISTLE

Russian thistle grows at low altitudes. Use the entire plant when it is young. It gives a dull olive-green color.

Procedure
1. One bushel of thistle will dye 1 pound of yarn.
2. Boil the thistle in 3 gallons of water until the plant is tender.
3. Pull off the stalks.
4. Add the wet yarn.
5. Allow the leaves to ferment in the dye bath for 1 week.
6. Rub the dye into the yarn often.
7. Place the yarn, still in the dye bath, on the stove and let it boil for 1 hour.
8. Remove the kettle from the heat and let the bath ferment for another week.
9. Rinse the yarn until the water is clear.
10. Place the yarn outside to dry.

GROUND COFFEE OR TEA LEAVES

Coffee will not produce a fast color in cotton.

Procedure
1. Use 1¾ pounds of ground coffee to dye 1 pound of wool yarn.
2. The resulting color will be a dark yellow-tan.
3. Boil the ground coffee in a strong water solution for 20 minutes (or boil a strong tea solution).
4. Strain the stock with cheesecloth to remove the grounds and then add cold water to make a 3-gallon dye bath. Add 2 teaspoons of vinegar for permanence.
5. Immerse the wool in the bath and heat it to boiling.
6. Simmer for 1 or 2 hours.
7. Rinse the wool and dry it outside in the shade.

ONION SKINS

The dry outer skins of onions make excellent dyes for fibers.

Procedure
1. One pound of wool dyed in 10 ounces of dry yellow onion skins will produce a gold or burnt-orange color.
2. Place the skins in a clean nylon stocking.
3. Cover the skins with water and boil them for 15 minutes. Remove skins.

Dyes, Tie-Dye, and Batik

4. Add enough cold water to the stock to make about 3 gallons of dye bath.
5. Immerse the wool in the dye bath, and heat and simmer it for an hour or more.
6. Rinse the wool and dry it outside in the shade.

Tie-Dye

Tie-dyeing is one way to create an explosion of beautiful color; students delight in the fast, dynamic results that are achieved.

Tie-dyeing is a resist technique. Fabric sections are either tied off, folded, clamped with blocks, or covered with wax to keep cloth areas from the dye. Protected sections do not absorb the dye, and an undyed pattern against a dyed background is the result.

Fabric that has been tie-dyed can be used to make lampshades, book covers, table covers, picture frames, window shades, gift wraps, wall hangings, clothing, and costumes, and it can be framed or mounted on cardboard. In addition, shirts, scarves, dresses, jeans, T-shirts, ties, hats, bedspreads, curtains, pillows, and sheets can be given new life by applying tie-dye techniques directly to them. Decorative stitching, beading, macrame, and weaving are effective combinations with tie-dye projects. Plan a tie-dye fashion parade today!

History of Tie-Dyeing

The craft of tie-dyeing began at least one thousand years ago in India and Japan. The Incas in Peru and Indian tribes in North Africa created tie-dyes, and it is still a favorite craft in the nations of West Africa. Marco Polo is recorded as having seen tie-dyes in China and India as far back as the thirteenth century. Here in the United States, pre-Columbian tie-dyed fabrics have been discovered in Utah, Arizona, and New Mexico.

The craft is as exciting to do today as it was for the Incas. The simple, inexpensive materials needed are the same: a stick, water, a pot, cloth, heat, and something to tie with. Originally, dyes were made from vegetable matter: madder, saffron, weld, Persian berries, and indigo. Today, modern aniline dyes are better suited to our fabrics. The simplest patterns and designs created with this dye craft have visual excitement and tactile appeal.

6–3 *In tie-dyeing forms and patterns are created instantly.*

Supplies Needed
bleach
blocks
clamps
100% clean cotton fabric (old sheeting); also silk, unbleached
    muslin, hopsacking, rayon, nylon, satin, burlap, velvet,
    and organdy; polyester does not absorb dyes well
crayons
heat source
household dyes
large tubs
pans: glass, metal, ·plastic, or enamel
plastic drop cloths
plastic squeeze bottle or eyedroppers
rags and sponges for cleanup
rubber or plastic gloves
rubber bands
sticks to stir dye baths
iron
string
salt
vinegar
spoons
stones, Popsicle sticks, bones, Styrofoam pieces, marbles
strong thread

Procedure
1. Wash the fabric first to remove the sizing.
2. Place the fabric flat on a work surface.

3. Knot, twist, and tie either a random pattern or one that has been sketched first. Follow the binding techniques described on page 193.
4. Tie any desired objects inside the knots to enhance the design. Use a shoe knot for easy untying.
5. Use available household dyes or order cold-water dyes from dye houses and mix them to specifications. To use household dyes, mix ½ cup liquid dye or 1 package of powder dye in each 1 quart of water, or dilute it further for lighter colors. Add 2 to 3 tablespoons of salt or vinegar to ensure the permanence of the dye (optional).
6. First, mix the dye with a small amount of very hot water, and, then, to complete the amount, add lukewarm water. Let the water cool.
7. The dye bath is ready when it has cooled to room temperature.
8. Dampen cloth before submerging the cloth in dyes. Many items can be put into a dye bath at once without crowding. For the classroom, small tie-dye projects are recommended as they are easier to handle. Use one pan or glass jar for each color.
9. Place the dye baths right in a sink while dyeing. (Do this outside when weather permits.)
10. Let the cloth remain in the dye bath until good penetration takes place (about 15 minutes). Stir while dyeing.
11. Submerge the cloth completely in the dye bath to ensure even dyeing.
12. Remove the cloth and rinse it in cold water until the water is clear. Undo the knots and rinse the cloth again.
13. Hang the cloth on a clothesline and allow it to dry. Keep the cloth out of direct sunlight.
14. Iron the cloth with an iron at a warm temperature.
15. If weather and space permit, work outside and rinse the cloth with a garden hose. Or hang the cloth on a clothesline and rinse it with a hose; leave the cloth on the line to dry.

6–4 *Rosette knot.*

a.

b.

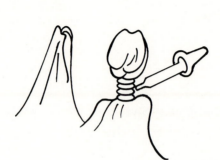

Note: If desired, mix ½ powdered dye color to ½ very hot water—enough to fill a detergent plastic squeeze bottle. Prepare several of these colors and let the water cool. During the dyeing procedure, pour various colors onto the cloth and into the knotted areas for an array of glorious colors. Then proceed to dip other sections into the pans of dye. (Use liquid dye full strength when pouring.) It is recommended, for permanent dye projects, that the cloth be simmered (over heat) in the final dye bath for about 30 minutes. Hot dyes produce brighter colors.

Design Through Binding Techniques

RUBBER BANDS

Rubber bands are used most commonly to bind fabric. Thick rubber bands give wide, bold designs. Thin bands create fine, spidery lines. String can be used as well, but it is difficult for young children to tie. Emphasize tying the rubber bands tightly, so the dye does not get underneath the tie, but not so tightly that the bands break. Practice first on rags to find out how tight the bands have to be.

ROSETTE KNOT

Procedure
1. Pinch up a generous section of cloth, about the size of a fist, and tie it tightly at its base with a rubber band. (See Figure 6–3a.)
2. By adding more ties along the fabric away from the top of the knot, you will get a sunburst effect. (See Figure 6–4b.)
3. Try tying over beads, sticks, Styrofoam, marbles, rocks, nuts, and beans. (See Figure 6–2.)

DONUT KNOT

Procedure
1. Form a rosette knot. (See Figure 6–5a.)
2. Take the top of the puff and push the center down inside through to the original rosette (think of a donut shape) and tie it with a rubber band. (See Figure 6–5b and c.)
3. Add liquid dye from a squeeze bottle into the banding before the final dyeing (as in Figure 6–4a).

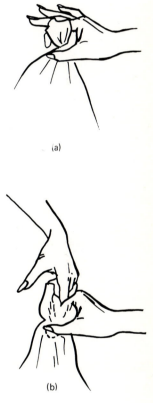

6–5   *Donut knot.*

(a)

(b)

(c)

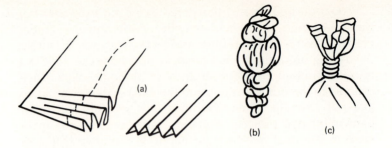

(a)

(b)   (c)

THE FOLD

Procedure
1. Gather or pleat the fabric in straight lines. (See Figure 6–6a.)
2. Secure the cloth with bands in random patterns. (See Figure 6–6b.)
3. Or wind the fabric tightly with rubber bands. (See Figure 6–6c.)

STITCHING

Sewing variations create intricate designs.

Procedure
1. Draw a design lightly on the cloth.
2. Do a running stitch along the line of the design.
3. Pull the thread tightly (use strong thread) and gather up the fabric.
4. Use rubber bands then to bind more patterns over the gathers.

6–7 Oversewing: roll the cloth and secure bands or oversew.

OVERSEWING

Procedure
1. Roll the cloth into a roll shape. (See Figure 6–7.)
2. Stitch over the roll.
3. Or just twist the cloth, tie ends together, dampen it, and place it in the dye bath. (See Figure 6–8.)

6–8 Twist the cloth, tie it in a circle, and then dye it.

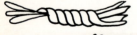

Design Through Dyeing Techniques

BLOCK DESIGNS

Procedure
1. Use blocks to create clear, bold, hard-edged designs. Use

two identical blocks. Design the blocks in simple massive shapes about 4 × 6 inches.

2. Fold the cloth into several layers, and place one block on top and the other exactly underneath it.
3. Clamp the blocks together tightly with C-clamps. (See Figure 6–9.)
4. The cloth, sandwiched between the blocks, is prevented from absorbing dye.
5. Masonite, wood, or plywood (about 1 inch thick) can be used for making these blocks in any shape. If you do not have a saw, ask the lumberyard to cut out the blocks.
6. Soak the blocks before using them.
7. Polyurethane meat trays can also be used as blocks.
8. Try creating clamp designs with tongue depressors and other scrap woods. Some Indian motifs include rain clouds, lightning, buffalos, and eagles, as well as geometric patterns.
9. Dishes and jar lids make good blocks, too.
10. Place the cloth into a simmering dye solution for 30 minutes. Rinse and remove the blocks.

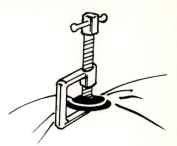

6–9 *Block designs using a C-clamp.*

PAINTED DESIGNS

Procedure
1. Wet the fabric and squeeze it to dampen it.
2. Draw the design right on the fabric with the full-strength liquid dye, using a squeeze bottle (such as a hair-coloring bottle, or use eyedroppers).
3. Or brush on designs with a paintbrush using the dyes by varying the colors in their strength. The colors will blend where they meet. When brushing on dyes, use paper cups or quart containers for each color and identify the color by writing the name on the cup. Place ½ package of powdered dye into a cup, or one package of powdered dye into a quart container. Add hot tap water to almost fill the cups or jars. Stir well. Let cool.
4. If the cloth is wet, the edges will be soft and blurry. If the cloth is dry, the edges of the dye will appear hard and firm.
5. Another technique is the batik process. Draw designs on the cloth with a paste resist or hot wax. These will resist the cooled dye when applying dye colors. (See page 202.)

DYEING TWO OR MORE COLORS

Use three or more bottles of full-strength liquid dye for pouring in various colors, such as yellow, gold, fuschia, and two or three prepared dyes in plastic buckets of other colors (for dipping). This technique works well for 30 to 50 students.

Dyes, Tie-Dye, and Batik

195

**Arts and Crafts for the
Classroom**

6–10 *Full-strength dye is
poured from the dye bottle onto
the banded cloth.*

Procedure

1. Tie, knot, and dampen the cloth.
2. Fill a squeeze bottle or an eyedropper with undiluted liquid dye (or pour it right from bottle) and squeeze the dye into the tied knots and under the rubber bands.
3. Dip part of the cloth into a light-colored dye bath.
4. Remove the cloth and squeeze out the excess dye.
5. Do not remove the rubber bands, but add more rubber bands to the fabric.
6. Rinse the fabric.
7. Dip the fabric into the second color dye bath and squeeze.
8. Rinse the fabric.
9. Tie some more knots and place the fabric in a third, darker bath.
10. Remove the fabric, squeeze it, rinse it well, and squeeze it again.
11. Untie all the knots and bands. Rinse well.

TIE-DYE ON A STICK

Procedure

1. Wet a large cloth and poke a broomstick handle into its center.
2. Wrap the cloth around the handle and tie it with string and rubber bands.
3. Have one person hold the handle.
4. Have a second person pour the dye from a bucket onto the cloth, holding the cloth over a second bucket. (Two quart-sized buckets are needed for each color used.)

5. As the dye is poured, the excess will fall into the second bucket.
6. Change the buckets under the cloth as the different colors are poured, so that the colors stay clean and can be used again and again.
7. For added designs, thinned tempera paints can be brushed on as well.
8. For variation, use dye on a large brush. As the brush is drawn across the cloth, turn the broom handle for a spiral design effect.

CRAYON-RESIST TIE-DYE

Procedure
1. Draw a crayon design on a piece of white fabric. Press hard.
2. Dampen the fabric.
3. Tie the fabric with string or rubber bands and dip it into watercolor or tempera paint.
4. Remove the string and rubber bands. Do not rinse.
5. Hang the fabric to dry, clothespin style, or place it in between sheets of paper toweling and press it with a warm iron until it is dry.

6-11 *Designs of all sorts are displayed in this tie-dye sampler. The threaded oversewing is left center. The dark section, top middle, was made by rolling the cloth, stitching it back and forth, and then bleaching it. (Courtesy of Jean Stange.)*

BLEACH DESIGN

The surprise effects of bleach design are very exciting. Plain washed cotton fabrics and dark colors such as blue (jeans) or black work well.

Procedure
1. Wash the fabric to remove any sizing. Keep cloth damp.
2. Tie it tightly with string or rubber bands.
3. Dip the tied portions into the bleach solution. (Equal parts of chlorine bleach and water.) Wear rubber gloves.
4. Leave the fabric in the bleach for only a few minutes.
5. Remove the fabric, rinse it in clear water, and hang it to dry.

GOOD COLOR-DYE COMBINATIONS

yellow, tangerine, fuschia, aqua, and black
fuschia, kelly green, and dark green
aqua, purple, and black
yellow, scarlet, fuschia, royal blue, and purple
yellow, navy, and aqua
rose pink, scarlet, yellow, and black
evening blue, fuschia, yellow, and dark brown
cocoa brown, gold, and black
fuschia, kelly green, yellow, and navy blue
tangerine, bright blue, yellow, and cocoa brown
fuschia, purple, and scarlet
purple, yellow, fuschia, and orange

Experiment to discover other interesting color-dye combinations.

Checkpoints

1. Cover all work surfaces and floors with plastic drop cloths. Work outside when possible.
2. Carry wet cloth over newspapers or a plate, in a plastic bag, or on an aluminum pan to catch the dye drips.
3. Hang tie-dyes to dry outside over grass or place newspapers under them to catch drips.
4. Remove any spills or stains with cleanser or household bleach. Identify each student's cloth with a name tag or felt-tip pen.
5. Most dyes today are permanent. If they are not, add 2 extra tablespoons of salt to the bath, or 2 tablespoons of vinegar to the works.

6. In the classroom, prepare colors in large containers and place them in a sink.
7. Tying in objects when binding fabric is fun and adds design interest. Styrofoam packing, pebbles, Popsicle sticks, coins, and marbles can be tied into rubber bands to create patterns.
8. Have separate working areas for tying and dyeing work.
9. Work with partners when tying knots; one person can hold the cloth while the other ties.
10. Wash all materials before dyeing them to remove sizing. Old shirts are easy to work with. Natural fibers, such as cotton and silk, absorb dye color best.
11. Make sure all knots are tight, especially on thin material.
12. Fabrics look darker when they are wet. Plan to make the dye color a little stronger, as it will get light when the fabric dries. Dyeing time will depend on the color desired.
13. After an item has been tie-dyed, wash it separately with cool water and cold-water soap or have it dry cleaned.

Batik

Unusual effects and colorful textures are part of the discovery process when students produce batik. The batik process is another popular dye-resist technique in which the design is applied to the material with a substance that will resist the action of the dye. This substance is commonly wax. The basic principle is that grease and water do not mix. Wax is applied to the cloth with a traditional tool known as a *tjanting*, or brush, and the cloth is then dipped or brushed with dye. The wax resists the dye, which fills the areas that are not waxed. This is the same process as crayon resist for tie-dye. Many teachers like their students to have experience with crayon resist before introducing the batik process. (Crayon drawings are brushed with dark tempera paint.) After dyeing, the resist (or wax) is removed from the cloth.

History of Batik

Batik is an ancient handcraft that is believed to be approximately two thousand years old, having originated in ancient Egypt and spread to India by way of Persia, where it is still a highly decorative art form. Small pieces of batik cloth also have been found in the ruins of old Javanese temples. As long as twelve thousand years ago, stone figures were decorated with patterns similar to those still being used today for cloth.

6–12 *Nigerian batiks reflect traditional tribal patterns created with metal stencils, printing blocks, and brushes. The dye color commonly made and used is indigo blue. This batik had a cassava paste resist applied on it and was then dyed.*

In Javanese, batik means "wax writing." It is believed that the name *batik* had its origin in the native cotton cloth worn by the Javanese before the Mohammedan and European conquests. It is also recorded that noblewomen in Indonesia did cloth batik before the thirteenth century.

As a contemporary art, batik gives handsome and decorative results and is popular among craftspeople as well as in school programs. In Japanese schools today, batik is taught as an important decorating technique for fabric to be used for kimonos.

There are two basic methods of doing batik: the Occidental and the Javanese. In the Occidental method, one starts with light colors and builds up to dark dyes. The Javanese use dark colors first. The main difference is the sequence of dyes; there are only minor variations in the tools and fabrics used.

The Javanese use traditional patterns and designs: birds, flowers, fruits, foliage, butterflies, fish, and shells. These are delightful motifs to use for the classroom as well.

In Africa, batiks often reflect symmetrical tribal patterns, for which metal stencils, brushes, and printing blocks are used. African cloths are well known for their blue indigo dyes.

6–13 *Batiks make handsome clothes (dress on the right) and can be used for decorative patterns on dolls, lamps, pillows, windows, and wall hangings.*

Batik in the Classroom

Batiking is exciting; it has that special "magical" quality of secret writing. Contemporary craftspeople have developed this craft into a personal art expression, and it is recognized widely for its unusual effects and creative possibilities. The teacher can introduce many related learning areas when doing batik, such as the study of various cultures and varied processes of cloth printing. (See color Figure 4.)

Batiks are found worldwide, and are used in many ingenious ways: as yardage for curtains, drapes, room dividers, blouses, shirts, scarves, wall hangings, window screens, tablecloths, napkins, place mats, stuffed pillows, toys, dolls, and even greeting cards. When batik is used as a window screen, drape, or lampshade, the light that shines through it adds a luminous, shimmering quality reminiscent of stained-glass windows.

Supplies Needed
paraffin wax, grocery store variety
beeswax (optional)
broken wax crayons (be sure not to include any plastic crayons)
liquid floorwax, lettering pens
candles
old roasting pan (or such) to place on a hot plate and to hold a muffin tin; or an electric fry pan (the water temperature can be controlled)
muffin tins that fit into pans
hot plate
nonflammable surface, such as a Formica table
waxed paper, cardboard, or foil under the cloth to protect working surface
tjantings (optional)
old brushes of various sizes (inexpensive bristle or soft hair)
plastic buckets to mix and hold dyes (or glass jars)
household dyes or inks or tempera paint
sticks
rubber gloves (or plastic)
lots of newspaper and paper toweling
electric iron
clothespins and clotheslines (optional)
water
100 percent cotton cloth such as old sheets, pillowcases, blouses, T-shirts, muslin (do not use crease-resistant or drip-dry fabrics as they resist dyes)

The Tjanting
The *tjanting* is a special tool used by professional batik designers. (See an example of the tjanting in Figure 6–15.) The tool produces interesting linear effects. Most of the designs produced in Indonesia are made by applying hot wax to the cloth with the *tjanting*. It looks like a metal funnel on the end of a wooden handle; it slowly dispenses the hot wax through a spout. To use the *tjanting*, dip the spout end into the melted wax pan and leave it there until it is good and hot. This keeps the metal bowl end hot enough to keep the wax flowing evenly through the spout. When the wax cools, place the *tjanting* again in the wax container, let it sit for about a minute, fill it, and draw freely again. Practice will help you keep the speed of the flow steady. Catch the drips from the *tjanting* with a jar lid.

PAPER BATIKS

At times, the simplest crafts are like classic treasures. They seem to be enjoyed forever.

The following procedure is an excellent one for introducing the concept of batik.

1. Be sure cardboard or waxed paper is under the paper when applying the wax.
2. Have the students brush on wax or apply wax with *tjantings* to simple paper toweling. Other papers, such as decorative wrapping paper, fine-quality parchment, and even drawing paper can be used. Apply cool household floorwax.
3. Or, draw a design on with crayons or candles.
4. Remove paper from cardboard surface and crinkle paper.
5. Float the papers in dye baths (or inks or tempera paint) or try sponging paint or dyes onto the paper.
6. Let the paper dry.
7. To remove the wax, carefully scrape or rub it off, or dip the paper into benzine or mineral spirits.

6–14 *Everyone enjoys expressing ideas in his or her own way. The smile on this girl's face displays her pride in her batik. The process is the one described, using felt-tip pens for the linear designs, clear wax over the lines, and a final brushed-on dye.*

These luminous papers can be used for message cards, wrapping special gifts at special times, book covers, window decorations, and holiday ornaments.

CLOTH BATIK PROCEDURE

Batiking should be done in a well-ventilated area. Helpers, newspaper coverings, and stations for varying procedures are a must. Keep watch on the water supply for the fryer, and keep electric cords out of the way. To introduce the project, display good examples of batik made by students and by professionals. Explain and demonstrate all procedures and tools before using them. (See color Figure 5.)

Procedure
1. Wash new materials to remove any sizing. Begin with a cotton piece about 12 × 18 inches. Local thrift stores and parent donations are a good source for old cotton bed sheets.
2. Suggest large patterns for designing batiks: butterflies, birds, flowers, monsters, geometric patterns, and imaginary animals. Consider large spaces as well as linear details when planning designs. Plan and draw the designs directly on the cloth with colored materials. Think of the design as a stained-glass window—bright, intense colors surrounded by darker outlines of color.

3. Materials for applying design can include:
    a. Felt-tip pens. Permanent or water-base pens will work. The colors are vibrant, and the design remains clear during subsequent procedures. When using water-base pens, wax must cover the drawing completely or the pen colors will run when the dye is applied. This can be a very attractive part of the batik, as the colors blend like a watercolor when the effect is planned for.
    b. Oil pastels, charcoal, crayons, and pencils for drawing.
    c. Crayons melted in muffin tins over low heat (electric fryer), then brushed into design spaces. Place the pieces of colored crayon in each muffin tin and add a 2-inch cube of paraffin to each tin. The paraffin helps spread the color during waxing and helps the wax to penetrate the cloth.
    d. Melted wax with a *tjanting* tool or lettering pen.
    e. Clear paraffin brushed on. The clear paraffin can be used to cover felt-tip-pen-drawn areas. This is the procedure we prefer when working with large groups of students. Remember to keep the container with paraffin over water (double-boiler style); it will smoke and even catch fire if placed directly over heat.
    f. Any found objects. Place an object such as a kitchen utensil into the hot wax and print it in repeat patterns on the cloth. You can also carve a design in wood or clay, cement the design to a long handle, place the handle in the hot wax, and print it on the cloth. When the waxed areas are cool, continue with the dyeing steps.
    g. Candles. Candles can be lit and droplets dripped on the cloth for drawing and texture. Brush dyes over the wax.
    h. Cool household liquid floorwax can be applied to cloth or paper.
4. Plan the drawing sketch one day, waxing and dyeing on subsequent days. Students or mothers as helpers can aid with supervision and attention to safety rules.
5. Divide the room into working stations. The drawing on cloth can be done at the student's seat. Provide a separate station for waxing, one with an inflammable surface. Six to eight students can work comfortably at one waxing table. Have two wax setups for a large table; place cardboard, waxed paper, or foil under the cloth during waxing.
6. Each setup includes one elecric frying pan containing water. Adjust the heat so that it is hot enough to melt the wax and keep it at this temperature during the entire process. Make sure that the wax penetrates the cloth deeply. To do this, check the underside of the cloth—the wax should come through. Keep clear paraffin in a 1-pound coffee can, and the muffin tin (containing wax

6–15 *Melted wax is applied to cloth with either a tjanting tool, brush, wide-ribbed lettering pen, found object, or stamp. After filling, carefully tip the tjanting tool back to keep the wax from running out. (See color Figures 4 and 5.)*

crayons) in the electric frying pan with heated water. Brush and apply the wax, as desired, to the cloth.

7. The crayons in the muffin tin method are more suitable for smaller groups of students. This adds large color areas quickly and gives the appearance of more color applications. Keep a brush for each crayon color so that students can trade brushes. Keep dirty brushes out of clean wax colors. Wash the color out of the brushes by placing them in the heated water in the fry pan.

8. After applying the wax, let it dry for 10 minutes until the wax is very cool (or try unheated household wax).

9. When the wax is cool and hard, take the cloth outside or hold it over a waste can and crinkle it into a ball. The crackling will later cause the dyes to run into the cracked wax lines, creating the spider-web effect that is the textural pattern so desirable in batik.

SUBSTITUTE PASTE RESIST FOR BATIK

Making a substitute paste resist is a simple and sometimes desirable procedure in doing batik, especially with very young children. A simple paste can be made with flour and cold water mixed smoothly until its consistency is creamy. (Gradually add 1 cup plus 3 tablespoons of flour to 1 cup of water.) Any lumps will slow down the process. The paste can be applied in any one of several processes. It can be spread with a blunt, smooth knife; brushed on; squeezed through the nozzle of a plastic bottle (mustard, catsup, or detergent); squeezed through a cookie or cake decorator; or spread onto the cloth and then, while wet, incised with tools such as a fork or stick. Use the paste resist on the day it is made.

The paste design on the fabric must be allowed to dry overnight. It is then crackled in the same way as wax.

Because dipping a cloth covered with a paste resist into a

dye would destroy the design, the dye must either be brushed or sponged on. Food coloring or prepared tempera can be used as a substitute for the permanent-dye process if desired.

When using water dyes, do not dip the fabric to wash out the paste resist. Instead, scrape, pick, or rub off the resist material. The fabric then can be dried and ironed.

DYEING BATIKS

For a class of about thirty students, mix more than one color. Apply the dyes at a separate station—such as one long table covered with newspaper containing three 1-gallon bottles of dye color. If there are three containers of dye—one scarlet, one navy, and one purple—the students have a good choice for background colors (bright colors are also fine). Consider the colors used in the drawing; for instance, red dyes will cover red pen marks. Cloths can be dipped into dye baths, or several colors can be applied to a background when brushing on dye colors.

6–16 *Dyes will keep for several weeks in covered bottles. The frame, right foreground, holds the cloth during wax application and keeps cloth from sticking to the table surface.*

Procedure
1. Prepare the dyes the night before. Mix dyes in simmering hot water, but use them when they are cool or they will melt the wax in the design.

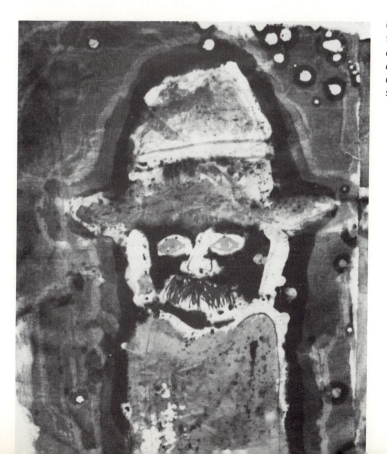

6–17 *Batik has a secret writing quality. The final design is not revealed until after the dye is applied. This cowboy is by a first-grade student.*

Dyes, Tie-Dye, and Batik

2. Prepare the dyes by placing 2 cups of simmering hot water into a container. Add powdered dye and mix it until it is dissolved; stir it well.

3. Wear rubber gloves and use a stick or spoon for mixing. Plan about one package of powdered dye to 2 quarts of water (or use quart jars for each color); the dye is prepared stronger than the package directions suggest. After the dye is dissolved, add hot water to complete the amount. Stir well.

4. Use at least one bristle brush for each dye color. More than one color can be brushed on the background for variety. The brush also produces a very interesting texture. If areas of color are kept separate, then the batik looks like it has been dipped into many dye baths. Colors will also blend and mix where they run together.

5. If you plan to dip the cloth into the dye, prepare the dyes as directed here but use about two packages of powdered dye to 4 quarts of water; mix the dye in a plastic container. Dipping is best done outside when weather permits, or place the dye baths right in the sink.

6. Immerse the cloth for about 15 to 20 minutes for color permanence. *Note:* As an alternative to using dyes, use acrylic paints on fabrics either by brushing them on or as in doing block printing.

7. Thin the acrylic paints when using a brush. When block printing, use thicker acrylic paints. Because the thicker paint is stiffer when dry, the cloth is better suited for drapery and hanging designs. Lacquer thinner or ammonia will clear off acrylic paints in unwanted areas or from dirty brushes (do not use on nylon brushes).

8. Let the dye dry somewhat on newspapers, or place the fabric outside on the grass and hold it down with a small rock to keep it from blowing away, or hang it on a clothesline.

6–18 *Student's expression reflects feelings of achievement in displaying his batik shirt.*

FINISHING BATIKS

To remove the wax, either

1. Scrape it with a blunt knife, or

2. Place a pad of newspapers on a table or an ironing board. Place paper toweling on the top of and underneath the batik. Place more newspapers over this. With a warm iron, iron the design areas. Change the newspapers as they become saturated with wax. Do not place newspaper next to the batik as the print sometimes rubs off. The heat also helps set the color. Ironing tables and helpers should be out of the line of traffic.

3. If needed, hang the fabric on a clothesline for further

drying. Spray the fabric with varnish or a plastic finish for protection, if desired. (If the wax crayon process has been used, place a clean piece of drawing paper over and under the fabric when ironing—this will produce a "batik print.")

4. Batiks are especially beautiful as lampshades and window curtains or coverings, for when the light shines through, they take on a special brilliance.

5. Batiks also can be used as pillow covers and on greeting cards; as swatches for patchwork, when cut up; or as appliqué on shirts. As a wall hanging, either stretch the batik over a cardboard or wood frame or hang it from a dowel (we glue ours right to the rod) and add macrame fringes.

Wax-Resist Eggs

Easter is time for flowers, bugs, planting vegetables in a garden, and painting eggs, but we can paint eggs at any time.

The egg has long been a favorite symbol in ceremonies. The decorated egg is a distinctive example of folk art, particularly from the Ukraine, where elements of folk tales are the decorations on the eggs. The Hutzels, who live in the western Ukraine, tell the story that, during the crucifixion of Christ, Mary decorated eggs as an offering for her son's life. Her tears fell on the eggs as she decorated them and the dots of brilliant color on the eggs represent her tears. Richly decorated eggs, then, are in the tradition of Christian ritual. Decorated clay eggs also have been uncovered in the ruins of pagan civilizations. (See Figure 6–19.)

Eggs can be decorated in much the same manner as fabrics are batiked. Applied wax resists the dye baths and the pattern remains.

Procedure

1. Blow out the eggs. (Make one hole at each end; blow through smaller hole. Puncture the egg yoke if blowing is difficult.)[1]

2. To apply the wax, use either toothpicks, small brushes, or place a straight pin into a pencil eraser (draw the head of the pin), or wax crayons. Favorite Ukrainian designs include spiral forms, the triangle, and overlapping circles; birds, such as the parrot, the mystic eagle, the peacock, and the phoenix; plant forms of all kinds; landscapes, clouds, and mountains.

[1]Or hard boil the eggs or use just raw eggs and decorate them. The inside of the eggs will eventually dry out.

6–19a *Applying wax to eggs with pin heads. Cups hold dye colors.*

6–19b *Wax-resist batiked eggs.*

3. Use rubber bands as guidelines. Or divide the egg into various shapes and include a pattern within each shape. These designs can be as simple or complex as you wish.
4. Melt the wax in a jar lid. The lid sits on a screen on a concrete block. Inside the block, a lit candle stands in another jar lid. Apply wax to the eggs with a pin head or a wide-nib lettering pen. Let the wax cool and harden. (See Figure 6-19.)
5. Dip the eggs into colored dye baths, the most common being the food coloring bath. Mix your own colors. Leave the egg in the dye bath for bright colors. Remove and let dry.
6. Add more wax and redye. Repeat these steps several times.
7. Remove the wax by placing the eggs in 250°F. oven. When the wax is shiny, it has melted.
8. Rub the wax off with a warm, lint-free cloth.

Checkpoints

1. Wear old clothes.
2. Study and discuss line effects, color theory, and color relationships.
3. Use simple motifs for designs: lines, dots, circles, squares, animals, suns, trees, and flowers.
4. For classroom use, the best material for batiking is unbleached muslin (or 100 percent cotton sheeting). Other suggested cloths are silks, velvets, linens, pellon, and even leather.
5. To transfer a design to sheer cloth, such as silk or organdy, place the cloth over the sketch and trace the design directly with chalk, pencil, or pens (the design shows through·the thin cloth).
6. Use a *tjanting* for applying the wax (See page 201.)
7. Use inexpensive brushes for waxing. Hot water melts the glue in the brush ferrel (the ferrel holds the hairs in the brush). Flat bristle brushes cover areas quickly, and soft hair brushes are good for details and lines.
8. Artists use about one part beeswax to two parts paraffin for waxing, but straight paraffin is fine for classroom use. Melted candles work well also.
9. Drawn lines are controlled. Crackled lines are uncontrolled, making a good contrast. For another textural application, apply the wax and let it cool. Scratch a design through the wax with something pointed, such as a nail or toothpick.
10. Use rubber cement instead of wax. Try masking-tape resist for sharp geometric shapes.

11. Other tools can be dipped into wax and used for patterns and designs: potato mashers, Q-tips, top edges of bottles, toothbrushes, forks, spoons, tin can edges, cardboard tubes, and even the edge of a piece of cardboard.

12. Use stretcher bars or embroidery hoops if desired to tack down the cloth. Use waxed paper under the cloth when waxing to prevent the wax from sticking to the work surface.

13. In lower grades, use paste resist or liquid floorwax, tempera paint, and watercolor on cloth instead of dye baths.

14. Be sure the dye bath has had time to cool before dipping the cloth.

15. When dyeing clothing articles, place the dye baths in or next to the sink so the batik can be rinsed in cool water to remove the excess dye.

16. Place the batiked fabric inside newspaper to remove excess water.

17. Colored inks can be used as dye baths.

18. Use gloves when dipping the cloth into the dyes and an old stick to take the cloth out of the dye. Have plenty of newspapers on hand.

19. Ironing can be done while the fabric is still moist. Be sure to change the newspapers frequently as you iron

20. If skimmed milk (either powdered or liquid) is brushed on the fabric before the dye is applied, the fabric will accept the dyes more readily.

21. Wax mixture: beeswax is added to the wax mixture to minimize the crackling effect. If adding paraffin to a crayon mixture, one 2-inch square of paraffin to crayon wax in a muffin tin is adequate.

22. Procion dye is a cold-water dye that is bright and permanent. Procion dyes work on cotton, linen, silk, viscose rayon, jute, wool, and other natural fibers, but not on synthetics. The dye comes in highly concentrated powdered form. Procion dye is packaged under different names. It is packaged in its original bulk form and salt and washing soda can be added when mixing the dye. It is a most economical dye. A 2-ounce package of the dye will dye between 10 and 30 yards of material. A weaker dye will give lighter color shades. You need only use a few teaspoons of the dye at a time; the rest can be stored until needed. The dyes are available in a variety of brilliant colors and can be mixed according to directions.

23. Steam fabrics to set the dye. Fold the fabric into a small and compact size. Wrap it in an old towel and tie it securely. Avoid touching the sides of the steamer. A steamer is any perforated pan placed over boiling water. Cover the batik with aluminum foil. After the water boils, steam the fabric for 45 minutes. Let it cool until you are

able to handle the batik. Place the batik in about 3 inches of water in a pan, face down. Soak it for 30 minutes to an hour. Remove the paste mixture or iron out the wax. Iron the batik and finish it for hanging.

24. To decorate polyester fabrics (including drip-dry, acrilan, and nylon) use specially prepared crayons for fabrics. Simply draw designs on paper, with crayons, and then iron the paper over the cloth to set the designs. Have the students add messages and designs with fabric crayon transfers on an old polyester shirt or pants for fun; everyone can add his special ingenious design.

Bibliography

ALBERS, ANNI. *On Designing.* Middletown, Conn.: Wesleyan University Press, 1971.

BELFER, NANCY. *Designing in Batik and Tie Dye.* Worcester, Mass.: Davis Publications, Inc., 1967.

DIMONDSTEIN, GERALDINE. *Exploring the Arts with Children.* New York: Macmillan Publishing Co. Inc., 1975.

KREVITSKY, NIK. *Batik Art and Craft.* Rev. ed. New York: Van Nostrand Reinhold Company, 1973.

LAUTERBURG, LOTTI. *Fabric Printing.* New York: Van Nostrand Reinhold Company, 1959.

MAILE, ANNE. *Tie and Dye As a Present-Day Craft.* New York: Taplinger Publishing Co., Inc., 1971.

MEILACH, DONA Z. *Contemporary Batik and Tie-Dye Methods.* New York: Crown Publishers, Inc., 1974.

NEWMAN, THELMA R. *Contemporary African Arts and Crafts.* New York: Crown Publishers, Inc., 1974.

ROBERTSON, SEONAID. *Dyes from Plants.* New York: Van Nostrand Reinhold Company, 1972.

WEIGLE, PALMY. *Ancient Dyes for Modern Weavers.* New York: Watson-Guptill Publications, 1974.

7

Yarns, Needles, and Cloth

Stitchery is the contemporary name for the ancient needle-and-thread arts of *embroidery* and *appliqué*. Modern stitchery is a combination of influences from the Orient, Europe, and Latin America. History tells us that the ships on the Nile were rigged with brightly colored patchwork sails. During the Renaissance, soldiers, kings, and horses met on battlefields wearing garments embroidered and appliquéd in gold. After trade routes were established with the Orient, rare dyes, silks, and designs influenced fashion.

American women pioneers are fondly remembered for their brilliant patchwork quilt designs. Every scrap of cloth was saved for this folkcraft; very little was ever thrown away. From these small pieces of fabric, beautifully designed objects were created; today, these quilt designs are recognized for their unique and handsome textures and patterns and are often displayed and treasured as fine wall hangings.

In Alaska, people still make coats, boots, and gloves from the hides of seals in order to protect themselves from the cold. In other parts of the world, people wear clothing for decoration as well as for protection. Creating your own fun fashions with just your hands, scissors, needles, and thread will help you to become that specially dressed person. You can stitch a shirt, tie-dye a shirt, batik a scarf, macrame a belt, string a necklace with beads, and design and appliqué a headband. These crafts will all be artistic expressions of your efforts.

7–1 *"Whoosh" by Pam Castano. Three panels, 42 inches × 60 inches each. Fabric appliqué. (Photo courtesy of the artist.)*

Stitching and embroidery are special ways to enhance your clothes. Your clothes are the nearest thing to you. They go with you everywhere you go, and everyone sees them on you. Stitchery can personalize them. Begin by thinking of embroidery as painting with colored yarns.

Designing with Cloth

Discovering, selecting, and working with fabrics and fibers offers the child exciting tactile experiences. Everyone likes to touch variously textured cloths from the wide selection available today. Cloth scraps and old clothes, and other sources such as cloth factories, can become a reservoir of ingredients for this never outgrown fun craft. (See color Figure 6.)

Students will especially enjoy rummaging through fabrics to select bright, happy colors and patterns, softly textured velvets, sheer chiffons, and rugged upholstery materials. Each of these tactile experiences can stimulate the imagination to a wide range of possible projects from small stuffed, lovable creatures to large, mural-sized panels. Class or individual projects can be done. To begin, design qualities

7–2 *"Felt Appliqué on Duffle," by Nanaug of Baker Lake. There is an expressive, rhythmic mood to these animals and figures that suggests the culture of the Canadian Eskimo. Duffle is a coarse woolen cloth with a thick nap that is used for cold-weather clothing. (Courtesy of The Hand and The Spirit Crafts Gallery, Scottsdale, Arizona. Photograph by Jerry D. Jacka.)*

Yarns, Needles, and Cloth

215

7–3 *Kindergartners had fun drawing on cloth with permanent felt-tip pens; their teacher made the cloth into a smock.*

should be discussed with the students. The following relate to constructing with cloth and thread:

1. Experiment with and choose color relationships: how one color will affect the color next to it; and how light and dark hues will affect the over-all design.
2. How do textures look and feel? What are their similarities and differences? How are textures in contrast to each other: rough-smooth and shiny-dull?
3. Shapes can be large as well as small, intricate and simple, and heavy and delicate. Encourage students to experiment with the placement of cloth before making final decisions. Shapes can be repeated to create rhythms and unity of design.
4. Many fabrics have busy print patterns and these will greatly influence the feeling of the final design.
5. The manipulative skills involved include cutting, sewing, gluing, and stitching. Many teachers find that both boys and girls are fascinated by the challenge of designing with needle, thread, and cloth. Many of the greatest past and

216

present designers, tailors, and tapestry weavers have been men.

Stitchery is an excellent introduction to making aesthetic decisions that are applicable to everyday living whether in personal dress or in our environment.

Happy Stitching

Embroidery is drawing with stitches. The very youngest student is able to glue threads and yarns in place. In Mexico, the children like to make yarn pictures; they glue the yarn onto a backing. Learning to thread a needle is a giant step to a first-grader.

To thread a needle, bend the end of the piece of yarn. Large-eyed needles are easier for youngsters to thread. Crease the point end with your fingernail. Insert the folded yarn end into the needle's eye, or make an eye with a piece of wire and pull the yarn through the eye.

Teach the few basic stitches shown here to get the class started. Before you know it, students will have mastered these stitches and will be on the way to inventing their own. Plan to spend time experimenting with different stitches. These experiments with stitches themselves are often decorative samplers. Involvement and enjoyment are often increased when there are no preconceived plans to establish boundaries. Manipulating materials becomes more creative when the materials themselves suggest the ideas and forms to be used. Start having fun by experimenting with different types of stitches and color combinations. Be adventurous and explore the materials; enjoy the doing as well as the finished product.

Instruct students how to achieve a straight line on cloth: pull one thread out from the cloth, and then cut along the straight line indicated. The teacher may choose to have the backing cloth cut into convenient sizes before beginning projects.

Basic Stitches

RUNNING STITCH

This is the most common and the simplest stitch. Pass the needle in, under, and out of the cloth along a straight or curved line. Take several stitches on the needle at once and

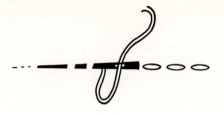

draw the needle through the cloth. Stitches and spaces can be uniform in length to achieve an even interval. (See Figure 7–4.)

COUCHING STITCH

Lay the strand of yarn to be embroidered along the planned line on the cloth. At uniform intervals along the yarn, bring the needle up on one side, across, and down through to the back on the other side. This holds the yarn strand firmly in place. (See Figure 7–5.)

7–5 *Couching stitch.*

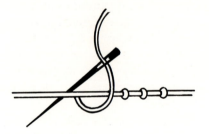

BACKSTITCH

Take one running stitch. At the end of the stitch go through to the back of the cloth; bring the back up at a distance twice as long as the length of the running stitch. (See Figure 7–6.)

7–6 *Backstitch.*

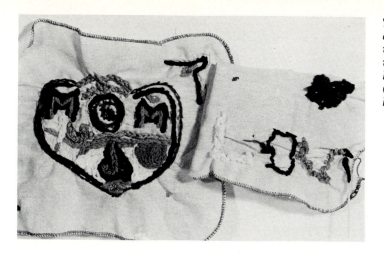

7–7 *The colorful and effective chain stitch on a loose weave dish cloth is produced with scraps of yarn and a large-eyed embroidery needle (the yarn was doubled and knotted at the end).*

CHAIN STITCH

Bring the needle to the front side of the cloth. Make a loop of the thread. Hold the loop down with the thumb. Bring the loop to where it just came up and bring the needle to the underside. Do not pull the thread tight. Bring the needle up to the front near the rounded end of the first loop. Create another loop and leave the thread over the first loop, thus holding the first loop down. Continue this stitch for a chain effect. (See Figure 7–8.)

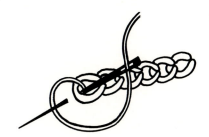

7–8 *Chain stitch.*

LAZY DAISY STITCH

Bring the needle up at what will be the center of the flower. Form a loop of thread the length of the flower petal. Go to the back of the cloth. Hold this loop down by making a short

Yarns, Needles, and Cloth

7–9 *Lazy daisy stitch.*

running stitch over the petal tip to keep it in place. Bring the needle back to the center to start the next petal. (See Figure 7–9)

FRENCH KNOT

Keep the point of the needle close to the cloth. Wrap the yarn three or four times (for the desired sized knot) around the needle. Insert the needle into the cloth close to where it came up; this forms the knot. (See Figure 7–10.)

SATIN STITCH

The satin stitch is used to fill the design shapes. Use small running stitches spaced next to each other to completely fill in a design shape. This also acts to put the stitch in relief, giving it bulk. Space the stitches close to each other, as shown, and fill in the design. (See Figure 7–11.)

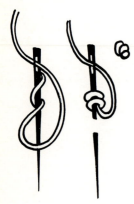

BLANKET STITCH

Bring the yarn and needle to the front of the cloth. Make half a loop, which is held under the thumb (at a right angle). Go to the underside of the cloth. Come up through the cloth in the center at the point of the angle. (See Figure 7–12.)

CROSS STITCH

Make a series of diagonal stitches. Work back across these stitches, creating the crosses, and fill in the opposite diagonals. (See Figure 7–13.)

7–10 *French knot.*

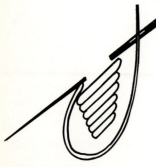

7–11 *Satin stitch.*

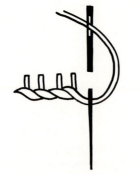

7–12 *Blanket stitch.*

7–13 *Cross stitch.*

SEED STITCH

Fill in an area with tiny stitches going in all directions. (See Figure 7–14.)

OUTLINE STITCH

Make a running stitch. Go under the cloth with the needle and come to the front before the end of the first stitch. Continue this stitch to create an outline. (See Figure 7–15.)

7–14 *Seed stitch.*

OVERCAST STITCH

Make a diagonal running stitch. Place the succeeding stitches next to the previous ones, working the needle up through the cloth to the front of the stitch, then down to the back and onto the top of the stitch. (See Figure 7–16.)

FEATHER STITCH

Make a loop stitch. Hold the middle of the loop with the thumb. From the back, go through the cloth in the center of the loop and make a half loop to one side. Move again to the center of the new loop; go through the cloth and make a half loop going in the opposite direction. Continue this stitch for the feather stitch. (See Figure 7–17.)

7–15 *Outline stitch.*

THREADED STITCH

Complete a row of running stitches. Using a different colored yarn, weave in and out of the running stitches.

7–16 *Overcast stitch.*

7–17 *Feather stitch.*

Yarns, Needles, and Cloth

221

7–18 *A sampler pillow of a variety of stitches. (Courtesy of Joan Melamed.)*

TASSELS

Supplies Needed
cardboard
scissors
yarns

Procedure
1. To make a tassel, cut a square of medium-weight cardboard.
2. Wrap some yarn around the center of the cardboard square twelve times. (See Figure 7–19a.)
3. Include a cord inside the top of the wrapping. This will be used later to tie the tassel onto a decoration.
4. Cut the bottom end of the yarn off the cardboard as shown in Figure 7–19b.
5. A short space from the top edge, tie a cord tightly to form the tassel. (See Figure 7–19c.)

7–19 *Tassel.*

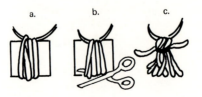

a. b. c.

POM-POMS

Supplies Needed
cardboard
scissors
yarn

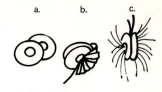

7–20 *Pom-pom.*

Procedure

1. To make a pom-pom, cut two cardboard circles of equal size.
2. Cut identical center holes in the circles. (See Figure 7–20a.)
3. Wrap some yarn through the center and around both pieces of cardboard many times. (See Figure 7–20b.)
4. Cut the yarn along the outside edge.
5. Tie the cut yarn through the center of the two pieces of cardboard. (See Figure 7–20c.)

Appliqué

Appliqué simply means sewing one cloth to another cloth. Like many contemporary craftspeople, you will want to create your own designs, whether abstract or representational. Cut your designs from one color cloth, and sew them onto cloth of another color, turning under as you sew along the edge. If you are using felt, pellon, leatherette, or blanket materials, it is not necessary to sew; just glue them down, as the edges of the fabric do not unravel. Then continue on with your stitched designs. The colorful scraps of cloth will build up a solid form quickly, while the stitching, which goes more slowly, will add linear quality. Young students can glue fabrics down and draw on linear details with felt-tip pens. See "Bold Wall Hangings, Banners, and Flags," pages 230–232.

Color prints add effective accents. Organdies, chiffons, laces, and nets also are interesting textural materials that can be applied in layers over other materials. Some students like to appliqué previously made weavings and macrames to cloth.

Stitchery and appliqué can be used on clothes, dolls, banners, pillows, toys, and flags. A very popular craft with young-at-heart people today is to stitch and appliqué all kinds of imaginative objects and designs on blue denim shirts and pants: bright swatches of cloth, sequins, jewels and beads, braids, buttons, and rickrack. Try giving an old shirt new life. Stitchery is an art to wear and enjoy.

There are many opportunities to incorporate cloth crafts into the classroom. The creative teacher will achieve a variety

Yarns, Needles, and Cloth

223

of results, from simple "feel it" pictures and cloth messages of happiness to school banners and flags. All carry with them the warm expressions of the children themselves. They are treasures of childhood to enjoy and keep.

Supplies Needed

needles: any large, dull, big-eyed needles: blunt tapestry, large rug, and plastic embroidery needles

wire wrapping (found on the end of bread loaves)

fabric for background: any kind is suitable—open weave such as burlap, muslin, and monk's cloth, and upholstery fabrics and felt

scrap materials of all kinds for appliqué in an assortment of weights, colors, and patterns

an old frame; embroidery hoops (some come with adjustable screws on the outer hoop); a meat tray or other Styrofoam sheets (optional)

pins, staples, or tape

scissors

thimble

threads and yarns: large rug yarns, common cotton skeins, raffia, string, and jute

decorative accessories: old jewelry, buttons, clay and glass beads, lace, braid, sequins, wire tassels, bells, and found objects

white glue or fabric adhesive

paper to plan design

white or black charcoal or colored chalks to apply design

wood dowels, lattice, picture frames, and mat board for hanging

plastic bags to hold different colored yarns

storage space, such as a basket or see-through plastic boxes to hold handwork

COLLAGE "TOUCH" PICTURES

This project is a never-ending cloth adventure with great tactile possibilities! Collecting and gathering cloth with different textures and patterns are the motivation to begin.

Share touching experiences with each other by talking about how objects feel and how they make us feel. Texture means the surface quality of an object. We all recognize the significance of touching; the infant rubs his cheek against his mother's skin; the three-year-old can't give up his favorite blanket, which he carries with him and delights in touching. Preschoolers and primary-age children gain much sensory learning information through feeling, and some reading programs use touching devices to teach letters.

Collage touch pictures are one way to invite "feeling" into

art. List words on the board that describe textures after exploring cloth samples, feeling walks, and texture-guessing boxes. The students can come up with all kinds of descriptive words such as *furry, bumpy, prickly, spongy,* and *bristly;* they often help with the spelling, too. Writing these words on the board helps us to remember them; they also serve as motivation for storytelling ideas. Invite the students to think of textures from their past experiences.

Collage touch projects include pictures, greeting messages, book covers, holiday jewelry, basket coverings (over ice cream containers), and large murals. A touch book made from each child's touch picture is an interesting group project. Old wallpaper books are excellent for backings.

Supplies Needed
cloth scraps of all kinds and magazine photo scraps
burlap, felt, yarns, beads, old jewelry, small old toy parts, rickrack, braiding, sponge, velour paper, sandpaper, and foils
white glue
scissors
cardboard backing

Procedure
1. Plan a project with a simple design.
2. Select the size of the cardboard backing. Try unusual shapes, such as round or tall ones.
3. Experiment with the placement of cloth colors, patterns, textures, and shapes.
4. Glue down a slightly larger backing cloth if desired, such as burlap or felt. Allow the cloth to extend over the edges of the cardboard; fold the fabric along the edge and lap to the underside and glue it down.
5. Cut out the pieces needed for the design.

Yarns, Needles, and Cloth

6. Glue and press down each piece onto the backing.
7. Add yarns and beads for decorative touches. Draw on details with permanent felt-tip pens.
8. Cover the entire cloth with waxed paper.
9. Press over the picture with a heavy object such as a book until the picture is dry.

For variation, try a patchwork picture. Cut scraps of cloth into geometric or free-form shapes. Be sure to cut them so that they fit together like a puzzle. Use a paper template (a pattern such as a hexagon) to obtain repeated shapes; in this way, the shapes will all be the same size but in a variety of patterned cloths.

EASY BURLAP STITCHING

Burlap is an excellent backing material for use with all ages of elementary students. The open weave of the fabric invites the sewer to add his own stitches and yarns to create expressive designs.

One fourth-grade teacher left a large piece of burlap out during the entire year and students added to the stitched mural as they wished. The finished fabric mural was presented to the school and hung in the cafeteria for all to enjoy. Another fifth-grade teacher requested each student to complete a 10 × 12-inch panel on their favorite American history story. These panels were then joined as a wall hanging and displayed in the school's entryway. Other possible burlap-

7–22 First-graders learn by doing a running stitch on each of these 10-inch burlap squares. Stitching around each square helps keep the fringe from raveling. As a mural display the squares reflect the charm and wit of each hand.

7–23 *Working in small groups, fifth-graders stitched individual units for this banner of the thirteen original colonies.*

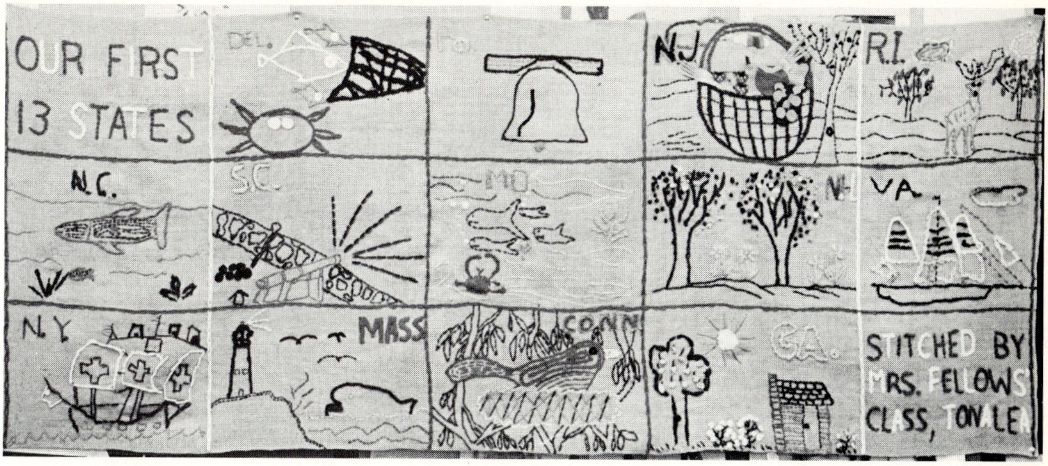

stitched designs can be used as individual wall hangings (on dowels); stretched over an old picture frame; matted as drawings; as curtains and pillow tops; and lined and used as carryalls.

Supplies Needed

burlap (or linen, upholstery fabric, or scrim)
yarn, string, thread, ribbon, found objects, beads, and bells
needles, such as embroidery, with large eyes
scissors
a sample of stitches
embroidery hoops and canvas stretchers (optional)

Procedure

1. Sketch the design on the burlap with chalk.
2. Demonstrate how to thread the needle and knot the thread.
3. Demonstrate some of the stitches you want the students to learn. Discuss how these stitches are used in the examples displayed. Discuss the place of embroidery in the Middle Ages and in our American culture. (See Figure 1–6.)
4. Encourage students to practice the stitches as well as to invent their own. Encourage exploring textural possibilities with various yarns, threads, and found objects.
5. Pulled threads will achieve another texture. To do this, pull the threads horizontally or vertically (pull several, about ten, next to each other). This will leave open window spaces; these can be pinched and tied off in clusters, glued open, or left as sheer designs.
6. Weave into the pulled-thread areas. Use the burlap as the warp, and weave with various materials; add beads and such if desired.
7. Appliqué brightly colored fabrics onto the cloth. Glue or stitch them down. (Pieces of appliqué can be folded under and ironed before stitching for easier handling.)

8. Yarn designs and found objects can be fastened down with stitches or glue.

BEADS ON CLOTH

An appealing decorative technique that captures the unpredictable spirit in art develops through the manipulation of beads and cloth. (See color Figure 7.) Beads are colorful and glamorous. They create jeweled embellishments that are a joy to wear. Adding beads to your cloths makes them become ablaze with designs of birds, flowers, and colorful shapes; and textures splash across shirts, pants, and belts.

Elegant native American Indian beadwork was a treasured art before Columbus discovered America. At that time, beads were primarily environmental materials such as bones, stones, clay, seeds, shells, and porcupine quills. When the European traders brought glass beads with them from Venice, the art of brilliantly colored beadwork became more decorative and graceful in design.

There are two basic ways of working with beads, either by weaving (see pages 281 ff.) or embroidery. The favored embroidery technique of applying beads is by the overlaid, spot, or couching-stitch process. (See Figure 7–25.) In this direct approach, a length of beads is threaded on a string, nylon thread, or beading thread. The backing material is commonly heavy cloth or leather. The length is then laid in position according to the design. Many of the designs are circular. Then, a second thread is stitched over the first, crossing horizontally over every few beads, which secures the strand to the backing, the same as in the couching embroidery stitch.

The Northern Plains tribes, including the Shoshone, the Assiniboin, and the Crow, as well as the Ottowa in Michigan, the Astakiwi in California, and the Apache in Arizona, are

7–24 *"Beaded whimsies." These heart and boot pincushions are part of the souvenir trade originally begun between 1890 and 1910 by the Mohawk and Mohegan Indians living around Niagara Falls, New York. The glass beads were sewn in a raised, three-dimensional loop on a shiny cotton cambric backing.*

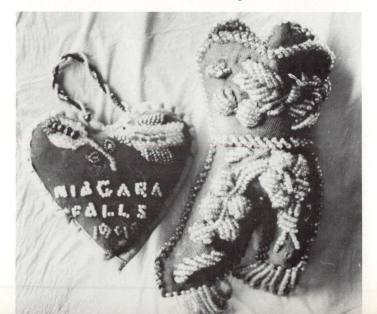

7–25 *Embellishing denim clothing is a contemporary folk art. Jewelry, old buttons, and beads were appliquéd to produce this inventive design on a denim shirt. Shirt by Patsy Lowry.*

admired for their magnificent beadwork. Adornment has played a major part in almost every culture of the past and present. Studying excellent artifact examples is an excellent way to uncover the history and art of the people.

Supplies Needed

beads, pearls, rhinestones, and buttons

cloth: denim shirts and pants, felt, any material heavy enough to carry the beads

nylon thread (beading thread is available at hobby stores)

needles that fit through beads (beading needles are also available at hobby stores)

paper cups, aluminum pie tins, or small ashtrays to hold the beads

embroidery hoop, small wood frame, or sewing bolt to hold the cloth taut (optional)

Procedure

1. Plan a simple design: consider large, simple shades.
2. Wash the cloth to remove the sizing, and then iron it.
3. Transfer the design to the cloth with chalk or a light pencil mark.
4. Plan for large design areas, but also let the design progress with colors and textures spontaneously as the student works with the available beads.
5. Thread the needle with a single thread. Knot the end.
6. Begin with a single bead and sew it on. Sew on this same bead two more times to anchor it.
7. Three or four beads can then be sewn on at the same time. Pick up the beads with a needle. Place the beads comfortably on the cloth, not so tightly that the cloth buckles.
8. Push the needle to the back of the cloth and resew the last bead to the cloth.
9. Lay the beads in the direction of the design. Continue beading with several beads. Never bead with more than five beads at one time, as the thread becomes too loose.
10. If the beading seems to be loose, use the couching

Yarns, Needles, and Cloth

7–26 *Large paper and cloth banners can rapidly transform environments. These original flags and banners are being displayed proudly by first-graders as part of a unit on flags of other countries.*

embroidery stitch to sew the beads onto the cloth. This is done by sewing small horizontal stitches across the beaded strand to hold it down.

11. Sew jewelry and larger beads into the work; be careful not to make the beadwork too heavy.

12. End the strand by tacking the thread several times through the fabric and knot it.

13. Be inventive and combine several techniques: appliqué, embroidery, and beading. Experiment and discover what possibilities are available.

BOLD WALL HANGINGS, BANNERS, AND FLAGS

Wall hangings, banners, and flags are festive additions when celebrating special times. The earliest banners were rigid standards, not flexible cloth. The Romans, Egyptians, and the Crusaders carried banners and flags to identify nobility and kings. They were widely used during the Middle Ages when warriors, hidden behind armor and helmets, carried banners to identify whether they were friend or foe. Merchants and craft guilds used banners to advertise. Today, many contemporary artists design cloth banners as a decorative and symbolic art form, and we find them displayed in galleries, homes, public buildings, and churches.

Banners can express various themes. They are gay, bright, highly decorative, and well-composed designs in fabric. They often express an idea, a name, a simple word message or quotation, a favorite book, a feeling, a symbol, or a theme from a study unit. Some even tell a story. The design is clear, elegant, delightful to see, and simple to make. Students are highly enthusiastic when creating banners and take great pride in seeing them displayed.

A successful approach to making a banner is one in which each student receives a square of cloth (all the same size, such

7–27 *"Sixteen Banners" by Pam Castano. Each banner is cotton canvas, 4 feet 9 inches high × 4 feet wide. (Photo courtesy of the artist.)*

as 10 × 10 inches). Have the class suggest themes, such as The Sun, Insects, Flowers, Santa's Delights, or Animals, and select one. Each person then creates his own interpretation of the subject. After all the squares are completed, they can be individually displayed or stitched together to make one large hanging.

Or, plan a theme for an extended project—possibly one that could continue all year—such as a mural about your school. All students can participate on the one project, such as what they like best about the school; try a mural of various interesting subject areas: an Apollo flight, the Wild West, going down the Colorado River on a raft, or ancient Greece.

Procedure
1. Consider the texture to be used for the background fabric: coarse or fine. In the elementary grades, burlap or loosely woven upholstery material works best because an open-weave fabric is easy to stitch on.
2. If burlap is being used as the background fabric, pull the threads to ensure straightness. Pull these threads on the edges for several rows if you desire a fringed effect on the completed hanging.
3. Sew down the row closest to the start of the fringe to avoid further raveling.
4. For an open effect in certain areas, the interior burlap threads also can be pulled and then tied; or add stitches, knotting, or beads to the open spaces.
5. Place a dab of white glue on the corners to prevent raveling.
6. Mount the background fabric on a fairly large frame, or lay it out on a project table.
7. At times you will want to plan the design first on paper that is the same size as the background fabric, indicating colors, textures, and so on. However, many times it's very exciting to begin sketching and sewing the material

Yarns, Needles, and Cloth

itself, letting the design happen spontaneously. Everyone can contribute, working during art periods as well as during their free time.

8. Keep a collection of scraps sorted and stored in easy-to-get-at places.

9. Work in a large area where design planning can be done and materials can be spread out and rearranged.

10. Have planning sessions with students to discuss variations in fabric textures, color relationships, plain and patterned fabrics, strong contrasts of lights and darks, and direct designing with cloth and fibers.

11. Sketch ideas on paper, but encourage the direct cutting of shapes with cloth scraps.

12. Keep cut shapes for appliquéing loose, until the final decision as to their placement.

13. Either sew or glue appliqués into place. Any all-purpose white glue is good—a thin coat of glue dries quickly and does not soak through cloth—or use any fabric adhesive.

14. Use scissors that cut cloth easily. Battery scissors are helpful on days when a lot of cutting is to be done.

15. Add running and other decorative stitches (use large tapestry needles for stitching yarns).

16. Add decorative items such as old jewelry, shells, beads, buttons, yarn, lace, rickrack, feathers, mirrors, and plastic eyes. These items relate to, and enhance, the final design.

17. Use yarns or draw with felt-tip pens to add linear quality to the design.

18. To hang the banner, turn down the top edge of the wall hanging and glue or stitch it closed, allowing room to insert a dowel rod. Or, hang the banner from short tabs of cloth, such as felt. Another way to display a banner is simply to glue or staple it to a wooden dowel.

19. When several hangings are stitched together patchwork style, it may be necessary to line the work with a backing. If the hanging becomes heavy, a couple of small drapery weights in the bottom corners will help it remain smooth. At other times, another dowel hung through a bottom hem will even the cloth.

20. Add fringes, beads, macrame, or tassels along the bottom of the banner.

Dolls

Of all the thousands of toys invented over the years, the one that captures the hearts of all children is the easy-to-love stuffed cloth doll. And what better doll to love than one the child can create himself? If you search your attic or favorite childhood toy box, you may come upon a weathered cloth creature that was once a dear playmate.

Dolls are found in all cultures. Homemade treasures are created from any materials available and all are intended for hugging and cherishing. Some dolls become "real life" friends to their creators and have special personalities. Fantasy animals may be a surprise character such as "Crazy Cat" or "Super Snake." Either type will be invented inspirations that can be storybook characters or delightful beginnings for stories and playing. Many contemporary artists produce giant "soft sculptures" as an art form by employing these same procedures.

CREATING PLAYMATES

All kinds of scrap material can quickly become fantasy dolls and animal pets. Try these examples, as they are simple to construct and encourage an imaginary approach. As part of the fun in making dolls, the personality does not emerge until the designer gives it meaning and life. (See Figure 7–39.)

Procedure
1. Stuff and tie a handkerchief with rubber bands, forming a head, body, arms, and legs. Draw with felt-tip pens to create facial features and clothing details.
2. Many favorite family heirlooms have been the sock doll. With a needle and thread and some rag stuffing, an old sock can be given new life. Stuff and tie off the head and body. A second sock can be cut, stuffed, and sewn for the legs and arms. Attach it to the body. Decorate the doll as simply or as ornately as you wish with clothes, stitched faces, yarn for hair, and other embellishments.
3. Fashion a friend from felt. Cut two identical sides, front and back. Stitch along the side seams—felt does not ravel—and glue on features and clothes.

7–28 *The delight on these happy faces reflects that their own handmade cloth dolls can become cherished playmates.*

4. Other doll heads can be made from bread or salt dough, papier-mâché, corncobs, nuts, and leather. They can be drawn on with felt-tip pens, painted, appliquéd, batiked, or stitched.

PILLOW PETS TO HUG

All varieties of colorful cloth shapes instantly can be turned into pillow pets. All that is needed are cloth scraps, trimming, and rags or old nylon stockings for stuffing. Plan the design on paper first. Instead of regular rectangular or square pillows, design fanciful animals, insects, butterflies, and flowers with interesting outside forms. Be sure to cut the shapes in duplicate.

Appliqué various cloth shapes to the front and back of the pillow pet. Running stitches ensure permanence; but young students can use glue. Add decorative stitches, beads, buttons, and other trims. For instance, create the whimsical face of a turtle with needles and yarn. Young students can draw on details with felt-tips pens. Sew the front and back together, leaving an opening the size of your fist through which stuffing can be inserted. After stuffing the pillow, stitch to close and finish it.

The pillow form becomes a three-dimensional, lightweight toy sculpture. Follow the same instructions, only in miniature, for pin cushions and jewelry. (See Figure 7–39.)

Supplies Needed
scissors
paper pattern
brightly colored cloth scraps
stuffing
needle and thread, decorative items
wire (optional)

Design your own "crazy cat" or "super snake."

Procedure
1. Start with a paper pattern. Provide 2" for a seam.
2. Form a wire skeleton to follow the design. Cover the wire with cotton batting or other stuffing material. Cover the wire ends with masking tape (optional).
3. Cut two identical silhouette shapes of your pet from one yard of brightly colored or patterned cloth (two heads, two bodies, four arms, and four legs).
4. Sew the shapes together inside out; leave a small opening.
5. Turn them right side out and stuff them with cotton batting, plastic foam, old rags, old stockings, or discarded plastic bags.

6. Appliqué the cloth shapes to the background cloth of the toy. Add felt-tip pen details.
7. Finish by sewing on decorative accessories and close the final seam opening.

CLOTH DOLLS

Supplies Needed

cotton sheeting	needle and thread
paper pattern	stuffing
felt-tip pens	decorative items

Procedure
1. Have students bring in old cotton sheeting.
2. Plan a design on a piece of kraft paper that will correspond to the chosen finished doll size. Provide 2" for a seam.
3. Cut out the design. For young doll makers, cut the head, arms, body, and legs all in one shape.
4. Transfer the design to the sheeting. (There is a front and back to the doll, so cut two identical shapes.)
5. Draw on all the details with permanent felt-tip pens.
6. Dress patterns and interesting faces can be drawn on. Leave extra cloth along the edges for outside seams.
7. Add decorative stitching.
8. With the two pieces of cloth turned inside out, sew up the seams with running stitches (a sewing machine helps speed up this step). Leave an open section of seam through which to stuff.
9. Sew up any dangling parts, such as arms and legs, when they are cut separately and put them into the body seam as you sew.
10. Turn the doll right side out.
11. Use the leftover sheeting to stuff the doll.
12. Glue or sew on yarn hair, fur clothing, buttons, jewelry, and plastic and leather scraps. Dress with old doll clothes.

STOCKING-FACE DOLL

One of the most amusing dolls to make is the one with a nylon stocking face. This doll also can be made from any soft material such as thin cotton or mesh.

Procedure
1. Stuff a nylon stocking with other stockings or batting.
2. With a darning needle and thread, start sewing facial features.

7–29a,b *Cloth dolls, life size, made by sixth-grade students.*

3. Catch some of the stuffing with the outside fabric as you stitch, pulling the stitches together to create a three-dimensional, sculptured face. As these funny features develop, they will surprise and delight you.
4. Sew additional features on, whether a nose or ears.
5. Straw, yarn, cotton balls, and pieces of a yarn floor mop can be added for hair and other details.
6. For further detailing, use pens, crayons, appliquéd cloth, and scrap box clothes.
7. Make the clothes yourself; large dolls can wear discarded infant's clothes.
8. Stuff and sew on other body parts and assemble them.
9. Older students might want to create dolls as large as 48 inches in height. Any of these stuffed dolls also make excellent puppets.

SPOOL DOLLS

As likeable insects, animals, and people, spool dolls are another folk toy. Other dolls can be made from clothespins, spoons, corncobs, and socks.

Supplies Needed
Empty spools (wood or Styrofoam)
pipe cleaners
string and sticks

Procedure
1. Place the pipe cleaners inside the spools.
2. Join the pipe cleaners with looped ends and twist.
3. Attach strings to a stick for a marionette if desired.
4. Attach strings to the pipe cleaners at the joints.

Yarns, Needles, and Cloth

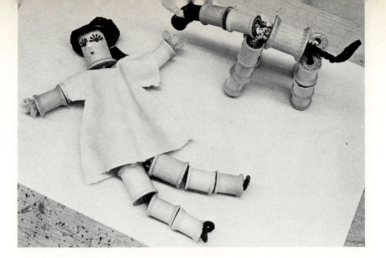

7–31 *Spool dolls are another folk art toy.*

YARN PEOPLE

String these up along a clothesline in the classroom in all colors, sizes, and styles. You will have fun in creating these simple, soft, make-believe little folk. They are easy to invent, easy to incorporate into learning areas, and easy to use as models in small environments such as in dioramas. Try dressing the basic doll in interchangeable costumes, as well as in folk dress from many lands. In almost every country this doll has been found to be a part of the culture. (See Figure 5–17.)

Supplies Needed
yarn
pipe cleaners
buttons and sequins
scrap cloth of all kinds
scissors
rectangular piece of cardboard 6 inches long

7–32 *Yarn dolls are lightweight enough to hang from a tree or to wear.*

Procedure

1. Basic body for any design: wind yarn around a piece of cardboard 6 inches long about 16 times.
2. Place an 8-inch piece of yarn through the top of the wound yarn and tie it tightly. (This holds the yarn together.)
3. Cut the yarn from the bottom of the cardboard and tie it off about 1¼ inches from the top. This forms the neck.
4. Tie the yarn again 1¼ inches down from the neck. This forms the waist.
5. Divide the remaining yarn in half for two legs; tie the yarn off about 2 inches from the waist for each leg.
6. Cut off any shaggy ends and fluff the ends for the feet.
7. The arms are made by again winding the yarn several times around the same 6-inch-long cardboard.
8. Cut the yarn from the cardboard, and tie 1 inch from each end for hands.
9. Insert the arms through the center of the body. Trim and fluff the ends for hands.
10. Dress and decorate each face differently. Glue or sew on features for the head, and create costumes with hats, capes, and boots. Add imaginative accessories.

APPLE-HEAD DOLLS

The apple doll is an old-fashioned favorite that was always found in farmhouses where there were children. This project is especially suitable for making witch faces at Halloween.

Procedure

1. Peel an apple.
2. Using a dull kitchen knife or popsicle stick, carve eyes, a nose, a mouth, and other features (carve hands from another apple). Add rice or peppercorns for eyes or teeth.
3. Make a hole in the bottom of the apple and insert a popsicle stick.
4. Place the apple on the stick into a soft-drink bottle or plastic detergent bottle.
5. Allow several days for the apple to air dry. To dry apple quickly, submerge it in baking soda for a few days.
6. Wrinkly character lines will form as the applie dries and shrinks.
7. If desired, draw lines on the apple or paint it. The character lines are very interesting as they are.
8. When the apple is dry, spray it with a plastic finish.
9. Form wire armature for body and attach to stick.
10. Construct simple decorative clothes from construction paper, corn husks, yarn, old socks, or cloth and glue or

7–33 *Traditional American folk dolls from Kentucky with dried apple faces.*

tape them to the wire armature. Add yarn or straw hair, pipe-cleaner broomsticks, and other details.

CORN HUSK DOLLS

Almost as old as corn itself, corn husk dolls have been found across this country and in many others. Every household can save the needed materials, which are obtainable in the fall of the year. Create small dolls, animals, and fantasy creatures with these simple materials.

Supplies Needed
six corn husks for each doll
corn silk for hair
string
felt-tip pens, bits of yarn, felt, and other fabrics

Procedure
1. Work with the inside layers of the husks, as they are easier to handle.

240

7–34 *A popular folk art in many countries, corn husk dolls and animals can be made in any shape or size. Corn silk and lines made with felt-tip pens complete the figures.*

2. Dampen four husks slightly in water and wrap them in a paper towel.
3. Place the four husks together.
4. Place the corn silk inside the husks (inside the center).
5. Tie them all together with string at about 1 inch from one end.
6. Turn them all inside out.
7. Tie another string 2 inches from the end, thus forming a head shape.
8. The corn silk becomes the hair and can be cut and shaped in any way desired.
9. Take two other husks for arms. Tie them at each end for wrists.
10. Place the arm piece inside the body husks, just under the head, to form the arms.
11. Tie the body again for the waistline.
12. Use the bottom of the husks for making skirts or legs. Add more husks if needed.
13. Add bits of decorative cloth and paper for the clothing and face. Draw on details with felt-tip pens if desired.
14. Use these fresh, appealing figures and invented animals for a number of things: family members in social situations, play activities, as figures for a Christmas crèche, dioramas, as small pins and necklaces, or to help celebrate special times.

Corn husks are also recommended as a weaving material. Dampen the husks in water to soften them and keep them in

Yarns, Needles, and Cloth

plastic bags. Split them lengthwise in ¼- or ½-inch widths. While damp, corn husks are pliable and are excellent for weaving on cardboard looms (see pages 271–272) and for building coiled baskets. (See pages 295–298.)

Patchwork Quilting: An American Craft Tradition

A cherished craft of our American heritage, patchwork quilting had its beginning primarily in New England with the early pioneer women and reached its peak between 1776 and 1876. Originally, women used whatever fabrics they had. They repaired quilts and clothes with colorful patches. Many of the patches came from scrap materials left over from making their own clothes. Soon after, the patches were not used to patch but to make new quilts and original patterns then developed.

Some designs and skills are acquired through hand-me-down artistic examples of patchwork quilting. Because of the flourishing of quilt making, we have inherited patterns that commemorate important events, such as the beginning of the West, the opening of the railroads, and the admission of states, as well as state flowers, and just everyday things. We have inherited a truly native art.

Today museums, galleries, and antique shops display beautiful examples of quilting that were used and worn. People continue to do this craft even though it requires many hours of patient planning and stitching.

7–35 *A bicentennial quilt is hand-quilted by Zella Harris. (Courtesy of The Hand and The Spirit Crafts Gallery, Scottsdale, Arizona.)*

Some of you may be fortunate enough to have an original handmade patchwork quilt. Join in and be part of this American folk craft tradition and create your own beautiful handcrafted patchwork quilt. Combining fabrics, colors, and patterns in designs offers limitless possibilities. The finished results are fun.

Patchwork means to form by joining separate pieces together. The design can also be formed with appliqué or by using both methods. A large quilt appears to be a major project; but keep in mind that the quilt top is a series of identical blocks. Each block is made separately. Sew one block together first to make sure that all the design pieces fit together properly. A finished block is commonly 12 inches square. Forty-two blocks will complete a double-sized bed cover. Blocks are placed six wide and seven long.

PATCHWORK QUILTING IN THE CLASSROOM

Begin with a small project such as a wall sampler, a "block," or a ball.

Choose your fabrics. They should be soft, firmly woven cloth such as cottons or polyester blends (fabrics must be colorfast). Calico prints, percales, broadcloth, muslins, or cotton sateens are all very good. These can be cut and sewn easily. Corduroys and velvets are too thick and bulky. Keep the fabrics similar in quality and thickness. Be sure to wash new fabrics before using them to soften them and remove the sizing (and to allow for shrinkage). Also iron them so that they are flat when cutting shapes.

Collect all kinds of magazine photographs to serve as ideas for designs. Mosaic tile designs, nature, or other quilts can serve as motivations for interpreting designs into geometric shapes for quilt making.

Study geometric shapes as an introductory lesson. Use rulers and protractors to make pentagons and hexagons. Begin with simple designs and simple geometric shapes such as rectangles, squares, and triangles. For the more complex

7–36 *Fourth-graders do felt-tip pen designs and quilting on squares and then stitch them together into a quilt.*

pentagon shape, draw a 4-inch circle. Divide the inside circumference into 72-degree sections, using the protractor. The octagon shape is made by dividing the circle with a 45-degree angle. The hexagon shape is made by dividing the circle into 60-degree angles. (See Figure 7–35.)

A good beginning project, for upper grades, is to make the circle ball by sewing together twelve hexagon shapes—six on each side—and then stuffing the shape with polyester fill. Rectangle or diamond shapes make interesting designs depending on the patterns and textures.

Supplies Needed
fabric scraps in a variety of colors, patterns, and textures
needle (size 7 or 8)
strong sewing thread (about #50 or #60)
paper
pencils
scissors
straight pins
pattern piece—heavy cardboard or plastic acetate pattern glued to a fine sandpaper pattern becomes a very durable and nonsliding pattern
filling (if a form is to be stuffed, use polyester fiber fill, old stockings, cloth scraps, or newspaper)
bias tape (optional)
rulers
tape measures, found objects such as dried flowers, netting, metal shapes, seeds, and wooden rings

Procedure
1. Design the number of paper templates you will need (twelve for the ball) for the entire quilted form, making them the desired finished size and shape. Place these aside.
2. Now draw and cut out three cardboard patterns (be sure to allow ¼ inch for a seam allowance on all sides of the pattern). Place these patterns on the wrong side of the fabric and cut the cloth pieces around them. When laying out the cardboard patterns, space them about ½ inch apart, thereby not wasting any fabric. If possible, lay the cardboard on the grain of the fabric.
3. Consider stripes, prints, and plain fabrics when organizing the finished design.
4. Place the patterns aside. You now have all the cut-out pieces that will be needed. Place the paper templates on the underside of the cloth. Paper templates should be the desired finished size, with ¼ inch of cloth showing around all the edges.
5. Pin the paper to the cloth.
6. Fold over the edges and baste the cloth to the paper. Do

not knot the thread for this basting stitch. The stitches can be large and done quickly. Instead of sewing, try scotch taping the cloth to the paper. Make as many of these pieces as are needed for the design. Press these shapes flat with an iron to get out any puckers.

7. Lay out shapes for the blocks as they will appear in the finished design. Do any changing before sewing them together. It is best to join the blocks together by rows.

8. With two pieces face to face, whip stitch with tiny stitches along the edges. Knot this thread and stitch a couple of extra times along the points.

9. Continue stitching the pieces (blocks) together until the design is finished.

10. Spray both the top and bottom sides with water, and iron them flat.

11. Now remove the basting stitches and the paper will fall out. Be sure to finish the piece before removing the basting and paper. After this, the quilt will need a final ironing.

12. If you plan quilting stitches, you will need the needle, thread, filler, top, and backing (old sheeting works). Use about an 18-inch length of thread—if it is too long it will tangle. Knot the thread and pull it through the top cloth so it is concealed inside the filler. With the help of a thimble, push the needle straight down through all the layers and back up again in *short running* stitches. Pushing the needle through at 90-degree-angle stitches will produce small stitches; 45-degree-angle stitches are used in ordinary sewing.

13. Finish the edges with 1-inch wide bias tape on the right side of the quilting.

Note: For a simple introduction to the concept, students can cut many pieces of the same shape and glue them to a backing. Or they can pin pieces together on the wrong side and then stitch them together with a running stitch. Found objects can be added to the front of the patchwork design when desired.

Needlepoint, Rug Hooking, and Fabric Flowers

NEEDLEPOINT

Needlepoint is enjoying a great revival in the craft area. Classes are popular and specialty shops have opened that cater to needlepoint designers and workers.

In the classroom, the materials needed are simple but varied. First do a felt-tip pen color design on paper, keeping it simple (a geometric design or a simplified animal). Each child will want to plan his own design. Young students can start to do needlepoint on a 4-inch square of plastic mesh. Older students can work on larger individual or group projects.

Supplies Needed
blunt needles

canvas mesh, loose burlap, plastic mesh, loosely woven dishcloths for beginners, screen hardware cloth, or scrim (rug canvas)

yarns, threads, raffia, sticks, weeds, string, cloth, rags, ribbons, lace, felt, pipe cleaners, and all kinds of paper

Procedure
1. Transfer the design to the backing: place the paper design under the backing and draw the design on the backing with a felt-tip waterproof pen.
2. Use a blunt, large-eyed needle. Experiment with stitches so that the stitching is done horizontally, vertically, diagonally, and in circles, using short and long stitches. Stitch with a variety of materials (see "Supplies Needed").
3. Fill in the mesh or screen as solidly as possible with stitches.
4. Needlepoint designs can be framed, mounted on felt, or made into small cushions. Try making a tiny needlepoint to fit into a round wooden drapery hook. These make delightful decorations for windows, Christmas trees, mobiles, and necklaces.

RUG HOOKING

One of the advantages of this project is that it can be done as a class effort. It is fun to see each individual's work added to the combined group product. And students can work at it in their spare time. If two or three needles are handy, more than one student can work on the rug at a time. Rugs take a great deal of yarn, so do not be too ambitious with your first rug project. Yarn scraps work well for color variety and for economic reasons. When hooked, small burlap pieces, about 15 inches square, are beautiful as pillow covers or wall displays.

Supplies Needed
backing: scrim or inexpensive burlap; plan 4 to 5 extra inches all around for hemming

simple wood frame (a little smaller than the backing)

tacks

felt-tip pen
rug yarns (skeins or yarn scraps)
rug punch needle, or hook (at most yarn and stitchery shops)
latex sizing and a brush

Procedure

1. Decide on the size of the rug you want to hook. A beginning size is about 18 × 24 inches.
2. Attach the burlap or rug scrim (allowing several inches along the sides for hemming) to a wooden frame. A simple handmade wood frame, a stretcher frame, or an old picture frame are fine.
3. Stretch the fabric tightly and tack it to the frame with staples or carpet tacks.
4. Plan your design. Reverse the design and transfer it to the wrong side of the burlap with a felt-tip pen.
5. Keep the design simple and use large shapes.
6. Transfer the design directly or use an opaque projector.
7. Thread the punch needle from back to front. Place a piece of yarn through the hole at the end of the punch needle handle and then through its point.
8. Extend the yarn 12 inches through the point.
9. Set the gauge for the length of the loop desired.
10. Point the needle into the backing and push it all the way through until the backing hits the handle. Point the needle in the direction you are going. All hooking is done on the underside.
11. Pull the needle out just to the surface of the backing and smoothly glide the punch needle to the next space.
12. Continue this motion of the needle back and forth through the fabric. For a thicker pile, use two threads at once.
13. For interesting textures and surfaces, vary the loops

7–37a *Rug hooking is an excellent group project, as several students can work on one large rug. The burlap rug-backing material is tacked or stapled to a wood frame. The rug punch tool is pushed in and out, working from the underside (note the rug tool, top center).*

formed by the punch needle in a low or high relief design.

14. Vary the weight and color of the yarns (rayon, cotton, and acrylic yarns are inexpensive). Place the yarn ends on the front side and cut them level with the rest of the pile when you are finished.
15. For tactile appeal, cut the loops on some of the yarns and leave others unclipped. A skein of yarn takes approximately 1½ to 2 hours to punch.
16. After the entire surface has been hooked, remove the backing from the frame.
17. Turn the edges under and stitch them down by hand with heavy thread.
18. Paint latex sizing on the back to keep the yarn in place and to prevent slippage if the rug is to be used on the floor.

A hand-hooked rug is so beautiful, one rarely wants to walk on it. Try a hooked rug as a wall hanging, for which the latex sizing will not be necessary.

7–37b   Pam Castano stands in front of her hooked rug hanging, "Dwellings," which is approximately 7 feet wide and 13 feet long. (Courtesy of the artist.)

POTS AND FLOWERS WITH FABRIC FLAIR

How do you bring springtime color into the classroom? One sure way is to create your very own gay bouquet of spring flowers. This project will catch the fancy of all spring-spirited people. Why not turn the whole school into a fanciful dream garden?

Supplies Needed
wire: pipe cleaners or baling wire or coat hanger wire
assorted scraps of cloth in bright patterns
white glue or starch
colored paper
aluminum foil, metallic papers, and colored magazine photographs (optional)
masking or green floral tape
decorative stitching
needles, thread, and yarn (optional)
real flowers, cornmeal, borax

Procedure
1. Decide on the flower design. Any shape and idea will work. Most flowers in nature are built with a number of petals. A beginning design might include a flower with

six to eight petals. Shape the pipe cleaner as desired, leaving some extra length where the petals are to be joined at the base. Twist the wire together.

2. Lay the shaped pipe cleaners on the cloth scraps.
3. Glue the pipe cleaners to the cloth with white glue. Let it dry.
4. *Then* cut out the flower shape around the pipe cleaner. Cut out several petals.
5. Join the pipe cleaners together in the center. Cluster any stamen material in the center, such as cut paper, beads on a wire, or the stamens that are available in hobby shops.
6. Use a pipe cleaner or wire to hold all the flower petals together at the base.
7. Add the flower to a long-stem wire.
8. Begin wrapping with tape from the flower end; add leaves of construction paper, foil, plastic, or dried natural leaves as you wrap the wire stem.
9. Make a whole bouquet of colorful patterned flowers. For variety, use magazine color photographs, foils, and metallic papers for petals. Build rose shapes and other flowers from aluminum foil. Try adding decorative stitches to the petal shapes before cutting them out of cloth.
10. Dry out real flowers by carefully placing them upside down into an equal mixture of borax and cornmeal.

Note: For burlap flowers, use burlap in a variety of colors, white glue, scissors, and about 20-gauge wire. Cut rectangular pieces of burlap about 4½ × 6 inches. Hold the piece horizontally. About ½ inch from the top (leave ½ inch along the bottom), pull out burlap threads. Place the threads aside to be used later as centers. Fold the burlap piece in half and glue the edges together. Now take the pulled threads and fold the pile in half; hook the wire around the center of the threads; the wire becomes the wire stem. Lay the wired center threads on top of the glued burlap and roll them around the stem. Glue the ends. Wrap the flower to the stem with tape. Fluff out the flower.

For patchwork pots, use a clean clay planting pot, colorful cloth scraps, white glue, or liquid starch. Cut fabrics into desired shapes. Paint the pot with diluted white glue or starch. Position the patches as you paint, overlapping them slightly. Wrap the cloth over the top of the pot. Add rickrack and lace and other embellishments. Let it all dry thoroughly. Finish the pot with clear coating of glue or starch. When dry, coat the inside of the pot with melted paraffin; this prevents moisture from real plants from seeping through and marring the patchwork decoration.

How to Crochet

Crocheting is another easy and exciting needlework craft. Learn these few basic stitches and then try making simple items such as belts, scarves, bags, and ponchos. Begin to invent imaginative forms and creatures by crocheting without preplanned designs. Try combining crocheting with weaving and macrame. Crocheting is fast, and assorted yarns and needles of various sizes can add infinite variety to your work. Beads, feathers, lace, and other decorations can be added as you go. It is fun to crochet a long chain and then pick up a random stitch to crochet onto. By doing creative crocheting you can produce round, free forms in any shape and size you wish.

CHAIN STITCH

Procedure

1. Tie a loop of yarn on the crochet hook. (See Figure 7–38a.)
2. Place a second yarn loop on yarn finger.
3. Pass the hook under the yarn on your finger and catch it with the hook.
4. Draw the yarn through the loops. (See Figure 7–38b.)
5. Repeat and enlarge the chain to the desired length. (See Figure 7–38c.)

SINGLE CROCHET

Procedure

1. Insert the hook under the top threads of the second chain from the hook.

7–38 *Chain stitch.*

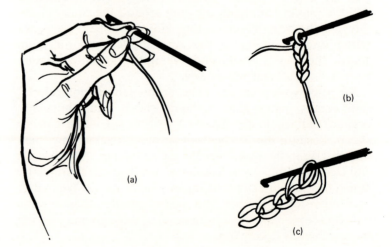

7–39 *Pet friends are stuffed cloth and knitted and crocheted forms.*

2. Catch the yarn over the hook and draw the yarn through the chain stitch.
3. There are now two loops on the hook.
4. Catch the yarn over the hook and bring it through the two loops already formed on the hook. This is one complete single crochet.
5. Insert the hook into the next chain stitch and repeat the single crochet. Repeat this across the row.
6. At the end of the row, chain one, then turn the work so the reverse side faces you. Continue with a single crochet stitch across the row.

For experimental designs, mix the single crochet stitch with the chain stitch to create inventive shapes; crochet long chains, and then single crochet for a while.

To enlarge the crochet, simply add extra stitches as you go. To make the work smaller, crochet two loops together. Build three-dimensional shapes by using large jute and superlarge crochet hooks. The large jute and hooks work quickly and produce forms that could even be suspended from the ceiling and separate spaces for an environmental effect. Integrate these spatial crocheted forms with colored lights and offer a modern dance and music presentation. The shadows from the stretched forms are as interesting as the form itself. If no hooks are available, crochet with the fingers.

String or Yarn As an Art Medium

STRING OR YARN PICTURES

This technique has long been a favorite tradition in Mexico to create cheerful, bright pictures. Instead of placing the yarn

Yarns, Needles, and Cloth

7–40 *Yarn is placed into glue on a firm surface, such as cardboard, in this traditional Mexican craft. The raised surfaces at the left build relief forms. Pencils are the base of the God's eye, top center.*

into softened wax, as is done by the Mexicans, we place the yarn into glue for the same effect. This project is a favorite one with students; designs can be simple abstract shapes, flowers, birds, scenes, suns, or other delightful motifs. (See color Figure 8.)

7–41 *Yarn pictures by third-graders.*

Supplies Needed
all-purpose white glue
cardboard, Masonite, or wood scrap backing, about 9 × 12
  inches
rug and knitting yarns in many bright colors

Procedure
1. Outline important shapes with thin lines of glue on the
   board.
2. Place the yarn onto these glue lines.
3. Fill in the outlined areas with other colors by brushing the
   glue down and working in sections; coil the string or yarn
   around and around until all the areas are filled in.

The same method can be used on bottles, clay shapes, clay
pottery, Styrofoam, or any three-dimensional form.

YARN MOBILES

This is a project that can be done quickly and is enjoyed by
all ages; the designs are free-form and can be completed with
yarn alone or combined with colored tissue papers and
colored cellophane for added brilliance. Consider a design for
a shape that will be suspended to move in the air. Smaller
yarn designs can be appliquéd with glue to a cloth backing
and worn as jewelry.

Supplies Needed
waxed paper
pie tins
various colored rug and knitting yarns or string in 2-foot
  lengths
undiluted starch

Procedure
1. Fill some pie tins with undiluted starch.
2. Place a piece of waxed paper and several selected yarn
   pieces in front of each student.
3. Ask each student to dip a piece of yarn into the starch and
   lay the yarn into an original design on the waxed paper:
   flowers, birds, hands, and free-form shapes.
4. Let the starch dry overnight.
5. After the yarn dries, lift off the waxed paper. The yarn
   designs will be stiff and light enough to hang from string

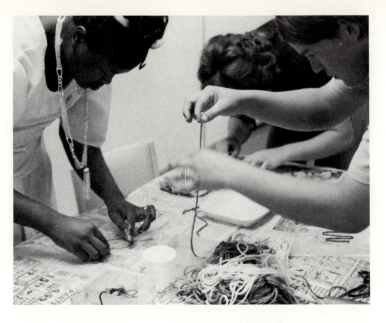

and move freely in the air. (Try wrapping yarn and string around balloons and other free-form shapes for more three-dimensional forms.) Shapes can be joined for giant mobiles.

Checkpoints

1. Plan time for sketching ideas on paper first.
2. Block out the design patterns on paper before cutting out the final designs.
3. Use materials that are strong enough to hold up with a great deal of handling.
4. Plan for inexpensive available materials for classroom use.
5. Use permanent paints and markers so they will not rub off, blot, or stain with use.
6. Plan for materials that are easily manipulated; for instance, use sandpaper, Velcro, or buttons so that objects can be removed and replaced at will when planning "stick-ons."
7. Plan for adequate working spaces.
8. Plan for discussion time and idea-interaction time. Motivation takes place during idea-storming sessions.
9. Sketch initial designs on the fabric with charcoal, chalks, or light pencil (pencil is hard to remove).
10. When doing stitchery, experiment with stitches for design effects.
11. Keep the designs simple. Add decorative details later.

254

12. When planning doll and doll clothes patterns, provide a supplemental fabric allowance for hems and seams.
13. Yarn can easily be dispensed in this way: use a cardboard carton and have balls of yarn in the carton. Punch a hole for each ball in the side of the carton and pull the end of the yarn through.
14. Iron projects with a warm iron when finished.
15. If desired, finish the edges of banners and wall hangings with iron-bonding cloth (optional).
16. Store needles, points down, in a Styrofoam block.

Bibliography

ALLARD, MARY. *Rug Making: Techniques and Design.* Philadelphia: Chilton Book Co., 1963.

BEITTLER, ETHEL JANE. *Create with Yarn.* Scranton, Pa.: Intext Educational Publishers, Inc., 1964.

BELFER, NANCY. *Designing in Stitching and Appliqué.* New York: Sterling Publishing Co. Inc. 1973.

BIRRELL, VERLA. *The Textile Arts.* New York: Schocken Books, 1959.

CHRISTENSEN, JO IPPOLITO. *Trapunto: Decorative Quilting.* New York: Sterling Publishing Co.: Inc., 1972.

COLBY, AVERIL. *Quilting.* New York: Charles Scribner's Sons, 1971.

ENTHOVEN, JACQUELINE. *Stitchery for Children.* New York: Van Nostrand Reinhold Company, 1967.

FELCHER, CECILIA. *The Complete Book of Rug Making.* New York: Hawthorne Books, Inc.

GRAVES, SYLVIA. *The History of Needlwork Tools and Accessories.* New York: Arco Publishing Co., 1973.

GREEN, SYLVIA. *Patchwork for Beginners.* New York: Watson-Guptill Publications, 1973.

GUILD, VERA P. *Creative Use of Stitches.* Worcester, Mass.: Davis Publications, 1964.

GUTCHEON, BETH. *The Perfect Patchwork Primer.* New York: David McKay Co. Inc., 1973.

HAMILTON-HUNT, MARGARET. *Knitting Dictionary.* New York: Crown Publishers, Inc., 1971.

HILTON, BEVERLY, ED. *Golden Hands: A Comprehensive Guide to Knitting, Dressmaking, and Needlecraft.* New York: Marshall Cavendish Corp., 1973.

KREVITSKY, NIK. *Stitchery: Art and Craft.* New York: Van Nostrand Reinhold Company, 1966.

LALIBERTE, NORMAN, AND STERLING MCILHANY. *Banners and Hangings.* New York: Van Nostrand Reinhold Company, 1966.

LAURY, JEAN RAY. *Doll Making: A Creative Approach.* New York: Van Nostrand Reinhold Company, 1970.

LAWLESS, DOROTHY. *Rug Hooking and Braiding.* New York: Thomas Y. Crowell Company, 1962.

MASON, ENID. *Embroidery Design.* Newton Centre, Mass.: Charles T. Branford, Inc., 1968.

MEILACH, DONNA. *Solft Sculpture.* New York: Crown Publishers, 1974.

MILLER, IREN PRESTON, AND WINIFRED LUBELL. *The Stitchery Book: Embroidery for Beginners.* Garden City, N.Y.: Doubleday & Company, Inc., 1965.

MURPHY, MARJORIE. *Beadwork for American Indian Designs.* New York: Watson-Guptill Publications, 1974.

NICHOLSON, JOAN. *Creative Embroidery.* New York: Gramercy Publishing Co., 1940.

RUSH, BEVERLY. *The Stitchery Idea Book.* New York: Van Nostrand Reinhold Company, 1974.

SIDNEY, SYLVIA. *Questions and Answers About Needlepoint.* New York: Van Nostrand Reinhold Company, 1974.

SONMER, ELYSE, AND MIKE SONMER. *Wearable Crafts.* New York: Crown Publishers, 1976.

WALLER, IRENE. *Designing with Thread: From Fibre to Fabric.* New York: The Viking Press, Inc., 1973.

WENDORFF, RUTH. *How to Make Cornhusk Dolls.* New York: Arco Publishing Co., Inc., 1973.

ZARBOCK, BARBARA. *The Complete Book of Rug Hooking.* New York: Van Nostrand Reinhold Company, 1969.

8

Weaving and Macrame

Long before recorded history, people discovered that plant fibers and animal furs could be twisted into strong cords and used together to produce cloth. Consequently, for thousands of years throughout the world, civilizations artfully blended fiber weavings by hand—a very slow process. In the mid-1700s, machines were invented that increased and improved the production of textiles. Today, modern textile factories with hundreds of electronically operated machines produce fabrics of infinite variety and design.

Weaving As Cultural Tradition

In the history of almost every culture in the world some weaving method can be found. The fundamental concept of over and under, the rhythm of in and out, and the basic loom concept have not changed much throughout history. From the simple prehistoric baskets of grass and straw to the ancient picture records found in magnificent woven tapestries, weaving has been and remains one of man's original and most significant crafts.

Early potters, for example, used woven baskets as molds, which they tightly packed with clay and then baked in the fire. On America's shores, the Indians of the Northwest wove remarkably tight baskets in which they cooked, stored food, and carried water. The basket-making techniques using reeds and grasses were then transferred to flat weaving for making blankets and mats. Linen fragments have been uncovered in Switzerland that date as far back as ten thousand years ago.

8–1 *"Arizona Mountain Vista," by Nancy Robb Dunst, is installed in the Phoenix Airport. Macramé and weaving is 15 feet × 7 ½ feet. (Courtesy of the artist.)*

The fine linens and ramie cloth discovered in Egyptian tombs (from about 1500 B.C.) were created for religious garments and indicate a high degree of talent and skill in weaving. The Chinese also were developing fibers from the silkworm and inventing the satin weave at about that time. And the Babylonians wore beautifully dyed, heavy woolens that they also traded in their journeys.

The Copts, who were the early Egyptian Christians, provided a record for us by burying their linens—as well as their spindles, eating utensils, and tools—in their graves. Their tapestry subjects were mostly religious scenes picturing Christ and the disciples.

Inventive and creative craftspeople developing a great number of weaving techniques and styles were found around the world. Along the shores of the Pacific Ocean in South America the textile craftspeople of the Inca Empire developed skills such as pattern weaves for tapestry, gauze, brocade, featherwork, knotted lace, and painted cloth. Fine fragments of these have been preserved because they were buried in sand. The colors from the vegetable dyes used on those fabrics are as vivid and beautiful today as they were thousands of years ago. The creative Peruvian weavers used a very simple loom for weaving complicated geometric designs from two horizontal sticks that were weighted down with stones, the warp threads stretched between them. A later improvement had a method of lifting the alternating warp threads added. With this, a belt or strap at the end of the loom was passed around the back of the person weaving; thus the popular "backstrap loom" was developed that is still used. This loom is similar to the looms used by the Navajo Indians—the vertical loom—and the Hopi Indians—the backstrap loom. In Africa, we find many varieties of both types of looms producing long strips of woven cloth that are later joined together, side by side, to make larger cloths.

8–2 *Long before machines were developed, weavers used inventive spinning methods, such as this rotating spindle, to twist fibers into strands for weaving. (Courtesy of Diane Harrison.)*

WEAVING AMONG THE AMERICAN INDIANS

North American Indians first made baskets at least nine thousand years ago; we have examples from tribes all across North America. The three basic techniques found are plaiting, twining, and coiling. Different plant materials were woven and the finished products were used for fish traps, ceremonies, storage, and carrying and serving food. Coiling and twining were generally western Indian processes; plaiting, generally eastern. Almost all tribes used simple plaiting and twining; it is in the techniques and decorations that we find differences. Baskets reflect the organic materials available in the environment. Some baskets were covered with resin so that they would hold water.

Twining and plaiting are found in the earliest of North American textiles produced by finger-weaving techniques. It is believed that the Indians of the East and Midwest wove textiles as early as 1500 B.C. But it was as early as nine thousand years ago that the Archaic cultures were weaving rush mats and fiber sandals. Loom weaving was done only in the Southwest. It first appeared in the Cochise culture about 1000 B.C. True loom weaving was thought to have been brought here from Mexico with the belt loom. Cotton was also brought at that time from Mexico. Prior to that, vegetable fibers and animal hairs were used in finger weaving. It is not known when the vertical blanket loom was brought to the Southwest, but it appeared in the Great Pueblo period, A.D. 1050–1300. The Southwest has long been an important weaving area.

In many cultures today, such as in that of the American Hopi Indian, it is the man who is the weaver. But in the American Navajo culture, for example, it is the woman who weaves. (They say it takes five people spinning yarn to keep one weaver weaving.) Since the early weaving of animal skins and pelts to the weaving of baskets, linens, and tapestries, the aesthetic qualities of a woven article have been as important as its functional qualities. The Indian's close relationship to the environment and his use of natural materials is an inspiration to all craftspeople.

Weaving wool began in about 1660, after the Spaniards introduced sheep into the Southwest. Navajo weaving reached a level of great artistry around 1850. From 1863 to 1868, the Navajos were confined at Fort Sumner, Arizona, and it was here that Navajo weavers began using commercial dyes, twisted yarns, and new designs. In about 1890, rugs took the place of thin blankets. The quantities desired by traders lowered the quality after 1900—when garish colors

8–3 *Plastic scrim, a stiff, open mesh, is the backing for this free-form weaving. The weaver has used artificial fur, lamb's wool, handspun and other yarns, and cloth in a variety of weaving techniques. Small shells have been sewn on.*

and unusual patterns were selected—until a revival of their original quality in about 1930.

The entire Navajo family works at shearing the sheep. It is the woman who washes, cards, dyes, and spins the wool. The spindle and looms used today have changed little from the ancient, primitive ones. The loom consists of two upright poles and two cross bars that support the warp frame. One weaves from the bottom up. The many colors of wool are achieved by using vegetable dyes made from berries, bark, fruit, roots, and flowers.

Every region has different patterns and designs. It is fascinating to study these and to select rugs from various geographical areas. The better quality rugs are disappearing today because the craft requires hard, time-consuming work.

The Art of Weaving

There is endless fascination in weaving. Birds weave, insects weave, and weaving was supposedly the first of man's crafts. The challenge exists in the manipulation of exciting textural materials and altering colors and textures into a visually aesthetic and tactile object. Although certain basic elementary skills are necessary for weaving, the rudiments are simple. The excitement builds when variations with materials and old and newly learned processes develop together. The spirit and joy of original designs can be enhanced by the simple skill of weaving over and under, employing inventively strung warps, using unusual weft materials such as leather, plastic, and grasses, tapestry techniques such as open slits, weaving free-form shapes, or inventive combinations of techniques. In some instances, preplanning is a must (thinking through the design to what will intentionally happen); in others, letting the materials dictate the expression and discovery stimulates creative weaving products. (See color Figure 9.)

Weaving is possible with very simple tools and materials; it is easy to store; it is available at the spur of the moment; it is an ancient process that is historically intriguing; and a pattern can be as simple or as complex as the weaver desires.

Weaving is enjoyed by people of all ages. Young students are fascinated by the process and the skill required and soon develop exciting creations from cardboard, straw, or wood looms. Large bulky yarns (such as rug yarn), rags, ribbons, and sticks can be woven quickly. The student must choose from various materials, select colors, and invent and compose patterns and designs. The objectives for everyone are mastering the color relationships, the varied textural qualities, and the challenge of construction skills in a handwoven article.

Weaving and Macrame

Thus, function and ideas are fused with fibers into an aesthetic whole.

Gather all the weaving materials you can find, from the tiniest silken hairs to string, ribbon, grasses, and sticks. Weave delicate webs such as the master spider, and giant room weavings that enclose an environment.

Textile Materials: Where They Come From

The great range of fibers available for weaving allows even the beginning weaver to choose from many fascinating sizes, colors, and textures. Listed here are but a few explanations of yarn production. Further study into the history, collecting, cleaning, and spinning of yarns into lengths would be a meaningful learning unit for any grade level.

The three kinds of natural fibers are animal, vegetable, and mineral. Synthetic fibers are chemically treated vegetable and mineral materials that produce those fibers that are called man made.

ANIMAL FIBERS

Wool

Raw wool is sheared from sheep and then packaged into bales. In its second stage, wool is soft and ropelike fiber strands; these strands are tightly twisted and drawn into a strand known as *roving*, which is then spun into yarn. Wool is a favorite because it is easily spun, dyed, and woven. It is soft, light, and warm.

Hair

Hair used for weaving is combed out of the soft undercoat of the goat, rabbit, dog, camel, or llama. Wool is usually added to it to give warmth and softness. Horse or cow hair is coarse and rough and is usually used in rugs or on sculptures.

Silk

Silk is a beautiful but expensive weaving material. The silkworm is commonly fed on mulberry leaves. (Wild silk is taken from silkworms fed on oak and other leaves.) It prepares a cocoon for its metamorphosis into a moth. Before the moth emerges from the cocoon, the cocoon is placed into hot water and the loosened silk is reeled off, several stands at a time. This is made into a filament. Later the filament is twisted into a silk thread.

Leather

Leather comes in short lengths, is expensive, and is used for small areas or used in strips. It can be dyed to various colors.

VEGETABLE FIBERS

Cotton

Cotton has been used for centuries. It grows as a plant and is cultivated from the seed pod of the cotton bush. It is harvested into large bales and then spun into yarns in mills.

Wool and cotton have been grown by man since prehistoric times. Cotton is available in many varieties, from string to rug yarn, and in many colors and weights: cotton butcher twine, cotton wrapping twine, and cotton rope. Cotton fiber is only half as strong as *hemp*, which is cultivated in the Philippine Islands and Africa. The hemp fibers, which grow to lengths of 10 to 12 feet, are peeled off the leaves of the abaca plant. They are stiff fibers, somewhat shiny, and often used for ropes and twine.

Jute

Jute comes from India and Pakistan. These fibers are taken from bushy plants that often reach heights of 10 feet. Jute is often used for macrame. It can be dyed but it may fade and shed. It is rough textured, which adds to its visual appeal, but it is sometimes prickly to work with.

Flax

Flax, which is linen, is grown mainly in Europe. The fibers are taken from the stalk of the flax plant. It is a strong, smooth fiber that has especially long strands. The fibers appear to gain beauty with wear and age. Linen is very nice to work with, but it is expensive. Waxed linen upholstery cord is also used for macrame.

Sisal

Sisal is imported mainly from Central America and East Africa. The fibers are white or yellow, about 5 feet long, and come from a species of the agave plant.

Coconut Fiber

Coconut fiber is taken from the hairy shells of the coconut. The fibers are resistant to moisture but do not have great strength.

Raffia

Raffia is a flat straw (from leaf strips from the African palm) that is fun to work and weave with; however, it does not show macrame knots well. It is used for baskets, mats, hats, and purses.

Ramie

Ramie is an ancient fiber. We have Egyptian remnants as examples. It is the strongest of all the natural fibers and is very thin and lightweight. It is produced from a nettle plant called China grass.

SYNTHETIC FIBERS

Rayon and Acetate

Rayon and acetate begin as trees. Wood chips are ground into wood pulp that is put into a chemical solution and then forced thorugh a spinnerette (this looks something like a shower head with very tiny holes) to make a filament fiber. Rayon, the first man-made fiber, was invented by a Frenchman, Count Hilaire de Chardonnet, in 1884. In 1910, the American Viscose Corporation first produced rayon for the American market. To make acetate, cellulose is obtained from wood pulp and combined with the main ingredient in vinegar, acetic acid. This combination makes acetate chemically different from rayon. Acetate was first made in the United States by the Celanese Corporation in 1924. Rayon fiber is tougher than acetate, but acetate is more elastic. Both are favorites for clothing because they are nonwrinkling, moth- and mildew-proof, washable, and spot-resistant. Both fibers are produced in a variety of sizes, textures, and weights.

Nylon and Acrylic

Nylon and acrylic fibers are developed from crude oil, water, and air through chemical processing. They go through

8–4 *The loom used here is a free-form one made from a tree limb and a large cow bone, with holes drilled in it, and warped with a cotton string. Fur, lamb's wool, twine, and handspun wools are the weft fibers used by this weaver.*

a spinnerette to form filament fiber. The main ingredient in nylon is a chemical called cyclohexane, which is derived from petroleum. Nylon was invented in the DuPont laboratories in the middle 1930s and first marketed in 1939. Acrylic fibers, such as Orlon, Acrilan, and Creslan, are derived from acryonitrile, another chemical made from crude oil. DuPont was also the first to produce these fibers in 1950. Nylon is an elastic and long-wearing fiber. Acrylics are soft, warm, easy-to-dye fibers.

Polyester
Polyester fibers are made from fiber-forming materials in elements derived from air, water, and petroleum. The raw materials are changed into a liquid and are pumped through a spinnerette. They solidify to form a fiber. This process was discovered in England and first manufactured in the United States in 1953. Other common manufacturer trade names for polyester fibers are Dacron, Fortrel, and Kodel.

MINERAL FIBERS

Glass
Glass fibers are used mainly in draperies and industrial projects. The fiber is made from sand into glass marbles. The marbles are remelted and the melted glass is forced through a tiny hole in a melt kettle and comes out a very thin filament. It dyes well and will not stain, wrinkle, fade, or burn.

Metallic Yarns
These fibers have been used for centuries. They are processed today from aluminum foil strips. They are used by themselves, or wrapped around a core of rayon or silk for strength. At other times, the metallic threads are coated with plastic so they will not tarnish.

Additional Materials for Weaving

A walk through the woods or along the beach can supply treasures of beautiful organic materials. You can weave with anything—your imagination will provide the ideas. Here are some suggested materials:

corn husk, stems, cattails, wheats, grasses, yucca, reeds, twigs, vines, bark, and leaves
cut plastic strips and dowels

fabric strips, felt, ribbons, and trimming
feathers
leatherette
nylon hose in different colors
papers: crepe, tissue, cellophane, construction, wallpaper,
  gift wrap, and magazine
plastic bags (from the cleaner's or grocery)
strips of bonded knit cloth (will not ravel), old clothes, and
  rags
telephone wire
wood dowels, pipe cleaners, Popsicle sticks, and bamboo
  strips (unravel old curtains)
yarns (all weights and colors): wool, cotton, acrylic, rayon,
  unspun wool, cotton string, twines, and cords

Spinning Wool

Spinning is an ancient craft and is an exciting way to introduce the weaving concept.

You may have wondered where the yarn in your sweaters comes from. What is used to make sweaters? Several fibers that are used include camel's hair, mohair—even dog's hair—and lamb's wool, which is called fleece. The wool is sheared from sheep. Our ancestors raised their own sheep to make fibers for blankets and garments they wore. Today, the Navajo people still raise great herds of sheep for their wool that they spin to make rugs and blankets. People gather to have spinning bees. Because the Navajo people live distances apart, families work together on this project.

Procedure
1. In order to clean the wool, use a comb and a stiff brush.
2. Hold a piece of wool in your hand and pull the comb through it. The dirt will fall out. Continue this until the wool is clean. It has an oily feel to it, as sheep have natural oils that help to hold the spin. This is called spinning in the grease. When you have cleaned the amount you will need, set it aside.
3. Many people today use a spinning wheel to spin wool. Using a wheel is much faster and produces a uniform spin. The early spinners used what is called a drop spindle. Use a 12-inch-long wooden dowel (about 1 inch in diameter) with a hook at the top end—like a crochet hook—and a disc near the pointed bottom. The disc will give the spindle momentum so that it spins like a top.
4. Take a piece of string about a yard long. Tie it around the bottom of the dowel and wrap several times. Catch the

Color Figures 1 and 2 *"Theater Games," a week-long workshop, combined original mask and costume making with improvisational drama and playmaking from a story plot. See pages 92-93 and 339. (Courtesy of Madelaine Shellaby, University Art Museum, University of California, Berkeley.)*

Color Figure 3 *A blind student at the California School for the Blind is involved with building structures, spaces, and textures. Boxes, sticks, tubing, and scrap wood were glued together. Students sometimes painted their sculptures with white gesso. See page 50.*

Color Figure 4 *At the waxing station during a batik class, students apply clear paraffin over a felt-tip pen drawing on cotton cloth. Wax is applied with brushes, tjantings, and stamps. The electric fry pan holds hot water, which heats the wax contained in the coffee can. Brushed-on dyes will be applied at another station. The older student is a helper. See pages 150-151.*

Color Figure 5 *Exploring themes such as the sun, flowers, apples, or oranges, each student can add an imaginative interpretation as part of a group project. Linda Deck created this handsome quilt by batiking each square and then sewing all the squares together. See page 152.*

Color Figure 6 *Stitching is fun for people of all ages. Self-taught artist (age 88) Helen Stice learned the same basic stitches (as described in text) from her mother when she was seven years old. As her grandmother quilted, Helen would save the scraps from which she made mittens and clothing for herself. French knots, bright colors, heavy yarn flowers, butterflies, and inventive designs are composed spontaneously in the sections first and then joined together. Starting at 4:00 A.M., this folk artist stitches all day, even when her fingers sometimes bleed. Her work is distinguished by the gathered cloth sections that gracefully catch the light and add a three-dimensional quality. See page 164.*

Color Figure 7 *"Beaded Royal Crown," Yoruba, from Nigeria, Africa, 36½". This king's crown contains symbols related to the myth of the origin of the Yoruba. Each kingdom expresses its origin and its relation to the creator God in a beaded crown. See page 176. (Courtesy of the Brooklyn Museum, New York.)*

Color Figure 8 *First-graders use yarn and felt glued to a wood backing to create these delightful yarn pictures. See page 199.*

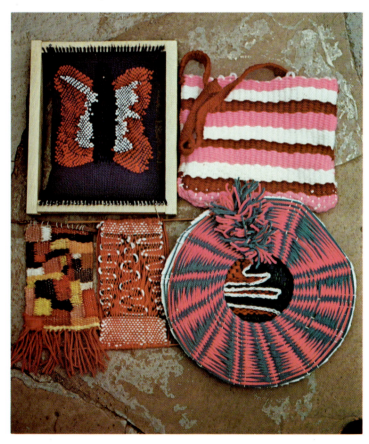

Color Figure 9 *Weaving is a fascinating art experience. Bright, colorful designs are woven on cardboard, frame, foam, and circular looms. Students especially like using fluorescent colored yarns. It is amazing how one's personality is reflected in the finished art. See page 207.*

A

B

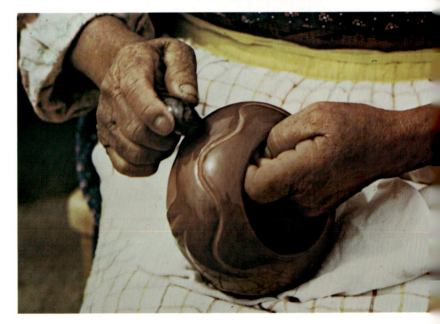

Color Figure 10. **A.** *Rose Gonzales, award-winning Pueblo potter, works with clay dug from timeless quarries. She sits in front of her backyard bread oven in San Ildefonso, New Mexico. First she makes a round patty of clay, which is placed into a dish form. Then she begins to form the clay into thick coils; her moistened fingers press, seal, thin, and smooth the coils into place.*
B. *Rose smooths and thins the bowl's soft wall with her wet fingers and hard gourd templates.*
C. *After drying overnight, the pot is carved. Hours of burnishing produce the shiny surface, which is polished to a smooth luster. The river pebble she uses to polish with is a prized possession. Such pebbles, selected for the complexity of their concave and convex curves, are often passed from mother to daughter. After drying the bowl is fired. See page 268. (Courtesy of Exxon Company.)*

C

Color Figure 11 *Baker's clay and salt ceramic are popular manipulative materials for elementary-school students. The imaginative forms shown were air dried and painted with acrylic paints, and then finished with a plastic spray. The light brown shape was browned as it baked in the oven. These can be worn as jewelry or hung as decoration. Note the hamburger. See page 279.*

Color Figure 12 *Kites are for special windy days. These floaters and flyers were used to harness various natural forces. Students worked with wind, water, air, and body movement. Materials used to make the kites were painted cloth, plastic, and paper on long rods. See page 312. (Courtesy of Madelaine Shellaby, University Art Museum, University of California, Berkeley. Photo by Nancy Hartner.)*

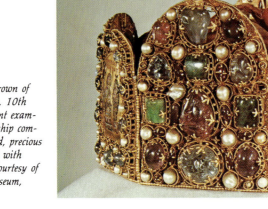

Color Figure 13 *"Crown of the Holy Roman Emperor, 10th Century." This magnificent example of medieval craftsmanship combines enamel work on gold, precious gems, and pearls mounted with prongs. See page 336. (Courtesy of the Kunsthistorisches Museum, Vienna.)*

Color Figure 14 *Crayon etching or scrath crayon, page 388.*

Color Figure 15 *"Berkeley and Me," a painted mural about the city. Young students work together to design and complete this huge painting.
(Courtesy of Madelaine Shellaby, University Art Museum, University of California, Berkeley. Photo by José Romero.)*

string on the dowel with a loop. Twist the unspun wool around the end of the string.

5. Hold the wool between the thumb and first finger of your left hand. With your right hand, twist the spindle like a top (holding it in the air) in a clockwise direction and you will feel the wool twisting. (See Figure 8–2.)

6. Keep pulling out stands of wool and twisting the spindle until the spindle drops to the ground. Twisting the fibers together adds greater strength. Yarn spun in this direction is known as Z-twisted yarn. Yarn spun in the counter-clockwise direction is called S-twisted yarn. The thickness of the yarn is controlled by how fast you move your fingers.

7. When there is a large enough amount of yarn on the spindle, take it off and wrap the yarn around a cardboard tube.

8. Now the wool yarn should be scoured. Use warm-to-hot water, and add about 1½ teaspoons of detergent to 1 gallon of water plus ½ teaspoon of salt. Soak the yarn for a couple of hours. Rinse the yarn.

9. Do not wring the yarn, but hang it in the sun to dry. Now, reread Chapter 6 to dye your own spun yarn into beautiful colors.

Weaving Terms

In order to begin this skill, it is helpful to master a basic weaving vocabulary. The construction of all fiber products is expressed in the following weaving terms. It is amazing to analyze the similarities between the most simple primitive looms, used since prehistoric times, and the huge mechanized power looms found in textile factories.

Weaving begins with a set of threads stretched on a frame. Essentially, all looms have a stretched *warp*, a method for making a *shed*, a *shuttle* of some kind to carry the *weft* thread across the wrap, and a *beater* to press the weft down. (See Figure 8–5.)

WARP

The warp threads are the skeleton, or framework, of the fabric. They are stretched up and down the loom, whether the loom is made of cardboard, Masonite, or wood. In choosing the warp threads, remember to choose a yarn that does not have much stretch. Also test it for strength. Ordinary cotton string (carpet string or linen thread) is fine for warping as it does not have much stretch. You can also use the same yarn for warp and weft. An interesting effect is achieved by using dark-colored warps with light-colored weft threads.

WEFT

The weft threads are the ones that cross over and under and are woven into the warp threads. At times they are also called woof or filling. Choose a fiber that does not have much stretch, and test it for strength.

SHUTTLE

The device that carries the yarn over and under the warp is the shuttle. Fingers are used on small looms. Large-eyed needles (weaving needles), hairpins, cardboard with yarn wrapped around it, and Popsicle sticks that have been sanded to a point and have a hole drilled on the opposite end all make good shuttles. Even a pencil can be used: simply tie the yarn to a pencil, cover the tie with tape, wind on the yarn, and you have a shuttle. A simple shuttle can be made from coat hanger wire. Cut wire into 8-inch lengths. File smooth any sharp ends. Turn one end into a loop. Thread yarn through the loop and start weaving.

SHED

A shed stick helps to lift the alternating warps through which the shuttle is passed. A ruler, dowel, or flat piece of cardboard will act as a good shed stick. The shed is the opening created.

HEDDLE

The heddle is a loop device that, like the holes in the Popsicle stick loom, raises and lowers the warp threads.

BEATER

A beater is used to push the woven thread into place. One can use fingers, forks, or a large comb as a beater.

BUTTERFLY LOOPS

When weaving, stitching, crocheting, or knitting, wind the yarn ends over and catch with the plastic clip from a bread bag. For larger ends, wind the yarn over two fingers—the index finger and the pinky—in a figure eight, and then slip a bobby pin over the center of the yarn. For even larger ends,

roll the yarn into a figure eight and tie a rubber band in the center. This works well when macrameing with long ends; they just slip open as needed.

Scissors are necessary tools for cutting yarns. Masking tape is used to tape down the warps in the top and bottom slits in the cardboard loom. Baskets, boxes, or ice cream cartons are effective for sorting and storing yarns for color and texture.

TAPESTRY

Tapestry is a weaving technique that indicates a pictorial design incorporating methods of joining areas of color and textures. (See "Weaving Techniques," pages 281–282.)

Types of Looms

The type of loom considered for the classroom will be decided on by the amount of space available for storage, whether students will work independently or in groups, and how much money is available for purchasing looms and yarns. Materials often are donated by parents or obtained from other sources. One imaginative teacher obtains material from a textile factory, which contributes discarded cuttings from clothing—the fibers are knit and do not ravel. Another source could be a thrift store for scraps, ties, and old sweaters that can be unraveled.

INTRODUCING THE WEAVING CONCEPT

Here are two simplified versions for introducing the weaving concept to young students. Many kindergarteners are delighted to be able to manipulate simple weaving successfully. One method of explaining the procedure is to have ten students stand in a line in front of the group. Have the first student hold the end of a long piece of rope. Place the rope in front of the first student, behind the second student, in front of the third student, and so on. Go back from the end with the same process, this time alternating the ropes to illustrate the weaving process. When the students begin their weavings, provide experimentation time and encourage trial and error. Errors in the alternating concept are easily corrected with simplified looms.

Having precut yarn pieces of a determined length makes it possible for the student to pick up a new piece of yarn as he or she completes each row. Weaving back and forth with a shuttle and long yarns is difficult for the young weaver.

After the concept of weaving is understood, the child will be eager to produce his own original patterns and designs. This over-under weaving concept is a favorite for students of all ages and one of which children never seem to tire.

PAPER WEAVING (ON PAPER LOOMS)

Weave party place mats, celebration cards, paper baskets, and large paper costumes.

Supplies Needed
papers: tissue paper, wallpaper, magazines, newspaper, old candy wrappers, metallic paper, shelf paper, oak tag, and brown paper bags to be combined for unique colors and textures

Procedures
1. Paper warps can be cut straight, curved, or angular as well as cut into irregular shapes.
2. Or fold a 9 × 12-inch piece of paper in half lengthwise. Cut equal slits along the folded edge, and cut slits to within a 1-inch border left on the outer edges of the paper. Slits can also be cut into curved, angular, or irregular shapes, but be sure to cut along the folded edge and leave the border on the other two sides. This serves as the loom.
3. Cut the wefts from a second piece of paper. They can be cut into straight, curved, angular, or irregular slits. The second piece of paper can be of various textures and colors to create interesting visual effects.
4. Weave the paper wefts (second piece of paper) into the paper warps in the regular under-over pattern.

To introduce weaving concepts, have young students weave with precut pieces of rug yarns and other materials into permanent fabric looms. See section on fabric looms, p. 275.

WEAVING INTO CLOTH

Supplies Needed
heavy string, raffia, reeds, grasses, jute, telephone wire, pipe
  cleaners, ribbons, fake fur, lamb's wool, plastic, and yarns
plastic and canvas scrim (backing)
cotton mesh, such as dishcloths
netting, onion bags, and potato sacks
burlap
loosely woven fabrics (curtain and upholstery materials)

Procedure
1. Plan a simple felt-tip pen design and transfer it to cloth with permanent pens or crayons. Or plan to have the design develop spontaneously without previous planning, as in a sampler.
2. Scrim is a stiff, lightweight backing used in making hooked rugs and needlepoint. The large holes are appropriate for beginning weavers, as the concept of under and over can be easily learned. No loom is necessary with scrim.
3. Use other backings as well, such as cotton mesh cloth.
4. Burlap is a good introductory backing material. Mount the cloth on a wooden frame or embroidery hoop for easier handling (optional).
5. Weave in the outline designs.
6. Fill in the formed outlines with more weaving.
7. Experiment with various weaving materials and yarns.
8. Add colored cloth (glue on) in the front or on the back of the scrim for variety.
9. Weave puffs and loops of yarn to give height and texture.
10. Stuff small pieces of cloth and sew them into the scrim or cloth.
11. Add finger weavings, spool weavings, and knitting or crocheting to the woven designs.
12. When the weaving is completed, attach it to another backing (glue or sew on) and use it as a banner or wall hanging; use it alone or combine several weavings together for a large wall hanging.

8–6 *A cardboard loom warped with string has a free-form center design woven first with a large-eyed embroidery needle. The outside areas will then be woven in. The round carpet rolls, with nails, are for spool weaving; cut slits could be substituted for nails. Supersized knitting and crochet needles make the forms grow quickly.*

MAKING A CARDBOARD LOOM

Probably the most commonly used loom in the elementary school is the cardboard loom. It is easy to make, lightweight, easily stored, economically feasible, reusable, and it can be made in various shapes and sizes. Individual weavings are handsome alone, but stitched together they become a rug, an afghan, or a large wall hanging. Often, these small weavings are used as samplers whose basic design is then used for larger weavings. Sampler weaving encourages experimentation with exciting and unusual combinations of colors, textural relationships, and weaving techniques.

Procedures
1. Provide a rectangular piece of cardboard for each student. A good sampler size for a beginner is about 7 × 10 inches.
2. Cut any number of slits across the top and bottom, as long as the number is uneven—between eleven and fifteen works well. (Or glue down lined notebook paper vertically on a cardboard loom to obtain equal intervals. Hold the warp in place with pins.)
3. These are cut ½ inch down and are spaced approximately ½ inch apart.
4. Warp the loom with string, tying on the first loop.
5. Run the warps down, around, through, and up.
6. Continue this procedure until all the slits are warped. Tie off the last warped thread.
7. Place masking tape across the top and bottom; the tape will help hold the warp threads in place.
8. Proceed with the weaving using any of the materials previously suggested. As the students weave, remind them to leave a slight loop at the end of each row. This helps to keep the weaving from moving in tighter, as in an hourglass shape.
9. Or, provide each student with two straws, wires, or sticks to place at the first and last warp; these will hold the sides of the weaving straight as the student weaves.

Older students may want to develop large-sized weavings, work on individual looms, or work in groups on one large loom.

PLANNING THE DESIGN

When a design is planned for a cardboard loom, draw the design on the cardboard first with a felt-tip pen (underneath the warp). Weave the design shapes in first, with a large-eyed needle and pieces of yarn. Interesting round, oval, and irregular shapes are created in this way. Various weight yarns provide textural quality. To finish the project, use one of these techniques: plain weave, dovetailing, lock stitch, or tapestry slit. (See pages 281–282.)

A variation of the rectangular cardboard loom is the round cardboard loom. Start with a 7-inch round shape. Cut out a

1½-inch circle from the center. Cut ¼-inch slits around the outside. Tie on the first warp and wrap the string from the slits to the center, through the center, and around the back up to the slits. Continue around until the warps meet at the starting point. (See pages 277–278.)

Unique cardboard loom shapes can also be cut, perhaps as a design for a neckpiece. Cut the outside shape into the design. Cut the ¼-inch slits around the outside shape, and string the warp threads from top to bottom on the front side of the loom.

Projects for beginning weavers can range from individual wall hangings to small weavings sewn together to be displayed as a group tapestry. Narrow looms can be used for making belts and exciting neckpieces.

A special favorite of young weavers is the marble bag. To make the marble bag, use a cardboard loom about 6 inches square. Warp the loom at about ½-inch intervals and warp around the loom, both in front and back. When weaving, work completely around the loom so that there are no exposed edges. Continue to the bottom; and remove the loom. Sew the bottom closed. Open the top of the loom and tie two warps together, leaving the top open. Then use a heavy piece of yarn to weave in and out around near the top. Use it as a drawstring. This project makes especially good use of yarn scraps; patterns emerge from the multicolored yarns.

STYROFOAM LOOM

Supplies Needed
a small Styrofoam meat tray

8–8 The drawstring marble bag was woven by a third-grader around a cardboard loom. The landscape weaving on the left is the result of a combination of techniques: the round sun shape is a free-form needle weaving worked from the round outside edge in; the stripe pattern in the sky was produced by weaving the row over two and under two warps alternately. Note the lock stitch where two colors of yarn meet.

string

precut pieces of yarn, felt, vinyl, or bonded fabric

Procedure

1. Cut ½-inch slits about ½ inch apart across the top and bottom of the tray.
2. Use string for the warp and run the string from top to bottom on the front side.
3. Cover the top and bottom of the loom with tape to hold the warps.
4. Tie the beginning and the end strings on. Or, they can be taped to the back of the tray.
5. Weave with precut pieces of weft or fillings (either yarns, or ½-inch strips of felt or cloth).
6. The ends will extend a short way out the sides, making a fringe.
7. Weave the first weft over and under the string warp.
8. Weave the second weft under and over the string warp, alternating from the previous row and, thereby, creating a checkerboard effect.
9. Complete the weaving.
10. Remove the warps from the loom by carefully lifting the warp strings out of the slits.
11. Place a wood dowel, a stick, or a metal rod through the top warp loops so that the completed weaving can be hung and displayed.
12. Add fringes or tie beads, feathers, and additional decorative elements onto the bottom warps.
13. A small weaving can be appliquéd to a larger wall hanging or can be worn as a neckpiece by slipping a plastic thong through the top warps.
14. An alternative meat-tray loom (4½ × 8 inches) is made by placing masking tape along the top and bottom of a tray. Using embroidery thread, tape on the initial thread and warp around the front and back with nineteen warps. Weave with threads, as well as yarns. This loom is good for middle and upper grades. When the front weaving is

8–9 Plastic Styrofoam looms: meat tray for flat forms and cup for spool weaving. The Popsicle stick, tongue depressor (with grooves), and plastic embroidery needle are shuttles.

finished, cut along the center back, leaving long threads on the top and bottom of the weaving. These can then be macraméd or tied as you wish.

FABRIC LOOM

Supplies Needed
vinyl, felt, or bonded cloth, approximately 6 × 9 inches
½-inch strips of vinyl, felt, or bonded cloth for the wefts, 10 inches long
thick cut yarn, precut into 10-inch lengths

Procedure
1. Use 6 × 9-inch pieces of vinyl, felt, or bonded cloth for the basic loom.
2. Cut ten vertical slits ½ inch apart. Leave ¾-inch borders on all four sides.
3. Weave with 10-inch precut pieces of thick rug yarns and ½-inch-wide strips of felt or cloth 10 inches long.
4. Leave alternating woven wefts on the looms. Complete the weaving. (The teacher can sew stitches along the side on a sewing machine for permanency.)
5. Display the weaving.
6. Or, remove the wefts from the loom and reuse the looms.
7. Plastic fruit baskets (grocery store variety) also can be used as looms. (See Figure 8–12.)

PERMANENT FLAT LOOM

Supplies Needed
Masonite
white paint
power or hand saw

Procedure
1. For a more permanent flat loom, cut some untempered Masonite (approximately 9 × 12 inches) and paint the surface white.
2. Cut slits with a power saw to a depth of 1 inch and space them approximately ¼ inch apart. The slits can be cut on the top, bottom, and along the sides of the Masonite piece.
3. Warp the loom by running string or yarn from the top to the bottom, tying it together at the beginning and at the end. The warp can go around just the front or it can go around the front and back. This permits one to weave around the board, as for a purse with three closed edges.
4. Space the warp at equal intervals, but for variation try spacing the warps unequally. The warp will suggest unusual shapes as you weave and will encourage new and varied patterns.

8–10 *This teacher explains how her special education students take pride in working together on a woven rug, using a wood frame loom with a supporting leg to permit it to stand upright. Donated knit fabric scraps were cut to size and woven using the Ghiordes knot. Note the nails along the sides to keep edges straight.*

8–11 *A straw loom. The straws are the warps. Hold the loom in the palm of one hand; weave with the other. Tie on the weft and begin.*

5. Another variation is to add warp threads along the sides.
6. Weave experimentally wherever your threads appear.
7. Place masking tape over the slits and warp ends to hold the threads securely.

A variation of a substantial loom can be made from a piece of plywood and two 2-inch-thick boards for end pieces. These boards are nailed or epoxied on the board ends and nails are placed across each end to hold the warp. This loom is similar to a box loom made from an orange crate. An old wooden drawer or a cardboard box also makes a good loom. Try building unusual loom shapes with wood.

FRAME LOOM

A sturdy picture frame makes a good loom. Nails or slits are used to hold the warp threads.

Canvas stretcher frames, used by artists to hold their stretched canvas, are inexpensive, strong, and can be assembled quickly for weaving. These can be found wherever art supplies are sold and are available in all sizes. When the weaving is finished, the frames can be taken apart easily and can be used again in any combination of sizes.

STRAW LOOM

Straw looms are a fast weaving technique to make long sashes, belts, ties, wall hangings, table runners, pillows, and even rugs (when the lengths are stitched together).

Supplies Needed
six straws
yarn
scissors

Procedure
1. Cut six straws in half. The warps should be equal in length, which will be determined by what the woven

(a)

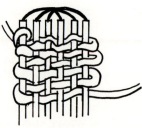

(b)

8–12 *A warp in a dark color produces an interesting pattern and texture. Strips of knit cloth are woven into the large weaving with the Ghiordes knot. The weaving on the right was woven on a plastic straw loom. Berry baskets and oak tag looms are used with rug yarns by young weavers.*

article will be. Six straws are commonly used (nine could be used, also); therefore, there will be six warp threads. (See Figure 8–11a.)

2. Tie all the threads together at one end. String makes a good nonstretching warp. (See "Overhand Knot," Figure 8–42.)
3. If there will be a fringe, allow some length for it.
4. Thread each warp thread through a straw. If there is difficulty getting a thread through a straw, suck the thread through gently (or use a piece of wire to push it through).
5. Push the straws to the end near the knot. Now begin weaving in the center of the straws.
6. Continue the over-under process until the weaving begins to fill the straws. (See Figure 8–11b.)
7. As you continue to weave, push the finished woven area up and off the straws onto the warp threads near the knot.
8. Continue weaving on the straws to the desired length.
9. Tie in new colors as you wish.

ROUND LOOM

A classroom favorite is a loom made from a cylindrical cereal or salt box. The warp runs from top to bottom. Try warping on a carpet roll for the same effect, or on a cottage cheese carton. Notch slits around the top at ½-inch intervals. Tie a warp to one notch. Proceed with the warp down the

8–13 *Weavings warped over old basketballs. Warps around a salt box or plastic container make good looms also. (Courtesy of Edna Gilbert, Mesa Public Schools, Mesa, Arizona.)*

side, across the bottom, up the opposite side, round the next notch, down the side, and so on. Continue around until the loom is warped. Begin the weaving underneath the box.

BACKSTRAP LOOM (POPSICLE STICK LOOM)

The backstrap, body, waist, stick, and belt looms are all basically the same loom. They all depend on the weaver for the warp tension. These looms are a little more difficult to use, as the weaver is very much a part of the loom.

Students in the upper grades or those with weaving experience will like the challenge of this loom. Start with warps about 4 feet long. After the weaving is finished, the long ends of the warps work very nicely into the macrame square knot fringe for a professional looking wall hanging.

This loom is popularly used in Scandinavia, South America, Mexico, Guatemala, and in Asian countries. Belts and other narrow and long articles are easily woven by this process.

Supplies Needed
wood tongue depressors or Popsicle sticks
yarn
stick (to hold the warps at one end)
cardboard shuttle (to hold yarn)
comb

8–14 *Backstrap loom and finished weaving. The heddle is made from Popsicle sticks with a hole drilled in the center of each. Warp tension is controlled by tying the weaving to the weaver. The finished weaving has a macrame fringe and appliquéd stars. (Courtesy of Margaret Burton.)*

Building a Backstrap Loom
1. Drill a hole through the center of the tongue depressors or Popsicle sticks—about six would be a good loom size for beginners. (See Figure 8–14.)
2. Space these about ¼ inch apart as they lie flat on a table.
3. Glue two sticks across the top edge on both the front and back.
4. Glue two sticks across the bottom edge on both the front and back.

The looms can be made as large as desired; just increase the number of added Popsicle sticks and the length of the cross sticks to accommodate them.

Procedure
1. Cut the warp threads about 2½ times the length of the finished weaving length. Double the warps (in half) over a holding stick with a lark's head knot (see page 302). Now the warp ends are about 1¼ times the needed length. The number of warps will depend on how many sticks are used in the loom. If there is one odd number left, simply tie the last warp to the holding stick.

2. Hook this holding stick to something stationary, such as a chair. (See Figure 8–5.)
3. Pass the loose warp ends through the heddle, alternating each strand through the drilled holes in the sticks and the open slits.
4. After the loom is warped, tie the remaining ends in an overhand knot and to a chair, doorknob, or stationary object.
5. Or, anchor the knot end to a belt or rope around your waist. Move back slowly until the warp threads are taut.
6. Attach the weaving yarn to a shuttle (tie it onto a pencil, or wrap it around a long thin piece of cardboard).
7. The Popsicle stick loom is the heddle. Push the heddle down. This causes the yarns in the holes to move down and the yarns between the sticks to move up. Thus, the warps form a shed, or open space, for the weft yarns and the shuttle to pass through.
8. Pass the shuttle (with yarn) through the shed.
9. Push the woven weft yarn up toward the stick end with fingers or a comb.
10. Now pull the heddle up and return the yarn through the separated space (shed).
11. Continue weaving by raising and lowering the heddle and passing the weft yarn back and forth. Complete the weaving.
12. When the weaving is finished, remove the wooden heddle.
13. With the remaining warp threads, tie a macrame square knot fringe along the bottom end.

FREE-FORM WEAVING

Free-form weaving depends on free-form warps. Any size or shape warp can be constructed using this technique.

Supplies Needed
sewing bolt or any soft board
pushpins
warp threads

yarns for weaving
needles (optional)

8–15 *Cardboard boxes, plywood sheets, and picture frames make good looms. Nails can be arranged straight across or in free form for variations in warps and weaving. Designs can be woven from original drawings placed under the weaving.*

Procedure

1. Place the pushpins in any shape desired: round, oval, or free-form.
2. With a short end, wind the yarn around a beginning pushpin.
3. Working in any direction desired, move the warp threads to the other pushpins; wind the thread around and go in another direction, winding around each pushpin.
4. Continue this procedure until all the pushpins have been wound and a warp is constructed. (Finish with an uneven number of warp threads. Tie the last thread.)
5. If there is a grouping of threads in the center, go over the warp threads with three or four stitches to hold them.
6. Begin the weaving toward the center of the design. Begin with about 2 yards of yarn; thread through the needle.
7. Where the warp is close, weave over and under two strands of warp at a time.
8. As it gets easier to weave, where the wrap is not so tight, weave over and under one strand at a time.
9. Keep the weaving loose so that the warps are not pulled out of line. If the yarn is pulled too tightly during the weaving, the finished shape will curl up when it is removed from the loom.
10. Keep a good even tension and push toward the center. Fill in any irregular shapes with yarn weaving.
11. To begin a new color, tuck the ends of the yarn underneath the worked areas and weave in the new yarn as you work.
12. The loose ends can be woven into the back after the product is finished and has been removed from the board.
13. Cut off any excess ends.

8–16 *Circular and oddly shaped looms encourage unique weaving solutions. The weaving at the upper left was done on a cardboard loom with outside and inside edges notched for the warp. The weaving at the upper right is over a wire frame. The weaving at lower left was done on a cardboard loom with the outside edges notched and the warps crossed in the center. Circular weavings are ordinarily done from the center out. Weaving at lower center is a wrapped embroidery hoop, partially warped and woven.*

14. Develop any shape in the weaving by placing the pushpins as desired. Flowers, animals, and free forms can be woven this way.
15. Remove the weaving by simply pulling out the pushpins. Add any ornamentation, such as cloth-filled puffs, beads, fringes, or feathers.
16. Suspend free-form weavings from twigs or dowels for display. Or appliqué the weavings to a backing such as burlap. For a group project, assemble several individual weavings on a large backing. After the project has been displayed, return the weavings to the designers to be mounted on individual cloth backings and framed, if desired.

Another kind of free-form weaving is done on a stick or twig loom. This is actually an ancient Indian method of weaving. Find some Y-shaped branches. String the warp back and forth over the forked ends. Weave through the warps.

FLAT CIRCLE LOOM (ROUND LOOM)

These looms can be made from cardboard, or embroidery hoops, wire, and even wheels. Coat hanger wire can be used to create unusually shaped looms—even three-dimensional ones. Two embroidery hoops will create a form within a form, with the warp within the two.

8–17 *Warps and weavings can be on three-dimensional forms such as this tree branch.*

Weaving Techniques

PLAIN WEAVE

The plain weave is the basic over-under procedure. For variation, begin the plain weave in the middle of the warps, beginning somewhere inside the warp. Weave in a curved design. Weave over and under several warps, turn around and come back under and over the same warps, and turn back again and weave adding rows to the curved design. Enlarge the design by including a warp thread as you come to the turnaround. After completing about twelve rows, turn the loom around and begin other curved designs. If an eye shape has been created, select another color and fill the open space with more plain weave.

TAPESTRY SLIT

In regular weaving, the weft yarn moves all across the warps. In tapestry slit weaving, the weft yarn moves partly

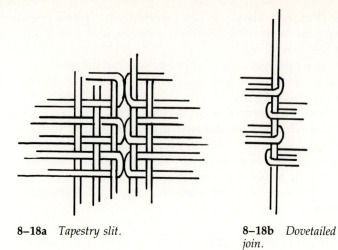

8–18a *Tapestry slit.*

8–18b *Dovetailed
join.*

across the warps and turns back. Then, the weft yarn weaves
up to the slit from the opposite side and also turns back. As
more rows are added, being completed in the same manner,
an open slit appears in the weaving where the two yarns
meet but do not interlock. (See Figure 8–18a.)

DOVETAILED JOIN

When a design is placed on a weaving, the weft threads
will meet. In this joining, the yarns meet alternately on the
same warp (see Figure 8–18b.)

LOCK STITCH

Two weft yarns that meet and interlock between the warp
threads are a lock stitch. (See Figure 8–19.)

GHIORDES KNOT

This knot can be woven first and then cut to the length
desired. Or it can be individually woven with strips of fabric,

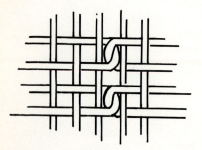

8–19 *Lock stitch.*

8–20 *Ghiordes knot.*

8–21 *Egyptian knot.*

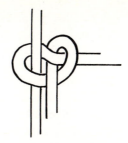

8–22 *Weaver's knot.*

as shown in Figure 8–10. After weaving, the loops can be cut for a fringed effect. (See Figure 8–20.)

EGYPTIAN KNOT

The weft cord loops around the warp resulting in a beadlike effect. (See Figure 8–21.)

WEAVER'S KNOT

The Weaver's knot is like a figure eight and also catches the warp. It is used to anchor a cord to the warp, as when adding a new weft cord. (See Figure 8–22.)

Unusual Weaving Techniques

WEAVING WITH BEADS

Beads are great fun to weave with to be worn as necklaces, bracelets, and rings or as decorations on clothing and shoes. Bead weaving is a craft appropriate to the intermediate grades. Many types of looms for weaving with beads are available commercially, but why not make your own?

MAKING A BEAD LOOM

1. Make a small wooden frame, or use an old wooden picture frame, making sure it is small enough for your design.
2. Make notches on both ends, at the top and bottom to attach the warp threads.
3. Begin at the right-hand notch, knotting the thread.
4. Wind the thread by passing it over the top, down the other end, under the bottom notch, and up over the notched end at the top.
5. Warp the frame until the desired threads are strung. Be

Weaving and Macrame

sure to warp (add) one more thread than the number in the bead design in the width.

6. Tie the last warp to the last notch in the loom (on the left-hand side of the loom).
7. Make sure the warp is secure and tight.

Supplies Needed

graph paper (optional)
beading loom
bead needles (or regular needles small enough to pass through the eye of the bead)
beading thread (available in hobby stores) or regular strong thread
assortment of colored beads, old jewelry, and pearls

Procedure

1. Plan your design. It can be a flower, a heart, anything whose design can be squared off—letters and words make good designs.
2. Organize the design on graph paper with ⅛-inch blocks.
3. Plan one square for each bead.
4. Beginners may want to keep the color plan simple, with one color for background and one or two colors for the foreground design.
5. A thin bead needle is used with a fine, strong thread.
6. Tie the thread in a small knot to the first warp thread on the top right (of the loom).
7. String on the beads needed for the first row.
8. Bring the beads and thread under the warp toward the left side.
9. Place each bead between a warp thread, and gently pull the bead string tight.
10. Bring the bead string up and over on the left side, and go back through each bead with the needle as you head toward the right side.
11. Continue this procedure, picking up the various beads according to your design, and finish each row.

8–23 *Finger weaving.*

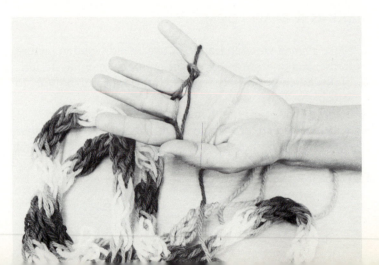

FINGER WEAVING

Supplies Needed
yarn

Procedure
1. Place the end of the yarn in the palm.
2. Pass the yarn between the thumb and forefinger.
3. Go behind the forefinger, in front of the middle finger, in back of the ring finger, and wrap the yarn around the little finger.
4. Then weave the yarn in front of the ring finger, in back of the middle finger, and in front of the ring finger.
5. Wrap the yarn around the back of the hand, across the palm, and hold it down with the thumb.
6. Starting with the little finger, take the yarn that has been woven in and out around the fingers and lift it over the top of the unwrapped yarn, one finger at a time.
7. When you reach the index finger, lift the yarn off and wrap a strand around the hand again.
8. Lift one strand at a time, starting at the little finger.
9. When you have the piece as long as you want it, cut the yarn and lift one strand at a time, looping it under the next finger's yarn (chain).
10. Loop the end of the strand through the last hoop to keep it from raveling.
11. Pull the yarn gently to straighten the weaving.

8–24 *In these examples of finger weaving, the yarn is used as the warp and the weft. On the left is the chevron design; on the right, the diagonal.*

THE CHEVRON

In the examples of finger weaving shown in Figure 8–24, the yarn threads are used both as warp and weft; the yarn commonly used is four-ply knitting yarn. The example on the left is the chevron design. This finger weaving begins with nine long cords that are doubled and placed on the dowel in a lark's head knot.

Procedure
1. Locate the middle of the cords and start with the first cord left of the center.
2. With one hand, start in the center and move toward the right, picking up the odd-numbered cords.
3. With the other hand, weave the first cord through the cords in the other hand.
4. Do the same with the center-right cord, moving toward the left.
5. The left-of-center cord always is woven to the right, and the right-of-center cord always is woven to the left.
6. Keep the warp threads in correct position.

Weaving and Macrame

285

THE DIAGONAL DESIGN

The example on right in Figure 8–24 is the diagonal design.

Procedure
1. Note the six cords mounted on the dowel with a lark's head knot.
2. Begin with the left outside cord and weave to the right edge.
3. Continue weaving always from left to right, being sure to keep the cords pulled in a straight line, as the diagonal pattern emerges.
4. For variety, try these patterns with variously colored yarns.
5. In both of these finger-weaving techniques, it is important to keep the warps and wefts in place.

TWINING

Twining is another form of finger weaving. The technique is inspired by the examples of the Nez Percé Indians of Oregon who excelled in twining handsome corn husks and other natural fibers into tote bags. We have interpreted twining for classroom use by using yarns and accessory beads or feathers. Actually, the Nez Percé revived an ancient craft that dates back to 2500 B.C., according to Junius Bird of the American Museum of Natural History. Other excellent complex examples of twining have been found in the Chicama Valley in northern Peru. This twining technique gives spectacular results when used for bags, baskets, floor mats, and lampshades.

Twining simply means to encircle a wrap thread (see Figure 8–25a and b); that is, to twist the weft yarns around the wrap thread. One weft thread comes from behind the warp thread, the other over the warp thread, and the two wefts cross each other between the warp threads.

8–25 *Twining.*

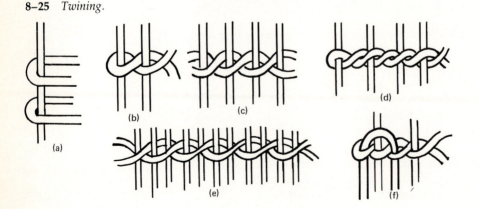

In *twining*, the warp cord is the vertical cord. It is cut twice the length needed, as it is folded and mounted with a lark's head knot to the top holding cord. Cut the mounting cord (horizontal cord in diagram) approximately three times the finished width. Find the middle of the mounting cord and place it around the warp cord. (See Figure 8–25a.)

Twist the mounting cord and place another warp cord through the center. Twist again and continue with the procedure as shown in Figure 8–25b and c. The half twist is shown in c; the full twist is shown in d; and a half twist enclosing two warp cords is shown in e. Figure 8–25f shows how to add additional warp cords into the twists as you are twining.

Encourage experimentation once the basic procedure is learned. You can create new and different patterns and designs.

Even young students can do twining, and everyone will be amazed at the success and beauty of the product. Older students will want to experiment by combining double half-hitch macrame knots with the twining as well as square knots, tying, beads, and found objects.

Supplies Needed
sewing bolt or cardboard (approximately 7 × 10 inches)
yarns
beads

Procedure
The purse in Figure 8–26 was twined in the round. In other words, the twining went all around the board that held the warp thread. (Warp cords are called threads here to differentiate.)

1. Tie a holding cord around the cardboard loom.
2. Secure the holding cord with pins or tape.
3. Add the warp threads to a free-hanging holding cord with reverse double half hitches.
4. Start twining by manipulating the fingers.
5. The weft cords are double cords, so either plan both to be of the same color, or alternate the color with two different colored weft cords.
6. Double the cord if it is the same color, or tie the two different colors with an overhand knot.
7. Begin twining. Twining can go around the warp thread in different ways:
   a. in a half twist in between the warp threads (See Figure 8–25c.)
   b. in a half twist between every two warp threads (See Figure 8–25e.)
   c. in a full twist between warp threads (See Figure 8–25d.)

8–26 *Twining around a sewing bolt. In the example at the right, the top yarn is the holding cord. The loose warps are doubled and mounted on the holding cord in a lark's head knot and remain loose. The weft cords are mounted as shown in Figure 8–25a. A variety of turns and yarn weights and colors add interest. Beads have been added to the finished purse and wrapping finished the cords at the bottom.*

   d. in a combination of half turns between and then full turns
   e. in a combination of turns and alternating rows
   f. in rows very close together or spaced far apart so that the warp shows
8. The unique variations possible provide opportunities to be creative and add excitement to the process. Many textures and patterns are possible by varying the threads, either in the warp or weft. (See Figure 8–25f.)
9. Try beautiful color combinations, too, or add beads to the exposed warp.
10. At the bottom of the purse, close the warps with a series of square knots. Twining around a rectangular soft board makes a beautiful purse.
11. Line the inside, and finger braid a handle. Twining is spectacular on a lampshade.

BRAIDING

Procedure (See Figure 8–27)
1. Knot four or five cords (yarns) together at one end in an overhand knot.

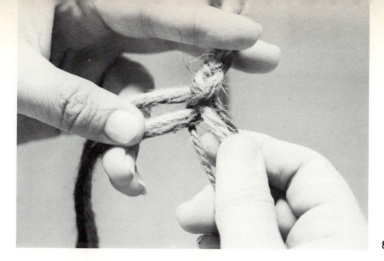

8–27 *Finger braiding.*

2. Begin braiding with an outside cord, going under two cords and forward over one.
3. Take the opposite outside cord and do the same thing in the opposite direction.
4. Continue braiding.
5. Finish with an overhand knot. This produces a round braid.

Braiding is commonly done with cloth scraps and has long been a favorite process in rug making. Scraps are about 1½ inches wide and about 1 yard long (sew scraps together to achieve this length). After braiding, the long braids are formed into a flat oval and loosely, but securely, sewn together to make a rug.

SPOOL WEAVING

It is great fun to spool weave on an empty thread spool. Spool weaving is simple to do, and very young, as well as uppergrade, children will enjoy it with equal fascination. As you weave, you will be compelled to see how long the coil can be made to grow.

The larger the spool hole, the thicker will be the woven cord. You can also vary the weaving by using various thicknesses of yarn. Yarn that is variegated produces designs with horizontally striped coils. Weaving with one color and then changing to another color results in an appealing two-tone technique.

Any number of nails can be applied to the top of a spool—from four to twenty. The fewer the nails, the faster and easier the weaving and the longer the cord will grow.

The same process can be used to weave fine metal on a spool. Thin, lightweight brass, copper, or steel wire, when woven, will produce wire cords that can be made into jewelry.

Weaving and Macrame

Use an empty thread spool. An empty carpet roll from a carpet store or a paper cup can also be used. Saw off several lengths of the roll and then carefully hammer five brads or nails along the circular top, spacing them evenly (be careful not to split the cardboard). If using a paper cup, cut out notches along the top, and cut the bottom off. The weaving can be done with another nail, a crochet hook, or with just the fingers. Remember to keep the yarn very loose as you weave and loop. Acrylic and wool yarns have the most elasticity. A variation can be made from a block of wood: saw out a circular center and hammer in the nails. (See Figures 8–6 and 8–9.)

Supplies Needed
nails
crochet hook (optional)
decorations
empty thread spool, carpet roll, or paper cup
yarn

Procedure
1. Drop the end of the yarn through the hole.
2. Wrap the strand of yarn around each nail once, going from left to right.
3. After wrapping all the nails, place the yarn around and on top of the first loops.
4. With a blunt nail or needle take the bottom thread and loop it over the top thread and over the nail. This leaves a single thread on the nail. (This process is the same as that used for the frame loom. See Figure 8–29.)
5. After the first round, continue in the same way.
6. Tug the tube as it grows.
7. To finish the tube, bind off by cutting the yarn, leaving enough thread to pull the yarn through each loop.
8. Take the tube off the spool and pull it tightly so that the top will close. (You may want to fill the woven tube with cotton batting or old stockings to keep it round.)
9. Now that you have the tube, add arms and tube legs (all kinds of wild animals can be formed). People, birds, fish, dolls, and puppets all take form and can be decorated by adding felt, beads, yarns and lace.
10. Try several different-sized tubes and create fanciful creatures.
11. Long tubes can also be used for belts.
12. Tubes sewn together can create other objects such as mats, purses, and pillow tops.
13. Add fringes, tassels, pom-poms, and beads for decorations to the objects listed in step 12.

FRAME WEAVING

Frame weaving is similar to spool weaving in that the woven article is produced by passing yarns over nails, and it emerges from a hole in the center. In this case, the object woven takes on a flat shape, as the loom is long. The object appears to have been knitted and grows very quickly. Weave purses, scarves, pillows, and doll shapes. Add decorative elements such as pom-poms, fringes, beads, tassels, handles, and appliqués.

CONSTRUCTING A FRAME LOOM

Supplies Needed
four pieces of wood: two long pieces about 12 inches long and 3 inches wide, plus two shorter pieces about 7 inches long (size is optional and depends on individual needs)
brads

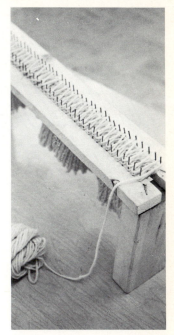

8–28 *Frame weaving. The loom in the photograph has 42 nails on each side.*

Procedure
1. Use the two long pieces of wood for the top and bottom, leaving about a ½-inch slot opening.
2. Place the two short pieces of wood on the sides and nail them to the other pieces to form a rectangle.
3. Mark the spots for the nails. They will be placed directly opposite each other, about ½ inch from each other, and ¼ inch in from the slot opening. Hammer in the nails.

WEAVING ON A FRAME LOOM

Supplies Needed
loom   yarns
nails   crochet hook (optional)

Procedure
1. Knot the yarn around the first top nail.
2. Move the yarn down and around the bottom nail.
3. Bring the yarn up and around the second nail in a zigzag fashion.
4. Continue warping until all the nails have been covered.
5. Bring the yarn up around last bottom nail, and go around the top nail again.
6. Wind the yarn back toward the left side of the loom, in a zigzag fashion, covering each nail twice. Continue winding over the nails until you are back at the starting nail.
7. With a nail, crochet hook, or fingers, bring the bottom

Weaving and Macrame

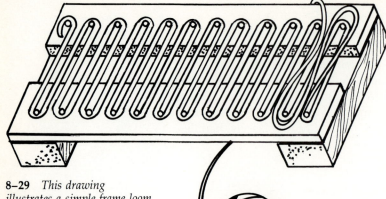

8–29 *This drawing illustrates a simple frame loom with 12 nails. The yarn is criss-crossed back and forth. The bottom loop on the nail is pulled over the top loop on the same nail and the weaving emerges from the bottom. Vary the yarn texture, the width of the slot, and the distance between nails for different effects.*

8–30 Ojos de Dios *over dowels, cotton swabs, Popsicle sticks, and Tinkertoys. Tassels, feathers, beads, and shells are often used for adornment.*

yarn strand over the top of the nail and off the nail to create a loop. Do this process on each nail to form the weave.

8. The weaving will grow through the opening in the loom. Gently pull the weaving as it progresses to keep it even.
9. Continue weaving until the desired length is reached.
10. Bind off, carefully removing the weaving from nails. Bring the two sides together and use the overcast stitch to close them. Knot the last thread.

OJO DE DIOS—MEXICAN GOD'S EYE

Do you wish for some good luck, health, happiness, and good fortune? Traditionally, in Mexico, the sacred "Eye of God" decorative weavings are hung above doorways to protect and bring good luck to the household within.

The original Sikuli prayer stick is diamond-shaped with a center eye. The tufts of yarn at the ends of the sticks represent clouds that will help to bring the rain. Tassels mean the wish for health and long life. The God's eye always represents good, and a prayer to God for good health, good fortune, and good crops.

In the 1950s New Mexico artists discovered the symbolic eye in Old Mexico. The artists brought the idea back with them and have enlarged upon it. Today many Southwestern weavers, including the women in the Navajo culture, practice this art.

The craft is exciting and fun for all ages and easily learned. The designs can be as simple or as complex as desired. The yarn ornaments are delightful to look at and add gaiety to a classroom when they are suspended individually from the ceiling and turn like mobiles. Hang them on walls, in windows, in your hair, or around your neck for good luck.

Supplies Needed
yarns, string, threads or raffia (use up odds and ends of yarns)

dowels, twigs, toothpicks, counting sticks, Popsicle sticks, cotton swabs, Tinkertoy rods, stirrers or pencils (two the same size)

glue

scissors

Procedure
1. Cross two sticks together, so their arms are equidistant; tie the sticks together at the center. A touch of white glue or a rubber band will keep the sticks together. Notch the sticks at their centers, if desired.
2. Begin at the center joint and wrap the yarn back and forth over both arms to keep it firm.
3. To start weaving, wrap the yarn once around one of the arms.
4. Span the open area between the arms, and then wrap the yarn around the second arm.
5. Span the area again to wrap the third arm, and continue to wrap the fourth arm.
6. Continue this procedure. Do not cross over the previously laid yarns.
7. For variety, wrap the yarn around an arm twice, leaving a wider space between the yarns before going on to the next dowel.
8. The tension created by the wrapping will hold the sticks together. Try to keep the tensions even.
9. To change color, knot a new yarn to old yarn on the underside of the ojo.
10. Another way to change color is to end a color on the same dowel on which you started (using a spot of white glue). Attach the new yarn to a different dowel by adding a spot of glue (or knot it on).
11. Experiment by wrapping two colored yarns at one time.
12. A beautiful design results by twisting two yarns together as you go.
13. Vary the thicknesses of yarns.
14. To backwrap, turn (reverse) the sticks and wrap them from the opposite side. This achieves a high and low relief, or sculptured effect.
15. Larger dowels create a deeper front-to-back space.
16. Try four sticks together for a more complex pattern.
17. Add pom-poms, feathers, bells, and beads to the ends of the sticks.
18. Experiment with new ways of crossing and adding sticks.

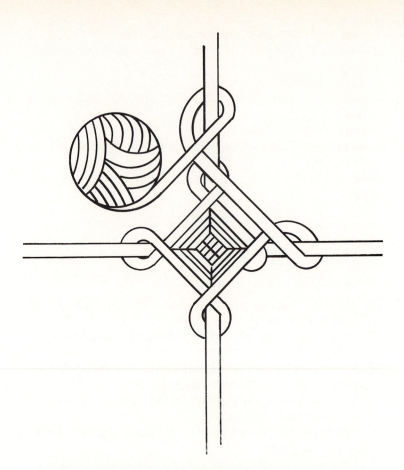

Try the same procedure on an irregularly shaped tree branch. Combine several small eyes to form a giant weaving.

19. For more complex designs, start with a long dowel and add cross sticks at varying angles; thus, when the wrapping is done, a more nearly three-dimensional sculpture is formed.

One fourth-grade teacher decided to do this good-luck symbol as a project for Christmas gifts. She used Tinkertoys as centers, which were donated by some parents. Other parents helped cut the ¼-inch dowels to fit the Tinkertoy—to a length of about 5 inches. Gluing the dowels in with a glue gun went quickly. With some of the 25-cents gift money she had collected at the beginning of the year, she purchased ten skeins of yarn. The colors she chose were red, white, and black. This amount was adequate for twenty-five God's eyes that measured eight sticks around, with stick lengths of about 11 inches. Another help was the common clip clothespin. This was used to hold the yarn in place and keep it from raveling whenever the students had to stop.

Marking the dowels at 1-inch intervals with a pencil helped

the students know when to change designs and colors. Running a small band of glue along the length of the dowel helped keep the yarns in place.

Along with adding cheerful holiday gaiety to the classroom, twenty-five students and their parents were very pleased. The designs were very beautiful and varied, the students had acquired a weaving skill, and a traditional art form had been explored from another culture.

Basket Weaving

Basket weaving is one of the oldest crafts on the American continent. It is known that coiled baskets were made by the Anasazi people as early as A.D. 500. Today, the Hopi Indians of Northern Arizona, Anasazi descendants, continue to make beautifully decorated, traditional coiled baskets and plaques

8–32 *"Vulture Basket" by Carol Eckert. The basket, 7 inches × 8 ½ inches, is made with the coil method using cotton threads over wire. The vulture is made the same way. (Courtesy of the artist.)*

out of fat, round coils of grass sewn with split yucca fibers. Some grass is dyed with native vegetable dyes (wild tea and sunflower seeds). The bright colors used in plaques are dyed with aniline dyes. The harvesting and preparation of plant materials require great knowledge and skill. Many basket makers travel long distances to find the most appropriate materials.

Pima baskets have wheat bundles as foundations and are bound with willow, cottonwood, or mesquite bark. The black decorations are small coils made by using devil's claw, a cultivated desert plant.

The Papago Indians of central Arizona are also noted for their basketry and use of the coiled technique. They use bear grass, young ocotillo stems, saquaro ribs, or straw bundles as the base, and sew with mesquite, yucca, and devil's claw. The decoration is usually simple geometric designs.

The Apache Indians produce coiled basketry for storage jars. They use three rods of willow or cottonwood and sew the coils together with splints of willow or cottonwood. Other rod baskets are sewn with split yucca leaves that are bleached to yellow, green, and white.

The Navajos produce a small number of baskets out of sumac. The baskets are primarily used for carrying, sifting, and washing grains.

The most beautiful baskets are aesthetic blends of shape and decorative designs. Designs are sometimes traditional, handed down from mother to daughter; the geometric, figurative, or symbolic designs represent people, plants, or animals in the weaver's life. Decorations of stones, shells, and bird feathers are sometimes added to the surface.

In Figure 8–33, Papago basket weavers produce baskets of fine craftsmanship, spending many hours perfecting their skill. As children, they learn how to gather, dye, and prepare the yucca leaves and devil's claw plant. Plastic dishes hold water in which to soak the grasses to make them pliable. The tools are simple; a knife to cut and split the grasses, and an awl to make the holes.

WEAVING RAG OR YARN BASKETS, PAPAGO STYLE

Most Indian baskets are woven with reeds and grasses. In the classroom, young students can weave with substitute materials such as clothesline for warp and cloth rags, string, or yarn for weft, in order to understand the coil concept and to create easy-to-construct baskets. This coil technique is the basket-weaving procedure of the Papago Indians.

Supplies Needed
clothesline (try corn husks, jute, or rags as a warp variation)

¾-inch strips 2 yards long of double-knit fabric in two colors
  (old skirts or pants will do)
3-inch yarn needle with a ½-inch eye, or large darning
  needles yarn

Procedure
  1. Use old clothesline, jute, or heavy twine for the warp and
     the knit fabric or yarn for the weft (which slips into the
     needle's eye for weaving).
  2. If lengths longer than 2 yards are necessary, simply sew
     or knot more fabric strips or yarn together and add them
     on. (Start with a warp 2 yards long and a weft 1 yard
     long.)
  3. To begin, sew a fabric warp strip and a weft strip
     together. If yarn is used, simply begin coiling around the
     warp (clothesline) with the yarn until a small circle is
     completed. The coiled process begins with a flat circle,
     called the mat.
  4. Thread the weft strip into the needle.
  5. Working counterclockwise, continue coiling the weft
     around the warp until you go around the small circle.
  6. For the second row, continue coiling around the warp,
     but sew the weft through each of the previous row coils
     until the circle is complete; or coil around the warp five
     times with the yarn warp. On the sixth coil, go around
     the previous row as well. Continue with five more coils;
     the sixth going around the two warps together. Continue
     this procedure.

Weaving and Macrame

7. Keep the weaving loose as you go.
8. To shape the basket, add or decrease the warp strip and coils in subsequent rows.
9. To begin shaping upward, hold the warp strip just out and a little on top rather than directly beside the previous row.
10. Continue up until you reach the desired width of the basket.
11. Then bring the shape inward (a little narrower) as you proceed upward, by subtracting (or skipping loops) and tightening the warp until the desired shape is reached. Add colors and designs as you wish.
12. To finish the basket, weave a few inches of weft inside several coils on the preceding warp.

Macrame

If you can tie a shoelace, you can do macrame. It looks complicated, but once you master the two basic knots—the square knot and the double half hitch—you will be amazed at your accomplishments. You soon will want to develop your own knot combinations. Macrame is a versatile handicraft, it is relatively inexpensive, and it can be carried about easily to be worked on anywhere. Teachers as well as children, even in the first grade, like this craftwork. With clear instructions, young students learn to manipulate the cords quickly and successfully. Starting with a simple project, such as key ring or neckpiece, the student will soon have fun discovering the many variations of the two knots and begin experimenting with imaginative designs. Before you know it, everyone in

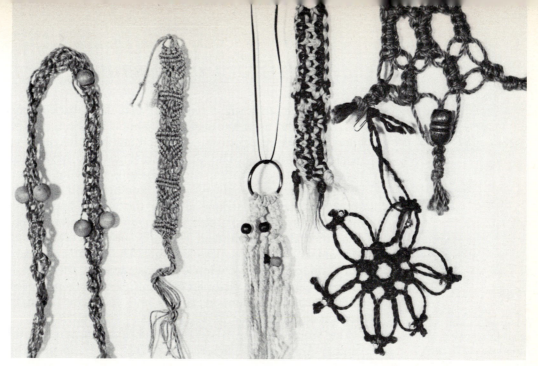

the class will be creating unusual and exciting macrame objects.

Today, macrame is enjoying a broad revival. Enthusiasts all over the world are creating masterful handcrafted pieces, from jewelry, to belts, to large sculptures and hangings. The craft appeals to people of all ages, and all enjoy producing items that are aesthetic as well as utilitarian.

8–35 *Examples of macrame completed by first- through sixth-graders; belts, necklaces, key rings (which can be worn as necklaces), and snowflake ornament. The snowflake is begun from a 1-inch curtain ring at its center.*

8–36 *Macrame belts, wall hangings, and necklaces. Butterfly loops, lower right, are held with rubber bands to keep the cords workable. Driftwood complements the textures and shapes of the yarn. Shells and beads are added.*

History of Macrame

8–37 *An inventive macrame design on a tennis racket. The handle is wrapped. Note the paper weaving in back.*

Macrame is an ancient handcraft that dates back to the Egyptians who used knots in their fishnets and fringes. The knots in jewelry, pottery, and clothing had religious or magical significance. The Greeks are known to have used these knots for recreation and in making slings for broken bones. Sailors have always done knotting and probably spread the art of macrame all over the world. They spent many hours creating knotted objects with which they decorated their ships and traded. The sailor's work is often called McNamara's lace, or square knotting. The Indians of northern California have evidence of macrame in their headdresses. During the Victorian era, European craftsmen used knots as a decoration on gowns and coats and even in household items such as bedspreads.

The word *macrame* is derived from either a nineteenth-century Arabic term, *migramah* (meaning "veil"), or from the Turkish word for "towel," *magramah*. Both items were decorated with a knotted fringe.

Macrame Supplies

WORKING CORDS

Working cords can be purchased in hardware, grocery, hobby, weaving, leather, and dime stores. They include any material that can be knotted easily, does not stretch too much, and can be obtained in long lengths—such as jute and cotton cord. These cords are constructed from fibers that come from plants and animals (see pages 262–264).

Acrylic rug yarns work well for some macrame articles, but they are too soft for large projects. Nylon, although it looks and feels silky and comes in a variety of weights from fishing line to heavy rope, does not hold the knots very well. The fiber is adequate when it is combined with cotton or wool, but it is difficult to work with for beginning students. If nylon is used, be sure to finish the ends off (as they will ravel) by either melting the end with a match flame or dipping it into nail polish.

WORKING SURFACES

To do macrame one needs any lightweight, rigid surface that will take pins (we like masking tape to hold the holding cords down): for instance, Styrofoam blocks; small, firm Styrofoam trays, such as meat trays; the bottoms of flat, sturdy cardboard boxes set upside down; clipboards; squared-off Celotex boards; three layers of cardboard taped together; wall board with taped edges; pillows; cork; and fabric bolts cut in half. The sailor's favorite knotting method is to tie a holding cord around the knee and macrame from it.

Macrame Knots

Supplies Needed
decorative accessories (beads)
a lightweight, rigid working surface
masking tape
rubber bands (string, or bobby pins to hold butterfly loops)
tape measure or ruler
T-pins
working cords

Procedure
1. Cut the working cord eight times the finished length of the sampler to be macramed.
2. Fold each cord in half. This means that each *working* cord will be four times the finished length of the sampler.
3. When demonstrating the knots, tape the working cords to the chalkboard.
4. Use cords of two different colors. Because the two inside cords do not tie in a square knot, tape them down with masking tape. Leave the two outside cords loose to be worked.
5. Demonstrate the "4" method of the square knot. (See Figure 8–39.) Ask the students to follow as you move the cords. Wait for everyone to catch up. Neighbors can help each other.
6. Instruct students to do half the square knot so that the twisted knotting appears. Complete about three half square knots.
7. Instruct students to do the rest of the square knot. Then have them complete three full square knots. Usually, they understand the knot by this method.
8. After making several of these knots, demonstrate the alternating square knot. (See Figure 8–40.)
9. Continue with a demonstration of the double half hitch in the same manner. (See Figure 8–41.)
10. The overhand knot can be used as a finishing knot after all the knotting is completed. (See Figure 8–42.)
11. If desired, comb out the ends to make a soft fringe along the bottom of the piece.
12. After the students have mastered the basic knots, plan a simple sampler necklace or key chain.

13. Encourage the students to develop further ideas, patterns, and sequences of knots.
14. Display numerous good examples and illustrations to help clarify the processes.
15. Artistic growth takes place when students learn to develop their own designs for pot slings, purses, belts, headbands, dog leash, wall hangings, and sculptures.

LARK'S HEAD KNOT (MOUNTING KNOT)

Procedure

1. Fold the cord in half and place the loop over the horizontal holding rod (wood dowel, wooden spoon, tree branch, or rope). (See Figure 8–38a and b.)
2. Reach under the loop and bring the two loop ends down under the holding rod and through the loop. (See Figure 8–38c.)
3. Pull down the two loose cords and tighten them comfortably. This attaches the cord to the holding rod. (See Figure 8–38d.)

SQUARE KNOT

Procedure

1. Bring the left cord over the two center cords. (See Figure 8–39c.)
2. Place this cord under the right cord, creating a "4." (See Figure 8–39b.)
3. Bring the right cord under the two anchor cords and up through the loop formed by the left cord. (See Figure 8–39c.)
4. Pull and you have half the square knot. By repeating just this half knot, you produce a spiral.
5. Bring the right cord over and to the left of the two anchor cords. (See Figure 8–39d.)
6. Place the left cord over the right cord. (See Figure 8–39d.)
7. Bring the left cord under the anchors and up through the loop formed by the right cord. (See Figure 8–39e.)

8–38 *Lark's head knot (mounting knot).*

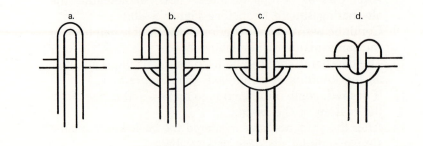

a. b. c. d.

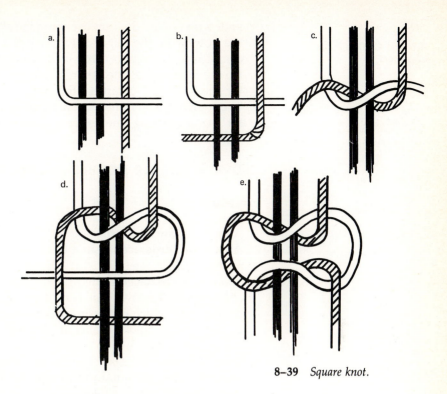

8–39 *Square knot.*

8. Pull gently and you have the completed knot. By making the knot tight or loose, a different visual effect is achieved. Repeat the square knot several times.

ALTERNATING SQUARE KNOT

Procedure
1. Make square knots across the row in the usual way.
2. In the second row, *leave* the first two cords, the square

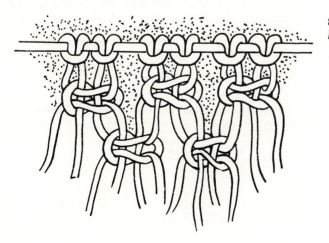

8–40 *Alternating square knot.*

knot with two cords from each previous knot. Knot across the row with the regular four cords until the row is completed. *Leave* two cords at the end of the row.

3. Do the third row as the first row, using the first four cords for the knot and complete the row.
4. The fourth row is done as row number 2. Alternate rows for the alternating knot. (See Figure 8–40.)

CLOVE HITCH, OR DOUBLE HALF-HITCH KNOT

Procedure

1. Attach the anchor cord.
2. Attach the cords needed in a lark's head knot around the anchor cord.
3. Make a "4" by placing the first left cord on top of all the cords across the row. This cord then becomes the anchor cord around which each cord will be knotted in a horizontal row. Pin or hold this anchor cord *taut*. Tie a small knot at the end of the cord to identify it and avoid confusion.
4. Bring the next cord *under* the anchor cord, loop it up over and around to the left and through the loop. Tighten the loop. This is half the knot.
5. The second half of the knot is made directly next to the first half. Bring the same knotting cord up and over the anchor cord, and loop around to the left and through the loop. Tighten the knot.
6. Push each knot next to the previous knot to achieve an even appearance. Pick up the next working cord. Continue the knots across the row.
7. This knot can be made horizontally, vertically, and diagonally by knotting around an anchor cord in the direction desired.
8. Vary the appearance of the knots by changing cords. Achieve patterns by changing the directions of the anchor cords; in this way crosses and V-patterns are achieved. (See Figure 8–41.)

8–41 *Clove hitch, or double half-hitch knot.*

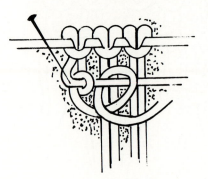

OVERHAND KNOT

Procedure

The overhand knot can best be understood by looking at the diagram, Figure 8-41. This knot is similar to the one used to tie one's shoelace.

WRAPPING PROCESS

Procedure

1. Form a long loop with the yarn as shown in Figure 8–43a. Place next to the cords to be wrapped.
2. With one end, wrap around the cords several times as shown in Figure 8–43b.
3. When at the top of the wrapping, place the end through the top of the loop as shown in Figure 8–43c.
4. To finish, pull the bottom yarn end which pulls top yarn loop down into the wrapped section and tightens it as shown in Figure 8–43d.

CIRCULAR MOUNTING

Procedure

1. To make a hanging pot sling or candleholder, begin from the bottom and work up.
2. Place eight lark's head knots on a plastic or metal ring that is 2 to 4 inches in diameter.
3. Work north, east, south, and west.
4. Bring the cords around the pot and up to finish.

8–42 *Overhand knot (used as a finishing knot).*

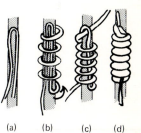

(a) (b) (c) (d)

8–43 *Wrapping process.*

8–44 *Circular mounting.*

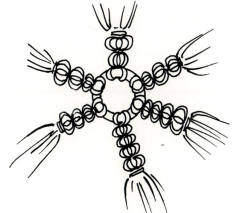

Weaving and Macrame

305

Checkpoints

1. Begin with simple projects requiring only a few cords.
2. Experiment with a variety of knots, materials, and sizes.
3. Remember which knot you just did and that, in the square knot, the two outside cords do the work.
4. Keep the knots pulled evenly with equal pressure. Work the knots tightly; but for textural variation try working them loosely.
5. Use an adequate working board. It should be long enough for the intended project, but not too large for small hands to hold.
6. Add objects to the macrame as you knot, such as bells, clay and salt beads, bones, feathers, straw and grasses, and any interesting textural object.
7. Combine macrame knotting procedures with weaving, stitchery, knitting, crocheting, and other fiber techniques.
8. Work with a minimum of twelve cords for an alternating knot pattern. A three-dimensional sculptured form can be built up with just the double half-hitch knot.
9. Use two or more colors in the macrame piece and watch the colors change as they travel through the knotting.
10. When making a pot sling, knot all the end cords (which will be the top) in a large overhand knot; hook this onto a coat hook to hold it firmly and knot away.

Bibliography

ANDES, EUGENE. *Practical Macrame*. New York: Van Nostrand Reinhold Company, 1971.

ALLARD, MARY. *Rug Making Technique and Design*. Philadelphia: Chilton Book Co., 1963.

AMSDEN, CHARLES AVERY. *Navajo Weaving: Its Technique & History*. Rio Grande Press, 1964.

ATWATER, MARY MEIGS. *Byways in Handweaving*. New York: Macmillan Publishing Co. Inc., 1968.

BELASH, CONSTANTINE A. *Braiding & Knotting*. New York: Dover Publications, Inc., 1974.

CROCKETT, CANDACE. *Card Weaving*. New York: Watson Guptill Publications, 1973.

DENDEL, ESTHER WARNER. *Needleweaving: Easy As Embroidery*. Philadelphia: Countryside Press, 1971.

DIAMOND, S. "All Out for Macrame," *School Arts*, **72** (Jan. 1973), 12–13.

DUNCAN, MOLLY. *Spin, Dye and Weave Your Own Wool*. New York: Sterling Publishing Co. Inc., 1973.

EDITORS OF FIBERARTS MAGAZINE: *The Fiberarts Design Book*. New York: Hastings House, 1980.

FANNIN, ALLEN. *Hand Spinning*. New York: Van Nostrand Reinhold Company, 1970.

GRAPF, RUSSELL E. *Card Weaving or Tablet Weaving*. McMinnville, Ore.: Robin and Russ, Handweavers, 1969.

HARVEY, VIRGINIA I. *Color and Design in Macrame*. New York: Van Nostrand Reinhold Company, 1971.

HELD, SHIRLEY E. *A Handbook of the Fiber Arts*. New York: Holt, Rinehart and Winston, Inc., 1978.

HOLDGATE, CHARLES. *Net Making*. New York: Emerson Books, 1973.

HOLLAND, NINA. *Inkle Loom Weaving*. New York: Watson Guptill Publications, 1973.

LABARGE, LURA. *Do Your Own Thing with Macrame*. New York: Watson Guptill Publications, 1973.

LYON, JANELLE. "Weaving on a Box Loom," *Arts and Activities*, **71** (Feb. 1972), 40–41.

MAHLER, CELINE. *Once Upon a Quilt*. New York: Van Nostrand Reinhold Company, 1972.

MARTHAMM, ALEXANDER. *Simple Weaving*. New York: Taplinger Publishing Co., 1969.

MEILACH, DONA Z. *Macrame: Creative Design in Knotting*. New York: Crown Publishers, Inc., 1971.

———. *Macrame Accessories*. New York: Crown Publishers, Inc., 1972.

THE NAVAJO SCHOOL OF INDIAN BASKETRY. *Indian Basket Weaving*. New York: Dover Publications, Inc., 1971.

PENDLETON, MARY. *Navajo and Hopi Weaving*. New York: Macmillan Publishing Co., Inc., 1974.

PHILLIPS, MARY WALKER. *Step-By-Step Macrame*. New York: Golden Press, 1970.

PLATH, IONA. *Handweaving*. New York: Charles Scribner's Sons, 1964.

REINEY, SARITA. *Weaving Without a Loom*. Worcester, Mass.: Davis Publications, Inc., 1966.

SHILLINGLAW, PHYLLIS. *Introducing Weaving*. New York: Watson Guptill Publications, 1972.

SHORT, E. *Introducing Macrame*. New York: Watson Guptill Publications, 1973.

TOD, OSMA G. *The Joy of Handweaving*. New York: Van Nostrand Reinhold Company, 1964.

TOVEY, JOHN. *The Technique of Weaving*. New York: Van Nostrand Reinhold Company, 1965.

TURNER, ALTA R. *Finger Weaving: Indian Braiding*. New York: Sterling Publishing Co., Inc., 1973.

VAN DOMMELEN, DAVID B. *Decorative Wall Hangings: Art with Fabric*. New York: Funk & Wagnalls, 1962.

WEST, VIRGINIA. *Finishing Touches for the Handweaver*. New York: Charles T. Branford Co., 1968.

WILSON, JEAN, *Weaving Is Creative*. New York: Van Nostrand Reinhold Company, 1972.

YOUNG, JEAN, ED. *Woodstock Craftsman's Manual 2*, New York: Praeger Publishers, Inc., 1972.

ZNAMIEROWSKI, NELL. *Step-by-Step Weaving*. New York: Golden Press, 1967.

Pottery and Modeling

Craftspeople all over America and the world have revived the ancient art of hand-built ceramics. Children and adults alike take pride in creating and using hand-thrown or hand-built ceramic objects.

Clay

Clay, a material that is found all over the world, has served as both an aesthetic and utilitarian form of expression since the beginning of civilization. We are fortunate to have many excellent examples of pottery remaining from past cultures whose decorations and degree of sophistication in craftsmanship tell us a great deal about the lives and customs of ancient peoples. The making of pottery dates back to the sixth or seventh millennium B.C., during which time, in Europe and in Asia, food containers were made from pure clay earth and fired in the sun.

The story of earth vessels, or pottery, is as ancient as humanity itself. Concerns with proportion, design, decoration, and color are visible in the earliest Chinese red vases of the fifth to fourth millennium and the contemporary forms

9–1 *Greek vase, ca. 750 B.C. (Courtesy of Phoenix Art Museum, Phoenix, Arizona.)*

produced by the artist/potter/sculptor today. Fine prehistoric examples are found in Mesopotamia, Egypt, and Crete. The potter's wheel, developed about 2000 B.C., provided the craftsman with a means of making more precise shapes and thinner walls than were possible using the coiled slab methods used previously. The pottery from Crete is called *Minoan*, after King Minos, and is well known for its decoration, which consists of stylized natural forms of seaweed, waves, and octopus. The *amphora* vase was a tall, two-handled jar that held wine or oil and was placed over the graves of loved ones for nourishment, with small holes permitting the contents to seep slowly into the grave. The amphora funerary was often more than 5 feet tall. Many examples were found in a cemetery in Athens, dating back to 750 B.C. The design is small and exact, with horizontal rows or patterns; geometric, figurative patterns and animals are repeated around the form. Favorite animal motifs included goats, deer, lions, bulls, boars, swans, griffins, sphinxes, and the horse and chariot. Another style of vessel is called *oinochoe* ("to pour wine"). The ancient Greeks created ceramics, with early designs being geometric patterns of squares, swastikas, and stylized figures. The golden age of the fifth century B.C. produced designs of Black and Red Figure styles. Each area of Europe and the Orient produced distinctive styles of pottery, with great artists contributing to the fascinating history of pottery.

Clay is dug from the earth. River beds, lakes, lagoons, and hilltops are all possible sources of clay. Dug clay can be worked for pottery if, when molded with the hands, no cracks appear on its surface. Clay is found in various grades

9–2 *Clay is an earth material that man reshapes for both utilitarian and aesthetic purposes. From lower left, clockwise: a clay stamp; a box made by carving into a solid form; a large mug made by a slab method; a pinch pot; a funny face slab, coil, and carved pot; and carved beads.*

of purity. Very coarse clay has a large amount of organic materials in it; the very purest clay has had most of the impurities removed.

Clay is the name used for mineral substances that are mainly aluminous silicate. Impurities may range from iron (which adds yellow, brown, or red), lime, magnesia, free silica, and alkali. Carbonaceous matter gives clay a gray or black color—most clays are pure white. Clay is the remains of rocks that have broken up over millions of years, and the exact composition depends upon the rock from which it was formed. Clay is also formed from the fine rock powder that was created by the grinding of the glaciers. All clays are not alike and some are better for pottery and sculpture. The two basic features of clay are the degree of fine individual particles as well as the plasticity that permits the clay to be molded into the shapes it retains after drying.

Clay is used in a moist form, but as it comes from the earth, it is sandy and sometimes rocklike. When clay is hard, it is ground and crushed for use. For thousands of years, man has devised ingenious ways of working with clay, and many of them are still used.

The primitive potter probably made his bowl or jar by pressing out the sides of a ball of clay. He may have used a rock to press into the ball for the basic form and then added coils for larger shapes. To make his pottery hard, the primitive potter probably placed it out in the open air to sun dry and bake. The potter's wheel was first used in ancient cultures. The formation of clay from a ball into a pot shape by turning it on a wheel is a skilled technique and is aesthetically exciting to watch. Visit a craftsperson's studio to see a pot "thrown" on a wheel.

Clay for Classroom Use

Commercial clay in ready-mixed moist form, usually in 25-pound bags, is the most convenient for classroom use. If moist clay is not available, mix 25 pounds of dry clay with about 3 to 4 quarts of water and keep it in an airtight container such as a galvanized garbage can or plastic bucket. Dry clay comes in cans. Add 2 inches of water to the can and sift the clay into the water until the top of the clay is covered. Use a strong stick for mixing and stir until it is well mixed. If the mixture is too wet, add more dry clay and continue to stir. Check the consistency, as the dry powder absorbs the water. After a few days, the mixture will be right for working. Keep it covered tightly and store it for later use.

The following discussion applies to beginning students

working with clay. For more advanced procedures, refer to the many sources listed in the references at the end of this chapter.

DISCOVER WHAT CLAY CAN DO

Clay is an exciting manipulative experience. All grade levels like working with it. It is a material that requires experimentation as well as skills and skill development. It is a direct avenue for self-expression and self-discovery; it is an earth material, easily worked and changed. Many schools provide the supplies and equipment necessary for clay projects. Its popularity in childhood and adulthood can be seen by the many clay enthusiasts who practice their craft. You can bring the wonder of past civilizations and how they explored clay properties into your classroom. Now you, too, can learn about and discover the possibilities inherent in this medium.

Play with the clay. Before you start to make things out of clay, experiment to discover its many possibilities. The first time you touch clay, you will find that it's not what it looks like. It is cold and wet and leaves dust on your hand as it dries. It easily finds its way onto your clothes and soon is in your mouth and eyes. Think about what clay feels like. What does it make you think of? What is its texture? Does it remind you of building in the sand? Push it, pull it, squeeze it, paddle it, bend it, roll it, flatten it, cut out shapes from it, and imprint forms into it. Clay is pliable; it is a very different experience from working with metal.

Students and craftspeople alike produce aesthetically pleasing clay forms for use and enjoyment. Much emphasis is placed on beautiful forms, interesting textures, and exciting glazes and finishes. Artists and students also use clay as a

9–3 *From the left: rolling clay with a dowel and a coil pot; cutting out a clay shape from a slab; modeling the clay and draping it over a plastic bottle; and making beads over a straw.*

Pottery and Modeling

9–4 *Cut carved porcelain bowl by Molly Cowgill. (Courtesy of The Hand and The Spirit Crafts Gallery, Scottsdale, Arizona.)*

material for use in sculpture. From very small items (such as beads) to large objects (such as sculptures and architectural murals), the only limit is the size of the kiln that fires the clay to harden it. Very often finished forms are stacked on top of forms to build massive clay structures.

WORKING WITH CLAY

1. As with all materials, discovery is the first step. Learn about the possibilities of clay by handling the material.
2. Work the surfaces and form textures by scratching, carving, and painting.
3. Work with your nails, fingers, sticks, wire, sponges, string, and kitchen utensils—anything that invites exploration.
4. If the clay is too wet, it will stick to the hands, but when it dries, it can be rubbed off easily.
5. If the clay is difficult to work, it needs more water and kneading.
6. Explore the clay's suppleness and manipulative possibilities.

Clay Terms

1. *Bisque* is an unglazed ware that has been fired once. Before clay is fired, it can be remixed with water to make it usable. Once it is fired over 500°F., the water evaporates and the clay can no longer be softened.
2. *Drying* a piece should be done as slowly and as evenly as possible. Leave it in a damp closet or cover the object loosely with paper toweling or plastic wrap. Larger pieces should be covered with a slightly moist cloth or paper towel. If the piece dries unevenly, uneven shrinking will occur and there may be warping or breaking.

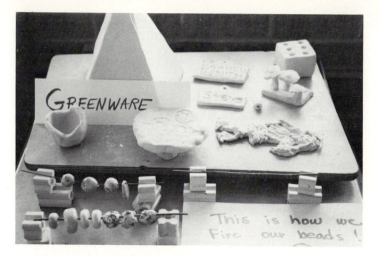

9–5 *Greenware examples ready to be fired.*

Two pieces that are joined during the forming must contain the same moisture content or they will separate during drying. In hand-built forms, all the wall thicknesses must be kept the same and this will help in the drying. If there are uneven thicknesses, uneven drying occurs and very often separating cracks will develop.

3. *Fired clay* has been fired in a kiln to its maturing temperature. Different clays require different firing temperatures.

4. *Greenware* is a clay shape that has all the water dried out of it, but has not yet been fired. It is very fragile.

5. *Hollowing out* an animal or figure shape that has been modeled from a form in a solid piece of clay is done after the piece becomes leather hard on the outside. Then the piece is turned upside down and the inside is scooped out with a spoon or clay tool, leaving the walls of the object an even thickness (about 1 inch). Be sure to scratch the student's name on the bottom of the piece.

6. *Joining* is the same whether for slab, coil, pinched, or modeled clay forms. Roughen the two surfaces to be joined with tools or fingernails. Moisten both with water or a thinned-out liquid clay called *slip*. Press the two surfaces firmly together. Smooth down the outside of the joint if desired. Leaving the joint visible adds interesting patterns.

7. *Kneading* or *wedging* the clay, which is mostly decomposed granite that has broken down over millions of years, must be done for good workability. The clay should be smooth and free from air bubbles. Start with a ball the size of your palm. Cut the clay in half with a wire or knive and slam the two halves together on a board (or on a Formica tabletop, plaster bat, or piece of canvas or linoleum—any surface will do that is not too absorbent). Then knead the clay as you would bread dough by

9–6 *Kneading the clay on a plaster surface.*

9–7 *Pottery can be made by "throwing" on a wheel. Note the position of the hands as this student builds up the walls of a cylinder on an electrically powered wheel.*

pushing, pressing, doing a double-over, and rolling the clay. Do this fifteen times, or until there are no more air bubbles when the wire is passed through. Then the clay is ready for working.

8. *Leather hard* is a stage during the drying (after about 2 hours). The clay is still moist at this point, but it is rigid and no longer plastic. It can now be carved easily, but if you were to move the form, it might break. The clay can now be carved with a tool, cut with a knife, and smoothed with a scraper. It is during the leather-hard stage that we often see potters use a wire to cut through the base of the object to loosen it from the working surface.

9. *Preparing clay* that has been cut into sections by drawing a thin wire or knife through it means to divide the clay in balls or blocks for the ready use of the class. Provide each student with a damp cloth with which to wrap his clay object and a board that is nonabsorbent (piece of Masonite). Use a plastic bag to cover the piece for slow drying.

10. *Slips* are clays mixed with water until they become a liquid form the consistency of cream. Slips are used in joining. They are also used as various colors for decoration on pottery. The slip is added to the surface of an object when the greenware is dry and before firing. Slips can be applied by painting, dipping, pouring, stenciling, dripping, or trailing. The slip can be applied to the surface and then scratched through to reveal the clay color underneath. This process is called *sgraffito.* Early potters used this method of decoration and students still do.

11. *Sgraffito* is a term from the Italian word that means to "scratch through." This is done by incising or scratching a design through a colored slip coating (or glaze) that then reveals the undersurface—either the clay body or an underglaze.

12. *Sponges* are used to add small amounts of water. They are also used to remove excess water from inside bowl forms.

13. *Shrinkage* occurs when clay dries. It shrinks again when it is fired. The original shape should always be made slightly larger than the desired finished piece. Different clays shrink differently. Some will shrink up to 20 percent in size after firing.

14. *Templates* are paper patterns, most commonly used to cut slabs for box forms.

15. *Throwing* is the process of shaping clay as it rotates on a potter's wheel. (See Figure 9–7.)

16. *Tiles* must be dried without warping. Dry them slowly on a piece of cloth. Remove some slices of clay from the back of the tiles before placing them out to dry.

Clay Textures and Finishes

One of the desirable characteristics of clay is its malleability. Shaping is the first step of the procedure. After forming, surface texturing can add aesthetic qualities to the clay piece. Texturing can be accomplished in these ways:

1. Press into the clay with sticks, fingernails, and pencils, or with any sharp or blunt tool. Use a simple ruler on the sides or edges to produce repeated patterns. Anything and everything can be used as a texturing tool.
2. Pat the clay with a spoon, stick, or tools for a softer effect. Use found objects to invent patterns.
3. Scratch a design into the clay with nails and tools.
4. Carve your own stamp from wet clay. Fire it, and use it as a stamp on other clay forms.
5. Or, make a stamp out of plaster. Mix 1 cup of plaster with 1 cup of water in a tin can or paper cup. Squeeze out all the lumps. When the plaster is hard, tear away the cup. Scratch and carve a design into the hardened end of the plaster with tools or a blunt knife. (Carve plaster just after it hardens for easier carving; complete the carving after a few hours when the plaster is very hard.) Carve the design about ⅜ inch deep into the plaster so it will leave an impression when it is pressed into the clay. Geometric designs, initials, and faces all make pleasing stamps.
6. Press cloth against the clay, such as burlap, for textural effects.
7. Add coils, buttons, and other shapes to the surface of the form. Score and join it as described, but lightly pat the smaller form to the larger form, making sure that the pieces are joined securely.

When all the forms are leather hard, remove them to newspaper or paper toweling to ensure even drying. Keep a sponge and water bowl handy to moisten the clay if it develops small cracks. Keep any remaining working clay in plastic bags to prevent it from drying out. Finishing procedures can be done now. Remove any unwanted edges with a wire or knife, smooth the bottom and sides, and add forms, such as handles to pots. Relief-carving, piercing, impressing textures, adding ornaments, and polishing greenware with a smooth object such as stone are done now. When the clay is all dry, it is called bone-dry greenware and is ready for firing.

Hand Building

The three basic methods of hand building are the hand or pinched form (ball of clay), slab construction, and coils of clay. Using these three procedures, practice on a flat, square piece of clay, 6 × 6 inches, to make a tile. Give texture to the tile by incising, adding, scratching, carving, or painting with slip.

HAND OR PINCH METHOD

The pinch method is the simplest way to work clay. (See Figure 9–8.)

Procedure
1. Whether making a simple pot or beginning an animal or other small sculpture, start by rolling a hand-sized ball of clay between your palms.
2. Push down into the center of the ball of clay with both thumbs.
3. Slowly force the thumbs out and begin to deepen and enlarge the hole the thumbs have made.
4. Gently pinch and rotate the ball to build out an even wall of clay.
5. As it turns, the ball will become enlarged and the surfaces smoothed, creating an interesting rounded shape.
6. Or form a ball shape by indenting your elbows into the clay or by using rocks to press in rounded shapes.
7. The very youngest student will enjoy creating simple "pottery" in this way. The method also can be used to make small sculptures by combining many pinched forms that are joined and built up and out.

Modeled forms are begun this way. To this beginning, the student manipulates the clay by pushing, pulling, bending, and indenting it to his own requirements. The final form can emerge from this one clay mass, but if other forms are to be added, the joining process should be used.

9–8 *Pinch pot on a Masonite board.*

Students will soon learn that large, heavy-bodied forms need strong leg forms for support. Detailing, texturing, and modeling for more complex objects can be done with simple tools, such as nails, bobby pins, and twigs. Because the clay material is so easily manipulated, encourage students to create action figures and animals in poses that suggest movement, such as dancing and bending. Be sure to carve out the insides of leather-hard figures if the figures are large and the clay is thick. Encourage students to invent whimsical sculptures by combining unusual shapes and forms—such as monsters with happy faces, or fat hippopotamus bodies and rabbit heads—and even to do self-portraits. Part of the fun of clay is the many surprise forms that emerge. (See "Clay Sculpture," pages 330–332.)

SLAB CONSTRUCTION

Slab clay construction is begun by rolling out clay as if it were pie dough. (See Figure 9–9.)

Supplies Needed
wire, 2 feet long attached to a small piece of wood at each
    end, or a knife
rolling pin, a length of dowel 2 inches in diameter, or a bottle
cloth (canvas, old sheeting, oil cloth, or burlap)
2 rulers or sticks
Formica tabletops or plastic sheeting
bowl of water (one plastic container for each table is fine)
a small bowl for slip
sponges and soft brushes for applying slip
stick, nail, or old paring knives

9–9 *Building a slab pot. Surface texture is achieved with the file in the student's right hand. (Courtesy of Perry Wray.)*

9–10 *Clay examples made with slab construction: masks, necklace, pendants.*

Pottery and Modeling

319

9-11 *Cups and lanterns have cut design perforations.*

scissors or incising tools, rulers, and sandpaper
pencils, forks, and other tools for giving texture to surfaces
newspaper to support forms as the clay dries
sinks and small Masonite boards for storing projects
kiln
glazes
paints and felt-tip pens

Procedure
1. On a flat surface, roll out the clay with a wood dowel until the clay is even in thickness, about ½ inch. (Roll the clay in between two rulers or flat sticks to achieve an even thickness.)
2. Now let your imagination dictate the form. Some possible projects are creating boxes, flower holders, mirror frames, dishes, tiles, and molding over forms. Incorporate the following procedures.

DRAPE MOLD

Anything can become a mold, and clay slabs can be draped over all flat or rounded surfaces. (See Figure 9–12.)

9-12 *Draping clay over a rock mold. (Courtesy of Perry Wray.)*

Procedure

1. Roll out a ball of clay until it is about ¼ to ½ inch thick.
2. Cut out the outside forms with a knife or stick.
3. A circle can become a pot. Use a bowl, a river rock, or an inverted quart jar as a mold.
4. Place a cloth, plastic wrap, or waxed paper over the inverted mold to prevent the clay from sticking. (Or use the inside of a bowl as a mold.) Make sure that the clay slab you use is large enough to cover the mold.
5. Drape the clay slab over (or inside) the mold and gently press and form it to the mold. Be sure that the mold you use has a flared edge and no undercuts, so the clay can be removed when it is leather dry.
6. Be sure to remove the clay after a few hours when it is leather hard and safe to handle.
7. Decorate and press in designs with tools and fingers while the clay is leather hard. Finish with a scraper, and sponge the clay smooth with water where a smooth texture is desired.
8. Add footings for handles to bowls and pottery if needed.
9. Flat dishes can also be made this way.

Large, irregularly shaped rocks are interesting forms to use as molds. Amusing animals can be built this way. To make a complete sphere, do one half at a time. Invert the rock and lay the clay on the other half. Join the edges with slip when the

9–13 *Artist Victor Verbalitis describes his craft to the author on a television craft series the author produced for the Rio Salado school district. He forms the two halves over two plastic bowls; then, while they are leather hard, he fits the two forms together. He says, "Each work appears to be age-old, historical, or archaeological, but is not. I regard them as contemporary relics."*

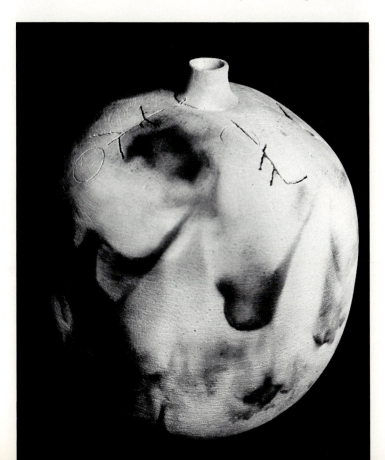

9–14 *"Records of Fire," dung-fired earthenware, 12 inches × 13 inches, by Victor Verbalitis. (Photo by Errol Zimmerman.)*

Pottery and Modeling

9–15a *Artist Tom Moore works on a slab form with various kinds of clay. The slab is then draped over the mound form (on the left) and is pressed to receive the texture. In the foreground is the finished wall plaque.*

9–15b *Students first drape slab clay over plastic bowls. (The bowls have been covered with aluminum foil and clear plastic.) The bowls (left foreground) are then fired in a kiln and painted with acrylics.*

two halves are leather hard. Smooth over the joined seam. Try making clay eggs over stones or over plastic egg forms. Incise, carve, and decorate them.

FLAT FIGURES

Miniature environments filled with interesting people can be created with these clay figures. Build towns and castles.

Procedure

1. Begin with a hand-sized ball of clay. Roll it out to a ¼-inch thickness.
2. If the clay is rolled over a burlap or other cloth surface, it will pick up the texture of the cloth.
3. If a cookie cutter is being used, grease and push the cutter all the way through the clay to the cloth. Use a knife or pointed stick to cut out your own original figure shapes.
4. Remove the cutter and lift out the figure; if it sticks, gently shake or push it out.
5. Add individual characteristics such as clothes and facial features.
6. Incise the figure with tools and add clay pieces with slip.
7. Place it aside for 20 minutes to dry leather hard.
8. Then carefully bend the arms, legs, and waist to add action and more character.
9. Build environments for the clay people to stand on; place these action figures "at the beach," for example.
10. Wadded up newspaper and cardboard supports help the figures and forms take shape as the clay dries hard.

9–16 *Family environments are the inspiration for these miniature clay sculptures. The flat, cut-out figures have hair that was formed by pushing clay through a garlic press.*

9–17 *"Woman in Bath," a wall piece 13½ inches × 18 inches, made of porcelain in a wood frame. The artist is Laura Wilensky. (Courtesy of The Hand and The Spirit Crafts Gallery, Scottsdale, Arizona.)*

11. Fire the clay.
12. Glaze or paint the clay with tempera or felt-tip pens.

Invent and build birds, animals, flowers, butterflies, houses, and cars using the preceding process.

FLOWER HOLDERS

9–18 *Flower holder with a textured surface.*

Procedure
1. Roll out a flat diamond shape, about 8 inches long.
2. Cut off the point of one layer.
3. Fold it in half.
4. Pinch and seal the edges of the sides together.
5. Inscribe a design on the surface.
6. Place a hole in the remaining point for hanging.
7. Insert crushed newspaper into the pocket of the clay to hold the hole open while it is drying.
8. Add clay decorations (flowers or insects, for example) to the basic shape with slip.
9. Fire the clay.
10. Use this as a wall hanging and add cloth flowers.

MORE POT ARMATURES

Use plastic bottles for slab-construction armatures; build the clay up around bottles and remove it when it is leather hard. Join the seams. Fill paper bags with crumpled newspaper or a wad of newspaper and tape them together for clay armatures.

Use blown-up balloons as basic molds for pottery shapes. Also experiment with other forms by making tall cylinder pots from cut slabs that have been joined (stuff them with newspaper). Use different-sized balloons to make various sized forms for slabs and build large sculptured forms. Or use small balloons and drape many slab shapes over them and build these shapes into a sculpture.

Styrofoam packing (as found in cooler boxes) can be cut, sawed, glued, or wired together as a base for clay forms. After the clay form is placed over the foam, the foam can be "melted away" with turpentine (slow) or gasoline (fast). Supervision and outdoor ventilation are advised.

COMBINING METHODS

Now try combining different building methods, such as slab with oil or pinch. Remember to stuff the inside of all shapes with paper while they are drying to hold the shapes open.

Sometimes it helps to make paper templates first. After cutting out a paper design, lay it out flat on the clay and cut around the shape with a paring knife. This will aid you in building irregular shapes as well as boxes. Score, pinch, and slip the edges together. When building box shapes, it helps to place coils along the inside corners and smooth them. This provides added strength. After the clay is leather hard, scrape and finish the edges and bottom. A lid should be made at the same time to ensure matching measurements, if one is desired, as the clay will shrink as it dries. Follow the pattern, or template; press a coil on the underside of the lid to fit inside the box rim. Add top handles or a knob to hold the lid. Place it aside to dry. Add textures and decorations. Dry and fire the clay.

CLAY DISHES

Procedure
1. Roll out a ½-inch slab. Cut out a dish shape.
2. Carefully cut out a center ring, leaving a frame edge of about 2 inches.
3. Lift the center out. The secret here is to gently pat around the outside perimeter of the center ring, thus enlarging and extending the size of the original center.
4. Bring the cut center ring back and place it under the circle frame. Be sure to score it and use slip to rejoin it.
5. Press the ring into place.
6. Place newspaper or cloth rags under the dish to give added support under the outside rim.

9–19 *"Happy Hippos" by Judy Smith display the combined techniques of throwing, pinching, coiling, and modeling. Surface textures were achieved by pressing burlap and tree bark into the clay. (Courtesy of Shop of Art, Tempe, Arizona.)*

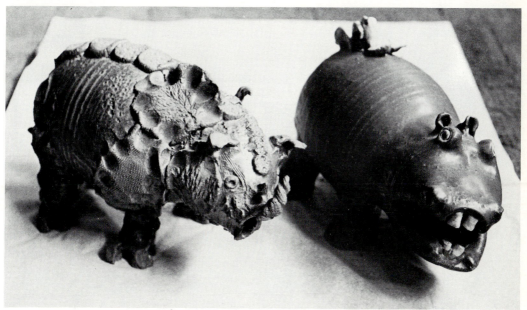

7. Decorate the dish with clay buttons, flowers, or painted slip. (A mirror frame is done this way, by gluing in a center mirror in place of the center ring.)

HANDMADE TILES

Clay tiles can be carved, stamped, and pressed. The tiles remind us of Sumerian writing, an ancient language, which was pressed into clay tablets. (See "Lettering," pages 110–112.)

Procedure
1. Roll the clay out into a slab about ½ inch thick.
2. Carve and press designs into the tiles.
3. Plan tiles as individual units, or cut them up like a jigsaw puzzle.
4. Let them dry slowly and thoroughly—this takes about 1 week if they are covered.
5. Cut strips of clay from the tile back (in an X shape) to prevent warping.
6. Lay the tiles out on canvas to dry and cover them with a weight the first night.
7. Let them dry, and then fire and decorate them.

9–20 *Carved, stamped, and pressed clay tiles are combined.*

COIL METHOD (INDIAN POTTERY): AN ANCIENT PROCESS

Pottery craft in the Southwestern United States, where broken relics have been unearthed at architectural digs in New Mexico and Arizona, dates back to 200 B.C. Pottery making is thought to have developed after fiber weaving, as pottery was used to line woven baskets. The pots were mainly functional: food containers, cooking ware, and ceremonial dishes. The motifs decorating the pots are of other-world spirits and geometric patterns. These designs are traditional for the ceramic craft. The ancient technique of coil building is still practiced in the same manner, and the traditional masterful creations are today acclaimed as works of art. (See color Figure 10.)

Most Pueblo craftsmen, for example, dig their clay from ancient quarries. At the Gila River Reservation in central Arizona there are many earth sources, such as a dry river bed, where the earth has been pulverized to the proper consistency, and a rocky hillside. In both cases, one digs under the top earth layer. Screens are used to sift the clay to remove organic impurities. The clay is brought to the working area and moistened to the proper consistency. Often, mesquite ash—a native desert tree—is added to the clay much as one would add flour to pie dough. This helps prevent the clay from cracking during firing.

Indian artisans keep their hands wet as they build with the clay. To make a traditional pueblo pot, the clay is shaped first into a palm-sized pancake for the base. An old inverted clay pot bottom is used as a mold to shape the base, thus forming a rounded bottom. The clay is then patted with a paddle, turned, spread, and thinned into an even shape. The paddle is hand carved from palo verde or mesquite, both desert trees. This is allowed to harden slightly for ½ hour. Then a fiber ring (this doughnut shape is made of rags twisted to form a circle) is placed on top of the clay pancake and the whole thing is turned right side up so that the pancake nestles inside the ring form. The clay pot mold is removed, and the coil building begins. The uniform coils are rolled either in the palm or on a tabletop to look like sausages that are 1 inch in diameter. The coil is the right size to cover the base shape. The surfaces of the coil and the cake shape are scored and dampened with slip; the coil is put into its place; and the fingers gently press, smooth, and rub the outside and inside surfaces until the coil is interlocked and is no longer visible. One hand places support against the opposite hand, on the inside and the outside of the coil to prevent sagging. Additional coils are added. The larger the diameter of a coil, the larger the pot size will grow. If the diameters of the coils

9–21 *The Papago Indians form their pottery with a pancake-shaped base and build the sides with the coil method. The doughnut-shaped cloth (on left of photo) is the mold for the base shape. Finished clay pot in foreground. Wood paddle (on right) helps shape the sides. A prized stone pebble is also used in shaping the sides of the pottery.*

9–22 *This young Hopi Indian holds her coil-built bowl, finished with her traditionally geometric but original design.*

9–23 *The study of Hopi Indian pottery was the motivation for this clay project. The students constructed coil pots, fired them, and applied original designs with acrylic paints.*

9–24 *For a traditional Indian firing, a hole is dug and wood, rocks, fuel slabs, and pots are stacked inside the tin wall. More wood is added to the outside, as shown; tin and wood are used to cover the top, and the firing is ready to begin.*

grow narrower, the shape of the pot will move inward. In this way, it is possible to change a pot's contour. Some Indians use gourds to further smooth the coils; others use a paddle or a prized river pebble that has been passed from generation to generation of potters. As the shape of the pot changes and moves inward to outward, it is allowed to dry and harden slightly so it does not collapse. The pottery is then set aside in the shade to dry for two days. Hopefully, there will be few, if any, cracks. Then the pot surface is dampened with a cloth and a scraper—a knife, bone, or flint chip—is used to smooth the outside surface. If any holes or cracks appear, they are filled with wet clay and rubbed with a stone or a dry corncob. The pot is wiped with a damp cloth and is ready for carving or decorating with slip. Some Pueblo potters wet the pot with slip and then polish the surface to a high, glossy smoothness by rubbing it with a prized stone or pebble for many hours.

If the pot is to be finished with painted symbols, the craftsman executes the finished decoration freehand, painting with eyeball precision. No mistakes are allowed. The red, yellow, and brown slips are made from manganese and iron oxides. Black is made from the Rocky Mountain bee plant. The Hopi Indians still paint their pottery with vegetable and mineral colors made from ground-up minerals and plant juices. The tool used is either a stick, feather, or, commonly, a yucca leaf whose end has been chewed and shaped and whose fibers have been cut to a desired size.

In firing pottery outside, conditions must be perfect or else the pot may crack. There must be no wind. A shallow hole is dug in the ground and rocks are placed into the hole. A fire is allowed to burn down to the wood coals. Prehistoric potters used wood for fuel, but today manure slabs, a slower burning fuel, are stacked below and around the pots and burned.

Large jars are fired separately. Small jars are placed upside down on top of rocks over the coals. Cans or a metal grill are sometimes used. More manure slabs are placed over the pots as well as a sheet of tin or galvanized iron to prevent staining and to keep an even fire. Twigs are stacked against and on top of the tin. Then the fire is made and the pot is fired. The firing can take from 30 minutes to 2 hours, averaging a temperature of 1,300°F. The potter removes a pot when he thinks it is ready, or lets it remain in the ashes to cool slowly. After the pot has been removed and has cooled, it is rubbed lightly with a greasy cloth to give it a shiny finish. As these pots are not glazed, they are never completely waterproof. If a pot has been fired correctly, it will ring like a bell when it is tapped.

COIL BOWLS

To create a coil bowl is an introduction to clay pottery and our Indian heritage.

Supplies Needed
clay
small bowls (glass, plastic, and pottery all work well)
burlap or other cloth scraps or plastic wrap

Procedure
1. If plastic, glass, or pottery bowls are to be used as molds, line them first with cloth to prevent any clay from sticking and cracking during drying.
2. Roll an 18-inch coil to about the thickness of your little finger.

9–25 *This coil dish was built inside a plastic dish lined with plastic wrap.*

Pottery and Modeling

3. Form the coil into a spiral shape and lay this on the bottom of the bowl.
4. Roll out these 12-inch coils as you need them. Place them around and up the sides of the bowl, allowing each spiral to touch.
5. Place marbles and buttons of clay in gaps where they are needed. Add other shapes where desired.
6. Carefully and gently smooth the inside of the bowl, if desired, so the spirals do not show. Too much pressure will spoil the coil design on the outside of the bowl. Add clay where it is needed so that the coils are blended together. A pot may crack during drying and firing if there is not a smooth surface inside the bowl.
7. Let the clay dry until it easily slips out from the bowl. Let it dry completely and then fire and finish it.
8. Larger bowls can be made by using larger coils, up to 2 inches in diameter, and by using larger bowls and many coils. Note: Coils can also be made by rolling out a slab of clay and then cutting ribbonlike coils for building.

Build free-form shapes using the coil method. Leave open designs and let the coils curl and move back and forth. Smooth the coils together where they touch on the inside. After the form is built up a few inches, let the clay harden for a short time until it is firm enough for you to continue with the coil building. Add coils until the design is finished. For beginners, pots should be kept under 8 inches high. Add buttons, beads, and other clay decorations where desired. Let the clay dry.

Clay Sculpture

The young child begins to sculpt with sand and mud. Rolling mud into snakes, pancakes, free forms, and balls starts the child thinking in terms of structuring the material. The balls soon take shape as snowmen do and, with many opportunities for working, the child begins to invent new forms and develop expressive sculptures. The early motor abilities of a child are very different from those of an adult. But each level of ability permits certain degrees of expression. The snake for a four-year-old is as significant a developmental step as a sculptured head is for an adult.

Clay sculpture is as old as clay itself. Today, artists like clay for sculpting as it takes form quickly and can be altered easily during the process. Aesthetic growth occurs, and ideas and skills improve as opportunities for practice with the material are given. The teacher should provide many working hours with the clay, talk about clay sculptors, discuss forms, and

look at and touch clay sculptures. Subjects for working in clay can be action figures, heads, animals, monsters, insects, cars, birds, and free-form shapes.

The three basic techniques of sculpting with clay are:

1. The additive method: building up the clay with simple shapes.
2. The subtractive method: starting with a large shape of clay and carving away clay to form the design.
3. Bas relief: working with a flat piece of clay (such as a 2-inch slab) and adding designs by using the two preceding methods.

Procedure

1. Start with a palm-sized ball of clay. Work on a surface such as a piece of Masonite. Shape sculpted forms by building them up or carving them away. Zoo animals, pets at home, people of many lands, living things, dishes, foods, cups, flowers, and nature forms all provide subjects for clay sculpture. Imaginary and humorous ideas are fun, too: such as moon creatures and invented insects and animals.
2. Emphasize ways of joining clay shapes together. There is nothing so discouraging as having a leg fall off of a sculpted clay figure during the firing. If the pieces of clay are joined properly (even the youngest can learn to do this well), all problems of this kind can be avoided. Use armatures when needed. (See page 324.)
3. When sculptures are textured and finished, let the forms dry under a loose plastic cover. Drying-out time varies, depending on the thickness of the clay pieces and the humidity in the air.

Pottery and Modeling

4. When the piece is leather hard, after a couple of days, remove it from the base surface. Invert the clay form and hold it gently. With a spoon or clay-sculpting tool, carefully carve out the inside of the form, leaving the walls of the piece about ½ to 1 inch thick. If the piece is a large one, the supporting walls should be thicker. Do not make the walls too thin or too thick. The reason for carving out the excess clay is so that there will not be any chance of air bubbles being trapped inside the form to cause it to explode during the firing process.
5. Continue to dry the piece under plastic until the forms are completely dry (usually about a week).
6. When sculpting a bas-relief panel, be sure to score the back side of the slab to prevent the clay from warping during drying. Do not allow clay shapes to protrude more than ½ inch. If there is not a high-relief built on the slab, place the slab under a weight overnight to dry it and prevent warping.

Decorating and Finishing Techniques

There are several possible methods of finishing clay forms. Some are very simple to follow and are desirable when there is no kiln available; others require some basic glazing materials with the use of a kiln.

GLAZES

Glazing is firing the clay a second time with a form of glass (a silica with added oxides for color). Glazes are available commercially in dry or moist form. If purchased dry, mix the glaze in jars as it is needed. Many commercial glazes are available; the choice depends on your colors, the clay used, and the firing range of the kiln. A glaze is a liquid coating whose special glass seals the surface of the clay so that it becomes nonporous and, thus, waterproof. Be sure that no glaze is on the bottom of the object or the object will stick to the kiln during the firing.

Dipping

Dipping is the simplest method of glazing. The clay object is dipped into the colored glaze (contained in a plastic bucket). Usually, the object is held at an angle and is partially placed into the glaze; this leaves some of the areas of the object uncolored, creating a design. Do not let the glaze become too thick, and touch up any missed spots with a brush. The designs formed are free flowing in effect.

Pouring

Pour the colored glaze over and around the object. Pour quickly, or the glaze will become too thick; the correct thickness of the glaze is that of a playing card. If the glaze becomes too thick, it will crack or lump during the firing. In order to coat the inside of a pot, pour the glaze into the pot until the pot is one third full. Rotate the pot and pour out the glaze, working as quickly as possible to avoid forming a heavy coating of glaze.

Brushing

With a wide, soft brush apply coats of glaze in varying directions to achieve an even application. Brush-on designs include bands of color as well as geometric and free-form designs. The use of small brushes on the last coat of glaze will create thin decorative designs. A turntable will rotate the pot to produce even bands and other patterns.

Alternate procedures for glazing include brushing hot wax (or crayons or candles) on a piece and then dipping it into a glaze for a wax-resist design; applying glazes through a stencil; and spraying on glazes.

DECORATING BISQUE CLAY

After one firing, follow these methods in place of glazing.

Procedure
1. Spray paint clay with a favorite color such as gold, silver, or fluorescent colors.
2. Polish the clay with a clear paste wax or with a cloth and colored shoe polish.
3. Rub bisque ware with cloth and wood stains or diluted oil paints.
4. Brush on diluted watercolor, tempera, or acrylic paints. One of our favorite finishes is a brushed-on thin brown tempera wash. Add a little white glue or clear latex paint to the tempera paint for permanence, or cover the clay with spray plastic.
5. Draw on a wax-resist design with crayons or candles, and then dip the object into the paint.
6. Draw designs on clay with felt-tip pens for colorful details. Finish with a clear plastic spray finish.
7. Paint clay objects with acrylic paints.

Firing Clay

THE KILN

To make clay hard, it must be fired at a sufficiently high temperature. The first hard firing is called a *bisque firing*. The second firing fuses a glass glaze to the clay and is called a *glaze firing*. Some clays require a high firing temperature, whereas others require a low firing temperature. The same is true of glazes—some are high and some are low-fire. Some kilns can only fire low-fire clays and glazes.

A great many kilns are available commercially. If you have a potter friend who can assist you, you may want to try building your own kiln with firebricks. Most teachers will want to begin with small commercial kilns, which usually are top loading. A small kiln can run on 110 volts, but an adequate classroom kiln needs 220 volts. Be sure to place the kiln in an out-of-the-way spot—away from the sink and the room's traffic pattern. Place the kiln out from the wall so that air can circulate around it. Many good kilns are available that come with proper instructions. If you are purchasing one, be sure the kiln has a peephole, a pyrometer to indicate temperature, and an automatic shutoff.

For outdoor firing, refer to "Coil Method," pages 327–329.

Checkpoints

1. If the clay is too wet, it will stick to your hands like butter and be difficult to work. Dry it out by first wedging it (like bread dough) on a canvas cloth. Or cut the clay into slices and leave them out on the canvas to dry.
2. If the clay is too hard, or large cracks develop, add some water and knead it, slice it, and place it on a tabletop or a cloth and sprinkle it with water. As the water is absorbed, sprinkle on more water; then wedge it.
3. Keep a pail of water handy for each table. Use small square sponges to add water to the clay as it is worked.
4. Do not add too much water as you work as this will weaken the clay and make it sag.
5. Store clay in covered plastic buckets or plastic bags.
6. While working with clay, keep it covered with a damp cloth or piece of loose plastic.
7. When working with sculptural forms instruct the student to keep the clay ¾ inch thick. If the form has been worked solid and the clay is leather hard, hollow out the inside, keeping the walls about ½ to 1 inch thick.

8. When adding forms in building, stress adequate scoring and wetting where the pieces are to be joined.
9. Place the name or initials of the student on the bottom of the piece to avoid mixing up the pieces.
10. When building a pot, tap its base gently on a tabletop to flatten it.
11. Build and join several pinch pots and decorative clay shapes to create unique animals, fishes, space creatures, make-believe zoos, farms, and cities.
12. Try placing a ball of clay in a plastic bag. Using your hands, try experimenting to create unusual forms inside the bag. When the clay is leather hard, pull off the bag, carve out the extra clay that is inside, finish drying it, and decorate and fire it.
13. Give texture to clay with wire, string, sponges, rope, pencils, sticks, kitchen utensils, fingers, and nails. Impress clay for textures with leaves, stones, and other objects from nature as well as buttons, gears, and other machine-made objects.
14. For a grainy texture add coffee grounds, wood ashes, and sawdust that will fire out. Vermiculite will not fire out.
15. Relief carving can be done on leather-hard clay.
16. Polish greenware with a smooth object, such as a stone.
17. Leave rough joints for interesting textures.
18. Try rolling clay into dirt or sand (try colored sands) for rough texture.
19. Cut off rough edges with knives or tools.
20. Use plaster bats as stands. Another variation is to use a stand from an old Victrola. Place a saucer on this rotating stand and turn it, or use large metal cans that held motion-picture reels.
21. Appropriate surfaces for working clay are oil cloth, plastic, linoleum tiles, canvas, old sheeting, wood planks, and Masonite.

Additional Modeling Media

SALT AND FLOUR

Mix equal amounts of salt and flour. Add water and food coloring until you develop the proper modeling consistency. Apply the medium to a cardboard or wood backing, building up forms in layers or masses, or let the sculpture stand freely. Textures and objects can be pressed into the medium and color can be painted on while it is still moist. This is a favorite material for aerial-view and topographical maps. Air dry the sculpture for a few days and then paint it or add details with a felt-tip pen. Finish it with shellac or a plastic spray.

SALT CERAMIC

Salt ceramic is an excellent medium for modeling and sculpting. It is much cleaner to use than clay, yet it provides an equally satisfactory result. The nice part about this medium is that it can be prepared in the kitchen with a minimum of effort and it air dries hard in a few days without being fired in a kiln. The following formula can be used for this medium:

Supplies Needed
1 cup of salt
½ cup of cornstarch
¾ cup of water
pan
stove
waxed paper
plastic bags
food coloring or tempera paint

Procedure
1. Mix 1 cup of table salt with ½ cup of cornstarch. Be sure to mix these dry ingredients first to avoid lumps.
2. Stir in ¾ cup of cold water. Add liquid tempera or food coloring, if desired.
3. Place this material inside a can; place the can in a pan of water.
4. Warm the water slowly over low heat. Stir the mixture constantly until it is thick and smooth (about 4 minutes).
5. Dump the mixture on a sheet of foil or waxed paper and allow it to cool.

9–27 *Fanciful story book characters are modeled from salt ceramic over toothpick armatures and decorated with felt-tip pens and paint.*

6. When it is cool, carefully knead the mixture into a ball or rounded form to remove any air bubbles.
7. Place the mixture in a plastic bag where it can be kept airtight until needed. (Kneading will prevent cracking later during the drying process.)

The recipe can be doubled, tripled, or otherwise increased to fit the needs of any class. If the salt mixture can be put together cooperatively, in the initial process, by having parents make one batch, the time saved can be devoted to artistic involvement.

There are positive aspects to working with this form of modeling and sculpting material: it is easy to clean up afterward, it dries very hard, and it doesn't shrink, so sticks and other armatures can be inserted to strengthen legs, bodies, or arms. It can also be painted easily after it is hard and dry, or color can be added by using a few drops of food coloring during the initial mixing stage (with the water).

Salt ceramic is a fascinating art medium with which children of all ages enjoy working. It lends itself well to successful expression as a modeling medium.

1. Salt ceramic can be modeled into three-dimensional animals or figures that stand.
2. Salt ceramic can be used in mosaic-type projects in which small objects such as beads, shells, beans, and pebbles are pressed into a salt ceramic flat surface and thereby are captured forever in an expressive statement. (Use plastic lids or meat trays for a base.)
3. Salt ceramic beads and jewelry can be created. To form beads, make a hole with a small nail or toothpick while the salt mixture is wet. Let them dry without touching each other.

9–28 *Salt ceramic and baker's clay are excellent for building dioramas.*

Pottery and Modeling

337

9–29 *Students work on a baker's clay mural on "Agriculture." (Courtesy of Barbara Herberholz.)*

BAKER'S CLAY

Baker's clay is a popular modeling medium and can be used to form beads, cars, heads, jewelry pins and necklaces, tree ornaments, baskets, and pictures. It dries very hard and is often used as sculpture material to sculpt delicate forms by the folk artists of Ecuador. (See color Figure 11.)

Supplies Needed

4 cups of flour	felt-tip pens, paints
1 cup of salt	plastic coating
1½ cups of water	

Procedure

1. Mix all the ingredients and knead them until they are the consistency of clay. If the dough is too stiff, add a few drops of water, but be careful not to get the dough too wet. (If you freeze the flour either before or after mixing, it will kill any larva in the flour.) Mix dough in large batches.
2. Add vegetable coloring or liquid tempera paint if desired.
3. Shape the dough into desired forms or use cutters such as paper cups or a blunt knife for free-form shapes.
4. Join any ends by moistening the parts with just a drop of water and gently press together.
5. Bake the forms in the oven at a temperature of 350°F. until they are hard and lightly browned—about 1 hour, or dry them in the air overnight.
6. When the forms are cold, paint and decorate them. Any paint can be applied (we use acrylic and tempera as well as felt-tip pens).

9–30 *Students contributed these gaily colored flowers, animals, and figures made from baker's clay and built on a cardboard backing. The head at the lower left could be strung and worn as jewelry or used as a tree decoration. (20 inches × 24 inches.)*

7. Spray the forms with a fixative, or paint them with a plastic coating for permanency.
8. The dough can be prepared ahead of time and stored in the refrigerator in an airtight container.
9. These forms can be strung and hung as mobiles, worn as jewelry, and used to make holiday decorations.
10. *The dough is not edible.*

SAWDUST MODELING MATERIALS

These recipes are good for making puppet heads, animals, masks, tree ornaments, and jewelry.

9–31 *Sawdust modeling materials are appropriate for tree ornaments, jewelry, puppet heads, and small sculptures.*

Supplies Needed
liquid starch or hot water
2 cups of sawdust
1 cup of flour
1 tablespoon of glue

Procedure
1. Add liquid starch or hot water to the flour and sawdust until a thick modeling consistency is reached.
2. Mix the ingredients well and knead them.
3. Add string, wood, or wire armatures before the modeled object is set out to dry.

Supplies Needed

2 cups of sawdust	*or*	2 cups of sawdust
1 cup of wheat paste		1 cup plaster
		½ cup of wheat paste
		2 cups of water

9–32 *Fifth-graders invent a maze game out of Plasticene.*

Procedure
1. Mix together either recipe.
2. Add enough water to create the consistency of clay.
3. Model forms.

NONHARDENING CLAY FOR MODELING

Nonhardening clay, often known as Plasticene, is especially suited to the primary levels where the emphasis is on ideas and expressions concerning the immediate unit being studied (as opposed to long-range projects).

Plasticene is easily manipulated and can be rolled, bent, and shaped into animals, figures, trees, dogs, and the like. After having been used for a unit in the classroom for a week or so, the Plasticene can be reshaped for the next barrage of expressive ideas from the class.

One first-grade teacher has each student keep a ball of Plasticene in his desk. Each time new words are learned, the students roll snakes with the clay with which they print the new word.

A fifth-grade teacher has Plasticene available for inventing games. Students create a snake maze on their tilted desk tops with the clay. Then, two or three students each pass a marble from the top down. The first marble through wins.

MAKE YOUR OWN REUSABLE CLAY

Supplies Needed
1 cup of water
2 tablespoons of oil
food coloring

1½ cups of salt
4 cups of flour
toothpicks for armatures

340

Procedure

1. Mix the oil, water, and a few drops of coloring in a cup.
2. Mix the salt and flour together.
3. Add the water solution to the salt and flour mixture, a little at a time, kneading with the hands until it is mixed thoroughly. If the mixture is stiff, add a few drops of water at a time until the clay is a workable, firm dough.
4. Place the clay in plastic bags or in a sealed container until you are ready to use it. It can be used again and again.

PLAYDOUGH

Supplies Needed

3 cups of flour
1½ cups of salt
3 cups of water
3 tablespoons of cooking oil
food coloring or paint
1 can of cream of tartar (1½ oz.)

Procedure

1. Mix all the ingredients together and cook them over medium heat until they form a ball.
2. Knead the dough on waxed paper.
3. Store the dough in a tightly lidded plastic container or coffee can.

Checkpoints

1. If an object is to be hung, such as a tree ornament, insert a paper clip, safety pin, wire, or string at an angle while the molding medium is wet.
2. If you are modeling a bird, for example, feathers and other accent effects should be added during the forming process. In some instances, white glue will provide sticking power for afterthoughts.
3. Foil provides a good working surface and prevents sticking.
4. Use armatures of toothpicks, wire, or pipe cleaners to ensure sturdier projected parts.
5. If kept airtight, salt ceramic can be stored for weeks.

Bake an Edible Sculpture

A special holiday bread sculpture can be made that can be eaten. It is highly manageable when being shaped and has a

9–33 Preparing this bread sculpture is as much fun as eating it. Dough coils, balls, and twists, as well as candy, nuts, and raisins, form this head of a witch to add to classroom festivities at Halloween.

springy texture when baked. Pull it, shape it into coils, slap it, shape it into balls, pound it, and twist it to create sculpted bread dough leaves. After baking, either freeze it for a later time or eat it within 4 or 5 days (wrap it well in foil). Experiment making angels, animals, birds, flowers, and storybook characters.

BREAD SCULPTURE DOUGH

Supplies Needed
1 package of active dry yeast
2 cups of warm water
3 tablespoons of honey or sugar
¼ cup of oil
2 teaspoons of salt
7 cups of flour
nuts, raisins, and candy decorations (optional)

Procedure
1. Dissolve the sugar in warm water. Dissolve the yeast in the warm sugar-water mixture for approximately 5 minutes.
2. Add the salt, oil, and flour a little at a time until the dough can be worked. (If the consistency is too sticky, add more flour.)
3. Knead the dough until it is workable and begin to sculpt forms.
4. Build forms on aluminum foil on a large cookie tray. Build the sculpture horizontally, not vertically.
5. Cut out shapes or build forms with patties, coils, and balls.
6. Decorate with nuts, raisins, and candy.
7. Let the dough rise for 10 to 20 minutes.
8. Moisten the parts to be joined with a small amount of water. Join the parts after the dough has risen.
9. If you wish, brush the surface with a beaten egg white. It will give the baked sculpture a shine.
10. Bake at a temperature of 350°F. for 20 to 30 minutes, or until the dough is lightly browned.

GLASS COOKIES

Celebrate holidays by baking, hanging, wearing, and eating these cookie decorations.

Supplies Needed
⅓ cup of sugar
⅓ cup of vegetable oil

1 egg
3 cups of flour
½ teaspoon of baking soda (to be sifted with the flour)
1 teaspoon of salt
⅔ cup of honey

Procedure

1. Mix all the ingredients together and knead them until they are the consistency of bread dough.
2. Roll the dough into ¼-inch-thick coils for outline shapes. Moisten one side and connect these coils securely.
3. Create designs on aluminum foil or a cookie sheet. Make a hole in any cookies designed to be worn or hung. (Use a straw to poke a hole.)
4. Break up lollipops for colored fillings by smashing them between sheets of waxed paper.
5. Sprinkle the crushed lollipops in the openings of the design. (The lollipops will melt in the oven and fill the spaces with a sheet of color.)
6. Bake at a temperature of 375°F. for 8 to 10 minutes or until the lollipops have melted and the dough is lightly browned.
7. Let the cookies cool and remove them from the aluminum foil.

PRETZEL SCULPTURE

Supplies Needed

1 cake of yeast	4 cups of flour
1½ cups of water	1 egg yolk
¾ cup of honey	salt

Procedure

1. Dissolve one package or one cake of yeast in 1½ cups of warm liquid and ½ to ¾ cup of honey. Let the mixture stand for ½ to 1 hour.
2. Add 2 cups of flour; beat for 100 strokes.
3. Add 2 more cups of flour; knead the dough for 5 to 10

9–34 *"Santa's Dream City" was constructed by seventh- and eighth-graders for an annual exhibit at the Phoenix Art Museum, Phoenix, Arizona.*

minutes. Let it stand in a warm oven until it is double in size.

4. Shape the dough into invented forms, using coils to make flowers, figures, animals, and designs.
5. Brush the dough with egg yolk that has been diluted with 2 tablespoons of water.
6. Sprinkle the shapes with salt.
7. Bake at a temperature of 400°F. for 15 to 20 minute for soft pretzels or at 500°F. for 15 to 20 minutes for hard pretzels. Makes 2 dozen.

Candy, Cookie, and Vegetable Art

CANDY CASTLES

The great chefs and candy makers all over the world create beautiful forms from edibles.

We are all children at heart when it comes to celebrations, festivals, and special times! Good things to cook and eat increase our awareness of and merriment at these occasions. (See Figure 9–34.)

Candy, cookie shapes, and vegetable forms can be used to build delicious and fun-to-eat sculptures. Varieties of sizes, colors, and textures are easily joined together with toothpicks or a little water. To join sugar cubes (as well as other candies), prepare a creamy mixture of confectionary sugar and water. Dip the sugar cubes individually into the creamy mixture and add cubes to build up inventive forms. The mixture will dry hard and firm, holding the sugar cubes in place—like glue.

HOLIDAY VILLAGES

Many festive holiday sculptures can be built with graham cracker or cookie shapes as bases. The three-dimensional forms are held together as well as decorated with the following tasty frosting.

Supplies Needed
½ cup of butter
dash of salt
1 pound of confectionary sugar (about 4 cups)
5 tablespoons of milk
1 teaspoon of vanilla
food coloring

Procedure
1. Cream the butter and salt.
2. Gradually blend in the sugar.
3. Add the milk slowly.
4. Add the vanilla until the ingredients are of spreading consistency.
5. Separate the mixture into batches and add various colors.
6. Decorate the candy and cookie sculptures. Add other candy delicacies for features and details.

ALTERNATE FROSTING

Supplies
3 egg whites
1 pound of powdered sugar
¼ teaspoon of cream of tartar

Procedure
1. Beat three egg whites until frothy.
2. Mix 1 pound of powdered sugar and ¼ teaspoon of cream of tartar together.
3. Add slowly to eggs. Beat until stiff, about 5 minutes.
4. Apply to the cookie base.
5. Add candy decorations.

Bibliography

BAYLOR, BYRD. *When Clay Sings.* New York: Charles Scribner's Sons, 1971.

BALL, CARLTON, AND JANICE LOVOUS. *Making Pottery Without a Wheel: Texture and Form in Clay.* New York: Van Nostrand Reinhold Company, 1965.

BARFORD, GEORGE. *Clay in the Classroom.* Worcester, Mass.: Davis Publications, Inc., 1964.

BEARD, GEOFFREY. *Modern Ceramics.* New York: Studio Vista and E. P. Dutton & Co., Inc., 1969.

DUNCAN, JULIA HAMLIN, AND VICTOR D'AMICO. *How to Make Pottery and Ceramic Sculpture.* New York: Museum of Modern Art, 1947.

HAUPT, CHARLOTTE. *Beginning Clay Modeling: An Approach for Teaching Elementary School Children.* Belmont, Calif.: Fearon Publishers, 1970.

JOHNSON, ISLE, AND NIKA STANDEN HAZELTON. *Cookies and Breads/ The Baker's Art.* New York: Bonanza Books, 1967.

KRUM, JOSEPHINE R. *Hand-Built Pottery.* Scranton, Pa.: International Textbook Co., Inc., 1960.

LEE, RUTH. *Exploring the World of Pottery.* Chicago: Children's Press, 1967.

MELLACH, DONA Z. *Creating Art with Bread Dough*. New York: Crown Publishers, 1976.

NELSON, GLENN C. *Ceramics*. New York: Holt, Rinehart and Winston, Inc., 3rd Ed., 1971.

NICKELL, MOLLIE. *This Is Baker's Clay*. New York: Drake Pub., Inc., 1976.

PETTERSON, HENRY. *Creating Form in Clay*. New York: Van Nostrand Reinhold Company, 1968.

PLUCKROSE, HENRY, ED. *Let's Model*. New York: Van Nostrand Reinhold Company, 1971.

RHODES, DANIEL. *Clay and Glazes for the Potter*. Philadelphia: Chilton Book Co., 1957.

ROETTGER, ERNST. *Creative Clay Design*. New York: Van Nostrand Reinhold Company, 1972.

SANDERS, HERBERT H. *Sunset Ceramics Book*. Menlo Park, Calif: Lane Magazine & Book Co., 1953.

SUPENSKY, THOMAS G. *Ceramic Art in the School Program*. Worcester, Mass.: Davis Publications, Inc., 1968.

VILLARD, PAUL. *A First Book of Ceramics*. New York: Funk & Wagnalls, 1969.

WILDENHAIN, MARGUERITE. *Pottery: Form and Expression*. New York: Van Nostrand Reinhold Company, 1962.

10

Sculpture: Constructing, Carving, and Casting

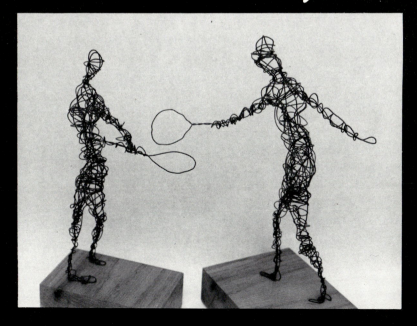

To sculpt means to form a three-dimensional design that has length, height, and width and that occupies a special space. This form can stand freely, can be built in low relief or high relief, or it can exist in the round. It can be constructed into a whole from parts, modeled with soft materials, or carved from firm materials.

Much of our prehistory is revealed in the visual images, shelters, and utilitarian tools that were left behind. Classic treasures include the huge stone heads on Easter Island in the Pacific, Stonehenge in England, and the Pyramids in Egypt. Each implies religious and spiritual beliefs of ancient peoples and can be enjoyed aesthetically today. We need only look to the Parthenon in Greece and to the Gothic cathedrals of Europe for inspiration from the past. As we reflect on these masterpieces, we are reminded of the simple, uncomplicated tools that were available to artists at the time. Before the industrial revolution and the advent of electricity, most constructions were crafted by human hands using basic tools.

Contemporary sculptures form with new materials such as plastics and steel. The modern materials and machinery are much more extensive and permit more experimentation and exploration. Man has always surrounded himself with hand-formed objects from very simple utilitarian to the most complex aesthetic forms.

Building is a basic and instinctive need. The young child begins with his food, the sandbox, blocks, and other building toys that become fantasy structures.

The adventure of searching out three-dimensional mate-

10–1 *A wonderful fantasy world of imaginative people and animals fills the work of artist Suzanne Klotz-Reilly. The sculpture is wood, fur, stuffed cloth, and old shoes and teeth; approximately 3 feet high. (Courtesy of Suzanne Klotz-Reilly.)*

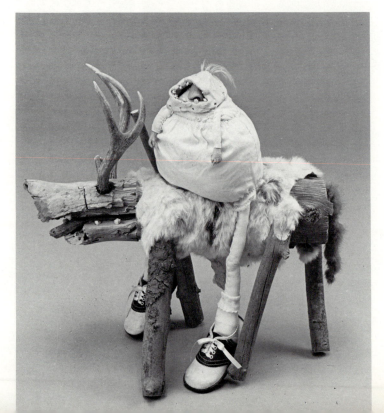

rials is in selecting, experimenting, and manipulating, and working through a plan to a new form. It is the feelings, ideas, and skills that we bring to the experience that determines what we do with the process.

All three-dimensional forms are viewed from several angles: front, side, bottom, and top; they interrelate within a space. Viewing should be a continuous process. Touching, handling, moving, changing, and reshaping are other goals to encourage. Each sculpting material has its own unique qualities with various textures and surfaces that add individual properties to the forms. Many ideas can be preconceived, and these should be explored through drawing sketches and making small models. Also, many art experiences should offer opportunities to explore without preconceived images—that is, to discover what the material can do and what can happen as the forms are developed and joined together into a composition and design is part of the creative process.

Opportunities for students to practice making qualified judgments and art choices are desirable objectives. Many discussions and practice sessions in forming aesthetic judgments help build a foundation in visual thinking.

Artistic considerations should include structural problems, the balance, the elements of design, the negative areas between shapes, any changing movement, and the existing space surrounding the sculpture.

10–2 *Found objects are partially embedded in sand inside half a milk carton. The sand will then be covered with plaster. Such casting experiences help describe how cast sculptures and jewelry are made with metals and plastics.*

Goals for Three-Dimensional Experiences

1. Sculpture encounters can begin with an open-ended exploration of materials and three-dimensional forms. Suggest to the students that they are cave people and are the very first to find a particular material. This may include "playing around," in other words assembling, taking apart, and trying new formations and structures, patterns and systems—the fascination of discovering the potential.
2. Focus on the ideas, concepts, and skills involved.
3. Evaluate the design and spatial construction and make changes. Continue to visualize and think through ideas.
4. Decide on the final structure and design; this is called *closure.*
5. Consider and evaluate the total experience: what has been gained, have the objectives been reached, and what will the future goals be?

Sculpture: Constructing, Carving, and Casting

Sculpture Terms

1. *Sculpture* is a general term meaning the practice of the art of forming substances into figures or designs, either in relief, intaglio, or in the round. (a) *Relief* is the projection of parts above the ground or plane on which it is formed. The projection can be in low, middle, and high relief. (b) *Intaglio* is a design carved into, or incised on, the surface; the design is sunk below the surface. An example of this is the plaster-incising project with the "scrimshaw" concept. (c) *In the round* refers to a sculpture that is a form apart from any background, as contrasted to relief. You can walk around something in the round.

2. *Mobile* is a term that refers to a three-dimensional design suspended by some means and that has free-flowing action, commonly caused by air circulation.

3. *Stabile* is a term applied to a mobile that is attached to a stationary base. It is constructed in such a way that balanced forms move by touch or in the air currents. It can be constructed of such materials as straws, wire, Styrofoam, balsa-wood strips, cardboard, string, plastics, and metals.

4. *Kinetic sculpture* is a term used for simple introductory experiences in the elementary grades, for to make sculpture move can be most intriguing. Movement is caused by touching or by the vibration of the air. Such materials as rigid wire, springs, and long plastic rods also move when a weight is added. Refer to objects that move when touched—such as a rocking chair, a seesaw, a pendulum, and a child's swing. Also refer to toys that move as a result of mechanical devices—such as clocks and wind-up mechanisms—batteries, and motors. Exciting ideas and challenging encounters will result as the students' kinetic sculptures begin to emerge. Interested students might want to demonstrate a process, such as electrical energy in wiring, battery input, and various types of motors.

5. *Casting* is done in a mold with a material that is in a fluid or plastic state. A casting is an impression from another form. The plaster sand casting and wax-candle casting are procedures described in the text. (See pages 394–396.) However, as an artistic tool, forms are often made in a soft material—such as clay. Then a plaster mold is made, the clay is removed, and the mold is injected with a hard material—like metal—that assumes the shape of the original form.

Forming Materials

Many of the materials used for sculpting in the classroom are collectibles from available resources. Those techniques described here require only basic art supplies and household

10–3 *The artist thinks of sculpture in terms of art in the round. The many ways to construct and assemble available materials in three-dimensional space offer numerous design possibilities.*

tools and materials. This means that the concepts, ideas, and feelings that we bring to a project can be as aesthetically simple or as complex as we want them to be. The procedural skills involved will aid the student to develop and accomplish his idea. The materials and tools are kept at an elementary level, although more artistic tools and supplies can be used. One teacher has a "collectatorium"—a special room filled with discards and throwaways from other teachers. These are kept in ice-cream cylinders and are intended for use by any teacher as his or her needs arise, whether for art projects or other related learning experiences. A favorite term today is *recycling*—the art teacher is a well-known recycler! Very often, the teacher has to use available resources in new ways, and this challenges the ideas of both teacher and students. Have fun filling your collectatorium.

Supplies Needed
pebbles and stones
boxes of all sizes and shapes: cardboard, wood, and plastic
cylinder-shaped cartons, cardboard tubing, oatmeal containers, and hat boxes
paper wrappings such as gift, foil, and tissue
plastics (sheet and shapes) and plastic wrap
straws, egg cartons, paper bags, and cups
wires of all kinds and thicknesses: coat hangers, telephone, baling, and copper
vegetables and fruit
wood: balsa, pine, twigs, driftwood, scraps, and dowels
yarns, threads, ropes, string, glass beads, and feathers
see-through papers such as acetate and cellophane

Sculpture: Constructing, Carving, and Casting

pipe cleaners, toothpicks, and Popsicle sticks
aluminum foil
buttons, labels, old jewelry pieces, and small mirrors
reeds, felt, lace, and carpet scraps
Styrofoam pieces, plastic packing materials, and old plastic
toys
metal objects such as bottle caps, nails, and kitchen utensils
decorating materials, such as paints and brushes
sponges and pasta of various shapes
glitter, sandpaper, decals, and stickers
tape, glue, thumbtacks, staplers, hammers, and scissors
rulers and knives for scoring and bending light cardboard

The following projects and procedures are successful for all learning levels. You can adapt them to fit the needs of your own classroom. Starting with simple tasks for small hands, these projects can become more elaborate projects for maturing hands. The concept of building in the round will excite and challenge all students. Working with three-dimensional materials offers another learning dimension.

Projects are intended for

1. Pure aesthetic pleasure and fun.
2. Enhancing the classroom or personal use.
3. Integration with other learning units such as science, math, reading, literature, social studies, and the related arts of music, theater, and dance.
4. Special gifts at special times.
5. Inventing play treasures.
6. Model building—from peepboxes to community models.
7. Creating changes in space and in the environment.

10–4 *Soft Styrofoam pieces are joined with spray adhesive to build large environmental sculptures.*

Constructing

PAPERS AND BOXES

Many household throwaways can be recycled into useful construction materials. Most of what we purchase in the stores is packaged, or boxed, and comes in a variety of shapes, sizes, colors, and textures. Start saving them, and discover the many ways you will find to use them in construction. Many throwaways contain unlimited hidden possibilities, once we start thinking about what they could become.

Supplies Needed
various square, rectangular, and cylindrical cardboard and
plastic shapes: cereal boxes, soap boxes, salt and sugar

10–5 *Constructing with boxes.*

boxes, small jewelry and medicine boxes, milk cartons, cookie and cracker boxes, unusual gift boxes, toothpaste boxes, match boxes, candy boxes, waxed vegetable boxes, cans of all sizes, Styrofoam packing material, carpet rolls, and thin cardboard for scoring and bending

various decorative objects: paint, old jewelry, pasta, mirrors, papers, foils, wallpaper, felt, cloth scraps, yarn, buttons, beads, spray paints

miscellaneous items: Popsicle sticks, toothpicks, wood dowels, Styrofoam, sponges, gift wrapping papers, cellophane, plastic scraps, string, yarn, chicken wire, metal and plastic

10–6 *From small boxes to large clay box forms, these unusual seats are organic and creative. (Courtesy of the Berkeley Museum of Art, Berkeley, California.)*

10–7 *A study unit about the northwest Indians was enhanced by an imaginative use of cardboard boxes, paper, and paint.*

rods and other shapes, egg cartons, glue, nails, hammer, wire, scraps of wood, ice cream containers, paper cups, plastic tubs, clay, sand, paper bags, pipe cleaners, paint, decals, stickers, carpet materials, balsa wood, tape, glitter, foils, acetate, thumbtacks, reeds, wires, tubing

joiners: glue, paste, string, wire, and tape

demonstrate methods of stacking, folding, scoring, bending, curling, cutting, tearing, fringing, slitting, and taping. Also demonstrate methods of constructing such shapes as cylinders, cubes, and cones

Constructing with Boxes

cars, trains, and buses—small ones to move, large ones to sit in

displays for paintings from large refrigerator boxes

all kinds of people, animals, monsters, and insects

towns and cities; students can design and build model houses and plan streets, schools, and public buildings—a total community

cages for animals in a zoo or a circus

totem poles

racing and antique cars

peek-through posters

a store, post office, and puppet stage

doll house with furniture

airplanes, helicopters, and an airport

masks, funny hats, and box costumes

cardboard boxes can be used as basic cubes on which drawings and magazine photos can be glued—spray them with a protective plastic coating; box environments can be built in which you can walk around

a "spook" box large enough to walk into can be filled with interesting visual and tactile objects

Methods of joining boxes that permit movement of parts will challenge your inventive thinking.

Environmental Spaces

These projects should be geared to the appropriate grade-level materials and manipulative skills. Drawing architectural plans, maps, backdrops, and murals as well as designing and building models are part of this sculpture experience.

We all have very personal spaces that we live in constantly. We are most familiar with our home spaces, although we often give very little though to the size of our bedrooms, the size of the classroom, the shapes of the windows we look through, the directions of the path we walk every day, the

placement of our furniture and objects at home and school, the shapes, contours, textures, and varying colors of the plants and trees that surround us and bring us pleasure and tell us of the changing seasons.

Our involvement with our personal spaces can alert us to all kinds of factual information in art as well as in other learning areas. Mathematical measurements; scientific data about plants; changes of seasons and temperatures; compositions of woods, fibers, clay, bricks, and cement; pollution; and the historical information about schools, homes, and community buildings can contribute to a broad and significant unit based on the environment.

To begin, invite public officials, architects, interior designers, and sculptors to your classroom to discuss relevant questions: What is being done now to maintain or improve the environment? Are there any new parks, playgrounds, recreation facilities, and buildings in the community? What is the architect's role in the over-all planning of a community? What is the architect's role in planning a new art center? What roles does the student have in determining the needs of a community? A good resource is *The American Institute of Architects* (AIA). The local chapter may be cooperative in providing maps and models, a speaker, and films for your needs.

Plan to visit the areas under study if possible: renewal areas, art centers, planning and zoning agencies, areas scheduled for demolition, outdoor sculptures, arts and crafts exhibit areas, and shopping centers. Ask students to consider the positive and negative points of view regarding the areas under study. A lively debate (have students choose sides) will bring forth varying attitudes and viewpoints. Keep notes

Sculpture: Constructing, Carving, and Casting

10–9 *Bridge builders are designing a suspended bridge during math and engineering studies, after researching its principles. The 40-foot bridge is made from straws, string, and glue. (Courtesy of Malorie and James Wiebe.)*

of pertinent information such as the sizes, materials used, and artists involved.

Many monthly magazines have articles devoted to new ideas for homes and beautiful inviting environments. Very often they include simple diagrams and floor plan architectural drawings. These are helpful, because they show the finished photograph of the completed structure as well as the plans for it. If students understand these symbols they can incorporate them into their own drawings and plans. Plans can generally be drawn to scale, using rulers and T-squares. If an architect's plans are available, use these as examples (if they are not too complicated). These should be introductory space-awareness studies, so the complexity of the unit should be geared for the grade level. First-graders can easily conceive of their individual home and school spaces and build simple relief panels with materials such as straws, seeds, cloth scraps, old magazine photographs, toothpicks, and sandpaper, with heavy cardboard as the base. Sixth-graders can complete group study projects by constructing simple three-dimensional models using such materials as paper, cardboard, corkboard, sponge pieces, birdseed, pebbles, balsa wood, sandpaper, acetate papers, and plastic wrap. (See Figure 10–9.)

In any construction project the following questions should be considered:

1. What is the purpose of the structure? What does it do?
2. Why have the building?
3. What do you do in it?
4. What do you do in one structure that you can't do in another?
5. How will you combine materials to create visual and tactile appeal in the structure?
6. How will you build, improve, and divide the working spaces?

356

FINDING ARCHITECTURAL DETAILS

Observe specific details: how the architect used levels and how one reaches them: kinds of ground cover—plants and trees; gardens; fountains; sculptures; water; benches; courts; types of wall constructions; shapes of window spaces; sizes and shapes of entrances and how one reaches them; provisions for heating, cooling, and water supply; walkways; grass areas; room dividers; and permanent building fixtures.

Point out what makes houses and buildings interesting; there are high spaces (skyscrapers) and low spaces (subways).

Consider how you enter a building; what kind of doorway there is; what enters through the doorway; and how you see in or out of a building (windows are also for air and light). They are of various shapes and may be spaced differently even within the same building. Consider structural additions there are to the building, such as columns, porches, or an extensive use of glass. Are there signs on the buildings? Do the roofs have gardens, antennas, smokestacks, chimneys? How is the city different from the country? Are there horses, farms and barns? How is America different from other countries? Where do the children play and where do the adults work?

All of these units can be studied and models built for individual spaces in a building, or as a whole complex community, depending on the abilities and needs of the students within an individual class. As always, each individual contributes his unique talents within the framework of the group and to its success.

DESIGNING CITY AND COUNTRY SPACES

We all move within constructions and spaces. Did you ever think about the many types, sizes, shapes, colors, and materials of structures in which we move? The city itself is a composite of spaces and structures that are planned for

10–10 *Redesigning a community our great architectural achievement relates the construction to history, literature, or imaginative realms. Castles, spook houses, and cathedrals can be idea sparkers.*

10–11 *Environmental bronze sculpture by Paolo Soleri is in front of the Phoenix Art Museum.*

varying functions. A city is a place where people meet, live, work, and play, and interact. It is where new and old exist together and where structures are constantly being built and torn away. A city is always changing. It is a place where different kinds of people live close together, mix, and exchange ideas. What do we find in a city? In the country? A partial list would include:

skyscrapers, office buildings, factories, individual homes, townhouses, apartment houses, shopping centers, signs, stores, hospitals, schools, libraries, theaters, amusement parks, pizza parlors, hamburger stands, gas stations, zoos, parks, fountains, playgrounds, benches, fairs, sports arenas, streets, culs-de-sac, beaches, ports, boats, oceans, cars, trucks, buses, motorcycles, parking lots, baseball diamonds, parades, machines, horse trails, gas stations, vacant lots, airports, freeways and throughways, football fields, sculptures, gardens, telephone booths, grass and trees, pathways, bicycle paths, crowds, barns, silos, machinery, animals, corrals, fields, rivers, and swimming pools

If you plan a model project about the city, you might begin by discussing and listing its various parts. Ask such questions as "What do you like about our city?" "What would you like to change?" "How would you change it?" (After thinking about an over-all plan, discuss the individual spaces to be built.) Draw maps and over-all layouts. Plan your city on flat surfaces and build the structures that are to stand on them.

PROJECTS RELATED TO SPACE DESIGNS

Personal Environments
1. My favorite room
2. My special dream house
3. The "zoony" house we found on Mars
4. My neighborhood from a see-through, bird's eye point of view

5. My neighborhood from an ant's point of view
6. My wildest dream school
7. A super space playground
8. An inviting school entrance; a new cafeteria
9. A scary haunted house
10. My own tree house or special hideaway
11. My dog house, my bird house, my monkey with banana house

Community Spaces
1. Redesign and rezone your neighborhood.
2. Design a shopping plaza.
3. Plan an expressway route.
4. Plan a children's park and zoo.
5. Study the historic structures in the community including hotels, city and county offices, railroad stations, farms, and residences.
6. Construct models of African communities; models of Indian communities; and models of prehistoric communities.

Imaginative Spaces
1. Design space cities of the future.
2. Study and construct models of cities of the past such as Dodge City, Kansas.
3. Reconstruct a medieval city.
4. Design a musical city in Mexico.
5. Construct magnificent cathedrals and churches.
6. Design an underground city; an Outerspace Platform City; an Under the Sea City.
7. Construct cities from books and stories.
8. Construct fairy-tale castles with kings and queens.
9. Design a contained city under the sea.
10. Design an Earth city under a plastic dome.
11. Design a fantasy sculpture and texture city.
12. Design a soft city made from foam rubber.

RELATED ART PROJECTS

1. Paint "on the spot" subjects from playgrounds and other recreational areas. Include good as well as bad features.
2. Select a room, house, school, or store in your neighborhood. Draw or paint a before and after scene of the subject. Include any improvements made, such as with colors, window designs, plantings, and signs.
3. Paint posters encouraging people to improve structures and environments.
4. Design signs and maps indicating shopping centers, supermarkets, schools, and mailboxes.

Sculpture: Constructing, Carving, and Casting

10–12 *Wood structure involves design, science (wood studies), and balance.*

5. Design a sculpture for the entrance of your school and another for the cafeteria.
6. Paint a mural of your neighborhood, including everyone's house, pathways, street patterns, signs, parks, and shopping areas. Paint another mural to include improvements made.
7. Structure and mathematics include measuring spaces, scale, and enlargement and studying geometric shapes.
8. Science can relate to structure in studying and comparing trees, the bones of the human skeleton, the muscles, veins, and arteries, and the differences and similarities in materials used for stress (wood frame as opposed to block), endurance, resilience, for building, and for decoration.
9. In language arts, descriptions of structure, environments, and design of local areas require vocabulary terms.
10. History requires the study of past historical structures and building procedures from the Greek column to contemporary steel and glass. The study of great architects, such as Frank Lloyd Wright, with books, films, and the viewing of structures, brings architecture alive. Included also could be a discussion of how the local environment affects structures. The Arizona desert is a vastly different environment from that of, say, Siberia and demands different materials.
11. How did various tools affect structures in the past? What tools are available today as compared to the past? How did life-styles and cultures affect structures, and vice versa?
12. Dance is affected strongly by the space involved; dance movements for the stage as compared to television or a hallway or bedroom influence the result.

10–13 *Concepts of structure can begin with found wood and glue (scraps available from lumber yards).*

360

GREAT ARCHITECTURE REVISITED

The architecture of the past and present represents some of man's greatest accomplishments. Every community we live in offers a wealth of historical structures right at our doorstep. Very often, study of structures such as old shops, city buildings, railroads, bridges, and homes reveals unique insights about our earlier culture and the people who settled and developed the community. Related old photos, records, stories, and newspapers provide a depth of belonging and a personal relationship to the community. Visits to selected sites can add dimension.

Some of the world's greatest moments in architecture can be relived again in the classroom. With cardboard, paper, and paste, the Parthenon, the Colosseum in Rome, medieval castles, great cathedrals, and/or the Capitol dome in Washington, D.C., can be reconstructed. Even lost cities such as Atlantis and Pompeii, or imaginary cities, can be created. What a wonderful opportunity to study our architectural heritage through the reconstruction of the buildings themselves. By using reference materials, diagrams in books, slides, inexpensive copying devices, and paintings of the originals, class members can work on such a project in groups or alone. This is an exciting way to make the history of art come to life. We all have a natural curiosity for the art mysteries of past civilizations.

Structures to Study

The Brooklyn Bridge (1869–83) by August Roebling

The Eiffel Tower in Paris (1887–99) by Alexander Eiffel

The Bibliotheque St. Genevieve in Paris (1843–50) by Henri Labrouste

The Marshall Field Wholesale Store in Chicago (built in 1885 and demolished in 1930) by Henry Richardson

The Wainright Building, St. Louis, Mo. (1890–91) by Louis Sullivan

The Auditorium Hotel and Theatre in Chicago (now Roosevelt University, 1887–89) by Dankmar Adler and Louis Sullivan

The Reliance Building in Chicago (1890–94) by Daniel Burnham and John Root

The Woolworth Building in New York (1911–13) by Cass Gilbert; neo-Gothic

The Chrysler Building in New York, (1929–30) by William Van Allen; art deco

The Daily News Building in New York (1929–30) by Raymond Hood and John Howels

The Empire State Building in New York (1931), 1,250 feet high

The Golden Gate Bridge in San Francisco, (1937)

The World Trade Center in New York (1971), 1,350 feet high

Sculpture: Constructing, Carving, and Casting

361

The Sears Tower in Chicago (1975), 1,454 feet high, currently the tallest building in the world

Supplies Needed
weights of cardboard and Styrofoam: grocery, shoe, and gift boxes
papers: textured, shiny, reflective, and transparent
paints and brushes
plastic wrap (for windows and waters)
paste or rubber cement and a stapler
scissors
papier-mâché
ruler for scoring
knife (for cutting out windows)
decorative elements for textures and landscape

Procedure
To begin this project, obtain a reproduction of an important architectural work. Some suggestions follow:

Historic structures in our community
Cathedral of Notre Dame, France
Parthenon, Greece
Colosseum, Italy
Taj Mahal, India
Capitol building, Washington, D.C.

Imaginative constructions also can be developed. Such a project can be combined with history and literature. The idea is to recreate with cardboard and paper, in stand-up fashion, the spirit of the structure and culture, that created great architecture. Papier-mâché can also be used to model specific forms (see pages 144–152). When the three-dimensional construction has been completed, it can be painted, drawn on, or otherwise decorated. Small salt dough figures dressed to reflect the times and culture will acquaint students with the various cultural aspects of the people of a region, their beliefs and customs.

Sculpting

WIRE SCULPTURE

Wire is another exciting material with which to work to form three-dimensional works. The interesting aspect about working with wire is that the entire image or form created is linear, like a drawing. That is, it is composed entirely of lines, which are both the contour (or outside surfaces) and interior forces of the figure being formed. By interlacing the wire

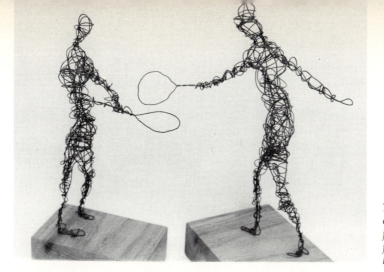

10–14 *Action figures made of wire are three-dimensional forms in a linear material. The figures are nailed to a wooden base.*

over, around, and inside forms, a feeling for body can be created. Wire has properties that are quite different from those of paint, clay, or any other material. It emphasizes the gesture and feeling for movement in the figure or animal form that is being created. Working with wire should encourage children to search for the roundness of the form and not to make a flat imitation of a drawing. The positioning will have to be such that the created form will stand. Having children think in terms of everything having a top, sides, and bottom will start them thinking about three dimensions. Wire forms need not be large, for working in reasonable sizes will enable children to better handle a piece. In working with wires, stress overlapping the wire to build up surfaces. Think also of cross contours, or the way in which the form goes around the figure or animal (the inside parts as well as the outline). Aluminum or stovepipe wire that is soft enough to be bent easily will work best. Be sure to stress care in shaping the wire so that accidents do not occur. Showing students movies of animals in action is a good way to motivate them to observe how animals jump, run, walk, move their heads, and generally function.

Supplies Needed
pipe cleaners
stovepipe, telephone, aluminum, baling, soft copper and
  brass wire, about 18-gauge
old scissors or pliers
tools to bend the wire (such as around wooden shapes)
felt and other cloth
wooden pieces, cardboard
Styrofoam shapes
aluminum foil
beads and buttons
plaster
papers
glue

Sculpture: Constructing,
Carving, and Casting

363

Procedure

1. Before class, prepare the wire by cutting varying lengths from 12 to 36 inches. Have a variety of lengths and weights available for use. Experiment with methods of shaping and twisting wire and how to achieve effects by beginning at and working out from the center core. Wrap added wire around the core and continue forming. Develop open, closed, and free-form shapes.
2. Have the students bend, twist, loop, curl, and wrap wires.
3. Form the wire around wooden shapes, if desired.
4. Or weave and shape the wires into a solid mass.
5. Join parts together by using thin copper wire or pinching the wire with old scissors or pliers.
6. Add other forms, if desired, such as Styrofoam shapes, crushed aluminum foil, or cardboard.
7. Staple or nail the wire to a block of wood as a base.
8. Or insert the wire into a clay base.
9. Or use thick plaster for a base and stand the wire in it until the plaster dries. Plaster can be added to parts of the wire sculpture to build up solid shapes. Paint the plaster if desired.

Use pipe cleaners and small Styrofoam shapes to create little creatures. Push the ends of the pipe cleaners into the foam and add other decorations for details. Aluminum foil adds a futuristic or mysterious quality to a sculpture and lends itself well to moon people, underwater creatures, and prehistoric animals.

Pipe cleaners can be used to develop imaginative insects, flowers, and animals.

BONE

Save the bones of animals and birds. Clean the bones by boiling or soaking them in a solution that is one half water to one half bleach. Rinse and dry them. Construct sculptural

10–15 Gladiator figures might be going into battle (made from bones and plasticene). Unusual materials can open up fresh viewpoints.

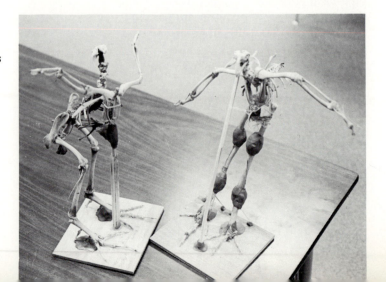

10–16 *Aluminum foil, toothpicks, plasticine, string, rubber bands, and feathers are combined to create new forms.*

forms with the bones and join them with glue or plasticene. Turkey or chicken bones make great necklaces; clean them, poke in holes with a needle, paint them bright colors, and string them for wearing.

ALUMINUM FOIL

Squeeze sculptural shapes from foil. Create fanciful insects, people, and animals. Add wire, feathers, and other decorative elements.

STYROFOAM

1. Stiff foam can be carved with sticks, knives, rasps, saws, and even with a hot soldering iron.
2. Individual shapes can be cut from stiff Styrofoam. Shapes can be glued together, or attached by joining with toothpicks or other sticks. Add decorative "stick-ons" to foam shapes.
3. Soft foam pieces can be cut with a scissor and attached with spray glue.
4. Stack forms to build large group sculptures.
5. Brush or spray paint.

MOBILES AND STABILES

Mobiles and stabiles are relatively new art forms, having been pioneered by Alexander Calder, one of the first to introduce the concept of motion in art (see Figure 3–6). Artwork of this type can be placed under the general heading of sculpture, or construction, as it is not done on a flat surface, and it can be viewed from all sides.

The most interesting characteristic of the mobile is that its lightweight individual parts move with the air currents, that is, motion is a prime feature of the mobile. As air passes against the parts of the construction, they turn gracefully

Sculpture: Constructing, Carving, and Casting

back and forth and around. In order for the mobile to be put into motion by the air currents, each part must be carefully balanced, almost as the parts of a clock are balanced. Do you suppose Calder got his idea for mobiles by watching the sensitively balanced parts of a clock? The difference between a mobile and stabile is that the stabile rests on a base.

Light is another major design factor in mobiles. The forms catch light as they move and reflect it. The forms also cast interesting shadows and these shadows become an important part of the over-all design.

Aesthetic considerations in the design of mobiles should include the structural challenges, the delicate balance, the design elements, the negative spaces between the shapes, the changing forms and their shadows, and the existing spaces surrounding the mobile.

Supplies Needed
lightweight wire
lightweight metal
straws
cardboard, balsa wood
string
tissue and colored cellophane paper
foil and metallic papers
sticks
yarn, reeds, and string
plastic
scissors, pliers, hammers, nails, and a saw
white glue or fast-drying airplane glue
nylon or monofilament thread (for hanging)

Procedure
1. String several wires across the classroom at convenient heights and have each student add hanging parts to it. In this manner, as each part is attached, it can be balanced on the spot. Design all the parts to be added and arrange them in units for balance, weight, movement, and shape.
2. Scissors or a knife can be used to cut out interesting flat forms. (If firm plastic sheets are used to make the forms, a coping saw may be necessary.)
3. Mobiles can be suspended from one spot in the ceiling. The remaining parts can cascade down at varying levels. These mobile shapes can be suspended from different armatures, such as a tree branch. Or, bend a coat hanger wire into various shapes and attach the mobile forms to it. For lightweight hangings, suspend shapes from plastic meat trays or plastic can lids. Simply poke holes in the plastic with a sharp object, suspend the forms from string, thread, or wire, and knot each string on the top side of the plastic.

4. Provide space and time to experiment with the materials; balancing and hanging a mobile is part of the building process. Many times, students want to work together to help each other carry out these steps.
5. Compose shapes, materials, and colors as the designs are formed with many of the materials listed.
6. Study the negative areas in between the forms in relation to balance and design.
7. Evaluate design as part of the mobile process, and experiment with changes in design as work progresses.
8. Many lightweight jewelry procedures and materials can be used to construct mobiles. (See Chapter 11.)

SPACE STRUCTURES

Supplies Needed
balloons (various sizes)
tape
plaster (see pages 388–389) to mix
string, yarn, or cloth
paint

Procedure
1. Inflate balloons and use them individually or attach balloons of various sizes with tabs of masking tape.
2. Mix the plaster as directed.
3. Dip string, cloth, or yarn into the wet plaster and then apply it to the inflated shapes.
4. Make sure the yarn crosses over itself frequently so that the plaster form is strong. Add decorative elements.
5. Let the plaster dry and then pop the balloons.
6. Spray paint the forms.

LINE-DESIGN BOARDS: STRING ART

Your students have probably made simple line designs using pencils and rulers, but they can be as simple or as complex as the designer wishes by using three-dimensional materials.

The fundamental idea is that a line is made by connecting pairs of points (in this case, stretched string) so that the design appears to be a curved shape. The simplest beginning design can be made by drawing a right angle. Mark off equidistant points every ½ to 1 inch so that each leg has the same number of points. If the points are numbered, the connecting points will be easy to see. This means connect point 1 to 1, point 2 to 2, and so on. The visual effect appears to be curved even though the actual lines are straight.

Sculpture: Constructing, Carving, and Casting

10–17 *With pencil or string, connect points 1 and 1, 2 and 2, and so on.*

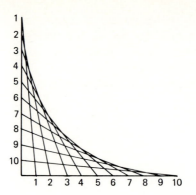

This art experience is appropriate for students of all ages—even preschoolers—if the concept is kept clear and simple. Such mathematical concepts as measurement, organization, and planning are necessary to make good line designs. (Very young students can prepare simple cardboard shapes and cut small slits into the outside edges of the cardboard. Attach the end of colored string, thread, or yarn into a slit. Thread it to another slit, and wind and weave several threads, string, or yarn to form designs.) From first grade up, students can use geometric shapes and V-, Y-, and X-shapes in their line-design boards.

A variation is to keep the right-angle concept in mind, and then to take one side of the angle and make it shorter. Keep the number of points on each side the same, squeezing up the points on the smaller size. Still match numbers 1 to 1, 2 to 2, and so on (the points will have unequal spacing). Now change the angle, making it an obtuse angle; change it again to an acute angle. There is no limit to the designs that can be generated once the concept is understood.

10–18 *Working with string art.*

368

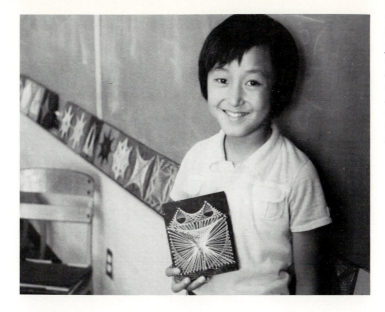

10–19 *This fourth-grade Korean student had difficulty at first with language communication, but was greatly admired and successful in creating line design boards as an inventive tool. Substitute cardboard with punched holes threaded with yarns for young artists.*

Supplies Needed
wood boards or fiberboard, about 6 × 6 inches
sandpaper
paper patterns, pencils, and a ruler
finishing nails and a hammer
spray paint
colored string or embroidery thread for designs (young students can use rubber bands around the points; then, if mistakes occur, they can easily be changed)

Procedure
1. Secure the boards from a lumberyard (pine scraps are fine). Sand them.
2. Spray paint the boards with an oil-based paint. Let them dry completely.
3. Plan a paper pattern first. Lightly glue the design onto the board on the corners.
4. Hammer nails through the design at designated points.
5. Tie the first string to the first nail.
6. Continue the design, going from point 1 to 1, point 2 to 2, as shown.

Creating Toys

Until the nineteenth century, toys were lovingly made by hand to delight and amuse young children. Today, toys are manufactured for us and are beautifully packaged by machinery. Making toys can involve everyone (adults too) in

Sculpture: Constructing, Carving, and Casting

10–20 *Five-in-one train set. This toy puzzle is also a pull toy. (Courtesy of Phil Van Voorst, The Hand and The Spirit Crafts Gallery, Scottsdale, Arizona.)*

continuously doing and solving. The toy is a play form, which means that the child brings past experiences to each new encounter. It is important to provide opportunities to create toys.

Costs can be kept minimal; the important objective is what we create. Simple materials, some recycled, can be turned into imaginative toy designs. The word *toy* flashes delightful fantasies and imaginings to our minds. Toys can be anything that requires manipulation and offers the user a challenge.

10–21 *Toys always have delighted the imagination of children. These Mexican handmade painted wooden horses have movable parts that operate when pulled by a string.*

Toys can move on the ground, fly in the air, hang and balance, have moving parts, make sounds, and create sensations. Playing with toys and games and doing arts and crafts procedures share many of the same behaviors.

They are self-motivating.
They are discovery-oriented.
They offer many possible alternatives.
They do not require adult approval.
They invite inquiry, exploration, and experimentation.
They invite original solutions and independent thinking.
They can modify behaviors.
They require decision making and making value judgments.

One fourth-grade teacher keeps a "toy idea box" in her closet. This box contains discards donated from home. To start yours, work from the following list, which suggests collectible materials that invite and challenge a child's thinking. The materials require the child's involvement to find unique solutions. The students manipulate the materials in fresh, new, and inventive ways. We talk of brain storming with words; here we brain storm with materials. The objective is to explore without predetermined outcomes.

marbles, batteries, propellers, rubber bands, wheels, old clocks and radio parts, all kinds of cloth and metal scraps, yarn, buttons, bells, beads, braiding, sequins, lace, linoleum, scraps, old cameras, typewriters, adding machines, pocket computers, springs, pulleys, gears, woods, rug samples, metal foil and gift wrap, papers, magnifying glasses, telescopes, all sizes and shapes of plastic containers, trays, bottles, lids, old jewelry parts, old toys, old photographs, old post cards, old doll parts, Halloween masks, old clothes and costumes, old furniture, old picture frames, boxes of all shapes, corrugated cardboard, nails, old signs, sea shells, wire, old lampshades, burlap, Styrofoam, carpet rolls, rocks, simple tools, bones, seeds, feathers, and glue.

Leave the box of collectibles available all year long. Offer display space for projects and encourage discussion and the interaction of ideas. Provide students with time for thinking and problem solving. Suggest ideas to expand those of the students and ask students to devise multiple ways of solving design problems. The artist and craftsperson often works through a problem while manipulating materials, exploring and "playing with" ideas. The artist is a self-motivator.

As soon as one idea gets under way, the ideas start flowing. Keep notebooks of your ideas and sketches for them. If we neglect to write down our inspirations, we often forget them. Sketches lead to thought building, and they can easily be referred to. Share your ideas with others. Reinterpretation and idea storming will lead to new discoveries.

You will be amazed at what will happen during the year to your class's "toy idea book."

We are still uncovering the many notebooks of Leonardo da Vinci. He was a hero in terms of being a self-starter. His many sketches indicate to us the original, inventive machines that he developed. The following is a list of possible toy inventions to include in your crafts curriculum.

a sound machine
a pulley machine with rubber bands
a push or pull toy
a "save the city" toy
"inventing a new tree"
time machines
a haunted house
a colonial miniature room
windups
flying machines
catch the wind toy
an ocean house
ride the clouds toy
three-dimensional puzzles
sensory toys: feeling boxes and smell bottles
space structures
fantasy sculptures
old toys into new ones
a "do nothing" toy

OPTICAL SPINNERS

These moving optical illusions will have everyone spinning. Excitement develops as the colorful, free-form designs on the cardboard move unpredictably. It's fun for all who spin.

Supplies Needed
cardboard, heavy paper plates, plastic lids or plastic meat trays cut into 4-inch circles
a 36-inch length of string
felt-tip pens or crayons

Procedure
1. Cut a 4-inch circle from cardboard, a paper plate, lid, or a plastic meat tray.
2. Create original bright, colorful designs all over the surface on front and back surfaces of the circle.
3. Punch two holes (with a pencil) about ¾ inch apart, near the center of the circle.
4. Thread the string through the two holes and tie the ends of the string together.

5. To work the spinner, place one loop of the string over each hand.
6. Twirl the strings until they are tightly wound.
7. Move your hands slowly apart and then back together again.
8. The spinner will spin quickly, causing the design colors to blend and change into new designs.

TOPS

English children create these toy tops for fun.

Supplies Needed
cardboard, paper plates, plastic meat trays
felt-tip pens
sharp pencil

Procedure
1. Decorate a 4-inch circle with unique and imaginative designs.
2. Push a sharp, pointed pencil through the center of the disc.
3. Spin the pencil with the fingers.

SCULPTURES IN THE SKY: FLYING KITES

We never outgrow the fun of flying kites, but how many of us have made our own? Did you ever wonder if kites were just for fun or had served other purposes? The best part of kites is that they need us to get them into the air and a windy day and open space in order to do their graceful dances.

A part of kite history is the fact that a gigantic kite flew a camera over the earthquake that devasted San Francisco back in 1906. In this way, it was possible to get aerial photographs of the city. Kite flying is an ancient art that was started centuries ago in East Asia. Legends tell us of warriors who used kites in clever ways to outwit their enemies. Bits of paper and cloth have long been used for aerial toys in folk tales and in celebrations in many cultures, including those of the English, Chinese, Indians, and Japanese. In the Bayeux Tapestry, a kite flies above the foot soldiers of William the Conqueror (see Chapter 1). Benjamin Franklin is said to have flown a kite in an electrical storm; Guglielmo Marconi, Alexander Graham Bell, Sir Isaac Newton, and the Wright brothers all experimented with kites. Kites have been used for recording temperatures, wind velocities, and humidities at altitudes of up to 24,000 feet. Kites were used to carry the first line of a suspension bridge across Niagara's gorge, and they have carried observers into the air and even pulled carriages. A popular hobby today is the soaring kite called the hang glider. People attach themselves to kites and fly with the wind from one point to another. Kite shops now sell bright, colorful kites imported from all over the world. Imported kites include the eleven-disc centipede kite that is 7 feet long (and can be made longer) with one hundred legs, and the 19-foot Indian dragon kite. Kite meets have been springing up all over the country. They give kite enthusiasts a chance to show the airworthiness of their latest creations. The object is to design kites to see which will attain the greatest altitude, longest flight, and quickest climb. The kite can also be thought of as a sculpture in natural motion, more abstract in form, large in size, and free to roam the vast space in the sky.

In order for a kite to fly, it must be balanced properly; therefore, trial and error are applied to balancing the unit. If the balance is not correct, differences must be checked in the rigidity, the paper or fabric tension, the amount of the bow, and the length of the bridle line (it may need shortening, lengthening, or shifting). One must always check for tears in a kite. Lengthening the tails may help to adjust a weight distribution. Further conditions for flying are wind, temperature, pressure, humidity, and gravity. Kites, therefore, offer ways to merge art with science, meteorology, math, and geography.

It is estimated that over 80 million kites will fly this year. Dinesh Bahadur, a proprietor of kite stores, says, "That feeling of contact from the kite through the fingers to the heart is what gives kite flying its beauty and value. I have had the feeling that kites are always lifting me up."

KITE I

Supplies Needed
lightweight sticks (a split yardstick is fine)
discards from the lumberyard
string and glue
butcher paper, or plastic sheeting (garbage bags), Mylar
cloth scraps
carpet warp
designs for kites—paint on or appliqué butterflies, fish, dragons, faces, moths, insects, flowers, and the like
drawing materials: crayons, felt-tip pens, tempera paints

Procedure
1. Each student needs two lightweight sticks: a 36-inch stick and a 30-inch stick. The students can work in pairs to tie the sticks.
2. First, measure 7 inches from one end of the long stick and mark it with a pencil. Also make a mark 15 inches from the

end of the short stick. Lay the short stick across the long stick matching the pencil marks.

3. One student can hold the sticks while the second ties the string firmly at the intersection of the sticks. Use a back-and-forth direction. If the sticks are still wobbly, apply some glue at the intersection.

4. With the carpet warp, wrap the end of each stick several times and move along the outside, going from stick to stick. Be sure the carpet warp is taut because the paper cover is later pasted over it.

5. Lay the kite frame on top of the heavy paper plastic or cloth. Draw around the frame; leave a 1½-inch margin all around.

6. Cut out the shape and draw and paint on designs. Let it dry.

7. Place the side with the design face down on the floor. Center the wood frame over the paper. Make ½-inch cuts in the paper where the four stick ends will be. Then bend the 1½-inch margin over and around the string and glue the paper down. Let it dry.

8. For stability a tail must be added. The tail length will depend on the wind, but it should be at least 8 feet long; tie cloth scraps together at intervals to strong string.

9. To bridle the kite, tie a string from one end of the long stick to the other end; leave enough slack so that the string stands out 5 inches from the frame at midsection. Tie the short sticks in the same way. Tie the flying string at the intersection. Adjust the bridle string during flight. Add or remove pieces of tail as the wind demands. Experiment and design your own kite. Have a school "fly in" contest.

KITE II

On May 5 of every year in Japan the Tango-No-Sekku, or the Japanese Boys' Festival, also called the Feast of the Flags and the Kite Festival, is held. On this day, all boys fly kites. In front of homes, symbolic kites fly from poles—the carp kite— one for each honored son (the largest kite is for the oldest son). The carp represents the qualities all boys hope to achieve: perseverance, strength, and bravery. The carp swims upstream each year against the current to lay its eggs and is, therefore, thought to be a worthy symbol. The kite is made of paper or cloth. (See color Figure 12.)

Supplies Needed
colored tissue, white tissue, or kraft paper
plastic sheeting, cloth
a strip of oak tag, 12 inches × ½ inch
paints, brushes, and felt-tip pens

newspaper and glue
string, ruler, scissors, and pencil

Procedure

1. Cut two identical fish shapes about 30 inches long, 10 inches wide at the middle, and 6½ inches wide at both ends (mouth and tail). The mouth must curve outward for the last 2 inches at the mouth ends.
2. Paint and draw decorative designs on both sides of the carp. Place one side down and glue the second one to it along the ½-inch edge. Do not glue the mouth closed.
3. Attach the round, fitted oak tag strip at the mouth: spread apart the mouth end, place glue along the inside mouth edge; press the oak tag strip onto the glued surface. (Leave enough paper or cloth along the edge—to fold over the oak tag.)
4. Fold over the cloth or paper glued edge so that the oak tag strip is covered.
5. The mouth should be round, open, and completely covered; the inside oak tag strip is for strength.
6. Draw three evenly spaced pencil marks on the mouth ring.
7. Make a small hole in each mark. With a 12-inch-long thread, tie into two holes.
8. With a 7-inch-long thread, tie into the remaining hole and into the center of the 12-inch thread.
9. All threads should be of equal length and meet in the center.
10. Tie a thread loop onto a longer kite string, or tie it to a tree, window, or pole outside and let the wind fly the kite for you.

10–22 *Kite flying is an ancient art and a popular sport today. More enthusiasts enjoy the challenge of designing their own creations.*

10–23 *"Kite Sculpture" by Pam Castano is made of metal and nylon rip stop, 8 feet wide × 17 feet high. It is installed at Honeywell, Inc., Phoenix, Arizona. (Courtesy of Honeywell, Inc.)*

KITE III

This kite is probably the most fun to fly. It is the "design your own flying sculpture" kind. Traditionally, most Oriental and East Indian kites are flat designs, such as Kite I. Three-dimensional kites such as the box kite, the tetrahedron, and the centipede are challenging to design as well. To begin, plan a general sketch of what appears to be a satisfying and feasible design. Design an imaginative outline shape with framing and add a light covering. A variety of materials to choose from are listed here. Construct a kite, add a flying line, and wait for a breeze to carry your sculpture to the sky.

Have a partner carry your kite about 100 feet down wind from you. Ask him to fan out the tail behind the kite and toss it up. Pull on the line as he does this. The kite will climb into the sky. Fly light kites in a light wind.

Supplies Needed

use materials that are lightweight, flexible to bend in the wind, inexpensive, and not easily broken or torn

for framing: either strong birch dowels about ³⁄₁₆ inch in diameter, rattan basket-weaving material, split bamboo poles cut into ¼-inch strips, bamboo garden stakes, bamboo strips from window blinds, or small sticks. (Balsa wood breaks easy, but sticks ¼ inch × 36 inches cut, bend, and glue readily.)

coverings: any size grocery bag (cut off the bottom), a plastic trash bag (24 × 36 inches or larger), polyethylene rolls (sold in garden shops), dry cleaners' bags for lightweight kites, light nylon fabrics, cotton sheeting, tissue paper, butcher paper, newspaper, Japanese rice paper and aluminized Mylar, which is a polyester with a reflective coating of aluminum or gold; it is difficult to tear it and very striking as it moves in the wind

decorations for plastics: crayons, permanent felt-tip pens, acrylic paints, or colored tape

fastenings: glue plastics to frames with hobby store cements, adhesive cellophane, or polyester or reinforced tapes; use white glue for papers; stitch cloth over a frame with a fast running stitch

lines: cotton string, about a 4-ply, nylon monofilament line from light to heavier line, depending on the kite weight (10- to 50-pound test), seine twine

reels: use a strong reel with nylon cord as it stretches; a 1-inch dowel piece or strong cardboard tubing

bridle: two or more strings tied to the kite frame (not the covering); the position of the ties determines the angle at which the wind will strike the kite; use cotton kite line

tails: long and lightweight to fly the kite better; tie on pieces of paper, lightweight rags, or plastic or Mylar strips, or use open-ended paper cups (with the wide ends facing the kite) tied to a cord every 8 to 12 inches

optional: helium balloons, crepe paper, streamers, surveyor's flagging ribbon

10–24 *More fish kites strung across the classroom to move in the air.*

Musical Instruments as Art Experience

Music is for all living creatures. It is a universal art shared by man and, possibly, by insects, animals, and plants.

One way to discover the world of sound and music is to construct your own instruments to produce different sounds and rhythms. Cultures throughout history have shared the dynamics of music with the visual arts. Every period in

Sculpture: Constructing, Carving, and Casting

10–25 *Ancient people used available materials for their musical instruments. Pictured from the drum, counter-clockwise, are prehistoric Indian instruments: Yaqui cocoon rattles, which are strung and wrapped around dancer's legs; a Hopi turtle-shell leg rattle; Hopi gourd rattle; Yaqui rattle; Hopi wood and strung-turquoise instrument; and a Pueblo wood and skin drum. (Courtesy of Heard Museum, Phoenix, Arizona.)*

history appears to have produced sounds in unique ways. Even today, African music has no rules about scales or order of notes. What is beautiful to the music maker is the sound created. What is important is not the complexity of the instrument, but the way the sounds are put together. Pueblo Indian music is thought to be one of the most complex of any music played by North American Indians. Its purpose is to bring supernatural help to crops and people. Much of the Pueblo music is choral. Their songs contain lines of varying lengths, and rather than a regular beat, there can be a different beat for each measure. Their musical artifacts, (made from bird-bone whistles, turtle shell, gourd and cocoon rattles and skin drums) illustrate the closeness of the Pueblo people to the earth.

Consider the following qualities before you construct instruments:

The sound qualities to be achieved
The aesthetics of the instrument to be constructed. The suitability of the materials to the desired sounds
The size and shape of the instrument in relation to the hand and mouth
The durability and cost of the materials to be used

Have fun constructing instruments—before you know it, you will be practicing music makers.

PERCUSSION INSTRUMENTS

Our first introduction to rhythm is as infants, slapping our hands on surfaces. And everyone enjoys beating out rhythms with their hands or feet. Any metal object makes a bell-like sound when it is hit with another object. Collect metal utensils from the kitchen or junkyard or use toy parts or old car parts. Drill holes in the metal objects and suspend them on string from a long stick or broom handle. Collect old spoons and forks in all sizes, flatten them with hammers, drill holes in them, and suspend them from various lengths of nylon cord. Hit them with another spoon. Discover the various syncopated notes you can create with these simple objects.

Cymbals

Try clapping pot lids together to imitate the sound of cymbals. Decorate them with paint for a visual effect.

Drums

The drum is the historical instrument of Africa. The Pueblo Indians also use the drum as their main instrument when they dance.

Procedure
1. To make a drum similar to the one used by the Pueblo Indians, stretch a leather skin over a clay pot.
2. Dampen the leather first and stretch it tightly over the pot.
3. Attach it to the pot with leather lacing. Other types of drums can be made from carved coconut shells and large gourds.

Hat boxes, tin cans, salt boxes, and round cereal boxes all make good drums. Decorate them with your own unique designs and play them with wooden spoons, dowels, bones, or just a pencil. The most effective of the simple drums one can make is the inverted wastebasket. Turn a metal wastebasket upside down on the floor or in your lap and beat away.

Or paint an old cookie tray and beat on it with a drumstick made from a piece of a broom handle, covered with an old sock that is tied on with string or a rubber band.

Bells and Chimes

Flower Pot Bells
Select (or make) a variety of sizes of earthenware flower pots. Build a holder such as a long wooden frame box. (Knock out the bottom of a wooden grocery box.) Tie each pot onto a piece of leather. Suspend the pots upside down, from their leather ties, into the holes in the box. Arrange them in sequence so that the dangling pots will make sounds from

low to high (larger pots have deeper sounds). Decorate them with acrylic paints.

Musical Glasses

Even famous musicians play this game. Select glass in a variety of sizes and shapes. Create a scale of sounds by filling the glasses with varying amounts of water. More water in the glass causes the glass to make a lower sound when it is struck. Color the water with vegetable coloring for a visual effect. Tap each glass with a spoon or fork. Bottles can be used instead of glasses in the same way. (Try blowing over both.)

Nail Chimes

Tie a variety of painted nails (of varying lengths and widths) with string to a long wood dowel. Vary the length of string. Space the nails about 3 inches apart and strike them with a metal object. Exchange old spoons or forks for the nails. Experiment for different rhythms and bell notes.

Bracelet Bells

Sew on small bells, shells, bottle caps, and other sound-producing objects to a strip of leather or cloth. Tie the cloth or leather to your wrist or leg. Listen to the sounds as you dance.

Xylophone

Procedure

1. Cut a 10-foot long and ¾-inch (or ⅞-inch) wide piece of electrician's pipe (either copper or steel) into graduated lengths with a metal saw (between eight to sixteen lengths of pipe).
2. Pad two strips of wood lattice (about 14 inches long) with felt or cloth.
3. Lay the various lengths of pipe perpendicular to the two wood strips (one strip across the top; one across the bottom).
4. Vary the distance between the pipes and experiment for sounds.
5. Use a wood bead on the end of a dowel for a beater.

Shakers and Rattles

All kinds of cans and boxes can be filled with seeds, rice, beans, pebbles, sand, metal objects, or anything small enough to make rattling sounds. The principle here is that of the papier-mâché maracas made by Latin Americans. Shake

the filled cans or boxes up and down, sideways, and in circles; tap them with your fingers; and gently strike them against each other. Paint designs on them.

The Pueblo Indians made rattles from gourds filled with pebbles. They decorated the carved gourds by painting on designs with clay slip. Other types of rattles were made from shells of the desert land tortoise.

Another type of rattle can be made by placing a Styrofoam ball at the end of a dowel or pencil. Cover the ball with decorative cloth and sew on any objects that will make noise when shaken. Use bells, tin can lids, or empty nut shells.

Tambourines

Join two pie tins at their centers with a brass paper clip, so that the bottoms are touching. Drill or punch holes along the edges of the plates. Hammer flat some bottle caps and punch holes in them. String the bottle caps with wire or string to the holes in the pie tins. Tie them securely so they won't shake off.

RHYTHM STICKS

Use ordinary wooden sticks or dowels about 12 inches long and of any diameter. Sand the sticks smooth and paint them. Strike or rub the two sticks together. For a different sound, carve small slots about 1 inch apart in the top surface of one stick. Rub the other stick across the grooves. To deepen the sound, rest the end of the notched stick on a basket or gourd. The Indians used the shoulder blade of a deer to rub across the notches in a stick of wood. Discover for yourself the varying sounds that can be made by rubbing various wood and bone objects together.

Sculpture: Constructing, Carving, and Casting

381

10–27 *Organic driftwood pieces can become handsome textured sculptures. Whittling, with a jackknife and soft woods, is a rewarding experience for students.*

Go on a stone hunt to find stones of different sizes and shapes. Paint the stones and cover them with a plastic finish. Rub or strike a variety of stones together.

Washboards are an old favorite as instruments. Just rub them with different tools to produce a variety of sounds.

STRING INSTRUMENTS

Banjos

Use a small wooden or cardboard box (a milk carton or cereal box about 2 inches deep works also). Cut ½-inch grooves along the top of two sides of the box that are opposite each other. Stretch string or rubber bands tightly across in the grooves (much like a warp). Rubber bands of various sizes will create varying sounds—the smaller bands will stretch farther and make higher sounds. Pluck the banjo gently with your fingers or use a toothpick to strum. A more elaborate banjo can be made from a carved gourd or painted cigar box.

Wood

WOOD CONSTRUCTION

Wood, being a natural material, is a special favorite among craftspeople. Using wood scraps and even old toys is fun and fascinating for students of all ages. It is through keen vision, experimentation, and imagination building that these shapes can form sculptures, skate boards, stilts, soapbox racers, whistles, and many other clever concoctions.

Supplies Needed
wood shavings, dowels
lumberyard scraps, pine boards
wood from trees, stumps, and branches
old wooden household articles
old toys
toothpicks
wood sticks such as counting sticks (comes in colors)
nails and hammers
tissue and cellophane paper and felt and cloth scraps
white glue
paint, stains, and brushes

Procedure
1. Collect interestingly textured wood shapes.
2. Discover what you can do with the wood: pound it with nails and hammers, point tools into it, and scratch and carve away at it with tools. Determine its hardness.
3. Arrange the wood shapes into the most pleasing arrangement, changing the shapes and reevaluating the design. See if the shapes of the wood can suggest designs. Consider line, spaces, and movement as well as planes.
4. Secure small and lightweight wood pieces by gluing them with white glue. (Fast-drying household cements speed up the drying process.)
5. Nail and hammer large pieces of wood together.
6. After completing a construction, sand any rough edges, if desired.

10–28 *Wood collage stresses form, texture, pattern, and repeated shapes. Use woods from tree limbs, pine boards, dowels, crates, and lumberyard scraps.*

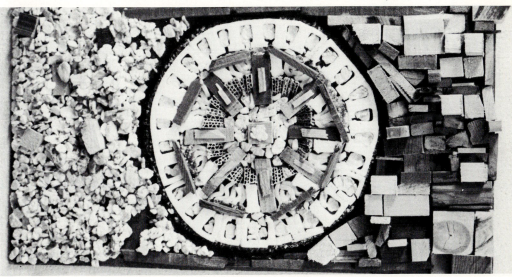

7. Paint or stain the finished sculptures. Add any further decorative pieces.

WOOD COLLAGE

Sand small wood scraps and gather wood shavings and driftwood pieces. Glue them to a surface of thin wood or Masonite (cardboard will warp from the weight). Build an entire environmental collage panel.

STICK OR STRAW SCULPTURE

Procedure
1. Lay out sticks into designs (squares, triangles, and free-form shapes) and glue them together on waxed paper or foil to prevent sticking.
2. After these small shapes have dried, begin to build a larger construction by carefully adding more shapes with glue.
3. Prop up the shapes, if necessary, or glue the sticks together into a constructed form adding each stick as you build.
4. Fill the insides of some of the created shapes with colored cellophane, tissues, plastic foil papers, or crayon shavings ironed inside waxed paper.
5. As straws are pliable and ideal building units, construct round and free forms with them; try twisting, pleating, and bending the straws into shape.
6. Attach the straws at the joints with the glue, nonhardening clay, marshmallows, or gumdrops.
7. Straws can also be strung on string, joined with 2 U-shaped pipe cleaners (one in each straw catching each other), and with paper clips. The paper clip used regularly will provide a flexible joint; open the clip into an S-shape (one clip in each straw) and join for a stiffer connection.

CARVING WOOD

There is something very special about working with wood. The feel of the texture, the look of the grain, and most expecially, the smell of the wood all combine to make for a unique sensory experience.

One of the best reasons for working in wood is to learn the various kinds of wood that are available in our environment. Looking for aesthetic shapes and forms and thinking how one can relate forms to achieve an interesting sculpture are also valuable experiences. Wood is available to students as a result of trips to forests and deserts. A search along paths on

10–29 *Carved cottonwood bird and fanciful wind thingamagig. Artists unknown.*

the way home from school also can provide wood scraps. Learn to classify various woods and grains.

When carving with a found piece of wood, first remove the bark. If the wood is still wet, it will be hard to work. Select pieces of wood that have been weather dried in the sun or dried in a warm basement or attic. It is fun to find woods that have unusual shapes and textures on ocean beaches, fields, or forests, and it is also fun to imagine where they originate. Try cutting into the wood to estimate its degree of hardness.

Balsa wood is handy for classroom use. Pine cut ends, available at lumberyards, and scrap branches are good for beginning woodcarvers. Often, the simple beautiful shape of the wood itself will determine the final carved shape. (See Figure 10–27.)

WOODWORKING TOOLS

In the elementary school classroom, simple tools can be used effectively: gouges, mallets, nails, rasps, chisels, saws, and dull knives. Typical carpenter's tools are the hand saw (coping saw), square, tape measure, and drill. Needed, too, are sandpapers, clamps, and a power hand tool for grinding, drilling and polishing. Power tools are very helpful, but they must be used under supervision. Dull knives are very practical, if used with caution, and are very versatile. Most of us, as young children, can remember whittling objects from branches with simple pocket knives as our basic tool.

WOOD TEXTURES

Use a wire brush and work with the grain to enhance the texture of the wood. The soft intermediate wood layers will brush out, leaving the harder grain and accentuating the natural forms in the wood grain. Another technique for raising surface texture is to use the flame of a candle, or a propane or acetylene torch. Burn the surface until the wood gives off a red glow under the flame but is not hot enough to

Sculpture: Constructing, Carving, and Casting

385

continue to burn after the flame is removed. Wipe the wood with a damp rag. After burning, use a wire brush to take away the softer woods. You will be able to see a difference in the color and shine of the wood.

Try brushing with different intensities, from soft to hard. You will find that you will be able to achieve a variety of textures and even colors with this technique. Burnishing is still another technique that is done by rubbing the wood with a hard object such as another piece of wood, bone, stone, or glass. You will probably have to rub fairly hard, but the wood becomes beautifully polished. Even wood shavings can be used for rubbing to achieve highlights in the wood.

For those times when you want a smooth finished surface, such as on parts of driftwood, or on an object you want to paint, gradually change from rough to finer-grained sandpaper until you have the finish you like. In certain instances, a contrast of rough and smooth textures is very beautiful.

WOOD FINISHES

1. Pure lemon oil is a simple and inexpensive polish that should be used sparingly. It is commonly preferred for furniture, especially antiques, and should be used about once a month.
2. Liquid shoe polish soaks into wood and produces dark colors. Solid shoe polish is a good wood finish, also.
3. Solid-type wax finishes give uniform colors.
4. Salad, olive, or mineral oil keeps wood from drying out. In kitchen utensils, it keeps wood from becoming waterlogged. Rub oil into wood with a soft cloth.
5. Use hard carnuba floor wax, then polish with a soft cloth.
6. Petroleum jelly is not sticky and gives a silky feel and look to wood.
7. Varnish, shellac, and lacquer are synthetic finishes and should be applied as directed on the cans or sprays.
8. Paint requires a smooth surface and the use of a filler sometimes before regular and enamel products are applied. On whittled figures, apply a coat of gesso first, or use a flat white ordinary house paint as a base. Glossy enamel paints give intense, high color.
9. Thinned watercolor, acrylic, and tempera paints can be used as stains. Brush them on or apply them with a soft cloth.
10. A simple permanent stain is a burnt umber oil paint, thinned with turpentine to give the desired color.
11. Powder paint can be mixed with water, linseed oil, or turpentine. Rub it on with a cloth.
12. Crayons can be rubbed into wood. Then run a cloth dampened with linseed oil over the wood.

Carving

SMOOTH GOURDS

Collect gourds in the fall of the year when they are ripe. Carve them with a nail or small screwdriver while they are still moist. Consider the all-around design of the individual shape and divide the gourd into interesting spaces. Then carve the designs into these spaces. Let the gourds dry. In Africa, carved gourd pieces are used to block print fabrics. The dry gourds are boiled in water until they are moist again and the outsides are cut to desired sizes and shapes. The block is then used as a repeated stamp print. If your gourds have dried out, try soaking or boiling them to make them soft enough to carve.

After the gourd is dry, rub it with a wax shoe polish (liquid shoe polish gives intense color; paste shoe polish gives a delicate tone). Colors that work well are oxblood, tan, and brown. Let the polish dry and then shine the gourd. Or try drawing into the incised lines with felt-tip pens. If you wish, drill the gourds and hang them on cords to display them.

WAX

The same carving techniques can be used on wax. Pour colored melted paraffin into greased containers such as milk cartons. If there are dips in the center, melt some more wax and fill them. Try pouring the wax into unusually shaped molds such as hollow plastic balls, plastic toys, and egg molds. Carve the hardened wax with simple tools such as nails, hard sticks, linoleum or wood carving tools, or dull knives. Scratch the design on the surface of the wax, and then carve the design to the depth desired. If you are making a candle, insert a thin candle with a wick into the mold before pouring the wax.

Sculpture: Constructing, Carving, and Casting

387

10–31 *Carved plaster head.*

SOAP

A traditional carving project is to simply carve a shape from a bar of soap. Use a nail or dull knife and carve the bar, turning it often to consider its three-dimensional surfaces. Carved pieces of soap can be joined by inserting toothpicks into them.

PLASTER

Students enjoy carving in three-dimensional media. Studying the art qualities of sculpture, both from real objects or pictorial examples, adds to the students' knowledge of sculpted design. Viewing art from all angles, feeling forms and textures, and considering both positive and negative design forms all add to the students' conceptual development. Sculpting some materials may require too much skill for students; plaster mixtures offer a lightweight material that provides the student with an opportunity to carve his ideas with simple tools. Skills developed in cutting, scratching, and gouging indicate the subtractive process as opposed to the modeling process. In working with plaster, the design forms are created by taking away from the whole.

Prepare a plaster mix as directed under "Plaster Casting," pages 391–393. If you want to, add color, coffee grounds, or vermiculite (from building supply houses) for interesting textures. Oil or rub with Vaseline any form you plan to use as a mold, such as a shoe box. A small milk carton is a good size with which to begin. Another interesting form can be created by pouring the plaster into a sturdy plastic bag; squeeze and

10–32 *From left to right, a clay head; a glue, tissue paper, and straw mobile; a carved and painted plaster block; and a sanded and painted wood block.*

388

alter this free-form shape as the plaster hardens. Or try building an interesting shape with a wire armature (coat hangers will do). Work quickly with the plaster, a spoon, and a knife to build on top of these wire forms.

When working with a mold, let the plaster harden and then tear away the outside mold. Carve the plaster with simple kitchen tools, nails, or chisels if they are available. Dip the plaster form in water to soften the surface for easier carving. When the carving is finished, sandpaper it for a smooth texture, if desired, and rub the sculpture with clear or colored shoe polish or with a cloth that has been dipped into diluted paint.

Try draping plaster-soaked bandages, which are available at drug supply stores, around wire, balloons, wood armatures, or molds.

No one tires of doing handprints or footprints in plaster. Simply mix the plaster as directed and pour it into a paper plate or aluminum pie plate. Rest a hand in the plaster for a few minutes. Remove the plaster mold when it is dry.

RECIPES FOR CARVING MATERIALS

Supplies Needed

1 part plaster	1 part cement	1 part sand
	or	or
1 part sawdust	5 parts Zonolite	2 parts plaster
or		1 part Zonolite or
3 parts plaster		2 parts vermiculite
2 parts vermiculite		
3 parts water		

Procedure

1. Mix the dry ingredients with water until the mixture holds together and is a smooth, creamy consistency. Stir well.
2. Pour the mixture into molds such as milk cartons or cardboard boxes that have been covered with shellac.
3. Let the mixture set until it is dry and hard.
4. Carve the hardened material next day.

Checkpoints

1. All plaster castings or carvings can be given a shiny finish by dissolving soap flakes in a bowl until they are like cream and then soaking the plaster in the solution for 30 minutes. Remove the plaster from the solution and polish it with a dry cloth until it shines.
2. Proportions can be changed to vary the hardness of the

plaster—the greater the amount of plaster, the harder the mix.

3. Mix the plaster in pliable plastic buckets.

4. After the mix has been poured into containers (molds), the plaster will harden quickly. Shapes can be carved after about 30 minutes. The blocks will keep indefinitely while they are in the molds.

5. If a plaster shape becomes too hard during carving, submerge it in water to soften it.

6. Have the students place their plaster carving inside of a cardboard carton as they carve. This helps control the dust and small cut pieces of plaster, which then can be thrown away.

7. Carving tools can be anything from spoons, nails, blunt knives, small old saws, files, chisels, or pocket or paring knives (for older students). Try carving coal.

8. Molds can be any container; milk cartons are already waxed, but other containers can be lined with wax paper or greased with oil or vaseline.

9. Sandpaper and fine steel wool remove rough textures.

Mosaics

Plaster grout is used for mosaics of all kinds. Seeds, tile, pebbles, rocks, wood, and scrap materials can be glued to any

10–33 *A mosaic table was made by gluing down glass pieces to a plywood base. Plaster grout was then poured around the shapes to fill in the open spaces. Wood pieces, stones, jewelry, and broken pottery also can be used for mosaics.*

hard surface such as Masonite, wood, or heavy cardboard. The grout is then poured around the objects and then hardens. Wipe off any excess grout. (Substitute baker's clay for plaster.)

EGGSHELL MOSAICS

Supplies Needed
eggshells
seeds (pumpkin, watermelon, and sunflower)
vinegar and water for cleaning solution
quart jars
food coloring
glue and small brushes to apply it
drawing tools (crayons or felt-tip pens)
plastic spray or shellac (for finishing)
cardboard backing

Procedure
1. Wash the eggshells gently in soapy water.
2. Soak them overnight in a vinegar and water solution to remove egg membranes.
3. Spread the shells apart and let them dry.
4. Crush the shells between sheets of waxed paper.
5. Divide them among several jars and add food coloring or tempera paint to each jar.
6. Leave the shells in the dye until they are desired color.
7. Prepare designs on a cardboard.
8. Apply glue with a brush or cotton swab in one area of the design.
9. Sprinkle on shells in a desired color.
10. Carefully shake off any excess shells and replace them in their jar.
11. Continue applying areas of glue and colored shells to complete the design.
12. Add areas of dried beans and seeds.
13. Let the glue dry. Finish the project by coating it with a plastic spray.

Casting

PLASTER CASTING

Plaster casting is best done out of doors in a place where water is available. The beach or a sand pile is a ready made place to do sand casting with plaster. Have the children wear old clothes and remove all jewelry from their hands.

10–34 *Cast ceramic tile, 6 inches × 6 inches, by Ken Goldstrom. (Courtesy of The Hand and The Spirit Crafts Gallery, Scottsdale, Arizona.)*

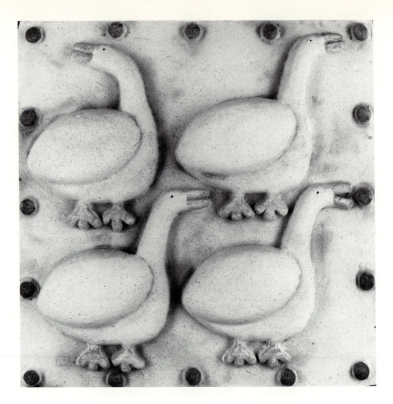

PREPARING PLASTER

Supplies Needed
forks and spoons
plastic bucket
water
stick (for mixing)
casting plaster (available at hardware stores; 4 cups of plaster to 1 quart of water)
sand
boxes of desired size: shoe boxes, plastic cups, milk cartons, and small boxes for jewelry-sized pieces and wall hangings

Procedure
1. Fill a container with sand.
2. Wet the sand with water, but do not get it soggy.
3. Smooth the surface sand with your hand.
4. Carve a design into the sand with a stick, about 1 inch deep.
5. Decorate the surface with other tools such as forks and spoons; embed old jewelry, weeds, bones, stones, and shells into the sand.
6. Carefully demonstrate how those objects embedded in

10–35 *Young craftsmen proudly display their hardened castings. After the plaster has set and the sand has been brushed away, the completed plaster casting is revealed.*

the sand will later project out after being cast with plaster. Most of the object will be placed into the sand with some part still visible; this part is captured by the plaster.

7. Prepare the plaster by first placing 1 quart of water into a bucket.

8. Add 4 cups of plaster slowly until a small mound stays above the water surface.

9. Stir the mixture with your hands until it is smooth. (Remove all lumps.)

10. When the plaster reaches the consistency of heavy cream, pour (or spoon out) the mixture quickly onto the top of the sand in the bucket to a thickness of 1½ inches.

11. While it is wet, quickly insert paper clips, looped string, or wire Us into the back of plaster so that the casting can be hung later.

12. Let the plaster harden for about 30 minutes, or until it is no longer warm.

13. Invert the bucket to remove the sand, rinse the cast off under a hose (outside), and your casting is ready to be hung.

14. Clean your utensils *immediately*, but never clean them in an inside sink or the drains will become clogged.

15. A small amount of salt in the plaster mix will speed the thickening; vinegar will retard the setting speed.

Sculpture: Constructing, Carving, and Casting

SAND CAST CANDLES OR SCULPTURES

Before the advent of electricity, candles were very important in people's lives. Our ancestors worked, ate, and lived by candlelight. Today, candles are used mostly for decoration. The initial candle shapes that you devise will entice you into inventing many more free-form candle sculptures.

Supplies Needed
a large sand pile, or a cardboard box filled with sand or individual, large plastic or tin cans filled with sand
wicks (or an old candle placed in the center for the wick)
enough paraffin for the class
broken crayons, colored candles, or food coloring wire (such as a coat hanger) or a pencil
driftwood, bark, jewelry, braiding, plastic flowers, and shells

Procedure
1. Place the sand in the container to be used. If a large box is used, mark the sand in units; then each student carves his shape in a unit.
2. Dampen the sand so it will hold its shape.
3. Sculpt out the desired shape. If the candle is to stand, plan three or four legs, or indent a jar lid into the sand to provide a level bottom.
4. Partially embed any decorative pieces into the sand. The embedded pieces are the ones that will show later; the piece you now see will have the wax around it. Natural forms such as weathered wood or pebbles work well. Plan some patterns, textures, and shapes pressed into the sand to add more interest to the finished candle.

10–36 *Either a large box or cans can hold sand for cast candles.*

5. Suspend the wick from a piece of wire or a pencil from across the rim of the container so that it touches the bottom of the mold. See Figure 10–37.
6. To make your own wick, soak a piece of heavy cotton string in a solution of 1 cup of warm water, 1 tablespoon of salt, and 2 tablespoons of borax powder for 2 hours; or use a string that has been dipped in paraffin as a wick.
7. Melt the paraffin in a large tin can over water, or use a double boiler, adding crayons for color, or melt a large amount of wax in a deep fryer.
8. Pour the paraffin into the mold cavities in layers, letting one layer cool slightly before proceeding. (This prevents holes and shrinkage in the wax.) To achieve multicolored layers, pour in various colored waxes.
9. Let the wax cool for about 2 hours.
10. Remove the candle from the sand, brush off the excess sand, or dip the outside of the candle into heated wax (this holds the sand to the candle).

Alternate Procedure

Candles can also be cast into wet clay molds.

1. Use a large ball of clay (the size of a large melon). Open a cavity in the center.
2. Press objects into the inside walls of the cavity (we used round meat bones).
3. Melt a large amount of paraffin in a deep fryer (add crayons for color).
4. Carefully scoop out cups full of wax and pour them into open clay molds. The wax must be poured slowly so that it settles into layers (various colors can be used if desired).
5. Let the wax harden—about 30 minutes. Then dig away the wet clay.

Sculpture: Constructing, Carving, and Casting

10–38 *A large clay lump is hollowed out and designs are carved into its inside. The oblong shapes in the photograph were made by pressing a bone into the clay. Then molten wax is poured into the clay cavity.*

Other candle shapes can be made by using various molds such as waxed, oiled, or greased cardboard tubes, oatmeal cartons, or milk cartons. An interesting skeletal effect can be achieved by placing ice cubes into a milk carton and then pouring hot wax around them. Another candle design is created by whipping the paraffin while it is still hot (with an eggbeater), and then placing it over two blocks of paraffin that have been tied together. The result looks like a whipped cake candle. Decorations such as glitter can be added while the wax is still warm. Try embedding objects into the wax as you pour it. Another way to work with wax is to cover a cookie sheet with a ¼-inch wax layer. When the wax is warm, break off pieces and shape them into birds, flowers, and abstract designs, with the heat of your hand.

Bibliography

ACCORSI, WILLIAM, *Toy Sculpture.* New York: Van Nostrand Reinhold Company, 1965.

ALLER, DORIS. *Wood Carving Book.* Menlo Park, Calif.: Lane Book and Magazine Co. 1951.

ANDREWS, MICHAEL. *Sculpture and Ideas.* Englewood Cliffs, N.J.: Prentice-Hall, Inc., 1965.

ARNOLD, JAMES. *The Shell Book of Country Crafts.* New York: Hastings House Publishers, 1969.

BAYLEY, THOMAS. *Model Making in Cardboard.* Harbor City, Calif.: Dryad Press, 1973.

BROMMER, GERALD F. *Wire Sculpture.* Worcester, Mass.: Davis Publications, Inc., 1968.

CALDER, ALEXANDER. *Mobiles*. New York: Museum of Modern Art, 1950.

CANEY, STEVEN. *Toy Book*. New York: Workman Publishing Co., 1972.

CHICHURA, DIANE B., AND THELMA K. STEVENS. *Super Sculpture: Using Science, Technology, and Natural Phenomena in Sculpture*. New York: Van Nostrand Reinhold Company, 1973.

ELISCU, FRANK. *Sculpture Techniques in Clay, Wax, and Slate*. Great Neck, N.Y.: Arts and Crafts Book Club, 1961.

FOWLER, H. *Kites, a Practical Guide to Kite Making and Flying*. New York: The Ronald Press Company, 1953.

GOLOMB, CLAIRE. *Young Children's Sculpture and Drawing*. Cambridge, Mass.: Harvard University Press, 1974.

HELFMAN, HARRY. *Making Your Own Sculpture*. New York: William Morrow & Co., Inc., 1971.

JOHNSTONE, JAMES B., AND SUNSET STAFF. *Woodcarving Techniques and Projects*. Menlo Park, Calif.: Lane Book and Magazine Co., 1971.

KLIMO, JOAN FINCHER. *What Can I Do Today?* New York: Pantheon Books, Inc., 1971.

LYNCH, JOHN. *Metal Sculpture*. New York: The Viking Press, Inc., 1957.

LEYH, B. *Children Make Sculpture*. New York: Van Nostrand Reinhold Company, 1972.

LIDSTONE, JOHN. *Building with Cardboard*. New York: Van Nostrand Reinhold Company, 1968.

MARKS, MICKEY. *Sand Sculpturing*. New York: The Dial Press, 1963.

MILLS, JOHN W. *The Technique of Casting for Sculpture*. London: Batsford, 1967.

MEILACH, DONA, AND DON SEIDEN. *Direct Metal Sculpture*. New York: Crown Publishers, Inc., 1965.

MOGELON, ALEX, AND NORMAN LALIBERTE. *Art in Boxes*. New York: Van Nostrand Reinhold Company, 1974.

REED, CARL, AND JOSEPH ORZE. *Art from Scrap*. Worcester, Mass.: Davis Publications, Inc., 1973.

RESMUSEN, HENRY, AND ART GRANT. *Sculpture from Junk*. New York: Reinhold Publishing Corp., 1967.

ROGERS, L. R. *Relief Sculpture*. New York: Oxford University Press, 1974.

ROSENBERG, S. *Children Make Murals and Sculpture: Experience in Community Art Projects*. New York: Van Nostrand Reinhold Company, 1962.

SELZ, JEAN. *Modern Sculpture*. New York: George Braziller, Inc., 1963.

STEVENS, HAROLD. *Art in the Round*. New York: Van Nostrand Reinhold Company, 1965.

STRIBLING, MARY LOU. *Art from Found Materials*. New York: Crown Publishers, Inc., 1971.

VERHILST, WILBART. *Sculpture: Tools, Materials and Techniques*. Englewood Cliffs, N.J.: Prentice-Hall, Inc., 1973.

WEISS, HARVEY. *Sticks, Spools and Feathers*. New York: William R. Scott, 1962.

Jewelry and Adornment

One of the rewards of an arts program is to hear the original designer say, "I made it myself." From the making of simple designs to the wearing of one's own handmade creations, from making strung clay buttons to painted pebble jewels, invention and skills are required. The treasury of art can be expanded into a lifetime of search and discovery for the student. Bring the wonders of past and present crafts into your classroom. The student is an open-minded, curious, and spontaneous person who is motivated by the offer of knowledge. You, the teacher, hold the key to success in art by your words, your inspiration, and your eagerness to encourage each child in the search and realization of his or her creative potential.

Wearing a disguise and "dressing up" can make us feel changed and capture different attitudes. There are special times we want to invent our personalities in a play drama or just disguise our appearance for fun. Behind a mask or costume we can become anything—a cowboy, a police detective, a spy-ring smasher, a circus clown, or even a famous television star. By mimicking characters we can become anything or anyone we wish. We can pretend to fly through space like Superman, jump back into time to chat with Benjamin Franklin, or float down the Nile River in Cleopatra's barge. So with costumes, masks, wigs, makeup, hats, old shoes, and jewelry, we can become "dressed up."

History of Jewelry

The earliest evidence of decorative adornment appears in cave paintings from the Paleolithic era. The materials used

11–1 *On left, woven choker necklace with wrapped cords procedure, by Susan Coffrey. On right, a necklace by Norma Hand. The design is cloth appliquéd and then stuffed. (Courtesy of the Scottsdale Fine Arts Commission, Scottsdale, Arizona.)*

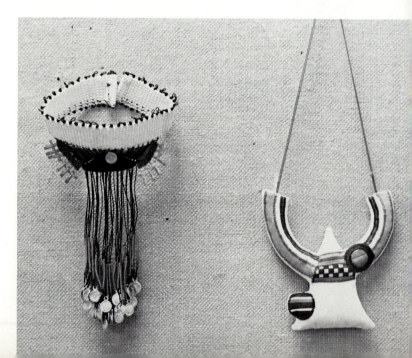

then for adornment were considered valuable. For instance, a 20,000-year-old necklace of seashells from a particular region was as valuable to its owner as a necklace of matched pearls is today. Other precious materials used were ivory, reindeer antlers, and amber (which is fossilized resin from pine trees).

Decorating oneself, thus, goes back to early man. His craft materials were bones, weeds, horns, wood, shells, teeth, and rocks. He assigned special meaning to these body ornaments, as well as to the painting of his body. Sometimes the ornaments recorded his experiences and at other times they had magical powers. Very simple tools were devised to drill holes and string objects for wearing. The same tools were used to carve hunting implements and intricate ornaments. As civilization progressed, many beautiful gems were found and were combined with rare metals. As more complex tools were developed, man changed the design of natural rare stones and metal. (See color Figure 13.)

Early in European history most of the jewelry worn had special meaning, such as a memento or as a sign of social distinction and, even more, of social privilege. In the nineteenth century, wearing jewelry that had no social significance was introduced. Up until the eighteenth century, both men and women wore jewelry; after the French Revolution, it became more of a feminine expression.

Today, in the handcraft revival, craftspeople are again enjoying using natural materials for jewelry for their textures and colors; bones, stone, metal, ivory, wood, and fibers all interrelate beautifully. Craftspeople are also practicing old techniques. For example, they are producing enamels, an ancient craft that became a highly refined art form between the fifth and twelfth centuries in the hands of Byzantine craftsmen.

11–2 *Painted velvet, quilting, and crochet make up the construction of this neckpiece by Betsy Benjamin-Murray. (Photo courtesy of the artist.)*

11–3 *Practicing the traditional craft of metal enameling, these students expectantly await the transformation that occurs when metal and glass are heated in an electric kiln.*

Jewelry and Adornment

401

11–4 *A second-grade artist holds his finished copper enamel piece, which he feels looks like a miniature painting filled with color.*

We are fascinated by the brilliance of some stones, from the textures, colors, and surfaces of a discovered pebble in the road to the multiple secrets uncovered from the deep earth of rare stones that are later polished. No matter where you live, beautiful rocks and perhaps gemstones rest beneath your feet and are waiting for you to discover their luminous and mysterious qualities.

INDIAN JEWELRY: OUR AMERICAN HERITAGE

The turquoise stone has been cherished by the Indians of the Southwest for many centuries. As the legend goes, the stone is said to have special powers. If even a simple stone were tied into the hair, it would ward off calamity, and the wearer could avoid many of life's misfortunes. It was a good luck piece. The Indians traveled long distances to obtain turquoise, the deeper blue and hardest stones being the most prized.

In about the middle of the nineteenth century, metal was introduced to the Navajo Indians. The first jewelry work done by the Navajos with metals was done in iron, copper, and brass. The Navajo men learned the craft while they were detained at Fort Sumner (1863 to 1868) and made copper bracelets and ring bits. Eventually, they took the craft home and began producing jewelry in silver. Silver is said to symbolize the gleam of the moon. Their equipment was very crude: a shovel or a prehistoric potsherd for a melting pot, scissors, a hammer, and a file. American dollars and Mexican pesos were rich in silver content and were malleable, so they were used by the Navajos in their silver jewelry. Today, most Indian jewelry is made of sterling silver. Although sophisticated equipment is available, many Navajo jewelers still work silver with primitive tools, such as an elementary forge and bellows, files, and anvil (from a section of iron rail) mounted on a box, and handmade stamp dies.

The jewelry was originally made for the gratification of the craftspeople, but soon it became an item desired by the public. A favorite necklace is the squash blossom. (See Figure 11–5.) The blossom design is taken from the Mexican trouser and jacket ornament that represents the young fruit of the pomegranate. The pomegranate design has been a favorite Spanish design for centuries, having been popular with the Moors. The crescent pendant, called a *najah* design, is found in the Old World as well as in ancient Pueblo ruin sites. The stamped and engraved designs have no symbolic meaning; they were merely taken from the Spanish and Mexican work. (See Figure 11–5.)

The Zuni Indians learned silver craft in about 1870. Until about 1920, most of their silver jewelry was traded or sold to

11–5 *Examples of contemporary Indian jewelry. At upper right are a Zuni inlaid stone and shell thunderbird and bracelet. A Navajo cast crescent is suspended from hand-formed (part of the traditional squash blossom) shallow silver beads. Since prehistoric times, hand-carved serpentine bear fetishes have been thought to contain a "spirit" that gives supernatural assistance to its owner. The hand-turned shell beads are drilled and ground on sandstone. The beaded deer head is of beads on cloth over a cow vertebra. The owl, lower right, is hand-carved and polished antler bone.*

other Indians. Before traders began buying the Zuni jewelry, there were not more than eight silversmiths in the community. During World War II, production increased until today hundreds of Zuni Indians and some entire Zuni families are at work at it. Zuni jewelry is distinguished by the many small turquoise stones, carved turquoise, shells, and inlaid pieces of many kinds of stone. The Navajo jeweler places emphasis on the silver design whose turquoise settings are secondary to it; much of the silver work includes stamped designs. The Hopi Indians also fashion silver jewelry, having begun in about 1935, using traditional designs found on their pottery and employing silver overlay techniques. The overlay techniques use two flat pieces of metal. A design shape is cut or sawed out from one piece of metal leaving a void, or negative shape. This metal piece is then fused on top of a second piece of metal by being either

Jewelry and Adornment

11–6 *Masks can hide us and change us by making us feel and look different.*

glued or soldered. In the classroom, this process can be easily adapted for student use by substituting a thin metal shim (hardware store variety of aluminum, copper, and brass). (See page 408–410.)

Masks and Costumes

The most inventive, creative face coverings can be made from anything and everything: from paper bags, papier-mâché (see pages 138–139), cardboard boxes, wood, weavings, feathers, shells, and an assortment of scrap objects. Study the facial masks and sculptures of Africa, Mexico, China, Indians of North and South America, and New Guinea as excellent motivations for mask making.

Masks can be used for pretending, for exaggerating, for frightening, or for hiding the way we feel. They are disguises. Sometimes masks can express the way we would like to feel. At other times they project us into another personality. They often provide us with ways to act out feelings we might otherwise be afraid to express. Did you ever notice that children's masks often reflect their own facial images as well as their inner feelings? Next time your class makes masks, take note of how similar the masks are to their own images.

Costumes also are body coverings. They can be made from any materials, such as sheeting, papers, old towels, and old clothes from home or thrift shops. Add decorative items such as chiffon, cheesecloth, feathers, old jewelry, and stuffed paper forms, to bring imaginative qualities to the costume.

Costumes are ordinarily designed as exaggerations to be used in plays and at parties, fairs, parades, and other social functions. They can be fun to make and wear and be the

11–7 *Dressing up in costumes and pretending are fun. Costumes, hats, makeup, and scenery change our appearances and cast us into an imaginary world.*

utmost challenge for the students' imaginations. They can also release inner feelings as the student assumes an identity, such as in role playing. Watch young kindergartners wearing their mother's or father's clothes and listen to the words and ideas expressed through this dramatic performance. Study clothing as part of history.

Decorating one's face with makeup and painted designs or objects was man's first effort at changing his image. We have evidence of primitive tribes that still paint their body parts to transform their images.

Whatever form we use to change ourselves—masks, costumes, or makeup—it is fun to imagine the many possibilities open to us.

Jewelry Terms

Anneal: To restore metal to its maximum softness by heating and allowing it to cool. With copper or silver, cooling must be done quickly and immediately after the metal gets red hot. This is done by quenching in cold water or pickle.

Bezel: A collar around a stone that holds it to the mounting (in a ring, for example).

Casting: To form an object by pouring or forcing molten metal into a mold.

Channel Work: Often practiced by the Zuni Indians; grooves, or canals, of silver are formed to hold stones.

Charcoal Block: Used for soldering and annealing, the charcoal absorbs and reflects the heat to achieve a more even temperature.

Chasing: Decorating the surface of metal by indenting it with a hammer and other tools.

Enamel: A vitreous glass in powdered form that is heated in a kiln and fuses the glass to a metal surface.

Engrave: To cut into a surface; to carve or to etch.

Files: Files are made in many sizes, shapes, and degrees of coarseness. They are used for removing burrs and rough spots, and for smoothing.

Fire Scale: A thin coat of oxidized metal that burns onto the metal surface during heating in a kiln.

Flux: A mixture of borax applied as a paste or liquid during soldering. It keeps the metal from oxidizing during the heating process so that the solder will adhere to the metal. It holds the solder in place and helps it flow when it reaches the proper temperature. Some fluxes are combined with pickle, which helps clean the metal as well.

Forge: To form by hammering; to beat into a shape with a hammer, anvil, or stake.

Forged or Wrought Metal Work: Jewelry objects are formed from a sheet of metal, wire, or fused masses of metal. Then they are sawed, hammered, tooled, filed, and polished.

Forming: The process of shaping and bending metal over stakes or forming blocks.

Gauge: A measurement—the thickness of the metal.

Graver: The cutting tool used in engraving, also known as a burin.

Jewelry Saw Frames and Saw Blades: The jeweler's saw frame is an adjustable frame into which the saw blade is clamped for sawing metal. The blades are very fine and make it possible to cut into small and irregular shapes. The size usually used for most work is #2/0.

Lapidary: Refers to cutting and polishing of stones.

Mallet: Made from wood and rawhide, it is used for many shaping processes because it will not mar, scratch, or stretch metal.

Mandrel: A tapered steel bar that measures rings for size. Lightweight mandrels are used as a base for wax forming. Heavy steel mandrels are used for bending metal.

Mounting: The top of the ring design that holds the stone.

Oxidize: To darken a metal surface, such as silver, copper, or gold.

11–8 *Found objects such as bones, feathers, beads, and bells can be made into jewelry. The pendant on the right is brass repoussé attached to a plastic backing. The necklace, bottom center, is made from antique drawer pulls and pins. The necklace, top center, is etched copper with copper enamel drops.*

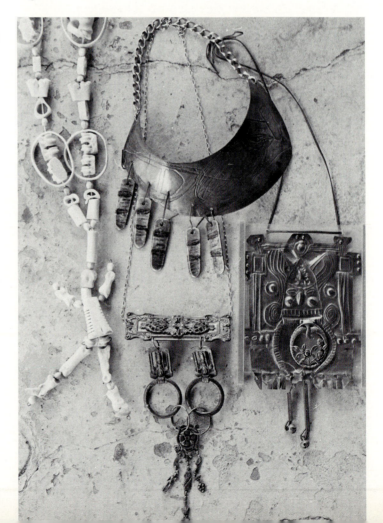

Pickle: An acid solution used to clean metal after the heating process.

Pliers: The flat-nose plier has flat jaws that are squared at the end; they are good for bending square corners. The round-nose plier is very good for bending wire; the tips are round and taper to a narrow point. The chain-nose plier has a flat jaw that tapers to a very fine tip and is used where a fine tip is desirable.

Polish: To give a shiny luster to metal by rubbing with progressively finer abrasives, which remove scratches from the surface.

Rouge: Red iron oxide combined with a base to make a very fine polishing compound. Rouge is the final polishing compound and will achieve the highest luster possible.

Shank: The part of the ring that circles the finger.

Snips: A version of the tin snips, they can be used to cut thinner gauges of sheet metal and solder.

Solder: An alloy of metal that has a melting point lower than that of the metal with which it is being used. Also means to join to pieces of metal with solder and heat.

Sterling Silver: An alloy of silver and copper composed of 92.5 percent silver and 7.5 percent copper.

Tripoli: A medium course compound that is used with a felt or muslin buff on a polishing wheel in the preliminary polishing steps. Helps remove scratches and fire scale and gives the metal a soft sheen.

Designing Jewelry

What makes us all unique is the way we place, use, and design everything in our lives. In making jewelry, we use design elements to uniquely organize materials in an effective manner.

When working with young people, the emphasis should be on the many inexpensive and fairly permanent materials that can be explored to construct jewelry objects. Dynamic adornment pieces can be created from organic materials such as rocks, shells, weeds, grasses, gourds, clay, wood, wood shavings, feathers, bones, teeth, leather, seeds, pinecones, and fur. Man-made materials can also inspire designs: papier-mâché, tissue paper, aluminum foil, pipe cleaners, beads, telephone wire, chains, bells, cloth scraps, fishing floats, metal washers, cereals, pasta, candy, fishing snap swivels, old jewelry pieces, tin cans, and many more found objects.

Gathering, selecting, adapting, and assembling materials are creative experiences for the young designer. Experimenting with tools and materials, sketching ideas, reorganizing through trial and error, evaluating, and exhibiting finished products are all worthwhile aesthetic endeavors for the student who designs any crafted object.

BASIC CONSTRUCTION METHODS

During the design process, methods of constructing and assembling parts should be explored. Very often, such basic procedures become an essential part of the design. The differing methods also require various simple tools. These are readily available tools found in the art or industrial arts centers of elementary schools.

Such tools include pliers, scissors, wire cutters, tweezers, tin snips, files, saws (coping or jewelry), electric hand tools (with drill, grinding and polishing bits), and a soldering iron (optional).

JOINING SKILLS

Use these simple skills with primary students.

Stringing is the most common method of joining. A leather thong is strong and versatile; check to make sure that the holes in the object to be strung are large enough. Plastic thongs, which are inexpensive and look like leather, are available from leather supply stores. Cotton string, yarn, shoelaces, nylon fishing line (which is inexpensive and comes in several weights), macrame cords, and wire are other materials.

Gluing with epoxy works well for heavy objects such a

11–9 *Jewelry-working tools include pliers, metal snips, leather stamping tools, leather hole punch, electric hand tool and bits, plastic lacing, and wire. Left front is a cut-metal shim design; right front is a spoon ring waiting for a stone to be set in it.*

leather, woods, reeds, metals, stones, and glass. Regular white glue is fine for cloth, yarns, string, and paper collage. Cements, such as model airplane cement, can also be used.

Tying, lacing, using snaps, sewing, and weaving are all good joining techniques. The joints produced can be designed to be invisible or as part of the visual and tactile spaces within the completed piece of jewelry.

Velcro is a material that is rough textured on both its front and back surfaces. It will stick to itself and pulls away to separate. It is good for joining small lightweight pieces, but it is expensive.

Upper intermediate students will find these skills challenging:

Chain links (or jump rings) made of any metal wire (copper, brass, aluminum, or nickel) that range in thickness from 12- to 22-gauge can be used. Wind the wire around a ¼- to 1-inch-wide wooden dowel. (Or use a pencil.) The size will depend on the design needs. Slip the coils off the wooden dowel. Cut up the center of the coils with snips or scissors. All the links will be a uniform size and perfect circles. They can be closed by simply pressing them together, or use a small amount of epoxy to secure the closure. The links can be used together to form a chain; the chain could be made of links of the same size or of varying sizes. They can also be used as jump rings, which are individual links that suspend an object from another shape (from a leather thong perhaps).

Tubing made out of plastic (hardware piping) or metal is available in various diameters. Different sizes can be used as a ring base, or small sizes as chain links. Simply saw off the desired widths from the tubing with a jeweler's or coping saw. File and sand the rough edges.

Jewelry and Adornment

Soldering with electric solder irons is an inexpensive procedure that can be used in the classroom following these instructions for safety.

1. Clean all joints with steel wool—be sure that the edges will be in full contact in order to join them properly.
2. Apply 50-50 type solder and paste flux. Heat them with the soldering iron until the solder flows.
3. Remove all irregular burrs and burnish with steel wool.
4. Polish the jewelry with a soft cloth and jewelry rouge.
5. To prevent tarnishing, dip the metal piece in Vinyl-on, a plastic liquid that dries in about 15 minutes to a hard, shiny finish. You may also paint with clear nail polish.

Findings such as backings are needed often to complete the object to be worn. These can be purchased inexpensively from hobby stores (pin backs, ring shanks, or necklace catches), or you can make your own. A large safety pin epoxied to the back of a piece of jewelry serves as an easy pin backing. Ring shanks can be made from old spoons, pipe cleaners, old jewelry, tubing, leather, old toys, and wire. Necklace catches can be improvised from two wire pieces. One catch is shaped out of wire into an S form; the opposite catch is simply a jump ring—the S shape catches into the jump ring.

JEWELRY PRODUCTION IN SIXTH-GRADE CLASSES

Two sixth-grade classes at a school in El Mirage, Arizona, have set up a jewelry firm as part of their study of "big business" and the free enterprise system. The corporation has a charter, a board of directors, and common stock certificates. The students are the salespeople, crafts bookkeepers, typists, and graph record makers. Workers are paid a fixed sum, and salespeople get a commission. The firm sold four hundred shares at a nickel each to establish their capital.

Crafting the jewelry is only part of the educational process involved here. Learning to make a business work is the fundamental skill practiced. The students incorporated as El Mirage Jewels and Crafts Corp. A retired attorney advised them on their corporate charter. Teachers Helen Cheek and William Hegler are advisers in the business. Many facets of the school curriculum are involved: mathematics, spelling, English, social studies, rock study, and producing the jewelry. Salespeople practice role playing and oral language study. Making job applications and figuring out commissions give excellent practice in arithmetic. The success of the project is indicated by the many sales of the items; this success provides further motivation and instructs the students in how to be better buyers, sellers, and producers. On the following pages, you will uncover a jewelry technique that has been waiting for your personal interpretation.

Multifunctional Jewelry: Wear It or Display It

The following procedures will produce jewelry that can be worn or displayed as mobiles. Many of the finished projects are transparent, such as those made from plastics and tissue paper. The attraction of these vibrant pieces is enhanced when they are placed against a window or suspended near a light.

DIP AND DYE JEWELRY

Supplies Needed
facial, rice, and tissue papers
paper towels
vegetable dyes or thinned liquid tempera
muffin tins
plastic crystals or liquid resin
newspapers

Procedure
1. Tear or cut paper pieces into 3- or 4-inch rectangles, squares, or circles.
2. Experiment with folding: fold a circle in half, in half again, and then again. Or fold a piece of paper into an accordion-pleated shape. Then start at one end and fold the pleats back and forth into triangles.
3. Mix or dilute colors, to achieve tints or shades, in muffin tins.
4. Dip the paper by points as well as sides into the various colors. You will soon discover how fast the paper absorbs the color. Try to leave some of the original white of the paper to add to the design. Also try blotting color onto the paper directly from a dye bottle. Make sure that the color goes through all the layers of paper.
5. After each color is applied, blot the design dry between some newspaper.
6. When dry, glue the design to a piece of cardboard. Spray it with plastic. Always use adequate ventilation.
7. Make holes in the designs or glue tabs on their backs so that the paper designs can be suspended from trees, hung

as a mobile shapes, or worn as jewelry. (See "Fold and Dye," pages 130–132.)

TISSUE PAPER JEWELS

Unusual tissue paper jewelry is easy and fun to make with just the addition of scraps of cardboard and lots of imagination. The directions here are for making pendants and bracelets. You can also use this process for making rings, hats, and hair decorations.

Supplies Needed

all-purpose glue (or water-lac, machê, or polymer gloss medium)
assorted colors of tissue paper and masking tape
flexible cardboard or oak tag
scissors

Procedure

1. Plan your design on a piece of paper that is the desired size of the jewelry. Consider background colors as well as which bright colors to add to the design.
2. Cut cardboard shapes to fit the size of the design. (The size of the bracelet is determined by hand size—make it snug enough so that it won't fall off, but large enough to slip over the hand.)
3. Shape the cardboard into a circle and tape the edges together.
4. Brush glue or polymer on the cardboard.
5. Apply a background tissue paper color over the entire outside and another color over the inside of the bracelet shape.
6. Reapply the glue.
7. Make 1-inch-wide strips either by cutting or by tearing tissue from the fold of the paper to its edge. All paper has a grain, so just tear along one edge and if it doesn't tear evenly, turn the paper sideways and rip from the other end.
8. Twist a strip of paper by hand.
9. Paint or squeeze on a glue line where the color strip is intended to go in your design. Press the strip into the glue line. If this is difficult to maneuver, try using small tweezers to apply the strips.
10. Vary the colors and the widths of your paper strips.
11. For the "jewels," wad tissue paper into a small ball and cover the ball smoothly with a piece of tissue paper of the same color. Be sure that the cover extends to the back and glue it down under the ball "jewel."

11–11 *Coloful tissue paper jewels made into neck pendants and bracelets.*

412

12. When dry, glue the whole jewel, or ball, into the design.
13. Try gluing down lace bits and then covering them with tissue and glue.
14. Decorate the piece with glass or plastic beads, sequins, yarns, and so on, or draw in details with felt-tip pens.
15. Cover the jewelry with a coat of water-lac, plastic spray, polymer medium, or thinned glue.

PAPER BEADS

Supplies Needed
colored beads
colored magazine photographs, toothpicks
cotton string
pasta forms
scissors
white glue

11–12 *Paper beads alternated with old jewelry beads. The bracelet is yarn wrapped around a ring of cardboard masking tape; lower right is a yarn design glued to a cardboard backing as a necklace.*

Procedure
1. Collect colored magazine photographs. The beads will all have the same "look" if they are from the same photograph.
2. Cut long triangles, 1½ inches across the base and 5 inches long, that end in a point.
3. Starting at the base, roll the triangle tightly over a toothpick to its point.
4. Glue it at the point.
5. When the glue dries, string the beads on a piece of cotton thread and add colored beads or pasta between the beads.
6. For variety, make a paper clip necklace or bracelet; seven clips make a bracelet. Wrap the clips with Con-Tact paper, colored tape, wallpaper, or gift wrap and hook them together to any length you wish. Dip beads in shellac, if desired.

CORN HUSK JEWELRY

Procedure
1. Remove the husks from the ears of corn.
2. Wrap the husks in wet paper toweling to keep them moist and flexible.
3. Cut one husk into thin strips.
4. Use the strips for weaving, make beads from them, and shape them into jewelry.
5. The forms can be tied or glued. If they are dipped into starch, the shapes will remain firm.

11–13 *Pasta and seeds glued to cardboard; a papier-mâché flower and ring made from telephone wire.*

SEED JEWELRY

Supplies Needed
seeds: pumpkin, squash, watermelon, and cantaloupe; popcorn; dried beans; and dried corn
colander needle
strong thread
paper toweling
old jewelry beads and pasta shapes (optional)
nail and hammer
dyes
nail polish

Procedure
1. All kinds of seeds and beans can be strung as beads to create attractive and unusual necklaces and bracelets. If you use fresh vegetables and fruits for the seeds, wash them in a colander and spread them out on paper toweling in single layers to dry. Collect an assortment so the children can share the varieties.
2. Carefully hammer a small threading hole into the seed.
3. String the beads as to colors, shapes, sizes, and alternate patterns.
4. Varieties of plants offer varieties of seeds. Some seeds such as dry corn or china berries can be dyed by soaking them in vegetable or aniline dyes.
5. A coat of nail polish gives a shiny finish.

STRING AND YARN JEWELRY

The procedure here is the same as that described for yarn pictures and yarn mobiles. (See page 251.) For jewelry, work on smaller shapes, such as a 3-inch cardboard round. Be sure to cover the edges with yarn. Secure all the ends of the yarn with glue. Add decorative items such as beads, dried flowers, sequins, and other jewels to the design. Cover the back with felt or cloth. Poke holes in the backing and string and wear it.

Supplies Needed
a tightly twisted, cordlike string
white glue
tempera paint and a small, pointed brush
waxed paper
clear nail polish or clear plastic spray
small bowl
ruler
scissors
pliers
a variety of cylindrical shapes (pencils, crayons, and tubing)
    and other cardboard forms
vaseline or oil

Procedure
1. Dilute the white glue: 2 parts glue and 1 part water.
2. Cut the string into varying lengths. Place the lengths of string into the glue and let them soak for 30 minutes.
3. While the string is soaking, cover the cardboard or foil shapes with a thin coat of Vaseline or oil.
4. As you take the string out of the glue, run the string through your fingers to remove any excess. Tightly wrap the string around and around the greased cylinders. If the strings meet, they will stick together where they meet.
5. Experiment with oval shapes, circles (large and small), and free-form shapes. Glue the shapes inside each other to form three-dimensional shapes. Try braiding three pieces of string together while they are wet with glue, and lay them over a greased form to shape a bracelet or a ring. Or glue several circles of the same size (side by side) around a dowel together to form a ring; add spiral and twisted designs later to the top surface of the ring.
6. Let the string dry thoroughly, for about 2 hours, until it is stiff. Then remove the shapes from the forms. If needed, cut through the coils and later glue the ends again to close the shapes. To make chain links, wind the string around a greased pencil or dowel several times. Cut them off, and then place the coils inside each other and glue the ends together.
7. Paint the string with tempera. Finish the jewelry with nail polish or plastic spray.
8. Glue on findings such as pin backings.

11–14 *Layered aluminum foil jewelry. The yarn pin at the upper right was dipped into starch and dried.*

FOUND OBJECT JEWELRY

Any and all interesting metals, beads, wires, bones, shells, stones, leather, or fibers can be combined and designed into handsome jewelry. Begin by looking for objects to be incorporated into good design forms. The "found object" necklace in the center of Figure 11–8 is made of brass drawer pulls and handles. Experiment and invent some new jewelry interpretations for your own wearing pleasure.

ALUMINUM FOIL JEWELRY, ANTIQUE STYLE

Supplies Needed
aluminum or gold foil
white glue and liquid soap or starch
lightweight cardboard or small box
string
scissors
lace
black paint: tempera or acrylic
brush

416

clear plastic spray for finishing (optional)
paper toweling or a cloth

Procedure

1. Cut out the basic forms from the cardboard. These shapes will go under the foil. They are to be built up in layers going from largest to the smallest. Any shape can be used: circles, flowers, birds, and even letters to form names. Cut out the largest shape for the bottom, and then pile on the smaller shapes. For instance, if designing a bird, cut out the basic shapes, and add a beak and wings (glue them down) onto the basic larger shape. A flower shape might have the basic outside shape with petals on top. Build up three or four layers if desired. Younger children should keep the designs simple. Also, add string and lace for linear effects: apply glue to the backing, lay on string, and press firmly.

2. After the forms are glued and have dried, cut out a piece of aluminum foil somewhat larger than the total cardboard surface.

3. Wad the foil, and then carefully unfold it. Do not tear the foil. Add glue to the cardboard, box, or picture backing.

4. Using your fingers, carefully press the foil into the multilayered areas of the design. Use a swab or a pencil eraser to get at the difficult spots.

5. Bring the alumunim foil around to the underside and glue it down around the edges. If covering a box, trim off any excess foil.

6. Paint the entire aluminum top surface with black acrylic paint. Leave the paint on for a few minutes. With a rag or

11–15 *Rings can be designed in all sizes and shapes, especially the "king's" ring. This one has a bent wire frame with beads. The shank is wrapped several times with wire to balance the large beaded form. Note the plastic braided bracelet.*

Jewelry and Adornment

417

toweling, gently wipe off the paint on the raised surfaces so that it looks like oxidized, antique jewelry. Black paint looks antiqued, but other colors are fun, too. Acrylic paint works well because it sticks to the aluminum surface. Tempera paint will work, too, if you first mix a small amount of liquid soap, glue, or starch into the paint. Or, try rubbing over the foil with a rubber pencil eraser. Then paint over the foil with regular tempera.

7. Let the paint dry. Finish the piece with clear spray.

This technique can be used to make holiday tree ornaments; the same procedure works well for pictures (foil over about a 9 × 12-inch cardboard); and the foil over a box looks like antique metal and can be used to keep jewelry in or to hold a gift.

RINGS

Supplies Needed

wire	rocks
ring shanks	tempera and a brush
plastic piping	epoxy
coping saw	masking tape
buttons, beads	nail polish or plastic spray

11–16 *Clay necklaces include stamped designs, a button, an acrylic painted pendant, and a free-form coiled piece that will be dipped into plastic film. The long beads were formed over a plastic straw. The stamp, upper left, is carved from plaster.*

Procedure

1. Purchase an inexpensive shank from a local jewelry parts, art, or hobby supply store, or use old spoons, wire, leather, pipe cleaners, or old toy rings. A simple shank substitute can be made from plastic piping purchased at a hardware store. The piping comes in diameters of ½, ¾, and 1 inch and is sold in foot lengths (it is very expensive). Slice off the desired ring widths with a coping saw, and sand off any rough edges.
2. Find a rock about 1 inch in diameter in an oval or other interesting shape.
3. Paint a design on it—such as an insect—in tempera.
4. Let the paint dry and then cover it with a coat of nail polish or plastic spray.
5. Let it dry again.
6. Glue the rock to the shank with a fast-drying epoxy.
7. Hold the rock in place with masking tape until it is dry.
8. Other rings can be made from papier-mâché, telephone wire, leather designs, and beads on wire. (See Figure 11–15).
9. Or find an old large button. Paint on miniature paintings with acrylic paints.

Alternate Procedure

1. Make a paper pattern that is the width of your finger.
2. With a jeweler's saw, cut off the cup end of an old metal spoon (measure the finger size from the paper pattern).
3. Overlap the ends, file them smooth, and hammer them into shape around a wood dowel.
4. Polish the ring with polishing rouge, or household metal polish and a cloth.

CLAY, SALT CERAMIC, BAKER'S CLAY, AND WOODEN ORNAMENTS

These clay and wooden ornaments can be strung as mobiles, can be worn as elaborate jewelry, or can be used to decorate holiday trees.

11–17 *Starting at upper left and going clockwise: a string necklace; brightly colored baker's clay necklace; salt ceramic pendant; examples of shrink designs; baker's clay ring (ring was formed over a pipe cleaner shank); and a cut-metal shim design, which will be stamped and mounted on a leather backing.*

Supplies Needed

clay, salt ceramic, baker's clay, wood, Styrofoam sheeting or
    meat trays
acrylic paints, felt-tip pens, and a brush
electric drill
plastic spray

Procedure

1. Hand shape a small mound of clay. Stamp or press
   designs on the clay and add decorative shapes to it.
2. Fire the clay in a kiln. Clay substitutes (such as salt ceramic
   and baker's clay) can be air dried overnight. If objects are
   to be worn, make a hole with the end of a straw.
3. Decorate the clay further with acrylic paints or felt-tip
   pens.
4. Finish the project with a plastic spray.
5. Or draw designs on ¼-inch plywood or balsa wood.
6. The teacher can cut and drill the forms with an electric
   drill.
7. Decorate the wood with acrylic paints and finish it with a
   plastic spray.
8. Follow steps 5 through 7 when using Styrofoam sheeting
   or meat trays.

Incised Jewelry

SCRIMSHAW

Scrimshaw is an old art form that was practiced by whalers
around the time of the Civil War, who scratched designs into

11–18 *The scrimshaw
process is adapted to these
plaster drop forms. The designs
are incised with a nail,
watercolor is painted on, and
the lines are filled with colored
inks.*

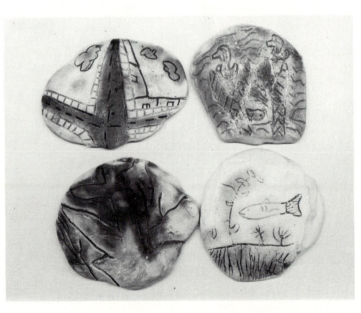

shark's teeth and whalebones. The same interesting effect can be achieved on small cast plaster shapes or on ordinary bones from the supermarket. Franklin D. Roosevelt was an ardent collector of scrimshaw.

Supplies Needed
cookie sheet
files, steel wool
shells, cow bones (cleaned and boiled) or cow horns, old ivory from piano keys, or white plexiglass
crayons, paint, ink, or felt-tip pens
nails or pins or sewing machine needle (for bones)
paper clips
plaster of Paris
oil or Vaseline
sandpaper
table knife
plastic finish

Procedure
1. Prepare a small amount of plaster (about 1 cup of plaster to ⅔ cup of water for about eight pendants).
2. Mix the plaster until it has thickened and then drop it by spoonfuls, like cookies, onto a waxed sheet of paper or a cookie sheet coated with oil or Vaseline.
3. Add paper clip hangers while they are still wet. Let the "cookies" harden for 20 minutes.
4. Plan your design to include textures and many lines.
5. Carve and scratch your design on the top surface with a nail, pin, sewing machine needle, or table knife. (You can use animal bones for carving, such as deer or cow bones, or shells, old ivory, or white plexiglass.)
6. When the carving is finished, rub the top surface with any medium, such as crayon, paint, felt-tip pens, or India ink, being sure to fill in the scratched lines with color.
7. Go back over the raised surface with sandpaper to remove the color and to reveal the colored incised lines. Add more painted or pen designs if desired.
8. If using bones, boil them clean and let them dry. Saw their surfaces flat with an ordinary hand saw. If the color of the bones is too dark, place them in diluted household bleach (½ water) to lighten them. Rinse and dry them. File and sand their surfaces smooth. Draw on design with light pencil marks. Scratch designs in with a sharp nail, or sewing machine needle—not the ball-point type. Sand off any remaining rough edges. Wash away any pencil lines with soap and water. Dry and fill in scratched lines using India ink with a pen or brush. Remove any unwanted color with soap and water or steel wool.
9. Cover the bones with plastic spray or shellac. Let them

Jewelry and Adornment

dry. Or rub the bones with paraffin and a soft cloth to a mellow shine.

10. String and wear.

SHELLS

This project, innovated by Nancy and Renny Mitchell, unravels the mystery of how the Hohokam Indians inlaid shells with turquoise and other precious stones.

Supplies Needed

shells with a smooth surface

wax (crayons or paraffin), vinyl paper or electrical tape

paper for sketching

acid bath (diluted pool acid can be used, which is muriatic, or vinegar will work)

a sharp tool (or a nail) for scratching through the wax and an X-acto knife or scissors for cutting through the tape

colorful rocks; turquoise, chrysocola, or malachite for blue-greens; coral for red; jet for black; and shell for white

epoxy glue

files

sandpaper

jeweler's cloth

rouge

walnut shells

Procedure

1. Sketch a design to fit the shell. Keep the design simple but interesting—birds, insects, butterflies, and geometric designs are all excellent.

2. Cover a smooth shell with vinyl paper, electrical tape, or a thick covering of crayon wax. Be sure to cover both the inside and outside of the shell. Take out all air lumps in the tape. (We dipped our shells into melted paraffin wax.)

3. Place your paper design over the shell. Draw through the paper onto the tape, or scratch out the design from the wax with a nail.

4. If using tape or vinyl paper, use an X-acto knife or scissors to cut out the design. *Note:* Keep the design for later use, as in step 5.

5. As an alternate step, apply the positive tape design to a shell.

6. Place the shells into the acid bath. Diluted muriatic acid etches in a matter of minutes. A vinegar bath solution will take overnight to etch the shell. Tape a long string to the shell to lower it into the bath. The vinegar etches around the design tape, leaving a positive raised shape, or an etched shape, depending on whether wax or tape

11–19 *Etched shells begin with paper designs. Felt-tip pen lines fill the bird design on top left. The bird design on the string is cut out of a tape covering the shell. The bottom center shell is a natural form used as a ring.*

was applied. (This project could be combined with a science lesson.)

7. Lift the shell from the bath and place it in clean water. Rinse it well. Remove the tape to find your design. (As an alternate to etching, the design areas may be filed away with small files.)

8. Crush some colorful stones with a hammer between cloth. Prepare some epoxy. Apply the stone mixed with the epoxy into the lowered design if desired (pick up with the end of a toothpick). Let the glue dry completely overnight. File down rough stones and smooth them with fine sandpaper and fine steel wool. Polish them with jewelry rouge and a cloth or leather buff. (Polish on an electric buffing wheel if possible.)

9. Coat with a sealer if desired.

10. If stones are not used, leave the tape on and color into the shell design with wax shoe polish, or apply crayon colors. Blend the crayon with some turpentine on a cloth. Then remove the tape; the color will be in the etched areas.

11. For variation, prepare a shape with round or square metal wire. The curves of the wire design must fit the curves of the shell. Hold the wire on the shell with clamps, tape, or clothespins, then fill the design areas between the wires with epoxy and crushed stone. This achieves a cloisonné effect.

12. Another variation is to inlay crushed stone in black walnut shells. Slice the shell about ¼ inch thick (cutting across either grain for differing patterns). Place the shell slice on waxed paper or foil. Prepare epoxy and fill the nut holes halfway with epoxy. Let dry. Fill the remainder

11–20 *More etched shells with inlay stones.*

of the holes with epoxy mixed with crushed stone. File, sand, and polish as described for the shell.

Plastics

Plastics have been called the look of the twentieth century. They are produced in a chemical laboratory from such basic materials as air, salt, natural gas, oil, coal, wood, and cotton. Plastic is a desirable material because it is lightweight, has a luminous quality, is easily formed into molds when heated, is versatile in terms of its possible uses, comes in a wide range of colors, and does not break easily. Artists paint with plastic base paint, and many of the clothes we wear are partly made of plastic. The two general types of plastics are *thermoplastic*, which becomes soft when heated and hardens quickly upon cooling (this can be repeated over and over again), and *thermosetting*, which sets in permanent shapes during the forming process.

Children love to look through colored plastics. Assorted shapes and sizes of plastics are available everywhere, from flexible packaging materials to transparent toys such as kaleidoscopes. Colored plastics and glass help make our environment aesthetically pleasing when used in stained glass for windows and for decorative panels. The processes used on plastic described here, such as carving, etching, and shaping, are employed by craftspeople who work with plastic as an art form. The colors and light quality of plastic are especially appealing to students. Using colored plastic sheets is an excellent way of teaching colors. By overlapping and viewing the world through special optical panels, much learning about colors, color preference, and color mixing takes place.

Plastic pieces can be purchased from commercial plastic manufacturers, often by the piece or by the pound. Paint on plastics with acrylic paints, or glue pieces together to create objects from tiny rings to see-through mobiles to lightweight pendants. You decide on the size of the plastic project to meet the needs of your curriculum. Any elementary age student will greatly enjoy building with this material. Plastic is an excellent sculptural material because it is easy to handle, portable, and lightweight. Also, plastics can be combined with woods, glass, metal, pebbles, shells, fur, and bones for unique jewelry and sculptured forms.

Plastic is available in sheets, rods, and tubes, all of which have polished surfaces and are covered with masking paper. For jewelry, we use sheets that are about ⅛ to ¼ inch thick. Plastic is also available as soft polyurethane, in liquid for casting, in cooking crystals (to be baked in an oven), in thin sheets (as found in plastic bags), in sheet plastic (which shrinks), and as Styrofoam (in meat trays or blocks).

PLASTIC JEWELRY

Supplies Needed
aluminum foil
coping or jewelry saw
asbestos gloves
awl
buffer
carver (optional)
cookie sheet
hot plate or oven
metal file
sandpaper
sheets, rods, tubes, crystals, bags, liquids, or soft boards of
    plastic
cement or epoxy
decorative items

Procedure
1. Draw the design directly on the masking paper (which covers the sheet of plastic).
2. Cut out the shapes with a coping or jewelry saw.
3. Strips of plastic can be bent by hand and then shaped over a form, or free formed, by heating them in a 360°F. oven for a few minutes.
4. When the plastic is taken out of the oven (*with asbestos gloves*), it can be formed *quickly* into the desired shape (plastic hardens as it cools). The plastic also can be hand held over a hot plate until it is soft and malleable, or it can be placed in a pot of boiling water for 4 or 5 minutes until it is soft enough to be manipulated. Bracelets, rings, necklaces, and pins can be made this way. Proceed with etching, carving, or gluing on other plastic or metal shapes. Initials, messages, flowers, hearts, and insects can be carved or etched on the basic shape. At other times, try cutting out forms from metal shim (see page 404) and cementing them to the basic plastic shape. Wood, bones, and found objects can also be cemented on. When complete, add findings where needed, and wear the piece.

11–21 *The center plastic shape was cut with a coping saw; the circle design is etched (scratched) onto the plastic. The ring, left center, was carved and polished with electric tools. Shape at upper center was made by stacking and melting plastic forms in the oven. Center right and lower center, plastic jewels and beads glued to a plastic backing and painted with acrylic paints.*

MELTED PLASTIC

Procedure
1. Make sandwich designs using two identical sizes of plastic sheeting.

11–22 *Small plastic vials are filled with plastic beads and then melted in an oven to form these tearlike designs. Wallpaper beads are wrapped over paper clips.*

2. Place the design objects in sandwich style between the two sheets of plastic. (Objects could be colored glass, plastic shapes, butterflies, drawings.)
3. Place the plastic "sandwich" on a cookie sheet that is covered with aluminum foil. Bake the plastic in a 350°F. oven for a few minutes. Watch it through the oven door as the plastic melts.
4. The piece is finished when the top plastic layer settles down over the design when it is touched with a metal spatula. The two plastic sheets melt together, thereby capturing the objects inside the sandwich.
5. Remove the piece from the oven and let it cool. The object will be hard and brittle.
6. Have good ventilation for all heating procedures.
7. All sizes and shapes can be glued together with a good household cement. Special plastic glues are available, but they are expensive for classroom use. Epoxy is commonly used.
8. Sand the shapes and edges or use a metal file. Then buff the plastic or place it near the heat, such as a torch or solder iron (which will give a smooth finish). A simple shining buffer can be made by covering a small block of wood with a strong cloth or piece of leather. Add jeweler's rouge to the cover and buff with it.
9. Holes for hanging can be drilled or made with a heated awl. Wear the piece or hang it for display.

Alternate Procedure
1. Melt down all kinds of plastic bottles, toys, and odds and ends to create new forms (using an oven set at 350°F.).
2. Fill old plastic medicine vials with small colored plastic objects and watch them melt down.
3. Keep an eye on the plastic vials and watch to see that they do not melt too long and become just a plastic puddle. When the desired form is reached, remove the plastic from the oven and let it cool.
4. Make holes in the shapes, or glue tabs on and wear these new abstract forms as jewelry.

Alternate Procedure
1. Secure some clear plastic lids from the supermarket butcher or thin plastic sheets (such as heavy acetate) from a dime store or hobby shop.
2. Draw designs on with permanent felt-tip pens (water-color-based pens will not work here). If you wish, draw original designs on paper first. Place paper under clear plastic and follow designs on the plastic with waterproof pens. The more lines drawn, the more interesting will be

the design. All pen colors work well, but dark colors, like the black, really show up.

3. With regular scissors, cut around the outside edge into any desired irregular shape that will shrink when heated.
4. If desired, turn the plastic cutout onto the back and color that side with a permanent pen marker.
5. Punch holes in the plastic with a paper punch.
6. Place the plastic on clean aluminum foil or in a pan and heat it in the oven for about 3 minutes at a temperature of 350°F. For classroom use, we use portable toaster ovens.
7. It's fun to watch the plastic while it is in the oven. As it heats, it shrinks into about 2-inch shapes. Before it flattens, the plastic will go through whimsical, humorous gyrations. If the plastic does not lie flat, gently touch it with a spatula while it is still warm.
8. Remove the plastic from the oven to harden.
9. Wear each plastic piece singly or combine many pieces on one necklace or bracelet to create unique jewelry. (See Figure 11–4.)

Alternate Procedure

Supplies Needed
plastic cooking crystals (available in hobby stores in clear and colors)
wire
cookie sheet
molds made from heavy aluminum foil, Pyrex dishes, or muffin or small pie pans

1. Cover a cookie sheet with aluminum foil.
2. Create a wire shape. (Any object could be embedded in the crystals.)
3. Place the layers of crystals into the spaces to fill in between the wires, or place designs in muffin tins.
4. Heat the crystals in 375°F. oven for a few minutes until the plastic melts.
5. The crystals will become a mass that will hold the wires together.
6. Remove the form from the oven and let it cool for a few minutes.
7. When hung in a window, these forms shimmer like stained glass.
8. Do this jewelry at gift-giving time.
9. For variation, pour the crystals into a pie pan, Pyrex dish, or aluminum foil molds. Embed any favorite items in the crystals. Heat the crystals as in step 4; remove them and allow them to cool. While the plastic is warm, mold it into free-form shapes (use asbestos gloves).

CARVED PLASTIC

If you have an electric hand tool in your classroom, you can directly carve plastic. Designs can be carved into the underside of the plastic. Three-dimensional effects are achieved by the depth of the designs (these cuts can be seen by holding the plastic sideways). Many industrial arts shops have this tool. Use regular hand tool drill bits and carving burrs to carve. Because these bits and burrs cut quickly into the plastic, care must be taken. Carving can also be done by filing away the design areas. Combine carving with other forming techniques to create jewelry.

ETCHED PLASTIC

Most of the time, care must be exercised not to scratch plastic, but designs can be created by intentionally scratching into it. Before you lift all the masking paper covering, etch a desired shape in the plastic with a sharp tool—a file or a nail. Initials, hearts, and abstract forms are fun to etch.

PLASTIC BAG ART

Clear plastic vinyl comes in sheets at hardware and fabric stores. Plastic food bags, old tablecloths, and raincoats will work, too.

Procedure
1. Draw designs on plastic sheeting with acrylic paints or felt-tip pens. Suspend large panels of plastic sheeting as environment spacers or banners. (Try rolling house paint designs on super sized panels.)
2. Or, collect pebbles and shells to fill plastic bags. Stitch the sides of the bags together on the sewing machine. Small bags can be exhibited or worn.
3. Plastic can be made to adhere to itself by gently pressing its two sides together with a hot iron.
4. For a giant sculpture, inflate plastic bags of assorted sizes with air or gas, and close them with a hot iron.
5. Attach bags to each other and suspend them from the ceiling. Project colored lights and slides on these "balloons" as they move in the breeze.

LIQUID PLASTIC FILM JEWELRY

Liquid plastic is available in colors in hobby shops. You have probably seen it used for making flower shapes. The same material can be used to create original jewelry forms. Form a shape out of wire and dip it into the liquid plastic. A thin film will fill the inside of the wire form (like a soap bubble). This will harden into a flexible film. (White glue colored with tempera paint can be substituted for the plastic film.)

For variation, create design shapes with liquid steel or silicone rubber sealant. Both are available at hardware stores. Silicone rubber comes in tubes of white, clear, aluminum or black. Squeeze line designs on waxed paper. Follow a design sketch placed under the waxed paper, if desired. The silicone rubber takes quite a while to set, so leave it overnight.

When the silicone rubber is hard, remove it from the waxed paper. Dip the silicone designs into the liquid plastic film for color fill-in. Or fill the spaces with tissue paper that has been covered with glue or starch. Finish the project with a plastic spray. Try dipping twigs, clay designs, baker's clay designs, pipe cleaner designs, toothpick shapes, clay coil designs, butterflies, and dried flowers into the plastic film. Wear these as jewelry or suspend them from hangers and enjoy watching the colors as they move.

STYROFOAM ART

Procedure
1. Cut jewelry shapes out of soft or rigid Styrofoam (meat trays, cups, and egg cartons).
2. Use a soldering iron to burn out shapes, or scratch designs into the plastic with nails or pencils.
3. Glue the shapes together. (Try spray adhesive.)
4. If desired, cover the plastic by dipping it into plaster or some spackle, to create rigid shapes.
5. Finish the project by decorating it with paint or felt-tip pen designs. Add "stick ons" such as feathers, seeds, and pieces of old jewelry.
6. Try carving into a large slab of Styrofoam, using dull knives and soldering irons, to develop it into a three-dimensional sculpture.
7. This process makes lightweight puppet heads. (See Figure 5–8.)

Metal

Most museum collections have examples of metal jewelry dating from all periods and cultures. Copper is a favorite metal that has been used since 8000 B.C. because of its rich color and durability. We find it used in jewelry and religious artifacts and formed for hunting and eating utensils. Today, we have a wide variety of metals and alloys that are suitable for jewelry construction.

For classroom purposes, inexpensive, easily available metals are desirable. We all admire ornaments formed in silver and gold, and studying these aesthetic forms from past and present cultures can help our knowledge of forming and joining procedures. Simplifying and adapting these processes for use with easily malleable metals are fun and a challenge in design and construction. Practice in these jewelry techniques can lead to a greater interest in, and understanding of, the history, uses, formation, and cultural practices of jewelry making.

TWISTED AND HAMMERED WIRE JEWELRY

Wire neck loops are very versatile pieces of jewelry. Study balance, form, and color in designing a wire necklace.

Supplies Needed
clear plastic spray
copper or brass wire in two or three thicknesses
round-nose and flat pliers
hammer (ball-pien)
wire cutter
metal rod or piece of pipe
beads or other items to be strung
steel wool
wooden dowel
steel surface (an old railroad rail)
ruler

Procedure
1. Cut a piece of wire to a length of 15 inches long.
2. With your fingers gently form the wire into a ring with a diameter large enough to fit around your neck.
3. With round-nose pliers, turn one end of the wire over into a small, closed loop. Proceed with steps 4 through 8. After the necklace has been strung with beads or other selected items, complete the neck ring by forming a loop on the opposite end. Do not completely close this end as it is to slip into the other end for a clasp.
4. Plan the shapes that will extend from the neck loop. Experiment with string (with the neck loop placed flat on a surface) to find interesting shapes for the wire. (String is a more flexible material and will bend into circles and spirals easily and quickly.)
5. After finding a pleasing design, bend the necessary amount of wire with the round or flat pliers (use your fingers for larger forms). Use lighter weight wire for these.

11–23 *Examples, from the left, are a hammered wire necklace, feather earrings, a brass shim stamped necklace, and, top right, a snake vertebra necklace.*

6. Hammer the designed wire loops on a metal surface to make the wire flat and to give it shape. File any rough surfaces.
7. String the shapes on the neck ring, keeping them in a planned order. Fill in any spaces between the shapes with beads or plastic tubing to hold the dangling shapes in place.
8. For variation, hang beads from the neckpiece wire. Attach them with a short piece of wire. To hold the beads on, wrap one end of the wire around the neckpiece wire, string on the beads, and then simply hammer the end of the dangling wire flat.

These free-form rings are fun to make and to wear.

Procedure
1. Begin with a piece of wire 18 inches long—20- to 22-gauge works well. (Telephone wire also will work.)
2. Use a wooden dowel whose diameter is the same as your finger or build the dowel up to the proper diameter with masking tape, and wrap the wire around the dowel three times.

Jewelry and Adornment

3. Leave extra wire on both ends. Form spirals and coils with the round-nose or flat pliers. Twist and shape the wire fancifully. If desired, hammer some of the shapes flat.
4. Add beads if desired. Extra shapes can be glued on with epoxy.

REPOUSSÉ COPPER TOOLING

Repoussé, literally "pushed back," is a design worked from the underside of thin metal. This forms a raised picture. (See Figure 12–12.) It is an ancient art. The Greeks and Romans beat and pressed thin sheets of gold and silver into molds to make jewelry and other objects of great beauty.

Supplies Needed
thin tooling copper (between 30- and 36-gauge, available in 12-inch sheets) cut into squares of any size; we used 4-inch squares. Brass or aluminum foil (discarded baking pans can also be used)
pencil, nail, ballpoint pen, wood dowel, leather working tool, or sharp stick (sharpened Popsicle stick)
liver of sulphur (available at hobby supply stores)
small brush
steel wool
newspaper pads and paper toweling
mounting background: wood, cork, leather, cardboard, or a picture frame
black oil or acrylic paint
clear varnish or acrylic spray

Procedure
1. Sketch a design on paper. Keep the design simple, but plan for a generous amount of textures.
2. Work on a thick pad of newspaper.
3. Place the design sketch on top of a copper square on the newspapers. Tape down.
4. Press into the lines with a pencil, nail, or a sharpened Popsicle stick (anything that is sharp).
5. After transferring the design to the copper square, remove the paper sketch and go over the lines on the copper to reproduce the design. Press hard.
6. Press down inside the design shapes on the copper, which will cause them to pop out. Turn the copper over and press again. Keep working from front to back until your design is in three-dimensional relief: the design emerges from the original surface of the square. This technique is called repoussé.
7. Imaginative birds and animals are recommended as designs because of the variety of textures they encourage.

8. Brush on a diluted solution of liver of sulphur. Leave it on until the copper gets black. If you are using brass or aluminum metal, brush on black paint and wipe off the top excess when it is dry.
9. Blot the square dry with paper toweling.
10. Use steel wool to brush the raised surfaces; this will remove the sulphur from the top and the deepened lines will remain black.
11. Cover the square with nail polish or plastic spray to keep it from oxidizing further.
12. Cut the copper into a circular shape and mount it with glue on a leather backing. Poke a hole in the leather and string it for wearing. It also can be mounted on a block of wood or cork or placed in a small frame.

COPPER ENAMELING

Young people love to enamel. It is one of the most exciting crafts and has been practiced for centuries. Enameling has in it the surprise element of color combinations. Although you can anticipate fairly well the color results, suspense remains as the kiln heats, blends, and releases in cooling handsome

11–24 *Copper enameling is fun to do and wear. These students are sprinkling powdered enamel on copper shapes through a small screen. The toweling under the copper captures spills.*

color combinations. As one young student has said, "Each enameled piece is like a small treasured painting." In planning the designs, have the students consider each piece as a fantasy painting. Teachers will find that demonstrating the process and displaying several completed examples will provide enough motivation for students. Both boys and girls enjoy wearing this art form.

We start this process with first-graders and plan to have several older helpers on enameling days. Successful designs are achieved even by the youngest or beginning enamelist.

Enameling is the process in which finely ground powdered glass, lumps, or threads are applied to the surface of a metal shape and then are heated in a kiln until the glass melts and fuses with the metal surface. In the classroom, the common metal used is 18- to 22-gauge sheet copper, or precut copper blanks. Pure silver and gold are used in fine jewelry.

Supplies Needed

sheet copper (18- to 22-gauge); or precut copper blanks (circles, squares, rectangles, or ovals); or copper cut into 2- or 3-inch shapes

metal shears

copper wire

powdered enamels in various colors

enamel lumps and threads

flux (a colorless enamel)

plastic bags

steel wool

gum tragacanth (commercial names are KYLR Fire or Enamel Ease)

tweezers

spatula

80-mesh wire sieves or nylon hose

drill for holes or a hole punch

small enameling kiln

firing fork

firing rack

a brick or an asbestos file

jewelry findings

epoxy

jewelry saw and blades

metal files

Procedure

1. Prepare three working-station areas.
2. The day before the enameling is to be done, have the students clean their piece of copper with steel wool. Two-, 3-, or 4-inch round or square shapes are good beginning sizes for pendants. Irregular shapes can be cut

or sawed from a flat sheet. Be sure that each piece is cleaned well, especially at the edges and corners.

3. Have the students initial their copper on the back with a grease pencil. Drill any holes now that will be necessary if the piece is to be worn as a pendant. Several copper pieces can be drilled to be joined later with wire jump rings (see page 409), as is commonly done in making necklaces or bracelets.

4. Paint a salt solution (1 teaspoon of salt to 4 ounces of water) on the back of the copper to prevent scaling in the kiln. (Or clean it with steel wool after the firing.)

5. Place the cleaned copper pieces (make sure all greasy fingerprints have been removed) in small plastic bags. Hold them at their edges. Use these bags in handling the copper from now on. The closed bags prevent oxidation and keep out dirt. Cleaning is an essential part of the process.

6. At another working space (on the next day), prepare each powdered color on a separate piece of toweling, with the hope of being able to reuse spilled enamels. Each piece of toweling holds one color. Students can change places for different colors, working carefully. An assorted variety of enamel lumps and threads can be added to the basic opaque primary colors: red, yellow, blue, white, and black. Shaking one color over another provides variety, too.

7. Have students work in groups of six or eight (by tables or rows) with an assistant helper to explain the processes further.

8. First brush on a coat of gum tragacanth, the liquid binder. Cover the copper evenly.

9. Using an 80-mesh sieve or an old nylon stocking, sift the powdered enamel onto the gum solution on the copper piece, making sure that the edges and corners are covered thoroughly with the enamel. (See Figure 11–24.)

10. Apply the enamel to about the thickness of a dime. Some areas can be thicker than others, and overlaying color will build up areas. Apply the enamel in any of these ways:
    a. Brush the clear gum tragacanth solution (a cleaner and binder) on the clean copper surface.
    b. Sprinkle it on with your fingers to build up color areas. This will give a bumpy texture.
    c. Cut a stencil design from oak tag. Sprinkle enamel through the stencil.
    d. Mix each color into a paste form (enamel mixed with water or gum) and paint the copper with a brush. Let the colors touch each other as they would in a painting.
    e. In the cloisonné method the copper is painted with

flux; it is fired, cooled, laid on wire forms on copper (20- or 22-gauge copper wire), and then refired. Both the flux and the wire adhere flat to the copper surface during the firing. When they are cool, the wire shapes are filled with enamel paste (enamel and water mixture) that is brushed in. The enamels in each space can be packed in with a small cupped tool or the end of a paintbrush. Fire.

   f. Add colored lumps and threads of enamel for various color designs. Place these carefully over the powdered color. Use tweezers or just drop them on carefully.

   g. The next two procedures are for more advanced upper-elementary students:

Sgraffito Procedure

1. Clean and coat the copper shape with gum tragacanth.
2. Fire a base color on the copper shape. When it has cooled, dust a contrasting color over it.
3. Use anything pointed, such as a toothpick, to scratch through a design to the bottom coat. Fire the copper again.

An Alternative *Sgraffito* Procedure

1. Fire a base color to the shape.
2. Let it cool.
3. Paint in a design shape with gum tragacanth.
4. Carefully dust on a contrasting color that will only stay where the gum has been applied.
5. To remove the excess, tap the side of the piece. The excess will fall away and the enamel color will stay where the gum has been applied.
6. Build as many color design areas as you wish.

COUNTER ENAMELING

To counter enamel is to enamel on the underside of a piece as well as on its face. The process is the same as the preceding for copper enameling, except that the piece must be placed on a trivet in the kiln, rather than on a firing rack. This is optional on small jewelry pieces.

Procedure

1. Lift the copper form with a spatula and place the piece on a firing rack. On a large rack, about four copper pieces (2 × 2 inches) can be fired together. Smaller kilns can fire two copper shapes at once.
2. Preheat the large kiln to a temperature of about 1,500°F. It takes the kiln approximately 1 hour to reach the firing temperature. The small table kiln heats to a melting temperature in about 20 minutes.

11–25 *This student is using a small kiln and asbestos blocks on a Formica tabletop. This kiln will adequately fire a few pieces at a time in about 3 minutes.*

3. Place the piece in the kiln. The firing should take from 1 to 3 minutes. When the enamel looks smooth and shiny, the piece is done. The lumps of enamel are the last to melt because of their thickness.
4. Remove the copper piece from the kiln with the firing tool and place it on an asbestos tile to cool for a few minutes. A brick can be used in place of the asbestos tile.
5. Place the cooling piece near the kiln and out of any drafts. Quick changes of air temperatures cause the enamel to crack and chip. Some of the very thick bubbles of glass will come off if they are too thick; they may need to be refired. In an emergency, glue them back on with white glue.
6. Finished pieces can be worn as jewelry or epoxied to a wood surface and displayed.

Leather

All young people are eager to handcraft objects from leather. They find delight in manipulating the leather and changing its form to their needs and wishes. The organic material itself has unique qualities, from its individual odor to its various colors. Students can begin at any age to stamp and paint leather with the simpler tools. It is hard to stop the students or keep up with their ideas when they work with leather. And a great part of their pleasure comes in wearing what they have made.

The advantages of doing leather-craft in the classroom are that leather is practically indestructible and only simple tools are required. Many leather shops sell inexpensive bags of scraps for classroom use.

11-26 *Examples of leatherwork. From top down: hair pieces and bracelets outlined with felt-tip pens and filled with acrylic paint; cut-leather pendant; braided suede belt; stamped leather key rings; and a tooled leather belt.*

Use leather to create jewelry (rings, bracelets, and necklaces), hair ornaments, key rings, belts, purses and wallets, to cover small boxes, and as table decorations. Combine it with other craft materials such as fibers, clay, and metal in wall hangings and sculptures.

Supplies Needed
pencil
paper
ruler (optional)
small sponge
bowl of water
soft rags
paper toweling
leather scraps of various thicknesses
modeling tools (with pointed and spoon-shaped ends)
metal stamping tools (various designs and letters)
hole punch
snaps
dyes and stain, permanent felt-tip pens, and acrylic paints
brushes
a flat, durable working suface: Masonite, marble, or a cookie sheet for stamping and tooling
a weight of any kind
neat lac (a commercially prepared lacquer finish to spray or dab on for a permanent water-resistant finish) or shoe polish

STAMPING AND PAINTING LEATHER

Procedure
1. Either use scrap pieces that are the size desired or cut preferred shapes with scissors or metal cutting shears.

11-27 *Detail of tooled leather by Bill Linderman.*

2. Dip the leather pieces into a bowl of water to dampen them.
3. Place the leather on the working surface.
4. Use leather stamping tools to create interesting designs. Students can select the tools they want and share others. Use a good sized leather hammer for stamps; the greater the pressure, the deeper the tool will stamp into the leather. A good stamp set of the alphabet will provide design possibilities for names and messages. Have the students work at various stations, such as one for stamping and another for painting.
5. Paint designs on the leather. Sketch a design on paper; flowers, birds, animals, and geometric shapes are all excellent. Place the sketch over the leather and draw over the design with a sharp pencil. Remove the sketch and draw over the design on the leather with a black (or any color) felt-tip pen. These outlines will be sharp. Then use acrylic paints to fill in the outlined areas according to the prepared design. Both the felt-tip pens and acrylic paints are permanent on the leather. Special leather dyes are available from hobby stores and, since they are acrylic based, the paints work just as well and can also be used in many other classroom projects. Finish the leather by staining or spraying it with neat lac.
6. Punch any needed holes.
7. Add snaps where needed.
8. Use copper jump rings to suspend a pendant and use a plastic thong when wearing the leather as a necklace.

LEATHER TOOLING

Procedure
1. Prepare a sketch of the design.
2. Prepare the leather by wetting it with a damp sponge and cool water on its flesh side, until it is uniformly damp and the grain side darkens (but do not saturate the leather).
3. Lay the leather grain-side up, until the water evaporates somewhat and the leather begins to return to its natural color.
4. Place the paper design on top of a piece of leather and tape it at its outside edges.
5. Go over the lines of the design with the pointed end of the modeler tool to transfer the lines to the leather. Use a ruler for straight lines if you wish.
6. Remove the paper.
7. Go over the design lines on the leather with the pointed end of the modeler.
8. To depress the background and create shaded areas or to raise the design, press the leather down, around, and between the design with the spoon end of the modeler.

Smooth down the background carefully. Press down fairly hard and continue to smooth the background areas until it forces the design to be raised to your requirements.

9. Keep the leather damp as you work by moistening it with a sponge on the grain underside.
10. When the tooling has been finished, the leather will be slightly warped. To flatten it, dampen it well and lay it flat with the design side on the paper toweling. Weight it down with something heavy (a book, perhaps) and large enough to cover the entire leather piece.
11. Let it stand for about 4 hours. If it is kept standing longer, the leather may get moldy.
12. Remove the weights and let the leather dry completely.
13. Mark and cut off any excess on the edges (use a good utility knife or metal cutting shears).
14. Stain the leather as the stain instructions indicate.
15. Finish the leather with neat lac (a commercial lacquer finish) or polish it with a soft cloth.
16. Punch holes where desired.
17. Add snaps where needed.
18. Use lacing and thongs if the leather is to be worn.
19. For variation, paint on leather designs with acrylic paints and when the paint is dry cover the leather with neat lac.

Simple Finishing Procedures

SANDING

Sandpaper is most commonly used to finish wood, plastic, plaster, rough paper, leather, and metal. As sandpaper is available in various grits, work from the roughest to the smoothest grit. To remove very small scratches on metal, use very fine steel wool; or a paste of putty and olive oil will remove light scratches. Clean metal with toothpaste and a cotton ball or soft cloth. Finish as follows.

Electric Sanding and Polishing

Any standard electric household drill can be used as a sander and polisher. Use a regular hardware vise and clamp the drill to a heavy table, which converts the drill into a standing position. Place attachments into the bit end. This is an inexpensive, safe way to create a stationary polisher and the drill will not become hot too quickly. You can use this device to sand and polish most materials, including metals, wood, and plastic, to a pleasing, shiny finish.

POLISHING METAL

Tripoli and rouge are two polishing compounds that are ordinarily used with a buffing machine. The tripoli helps to remove any unfinished edges, and the rouge is the final polishing material. Attach a buffing wheel to the electric drill, and you have an excellent polishing machine. A small electric hand tool has various attachments, including drills, grinding bits, and polishing wheels, that are all handy for jewelry construction (which includes working with metal, plastic, and wood). When no electric tools are available, polish the metal with a household metal polish, which is sold in grocery stores. Rub with a soft cloth, and polish with a chamois.

OXIDIZING METAL

Oxidizing metal makes it look like an antiqued piece with shiny, high places and dark, indented places. Silver and copper can be oxidized by brushing or dipping boiled spinach juice on the metal. Liver of sulphur (see "Repoussé Copper Tooling," pages 432–433) will deliver the same effect and is available at drug or hobby stores. When the metal darkens, rinse off the excess. Rub away the high surfaces with steel wool or pumice powder on a cloth and polish the metal as desired.

WOOD FINISHES

A light coating of linseed, olive, mineral, salad, and pure lemon oil are all appropriate finishes for wood. Allow oils to absorb, pat with paper towels, and wipe carefully. Petroleum jelly, varnish, shellac, paints (both water soluble and oil based), shoe polishes (both liquid and cake), and wax are all excellent finishes, depending on the finish desired.

LEATHER FINISHES

A neutral shoe polish is one finish for leather. Neat lac, a commercial product, is a commonly used finish and is a water-resistant lacquer that can be conveniently sprayed on or dabbed on with a wool dabber. The teacher can place the almost finished leather objects on newspaper outdoors. Then the neat lac can be evenly sprayed across all the objects at once; use neat lac outside as it is a lacquer product with fumes. Colored stains are another commercial finish.

PLASTIC FINISHES

Clear Vinyl Acrylics

Clear vinyl acrylic is a water-based finish that appears to be opaque white but dries clear. It is available in gallon and quart paint containers. It can be brushed on any paper, wood, plastic, plaster, metal, or clay object to give a water-resistant finish (when dry). Vinyl can be cleaned up with water before drying. This product can be used with papers for montage, collage, and decoupage. Commercial products are Deft and Water Lac.

White Glue

White glue can be diluted with water so it can be brushed on. It will give the same shiny quality as water lac. It can be used for montage, collage, and decoupage.

Paints

Acrylic paints can be brushed on with water, yet will dry to a permanent, water-resistant finish. They are excellent on all clays, leather, and wood. Enamel paints, from hobby supply stores, are permanent but do need turpentine for cleanup. Watercolor paints (tempera as well) can be thinned and brushed or rubbed on clay, wood, leather, and plaster.

Felt-Tip Pens

Permanent pens do not smear. Water-based and permanent pens can be used on clay, plaster, wood, salt ceramic, baker's clay, and papier-mâché, but water-based pens need to be finished with a polymer coating.

Polymer or Acrylic Gloss

A variety of plastic finishes is available in hobby supply stores. These can either be brushed, dipped, or sprayed on. A plastic finish is needed where water-based pens and paints are used for permanency. Acrylic gloss is another name for the same product.

Checkpoints

1. A small amount of toothpaste or cleansing powder on a soft cotton cloth dampened with water will clean silver, pewter, copper, and brass. Rub the metal gently until the surface is clean and smooth. A pencil eraser will also rub off any oxidation on silver, copper, or brass.
2. Toothbrushes are effective for cleaning deep surfaces.
3. Dip jewelry in clean water and dry it before buffing. Then spray it with a plastic coating, or dip it into a vinyl for a

hard coat finish, or cover it with a coat of clear nail polish to prevent air tarnishing and oxidation. Spray any plastic coating out of doors.

4. To remove scratches from plastic, rub it with an automobile rubbing compound or toothpaste on a wet cloth. Dry and buff it with a dry cloth. Polish plastic with carnuba paste wax or lemon oil polish.

Further Suggestions for Creating Jewelry

1. Weave unique neckpieces on a small loom.
2. Sew beads on felt and back with cardboard.
3. Dye bottle corks with bright vegetable dye colors or tempera paints. Add decorations with pipe cleaners, straw, yarn, and buttons.
4. Use a brass rod (⅛-inch diameter) as a base for a choker necklace, round it out with your fingers, bend hooks on the ends with pliers, and hammer the ends flat.

11–28 *Glass cookie art; and a bracelet, beads, and necklace made of pasta and cereal decorated with felt-tip pens.*

5. Cut ¼-inch pipe with either a hack saw or a plumber's pipe cutter to make metal beads.

6. Bones are beautiful shapes. Wash and soak them in a solution that is one-half water and one-half bleach. Polish the bones with a white polishing compound and buff them.

7. Glue seeds onto a tin can lid (with bound edges such as a tennis ball container lid) in a mosaic pattern. Add feathers, pop top fasteners, nuts, bolts, leather and cloth scraps, or string seeds for a necklace. (see Figure 11–13.)

8. Slice walnuts in half with a hack saw to uncover the beautiful lacey design inside. Sand them with sandpaper and paint them with polymer or clear nail polish. Glue a backing on and wear one.

9. Cut balsa wood into interesting shapes; sand them smooth. Paint designs on the wood with acrylic paints or draw on them with felt-tip pens. Cover the painted wood with an acrylic gloss medium.

10. Dye ordinary poultry feathers to add to homemade jewelry forms in salt ceramic, baker's clay, and Styrofoam.

11. Use colored yarns for wrap technique necklaces.

12. Create small papier-mâché bracelets, rings, or free-form shapes. Paint, decorate, string, and wear them.

13. Necklaces can be strung with pasta forms. Decorate with felt-tip pen designs.

14. Use fabric crayons on typing paper. Iron onto a polyester fabric. Place cloth design on top, polyester fill in between and thin cotton on bottom. With a running stitch, quilt the design together. Wear as jewelry.

15. Use a felt backing and stitch on a beaded design. Mount the finished beaded work on leather or balsa wood. String and wear it.

11–29 *Selection of jewelry. From left, clockwise: fabric crayons on cloth, then quilted; weaving on a coathanger; telephone-wire necklace (wrapped around a pencil); needlepoint "JOY"; painted button on a pipe cleaner ring; and potato parts strung on a needle and thread (when parts are dry they shrink and look like teeth) for a necklace. Note the tied-on warp on the coathanger.*

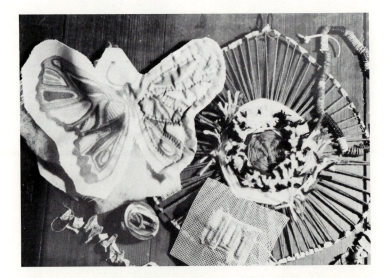

16. String shells into which holes have been drilled or made with a hot needle.

Bibliography

BARSALI, ISA BELLI. *European Enamels.* New York: Paul Hamlyn, 1969.

BOULAY, R. *Make Your Own Elegant Jewelry.* New York: Sterling Publishing Co., 1973.

BOVIN, MURRAY. *Jewelry Making for Schools, Tradesman, Craftsman.* Forest Hills, N.J.: Murray Bovin, Publisher, 1967.

CHOATE, SHARR. *Creative Casting.* New York: Crown Publishers, Inc., 1966.

COARELLI, FILIPPO. *Greek and Roman Jewelry.* New York: Paul Hamlyn, 1966.

COLEMAN, ROBERT R. "Jewelry Creations." *School Arts,* **67** (March 1968), 30–33.

CONWAY, VALERY. *Introducing Enameling.* New York: Watson-Gupthill Publications, 1973.

DALI, SALVADOR. *A Study of His Art-in-Jewels.* New York: The Graphic Society, 1959.

DHAEMERS, ROBERT, AND HOWARD A SLATOFF. *Simple Jewelry Making for the Classroom.* Palo Alto, Calif.: Fearon Publishers, Inc., 1958.

GENTILLE, THOMAS. *Step-by-Step Jewelry.* New York: Golden Press, Inc., 1968.

GREGORIETTI, GUIDO. *Jewelry Through the Ages.* New York: American Heritage Publishing Co., Inc, 1969.

HUNT, W. BEN. *Indian Silver Smithing.* New York: Collier Books, 1960.

KAIN, JAY D. *Cast Pewter Jewelry.* Worcester, Mass.: Davis Publications, Inc., 1975.

LA CROIX, GRETHE. *Creating with Beads.* New York: Sterling Publishing Co., Inc., 1973.

MERIEL-BUSSY, YVES. *Repoussage (The Embossing of Metal).* New York: Sterling Publishing Co., Inc.

MORTON, PHILIP. *Contemporary Jewelry: A Studio Handbook,* 2nd ed. New York: Holt, Rinehart and Winston, Inc., 1976.

NEUMANN, ROBERT VON. *The Design and Creation of Jewelry.* Philadelphia, Pa.: Chilton Book Co., 1972.

NEWMAN, THELMA R. *Leather As Art and Craft.* New York: Crown Publishers, 1973.

PETERSON, GRETE. *Leathercrafting.* New York: Sterling Publishing Co., Inc., 1973.

RICHIE, CARSON I. S. *Organic Jewelry You Can Make.* New York: Sterling Publishing Co., Inc., 1973.

ROUKES, NICHOLAS. *Crafts in Plastics.* New York: Watson-Guptill Publications, 1970.

SCARFE, HERBERT. *Cutting and Setting Stones.* New York: Watson-Guptill Publications, 1972.

SEITZ, MARIANNE. *Creating Silver Jewelry with Beads.* New York: Sterling Publishing Co., Inc., 1973.

SEYD, MARY. *Introducing Beads.* New York: Watson-Guptill Publications, 1973.

SOLBERG, RAMONA. *Inventive Jewelry-Making.* New York: Van Nostrand Reinhold Company, 1972.

UTRACHT, OPPI. *Metal Techniques for Craftsmen.* New York: Doubleday & Company, Inc., 1968.

WARD, VESTA B. "Jewelry to Shoot For," *School Arts,* **69** (Jan. 1970), 26–27.

WHITEFORD, ANDREW HUNTER. *North American Indian Arts.* New York: Golden Press, 1970.

WINEBRENNER, D. KENNETH. *Jewelry Making As an Art Expression.* Scranton, Pa.: International Textbook Company, Inc., 1953.

ZECHLIN, KATHARINA. *Creative Enameling and Jewelry Making.* New York: Sterling Publishing Co., Inc.

12

Fundamentals of Printmaking

Picture one of those times that you walked on wet sand at the beach when the tide was out. Remember how you left your footprints in the wet sand? Seagulls and shells leave marks in the sand until the water seeps up to erase them or the tide washes over them. Such impressions are also called prints. The process called printing is an ancient one of pressing to reproduce images.

History of Printmaking

The ancient Chinese carved seals that were either flat or cylindrical. They carved the seals in stone and used them widely as identification, much like a signature, before writing developed. The seals then were pressed on clay tablets and papyrus documents. The Chinese also carved woodcut prints as early as the sixth century, thus producing texts.

In the fourteenth century, paper was manufactured in Europe; and, in the fifteenth century, the Gutenberg press was developed. Printing subsequently changed the course of history.

Relief printing (or printing from a raised surface) was

12–1 *"Ulrich Varnbuler," woodcut, 1522, by Albrecht Dürer. This German Renaissance master created many magnificent woodcuts utilizing technques similar to those described in this chapter. All the images, including the lettering, are carved in reverse. (Courtesy of the Art Institute of Chicago.)*

developed by the master artist Albrecht Dürer and his contemporaries during the sixteenth century. He engraved (cut) into the end grain of wood, leaving fine lines and forms. (See Figure 12–1.)

The woodcut is the oldest print medium; it was used in the Orient in the seventh century. Paul Gauguin (1848–1903) revived the art of the woodcut in visualizing many of his well-known South Seas subjects.

The most popular print medium during the sixteenth to eighteenth centuries was the copper engraving; Rembrandt created many important etchings. At the same time, the English School produced popular engraved portraits by Reynolds, Gainsborough, and many other famous artists.

The well-known American patriot Paul Revere (1735–88) was an expert engraver and produced an interesting historical account of the Revolutionary period, an engraving titled "The Boston Massacre." Revere, well known for his mythical ride to spread the alarm of the advancing redcoats, was an accomplished silversmith and a publisher of copper engraved prints, as well as paper money. The engraved print is hand colored with watercolor.

Lithography, a printing process done on stone with a grease pencil (see "Terms") was invented in 1798 by a Bavarian, Alois Senefelder. In America, the Currier and Ives Company (founded in 1852) brought hand-colored lithographs of popular subjects to the American people; prints could be bought for 15 to 25 cents. The company employed some staff artists, but most images were paintings made by artists that were copied on the stones by expert draftsmen. One of the many famous artists whose charming paintings were copied was George H. Durrie of New Haven, Connecticut. His works were of snow scenes and the countryside, and included pleasant figures of people and animals.

One of the most recent printing processes (an adaptation of the ancient stencil) is the silk screen, often called *serigraphy*. This process was an outgrowth of the 1932 Federal Arts Project, when artists, because of the economic depression, were encouraged to use less expensive media. The works were then distributed to schools and the public. The term *silk screen* was coined by Carl Zigrosser, curator of prints at the Philadelphia Museum of Art. The process has been popular with many outstanding artists since that time.

Today, many innovative printing techniques and materials are being developed by artists and students. New tools and advanced processes are constantly made available to challenge our creativity. Printing techniques are applied to a variety of surfaces, such as papers, cloth, plastics, and metal. Printmakers in elementary school classrooms and contemporary artists find incentive in printmaking processes that allow them to reproduce multiple art images.

Printmaking, as an art form, is filled with surprise and suspense. The process invites discovery for, after following a sequence of printmaking steps, the student is still unsure of what the exact final image will look like. Watching the development of the plate, the inking of the surface, and the printing of the plate is intriguing, and the moment of pulling a print is always filled with eager anticipation.

The process demands cutting skills to achieve textural qualities and shape dimension and designing with positive and negative forms. By incorporating various processes, the print can be either stamped, cut away, cut into, or have parts added to it.

How Prints Are Used

Even the youngest student enjoys making and repeating forms. There is much pleasure in placing a palm into mud and then transferring that image to a sidewalk surface. Children become eager to repeat the process by making multiple images from their hands. The process is endless, and soon children print fingers, arms, and feet with any wet materials they can find.

In the same way, the artist can produce a quantity of his own drawings and designs by inking the same incised surface over and over again to produce prints. Several copies can be made from the same block; as a result, the original print is available to more people. Today, the artist-printmaker often produces an edition, or a limited number, of prints. For instance, he says, "I will print 150 prints from this block." On the print the number 73 may appear over 150. This means that the print is the seventy-third of 150 prints from the original drawing.

Films, filmstrips, books, artist's works, reproductions, and gallery exhibits motivate children at every grade level. Supplying the answer to the question "How was it done?" will give impetus to the endless possibilities open to the printmaker.

Objectives

The main objectives in printmaking are to become familiar with (1) commercial reproduction processes, (2) artist's techniques, and (3) methods of reproducing one's own drawing or design. There are many ways of incorporating the reproduction techniques into the arts curriculum, and only basic materials are needed. The creative teacher should be innovative with the tools and materials he has available.

In the classroom, there are times when you will want to create a single-print technique in which design and composition are the main goal. Such a print design might appear as a program cover, stationery, or a message card. At other times, techniques for repeated designs, such as for fabric printing (for curtains and clothing), will be needed.

Printing as a decorative procedure is effective for gift wrapping papers, stationery, gift boxes, doll clothes, kites, storybook covers, and even oak-tag frames to hold other art. Think how personal a work paper would be with a student's individual seal stamped on it, cut from a cork or eraser—in theory, a process similar to that used by the Chinese.

Printmaking Terms

Blocks: Any object that will hold its shape under pressure can be used as a printing block: cardboard, clay, stiff plastic, linoleum, wood, rubber, acetate, wax, soap, and many found objects.

Brayer: Used to apply ink to the printing block. It most often is a rubber-surfaced roller. A clean brayer can also be used to apply pressure on the back of paper when printing.

Calligraphy: The print is made from a collaged surface created with various materials, such as fabrics, cardboards, string, glue, tapes, and papers.

Engraving: A method of scratching or incising into a surface (often metal) with a sharp tool. The scratched lines will hold the ink during printing, and the print is made.

Etching: A process whereby the design is bitten into a metal plate with acid. Prints are made from the etched areas that hold the ink.

Inks: Water-base ink is most commonly used in the classroom as it is easy to clean up. Oil-base inks can be used but require a turpentine cleanup. Oil-base inks are necessary when printing on textiles, but water-base inks are preferred for paper. Finger paint can be used for silk screen paint. Powder or liquid tempera mixed with liquid starch is also a good printng ink.

Ink Pads: A simple stamping pad can be made from a sponge, several layers of paper toweling or newspaper, or felt or scrap cloth that has been dampened with water and saturated with either dry or moist tempera paint.

Intaglio: A method in which the printed image is lifted from the ink deposited in the incised, engraved, or etched areas.

Lino Block Print: A print is made from the surface of a piece of linoleum in which the design has been cut with tools. (See Figure 12–14.)

Lithography: A method of surface printing from a stone (or metal) block. A grease crayon or grease wash is placed on the stone. An acid/water solution is then placed on the stone. The greased areas repel the acid/water solution, and the rest of the stone is bitten. The grease is removed, and the raised surface catches the ink and produces the print.

Monoprint: the process of making one print from a plate that has an impression made with fingerpaint, oils, or printing inks. (See Figure 12–23.)

Palettes: Any surface that is water repellent and smooth. Such surfaces include flat metal trays, TV trays, glass, plastic trays, linoleum, plastic sheets, cardboard surfaces covered with aluminum foil or waxed paper, dishes, or old metal movie film cans.

Relief: The printed image is lifted from the raised surface by:

   Additive Relief: The raised surface is the result of adding items of equal height to a foundation, glue, collage, etc.

   Subtractive Relief: The raised surface results from carving away part of the base (lino, wood, etching).

Silk Screen: A process in which paint is forced (squeezed) through a silk screen in areas left open to the paint.

Squeegee: A tool edged with rubber used to squeeze the ink across and through a silk screen. Printing procedures are: to stamp an object into an ink pad then onto a paper surface; to place paper on an inked block and rub the back of the paper with the bowl of a spoon; to place an inked block directly onto paper and apply pressure to the block (by standing on it).

Stencil: Paper, metal, or another material that is perforated. When it is laid on a surface and paint is applied, the paint goes through the perforated image onto the print.

Wood Block: The background design is cut away with gouges. The areas left raised will receive the ink and create the print, as in the lino block print.

Getting Started

1. Organize the tools, materials, and working spaces for printmaking activities.
2. Establish these working stations: a cutting area, an inking area, a printing area, and a hanging area.
3. Store and display materials and tools in convenient and accessible locations in stackable boxes, such as clear plastic trays or shoe boxes, and clearly label them.
4. Collect and keep found objects such as sponges, corks, wood scraps, felt, and jar lids.

5. Plan the designs. Discuss ways of using repeated patterns.
6. Discuss and demonstrate the cutting skills involved, methods of inking, and ways to pull prints. Textures are especially exciting in a print. They will vary according to the tool, the paper used, and the paint or ink used.
7. Use the type of paper that is appropriate to the printing project. Tissue paper, for example, can be used for printing and makes excellent wrapping paper. It can also be mounted on a backing such as white construction paper. Kraft, or butcher paper, is good for large murals, on which several people print. Standing on a block is helpful when printing on a large area. Apply equal pressure over the block or blocks so that the group print has a uniformly inked surface. Colored construction paper, newsprint paper, typing paper, paper bags, manila paper, magazine or newspaper pages (want ad sections), phone book pages, and wallpaper samples are all good for printing.
8. Experiment with the proper consistency for printing paint. The best consistency is like that of thick cream. Finger paint is a good printing ink, or acrylic paints can be used for permanent color. Make printing ink by adding tempera paint to thick starch. Special block-printing inks are available that are either water-soluble or permanent.
9. The paint can be either brushed on or rolled onto the block with a brayer, or the printing block can be stamped on a pad.
10. Experiment by applying several colors to the same block.
11. Have students work in small groups.
12. Prepare the students' desks with thick pads of newspaper under the paper to be printed. The thickness provides a spongy pressure that helps produce a good clear print.
13. Print the design on a scrap piece of paper first to see what the print looks like.
14. Hang prints on a clothesline with clothespins to dry.

THE PRINTING PAD

There are several ways to prepare a stamping pad.

Supplies Needed

brayer
cookie sheet
inks
paper toweling or newspaper
pie tins

plastic floor tiles
sponges
tempera, dry or creamy
water

Procedure

1. Place some water in an aluminum pie tin, cottage cheese lid, or bread or cake tin large enough to hold printing tools (enough water to cover the bottom of the container). Into this water place a common kitchen sponge. On the sponge, place either dry tempera or creamy tempera paint. Stamping into this is easy, and the tin can be shared by three or four students. Several dishes with other colors can also be shared. An inked stamp will print several times.

2. Place several pieces of paper toweling or several thicknesses of newspaper in a pie tin. Dampen the paper and pour on liquid or dry tempera.

3. Place some ink on a plastic floor tile, on aluminum foil, or on a cookie sheet (if you use a sheet of glass, tape it around the edges). Spread the ink with a roller brayer until the ink is the proper consistency, an even thickness with puckers.

Introducing the Print Concept

RUBBINGS

Rubbings are excellent techniques for discovering visual and tactile forms in our environment. Often there are textural and visual qualities belonging to an object that cannot be seen until a "print" is made. Multiple print rubbings can be taken from one surface, and in this way the concept of printing is learned. Ask students to bring in hidden textures for the class to discover. Or, take a short field trip with the class to an interesting site. Crayons and medium-weight paper make very good tools and surfaces for doing print rubbings. Some good beginning surfaces for rubbings include:

IN THE FIELD	IN THE CLASS
Railroad cars	Coins
Old buildings and walls	Silverware
Manhole covers	Embellished rifle barrels
Tombstones	Wrought iron
Items in antique shops	Kitchen utensils
Fences	Wood grains
Name plates	Leaves
Old signs	Mosaics

ROLLING PRINTS

This technique permits you to make a mirror image of an object. Objects from nature make good prints, especially those that have fine details, such as ferns, feathers, and fish. Details print clearly and you can make several prints.

Procedure
1. Ink both sides of the object (when flat forms are used).
2. Place the item between two sheets of printing paper.
3. Apply pressure by rolling over the paper with a rolling pin. This process reveals unusual and sometimes unknown textures. Rarely are there two objects whose images are alike.

The Stamped Print

The stamped print tool is any object that is small enough to be placed onto the inked pad. Many found object tools are used to stamp print.

If a repeated pattern is planned on a large-sized surface, have students divide the spaces before they begin to print by

Fundamentals of Printmaking

either marking off the spaces or folding the paper gently to indicate division. Plan alternating designs every two or three folds. Numerous patterns and separations are possible; or ask the students to think of the tool "walking" or "dancing" across the paper to achieve rhythms or variety.

PRINTING WITH VEGETABLES AND FRUITS

One of the teacher's classic printing tools is the good old potato. (The same effect can be achieved with a carrot, a turnip, or any other vegetable that can be cut to a flat surface.) (See Figure 12–4.)

Procedure
1. Cut a potato in half to get two flat surfaces that can be incised and that are broad enough so that either side of the potato can be gripped. To cut into the potato use a paring knife, a melon ball cutter, or scratching tools such as pencils, nails, dull scissors, and sticks.
2. Keep the design simple: geometric designs are good motifs.
3. Incise fairly large shapes so that pieces of the potato do not break off during the printing process.
4. The design can be incised at least ⅛ inch into the potato. (The outside edges of the vegetable also become part of the design.) The tool cuts away parts of the smooth surface, leaving the remainder of the surface with which to print.

One teacher enjoyed printing the textural design of half of a lemon, so she planned a design and printed the lemon on white fabric, which she then made into a blouse. For a permanent ink, she used refillable felt-tip pen ink. She poured a small amount in a cup, and dipped in the lemon. Children may want to create more lasting prints as well, by stamping designs on fabric to make curtains, kerchiefs, scarves, or shirts. Lemons, oranges, and grapefruits give exciting organic designs and can be used in conjunction with other printing tools.

12–3 *Natural textures in our environment are revealed, and the details and structure come into focus by inking the objects and printing them on paper with a rolling pin.*

12–4 *Potatoes, carrots, and green peppers are carved into designs, dipped into a stamp pad, and printed into repeated patterns. Aluminum foil trays hold toweling with creamy paint on top.*

PRINTING WITH FOUND OBJECTS

Every kitchen and toy box is a wealth of found objects for printing: utensils, toys, wooden spools, jar lids, chicken bones, keys, washers, nails, and sink stoppers can be used to develop an interesting design that will lend itself to repetition. Dip the four wheels of a toy car into an inking pad and roll it across paper. The parallel lines made by the wheels— either vertically, horizontally, or diagonally—will divide the paper into equal and patterned spaces. Then a stamp design can be added between the lines. These designs are a finished product in themselves, but they can provide further inspirations in stitchery and ceramics. Use buttons, a toothbrush, animal stamps, letter stamps, plastic toys, objects from nature, dowels, wooden clothespins (both ends), plastic curlers with many teeth, designs cut from art gum erasers, and erasers on the ends of pencils to stamp designs. Water-base paints and inks leave the objects as good as new. (See Figure 12–5.)

PRINTING WITH PLASTICENE AND CLAY

Procedure
1. Turn a ball of clay into the desired shape (commonly a pancake about 1 inch thick).

12–5 *A toy car divides spaces for patterns. Other designs will then be printed in the divisions.*

12–6 *Designs from the simple to the complex can be carved from vegetables, sponges, and clay.*

2. Draw into the flat surface with a tool such as a toothpick, pencil, hairpin, nail, or stick.
3. Remove the cutout clay, particularly the clay crumbs.
4. Use a good thickness of padding under the paper on which you will be printing.
5. Gently press the clay onto the ink pad (the paint pad) and stamp the clay on the printing paper.
6. When you are finished, wash off any paint that remains on the clay. The clay can be used again and again.

MORE STAMPING TOOLS

12–7 *Found objects for printing. The tree wood block, top center, has cut pieces of rubber tubing glued on; the tree print is made from the block. The roller at bottom can hold foam tape, string, rubber bands, or cardboard designs to be dipped into ink.*

Cut designs into finely grained sponges that have been cut into small pieces. Use a separate sponge for each color designed for printing. Jar lids, sticks, wood scraps, and wooden spools also can be used. Glue cutout felt or cardboard designs on the jar lids and then stamp print with them. Carve simple designs on the ends of wood or Styrofoam

thread spools. Print with other objects such as shells, forks, nuts, gears, jewelry, and doilies.

The Relief Print

In this reduction process a line is incised with a tool into a block surface. If the block is small, the surface can be inked on a pad. Most large blocks are printed by using a brayer and water-base ink (available in many colors) or finger paint.

Procedure
1. Squeeze the ink onto a flat surface such as a cookie sheet.
2. Roll the brayer over the ink until it is covered evenly.
3. Roll the ink from the brayer onto the block and cover it evenly.
4. To print, press the inked block onto the paper, turn the block and the paper over, and gently rub the paper against the block with any dull tool such as a spoon or a tongue depressor. Press the paper carefully onto the inked block and rub.
5. Peel the paper back.

STYROFOAM TRAY

This is a good process for small children.

Procedure
1. Draw or press in a design on the smooth side of a Styrofoam tray with a pencil, pen, scissors or paper clip—any simple tool works. Be sure to press firmly so the grooves are deep.
2. Prepare the ink and brayer and print as described in "The Relief Print."

12–8 *Prints made from designs incised with scissors on Styrofoam trays.*

Fundamentals of Printmaking

459

12–9 *Relief block examples (left to right): cork, linoleum, Styrofoam, wax, soap, and paraffin.*

3. A variation is to cut the outside edge of the tray as well, so that the outside form becomes part of the design.

Note: Press the Styrofoam against a sharply textured surface (wire mesh or twine). The texture will be imprinted on the Styrofoam. Proceed with the incising of the design, press the tray into the ink, and print.

SOAP BLOCK

Procedure
1. Remove the label or trademark from a bar of soap with a straight-edged scraper. Be sure the surface of the bar is flat.
2. Transfer a design onto the soap by placing a paper sketch over the bar and inscribing onto the paper and into the soap.
3. Carve the design, eliminating all areas that should not print.
4. Ink as before and print.

PARAFFIN BLOCK

12–10 *This student has incised a design into a paraffin block.*

Procedure
1. Use small boxes or cartons as molds for paraffin blocks, or use paraffin blocks as they come in their packages.
2. Melt and pour the paraffin into a mold (to a level of about 1 inch). Let it harden, and then remove it from the mold.
3. Smooth the surfaces of the paraffin block with a scraping tool (a tongue depressor is fine).
4. Prepare a sketch of your design and place it over the block.
5. Inscribe the design directly on the block through the paper with any suitable tool—points of scissors, nails, or pencils.

6. To check your design, place a thin piece of paper over the block and rub the surface gently with a pencil point. This will give you a rubbing.
7. Cover the face of the block with ink. (Add a small amount of liquid detergent to the ink to make the ink adhere to the paraffin.)
8. Place the printing paper carefully over the block and rub it gently but firmly.
9. Check a corner of the paper (lifting a small area carefully) to see if the block is printing well.
10. Reink the block for subsequent printings.

PLASTER

Procedure
1. Mix plaster with water (approximately ½ pound of plaster per child) and pour it into a waxed container, greased box, or clay mold.
2. Let the plaster harden overnight.
3. Brush the top surface of the plaster with a color.
4. Sketch your design directly on the block.
5. Carve into the plaster block with a sharp tool, such as a nail or hairpin.
6. Roll the ink on a plate with a brayer until it is spread uniformly. Roll the brayer horizontally, then vertically, and then back again. Do not spread the ink too thinly; keep enough ink contained within an area suitable for the size of the brayer.
7. Roll the brayer over the plaster surface, alternating the direction of the brayer to ensure even coverage.
8. Carefully place the printing paper over the inked plaster surface and gently and evenly rub the paper with your fingers or any flat, smooth object. Fairly hard pressure must be applied to transfer the ink to the paper.
9. Lift up a corner of the paper to see if it is printing well. The first one or two prints do not print as well as the later ones.
10. Reink the surface of the plaster block for more prints.

METAL FOIL
(See "Repoussé Copper Tooling")

Procedure
1. Place a heavy, flat, metal foil tray (such as the ones that come with frozen pies, cakes, or breads) on several thicknesses of newspaper.
2. Draw on the foil with a hard tool, such as a sharpened lead pencil, nail, or pointed stick. By applying firm and even

12–11 *Soap, paraffin, plaster, and Styrofoam blocks, can be carved for printing.*

12–12 *Metal foil designs are inscribed with a pencil-like dowel. The metal is then attached to a backing and printed.*

pressure, a raised (embossed) line will appear on the underside of the foil.

3. Large forms as well as minute details are possible with this process.
4. After the incising, attach the foil to a piece of cardboard, such as a shoe box bottom. (Staple or glue it on.)
5. Roll on the ink with a brayer and print. After printing, these pieces of foil are sufficiently attractive to be mounted on wood and exhibited as repoussé (see Chapter 11).

ETCHING PLASTIC

Supplies Needed
heavy acetate
sewing needle or nail
tray
medium-weight paper ink
rags

Procedure
1. Draw and scratch the design into the acetate with a nail or sewing needle.
2. Ink the plate generously with the brayer so that the incised lines are filled with ink.
3. Wipe the ink from the acetate plate, but let the ink remain in the incised lines.
4. Dampen the printing paper in the water tray and place it on the plate. Be sure the plate is on newspapers.
5. Rub the back of the paper surface carefully with your fingers or a spoon. Go over the lines carefully, making sure that they are printing.
6. Remove the paper from the acetate and let it dry.

Note: All of the preceding printing surfaces used—wax, plastic, foil, Styrofoam, linoleum, wood, and soap—can be given texture by marking their surfaces with nails, screws, wire, and other pointed objects. For unusual background patterns and textures, take rubbings from wall surfaces, or ink print sandpaper and leaves and other surfaces. Then one can proceed with the other printing steps described here.

12–13 *Linoleum blocks are carved with a variety of carving tools. Note that the left hand is holding the block and is behind the path of the knife.*

LINOLEUM AND WOOD BLOCK

At the upper grade levels, linoleum printing is an art experience that offers a unique and satisfying challenge. Studying the history of printing techniques and elaborating on the work of many contemporary as well as historical block print artists are essential to the curriculum. (See Figure 12–13.)

Printing becomes more meaningful for the elementary student when he uses the block prints as art forms or for specific learning areas that require repeated designs. Examples of the latter are planning and producing fabric designs, a small newspaper or book illustrations, posters, holiday cards, and other career-related projects.

The printing process for linoleum and wood blocks is the same. However, it is not practical to use wood blocks in the elementary classroom as the tools for wood carving are expensive and blades for them cannot be replaced easily. Also, wood is more difficult to carve than linoleum. If wood is used, cut the wood according to the grain. (Cross cuts will cause the wood to splinter.)

Only a few sets of tools are needed in the average classroom for cutting linoleum, as tools are easily shared.

Supplies Needed
design
carbon paper
brayer
water-soluble or permanent inks
a knife for trimming edges

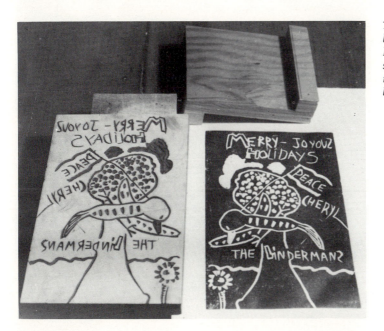

12–14 *An inked linoleum block and the reverse print. Note the lettering. The wood Z shape on top is placed against the edge of a table and holds the block in position for carving.*

Fundamentals of Printmaking

battleship linoleum (blocks or vinyl floor tiles)
paint and a brush
papers
U-shaped gouges (various sizes)
V-shaped gouges (various sizes)

Procedure
1. Plan the design carefully, after studying several fine examples of linoleum block printing and making several sketches. Consider the placement of the darks and lights, positive and negative shapes, and the textures. Transfer the design to the block by placing carbon paper between the design and the block.

12–15a *The linoleum block has paint applied to it with a roller and a brush.*

2. Various tools create various tool marks and unusual effects; therein lies the excitement of this type of print making. (Experimenting first with tools or linoleum scraps helps inform students as to tool-mark possibilities.) Some

12–15b *The block is placed beside the etching press.*

12–15c *The print paper is placed on top of the block, and then both are rolled through the press. (If there is no press, the back surface is simply rubbed to transfer the ink to the paper.)*

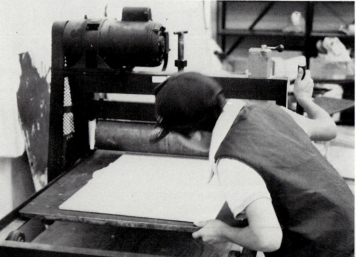

marks are not seen until the first print. Then they may be cut further or otherwise altered. Use battleship linoleum if it is available, but vinyl floor tiles can also be used.

3. Darken the linoleum block with ink or tempera or acrylic paint. When the block is cut into, the cutting marks will be visible, as white areas. In this way, the design can be seen as you progress.

4. If any lettering is planned in the design, remember to cut the block *in reverse.* To check lettering hold the block up to a mirror. The design can also be checked by making a rubbing over the surface with a pencil and paper.

5. Cut away all the unwanted areas. If the linoleum is difficult to cut, warm it a little to allow for easier cutting: leave it out in the sun; place it near a radiator; or place in a 300°F. oven for about 10 minutes, with the oven door open slightly. When the linoleum is just about too hot to hold, it will cut very easily.

6. *Keep the hand that is not holding a cutting tool away from the cutting hand.*

7. Ink the linoleum with a brayer, using water-soluble or permanent ink. Distribute the ink evenly and print as directed for relief prints. (See page 459.)

8. Reink the linoleum for more prints.

9. Acrylic paints can be substituted for inks; use thickly.

Alternate Procedure

1. Cut a piece of thin linoleum to measure around a spool, wooden dowel, or small can.

2. Lay the cut piece flat and cut away a design.

3. Warm the linoleum, glue the underside, and place it around the spool or can, tie it, and let it cool and dry.

4. Prepare the ink with a brayer.

5. Place a pencil or wooden dowel into the spool. This acts as a handle to control the movement of the spool.

6. Roll the spool in the ink and rotate it until the linoleum is well covered with ink.

7. Roll the spool, dowel, or can over the paper, transferring the design.

12–15e *When the ink is dry, the students sign and number the prints. Students are from the Children's Art Workshop, Jon Sharer, director, Arizona State University.*

Checkpoints

1. Keep a small carborundum on hand for sharpening tools. Dampen the stone and then rotate the tool.
2. Print on newspaper, wrapping paper, paper bags, paper toweling, magazine paper, rice paper, and typing paper.
3. Rub with smooth objects: paddles, tongue depressors, or household spoons.
4. Discuss safety measures with the students. Always cut *away* from your body. Turn the linoleum block as you work. By turning the block, the cutting marks will go in various directions, and add to the design interest.
5. Floor tile and ⅛-inch battleship linoleum can be mounted on blocks of wood with double-face tape or glue.

The Collage Print

In this type of printing, one material is added on top of another. It is the raised surface that prints, and is often rich in texture. This raised surface can be fabric, metal, paper tape, masking tape, acrylic modeling paste, or various papers, as well as the glue, foam tape, and cardboard procedures described. Glue the raised materials to a base such as wood scraps, Styrofoam (meat trays), jar lids, inverted cottage cheese containers, or small pieces of pressed board (Masonite). Either stamp or roll ink on a surface with a brayer, and print.

CARDBOARD ON CARDBOARD

Procedure
1. Give each student two pieces of lightweight shirt cardboard, index cards, chip board, or mat board.
2. Plan a design, considering both the positive and the negative spaces (inside and outside spaces).
3. Cut out forms from the sheet.
4. Glue the forms onto the second sheet with rubber cement.
5. Use creamy tempera paint (add a little starch) or use water-soluble printing ink.
6. Spread the paint or ink with a brayer on an aluminum tray or cookie sheet. Roll the inked brayer onto the raised forms. Some lower shapes will print also.
7. Place the paper on top of the cardboard. Newsprint, tissue, or any lightweight paper works well.
8. Rub the back of the print with a dry brayer, a wooden spoon, or jar lid. Be sure to press hard enough to pick up

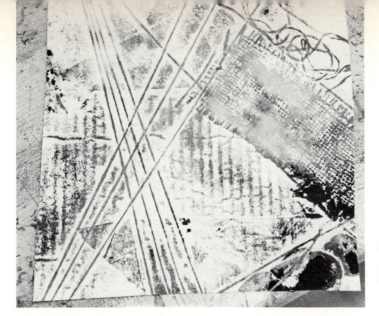

12–16 *A corrugated cardboard, burlap cloth, and string collage was rolled with ink and a print was taken from it.*

the print but not so hard as to tear the paper. Practice will teach you the correct pressure.

9. Look under a corner of the paper to see if you are picking up the ink. Pull a print from the cardboard surface.

GLUE, STRING, CORRUGATED CARDBOARD

Procedure

1. Apply glue line designs directly from a squeeze-bottle applicator to cardboard or a card.
2. Let the glue dry and harden overnight (provide sufficient time for drying).
3. Experiment with rolling string in glue; then apply to cardboard and let it dry.
4. When using corrugated cardboard, plan the design and then cut away some of the surfaces with scissors, leaving positive and negative forms.
5. Roll the hardened forms with an inked brayer and print.
6. A variation is the collagraph technique. Here, one applies white glue, either with a spoon, knife, brush, or squeeze-bottle, to a backing surface such as cardboard, wood, or Masonite. Let the glue set up slightly, then incise lines, and textures into glue. When glue is hard, ink the surface and print.

12–17 *Glue is squeezed from a bottle over a pencil design onto a computer card and is ready for the brayer, ink, and printing.*

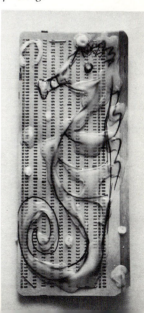

FOAM TAPE OR FOAM SHEETING

Procedure

1. Cut design shapes out of foam tape (available in hardware stores), foam sheeting (available in hobby shops), Styrofoam meat trays, or sponges.

12–18 *Foam sheeting, firm Styrofoam, sponge, and cardboard were cut and glued to jar lids for printing purposes. A margarine tub holds the tempera.*

2. Glue the shapes to a cardboard backing or jar lids. (Rubber cement is good for the sheeting as it is waterproof. Foam tape is already backed with glue.)
3. The foam absorbs a good deal of paint, so be sure to cover the shapes well. The denser foam makes a better print.
4. Brush the paint on the individual surfaces to print several at one time.

CYLINDERS

Procedure
1. Build up designs with thin cardboard, string, rubber, felt, or tape on any size cylinder that can be inked.
2. A cardboard tube, a wood dowel, a tin can, a glass, a jar, a brayer, an empty thread spool, a broom handle, a cardboard carpet roll, a piece of plastic tubing, and even a pencil are simple and lightweight cylinders. (Styrofoam thread spools can be either added onto or incised and then rolled in ink.)
3. If small enough, the cylinder can be dipped and rolled into the paint in an inking pad. Otherwise, use a brayer to smooth the ink in an aluminum tray and roll the cylinder directly into the ink.

SUPER CYLINDERS

Procedure
1. A large wallpaper roller (used for taking out air bubbles in wallpaper) is good for large projects such as decorating backdrop scenery and creating murals. They are hard plastic and are available at hardware stores.
2. Materials such as felt and twine can be glued to the surface.
3. Instead of ink, use latex house paint (water base).
4. Print on large kraft paper or on clear plastic sheeting.

INNER TUBES

Procedure

1. Give each student a piece of rubber cut from the inner tubing of an old tire.
2. Plan a design, sketch it onto the rubber, and with scissors cut out the chosen shapes from the tubing.
3. Glue these shapes to a block of wood.
4. If the design is small enough, the block can be stamp printed; otherwise, proceed using a brayer.

The Stencil Print

The use of repeated visual images brings us to a method of reproduction that goes as far back as the cave man. Thousands of years ago, a cave painter in Lascaux, France, made a stencil by placing his hand flat against the wall and blowing a mixture of fat and pigment, through a hollow instrument such as a bone, against his hand.

In American history, stenciling has played an important role as a decorative art technique, having been used on walls, furniture and floors. Some of our most treasured antiques are pieces of furniture finely stenciled by Pennsylvania Dutch craftsmen.

Exploring this process is as intriguing as its result. Repeated images suggest designs for cloth, holiday cards, and murals. Repeated images in sequence also suggest movement (such as a horse galloping), clouds, and concepts of space—where objects overlap and recede.

Stenciling is a simple procedure where color (paint, crayon, or chalk) is forced through a cutout shape onto the material underneath it (paper or cloth). The cutout material usually used is waxed paper, oak tag, or computer cards. Found objects such as doilies, plastic fruit baskets, metal forks, and

12–19 *Super-roller prints cover large areas quickly. String is glued to a rolling pin and rolled over a sponge pad and then printed.*

12–20 *Stencil prints are favorites for all ages and can be used with crayon, chalk, paints, and spray techniques. In this crayon print, the stencil was overlapped and shifted to produce the image. Note: Use a stencil design on a T-shirt (backed with cardboard) and spray the design with a can of interior/exterior spray enamel for permanent projects. (Spray outside.)*

other kitchen utensils make good beginning stencils to introduce the concept.

Supplies Needed

stencil paper, mimeograph stencil, oak tag, or waxed paper (for a more permanent backing run typing paper through melted paraffin in a wide, flat pan)

white drawing paper, construction paper, tissue paper, or cloth

cutting tools: scissors and a mat knife

chalk, crayons, or pencils

sponges, cotton, and paper tissues

tempera and spray paints

newspapers

jars of water

muffin tin

stenciling materials: crayons, paints, chalk, stiff brushes, a toothbrush, and a spray bottle

found objects

CHALK

Whether stenciling with chalk, crayon, or pencil, the technique is the same.

Procedure

1. Cut or tear a stencil from oak tag, waxed paper, or plain white drawing paper. You may want to use both the

positive and the negative stencil, so use care not to destroy it after using it once.
2. Lay the stencil down.
3. With chalk, rub from the outside into the center.
4. The application and blending can be done with a piece of cotton, a cleansing tissue, or a finger.
5. Before stenciling, always be sure that your stencil is flat on the paper.

SPRAYING A STENCIL

Procedure
1. Thin some tempera paint in a shallow pan or muffin tin.
2. Put plenty of newspapers around the stencil and place it either on the floor or a table.
3. Spray the stencil with one of several items: dip a toothbrush in the paint, hold it over the stencil and rub the brush with something flat like a stick or nail (or rub the toothbrush over a piece of screening-tape outside the screen). The paint will spatter and fill in the stencil. Or use a fixative sprayer, or an atomizer filled with paint.
4. By applying heavy or thin areas of spray, various textural effects occur.
5. If you are overlapping shapes, be sure that one color is dry before applying another.
6. Objects from nature can be placed on the paper, sprayed, and removed. (These create interesting silhouettes.)
7. Try combining nature's patterns with your patterns.

CRAYONS

Use crayons with paper stencils on muslin or sheeting. Fix the crayon by ironing it on the fabric. Do not wash the fabric often. Use crayon stencils for place mats, window curtains, wall hangings, or in combination with batiking.

PAINTS

Use firm, waterproof stencils out of oak tag with paints. Use inexpensive hardware variety bristle brushes to apply the paint. These are stiff and penetrate cloth or paper easily. Be sure to use thick paints. Use sponges to fill in the design shapes, but be careful not to load on the paint and have it squeeze under the stencil as this creates ragged edges.

When using tempera paint, use a stiff brush dipped lightly into the paint. Wipe off any excess paint. Start from the edge of the stencil and brush or dab toward the center of the paper, holding the brush in a vertical position (this prevents paint from going under the stencil). This technique achieves a soft blending effect that goes from dark at the edge to light at the center.

Use the same approach for permanent paints, such as acrylics, or inks on textiles. Use very little paint on a stiff brush, stroking or stippling the paint onto the fabric. Experiment to find the most satisfactory approach for you. Solid forms are exciting as well.

If using several colors, keep one brush for each color. Remove all sizing from fabrics before using them. Common cotton is best for any textile painting. (Polyester fabrics tend to resist paints.) Paint over printed cloth as well. Gingham or polka dots are fun. Keep the designs and projects simple in the elementary grades. For polyester and cotton cloth try this process: place your cutout stencil on the cloth (T-shirts or curtain material) backed with cardboard and tape down tightly. With a can of interior/exterior spray enamel, held upright about 12 inches from the cloth, spray lightly with short spurts. Paint dries quickly, is permanent and designs can be overlapped. Do this outdoors.

The Screened Print

The silk screen process is an extension of the paper stencil technique. This printing process permits a large quantity of designs to be run quickly, as in an edition. This is possible because more permanent tools and materials are used. (See Figure 12–21.)

The procedure often is called serigraphy. *Seri*, in Greek, means "silk." The process is basically a blockout method. A pigment is squeezed through a fine mesh, commonly silk, to produce the image. Several screens can be made to provide several colors; each screen is used for each color. This is a popular printing method with contemporary artists and also

12–21 *Screen printing is done with a wood frame hinged to a backing. The fabric is stretched across tightly, stapled, and taped.*

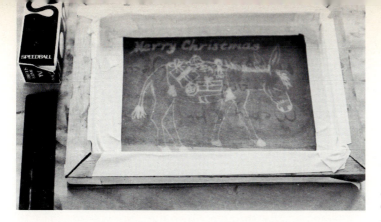

12–22 *The rubber squeegee on the left will carry the printing ink across the screen and print. These screens can be cleaned and reused.*

is used to produce posters. Many school theater productions and art shows advertise with silk screen posters.

Silk screen printing is used on cloth as well as on paper. Art teachers like this repeated procedure for designing curtain and simple costume fabrics. For permanent projects, use commercially prepared inks or textile paints. Large areas can be printed on the muslin backing used for stage curtains; this material is very wide, is lightweight, and does not have visible seams. If the material is for temporary use, print with water-base inks, paints, or finger paints on old sheeting.

Supplies Needed

a frame: either a small wooden frame, a cardboard box with a
   rectangle cut from it, or an embroidery hoop
screening material: fine mesh silk (expensive), permanent-
   finish organdy (a good beginning substitute), or dotted
   swiss cloth, cheese cloth, or nylon stockings
stencil paper: typing or mimeograph stencil backing, waxed
   paper, or commercial stencil paper
squeegee, tongue depressor, spatula, or plastic windshield
   wiper (or cardboard)
scissors
inking pad (a tile)
shellac
paint: finger paint, commercial silk screen paint, inks or dyes,
   or tempera (add water and starch for the consistency of
   toothpaste) or tempera mixed with wheat paste
printing paper, construction paper, or any paper or cloth
scissors or knife
masking tape, gummed stickers, or paper reinforcements

CONSTRUCTING A SCREEN

Procedure

1. To make a screen, use a wood frame base or a cardboard box with a center rectangle cut out from it.
2. Or, use an embroidery hoop and stretch the material tightly across it.
3. Stretch the material tightly over the wood or cardboard frame and staple it on. Cover the edge of the frame and

Fundamentals of Printmaking

cloth with tape. (Leave the center open.) Cover the tape and an overlapping of the cloth with shellac to waterproof the edges and add strength to the screen.

CONSTRUCTING A STENCIL

Procedure

1. Cut or tear a design out of the stencil paper. A negative shape results, through which the paint will go. (Place the stencil in between the printing paper and the screen. Place the paint on top of the screen, and squeeze the paint across and through the screen with a squeegee. The stencil design is then passed through onto the printing paper.)
2. Place the printing paper on a flat surface.
3. Place the stencil design on the paper.
4. Place the screen (either the hoop or box) on top of the stencil, making sure that the stencil is tight against the screen.
5. Place the paint on top of the screen at one end (about 2 tablespoons of paint—the size of design determines the amount of paint needed).
6. Squeeze paint from one end across to the opposite end, making sure that the paint goes into the open areas onto the printing paper. When using this process, the paint goes through the screen and adheres the paper stencil to the screen (not where the design has been cut away). The paint thus goes through these spaces and will print. Lift up the screen, and you will find that the stencil has clung to the screen.
7. Gently lift off the screen and stencil and you have your first print.
8. Place the screen and stencil on the next sheet of paper and repeat the process, as many times as you need to make the desired number of prints.
9. If you want to make a second color, print the first color, and let it dry. Use a new stencil with a clean screen and print a second color over the first color.
10. Work quickly as the paint will dry and clog the stencil if left too long.
11. As a variation, cut shapes out of gum-backed paper and glue them to the bottom of the screen, with the gummed side on the screen.

| crayons | paint thinner | tousche |
| glue | masking tape | |

Procedure

1. Draw directly on the screen with a crayon design where you want to print your design. Press down heavily on the crayon.
2. Pour Lepage's glue (thinned to one part water, one part glue) on one end of screen. Drag the flat edge of a piece of cardboard across the screen. Be sure the screen is resting on sticks, or on anything to raise it, or it will adhere to the work surface.
3. When the glue is dry, hold the screen up to the light and check to see that all the pin holes are filled. If necessary, repeat the procedure with more glue.
4. Let the glue dry.
5. Remove the crayon designs with a piece of cloth that has been dipped into paint thinner or turpentine. This opens the crayoned areas and permits the paint the pass through.
6. Now the screen is ready to print. This screen can be cleaned and reused as long as the glue-blocked areas remain.
7. As a variation, draw or paint glue directly on the screen with brushes. Leave openings for the paint to pass through.
8. Other blockout techniques use masking tape designs for straight-edged as well as irregular shapes. Gummed stickers and round paper reinforcements will also block out areas. When they are removed, open areas are left for the paint to pass through. *Note:* Tousche and film screen can be purchased from commercial stores. Tousche is used like crayon, and film screen is used like a cutout stencil.
9. For a line design in the screen, draw or type a design on a mimeograph stencil. Or draw with a fine-tip ball-point pen or mimeo stencil tools. Proceed as before by taping the stencil to the bottom side of the screen.

PAINT FOR SCREEN PRINTING

Supplies Needed
liquid starch	laundry starch
tempera paint	1 quart of boiling water
soap flakes	1 cup of soap flakes
water	

Procedure
1. Add the liquid starch to the powder paint until it is the consistency of thin paste.

2. Add a small amount of soap flakes to the tempera paint to give it body; mix well. Only add water to the tempera paint when necessary.
3. Finger paint also can be used, either commercial preparations or homemade. Mix 1½ cups of laundry starch and a small amount of boiling water. Add the rest of the boiling water to it. Stir in the soap flakes and tempera color.

The Monoprint

The monotype print is one way to apply paint on paper. The first artist known to use this print technique was Giovanni Bennedetto Castiglione (1616–70). Degas was said to have produced more than 300 such prints, exploring the medium to its fullest. In 1968, the Fogg Art Museum displayed 79 Degas prints. Artists were fascinated with them and started to experiment with the medium.

The paint is applied to a zinc plate. Parts can be wiped away or rubbed off. After the image is completed, dampened paper is carefully placed on the plate before the paint dries. Pressure is applied to the plate either in a lithograph or etching press or by hand. The paper is then removed, with the paint transferred to the paper.

Monoprinting is a spontaneous and exciting process that gives an instant, direct, and unexpected print. Children in every grade from preschoolers on enjoy this technique.

Supplies Needed

paints: tempera, finger paints, acrylics, or water-base block-printing inks (oil paints are interesting but are impractical for elementary-school classrooms)

smooth, flat nonporous surface: glass sheet (with taped edges)

12–23 *Students pulling a monotype print.*

tabletops
Formica surfaces
aluminum cookie sheets
brushes, sticks, and sponges
papers: newspaper, tissue, butcher, newsprint, wrapping,
  magazine, and cardboard

Procedure

1. Roll the paint out evenly on the work surface. Encourage the students to experiment with creating textures and color combinations directly on the work surface. Scratch through the paint with pencils or fingernails. Lay on string or sprinkle on sand for textures.
2. When the design is to your liking, carefully place the paper on top of the paint and rub it gently and evenly with the hand, making sure that the print is being transferred to the paper. Often, more than one print can be taken from each paint application.
3. Many unusual textural and color effects occur as the wet paint blends and moves as it is rubbed with the hand.
4. These prints are beautiful in themselves but often are combined with other printing techniques such as block prints.
5. After printing with a brayer or other process, if there is ink left on the work surface, experiment by taking a mono-print from it.

Checkpoints

1. Print on a variety of papers.
2. Paper textures create interest. Try tissue paper, paper toweling, brown paper bags, sandpaper, pages from old telephone books, construction paper, magazines, and the backs of wallpaper. For other interesting textures, apply sand, salt, or sugar to the paint while it is still wet.
3. For added interest mount prints on oak tag, sheet plastic, Styrofoam, or cloth.
4. Use water-base fluorescent paint (available in tempera as well as in gold and silver).
5. Pour different colors of paint on the pad, one on top of another. The colors will blend.
6. For a shadowlike effect, apply the design with one color paint first; then reapply the design slightly off center in another color. This is called *off-register printing*.
7. Try various colors with the same block print to see how the design appears with different colors.
8. Plan a design before printing. Then print without pre-planning a design.

12-24 *Monotype print, "Another American Warrior #2," 40 inches × 30 inches, by Fritz Scholder. (Courtesy of Marilyn Butler Fine Art, Scottsdale, Arizona.)*

9. Collect objects of unusual shapes and textures (see page 457). Many times an object will not print as expected. Glue objects to jar lids, cottage cheese containers, plastic meat trays, wood, and Masonite for easier handling.

10. Use a large paint pan (a cookie sheet is good) with many sponges (or paper pads) so that many colors can be experimented with at the same time.

11. Attach water- or oil-base clay to a scrap piece of wood before incising a design. This becomes a sturdy handle for grasping the printing clay.

12. For additional stamping tools, cut into corks, small sponges, and wood scraps.

13. Use practice sheets when experimenting with color. Sometimes these are more visually exciting than the finished sheet.

14. Blot the paint from blocks on paper toweling or newspaper to remove excess paint. Try wetting the paper before beginning the printing process.

15. When using cutters with metal surfaces, such as cookie

cutters, for printing a design, glue string to the edges of the cutter so the ink or paint will adhere evenly.

16. Watercolor or thinned tempera paint gives soft, blended designs, whereas acrylic paint creates bold color designs.
17. Be sure to cut the design deep enough.
18. Have the paint the consistency of thick cream for printing.
19. Use enough newspaper or paper toweling under the printing paper for padding purposes.
20. Limit the number of students working in a group to eight.
21. Spread enough newspaper under the working areas to catch glue, paint, or water and to speed the cleanup process.
22. Add starch (half and half) to tempera paint and then saturate a 1-inch sponge with the paint to make an effective stamp pad.
23. Do a spontaneous print mural. Have each child participate, printing on one large mural surface. Have the design forms develop as the children work. Some mural themes are the City, A Flower Garden, Moonwalks, The Bus Stop, Crowds in the Elevator, Under Water, and In the Heavens.
24. Encourage the use of new and exciting materials alone and in combination.
25. Preparing the media, demonstrating procedures, and discussing print examples beforehand help the printing experience. Use large tables as stations and have materials laid out on them for initial designing, cutting and gluing, inking, and printing.

Printmaking Bibliography

ANDREWS, MICHAEL. *Creative Printmaking.* Englewood Cliffs, N.J.: Prentice-Hall, Inc., 1963.

CAPON, ROBIN. *Introducing Abstract Printmaking.* New York: Watson-Guptill Publications, 1973.

CRAVEN, THOMAS, ED. *A Treasury of American Prints.* New York: Simon & Schuster, Inc., 1939.

ERIKSON, JANET DOBBS. *Block Printing on Textiles.* New York: Watson-Guptill Publications, 1961.

————, AND ADELAIDE SPROUL. *Print Making Without a Press.* New York: Van Nostrand Reinhold Company, 1974.

GORBATY, NORMAN. *Printmaking with a Spoon.* New York: Van Nostrand Reinhold Company, 1960.

GREEN, PETER. *Introducing Surface Printing.* New York: Watson-Guptill Publications, 1968.

HELLER, JULES. *Printmaking Today,* 2nd ed. New York: Holt, Rinehart and Winston, Inc., 1972.

KAFKA, FRANCES J. *Linoleum Block Printing*. Bloomington, Ill.: McKnight & McKnight, Publishers, 1955.

KAMPMANN, LOTHAR. *Creating with Printing Materials*. New York: Van Nostrand Reinhold Company, 1969.

NELSON, ROY PAUL. *Cartooning*. Chicago: Henry Regnery Company, 1975.

MCARTHUR, JEANETTE. *Printing Without a Press*. Hollywood, Fla: Dukane Press, Inc., 1970.

PATTEMORE, ARNEL W. *Printmaking Activities for the Classroom*. Worcester, Mass.: Davis Publications, Inc., 1966.

RASMUSEN, HENRY N. *Printmaking with Monotype*. Philadelphia, Pa.: Chilton Book Co., 1957.

SACHS, PAUL J. *Modern Prints and Drawings*. New York: Alfred A. Knopf, Inc., 1954.

SAFF, DONALD. *Printmaking: History and Process*. New York: Holt, Rinehart and Winston, Inc., 1978.

SCHACHNER, ERWIN. *Printmaking*. New York: Golden Press, 1970.

STERNBERG, HARRY. *Woodcut*. New York: Pitman Publishing Corp., 1962.

WEISS, HARVEY. *Paper, Ink and Roller*. New York: William R. Scott, Inc., 1958.

WOODS, GERALD. *Introducing Woodcuts*. New York: Watson-Guptill Publications, 1969.

Photography

Photography starts with your own special vision. For one moment, your eye selects something meaningful to you from out of the world and you keep its memory forever. Today's camera is a third eye. The excitement and anticipation in snapping the shutter and waiting for the captive image to be developed is always suspenseful and often rewarding. We communicate and share personal ideas through these images, which help us to develop a visual language and visual literacy. Through the camera, we learn ways of seeing, of expressing significant feelings, and of communicating important thoughts.

One of the first records of a box for viewing or projecting pictures was one constructed by L. B. Alberti in 1437, a rough form of the camera obscura or magic lantern. Leonardo da Vinci also left manuscripts containing a diagram and notes on the pinhole camera. Giovanni Battista della Porta is named as the inventor of the camera obscura, described in his book, *Magica Naturalis*, published in Naples in 1558. Daniello Barbaro gives us the first account of a camera with a lens in his *La Pratica della Perspettiva*, published in Venice in 1568.

In the latter half of the eighteenth century, cameras became quite common as a show and for sketching purposes. Some were large enough for the observers to get inside them; others were small and portable and fitted with mirrors on the inside that reflected the image on a horizontal screen on the top of the box. Such a box is pictured in *Leçons de Physique*, by Abbé Nollet, published in Paris in 1755. The diagram illustrates the similarity between the camera and the eye and the fact that the nearer the object is brought to the lens, the further away on the other side of the lens is the sharp image.

Many others contributed to the development of the photographic process, and in about 1824, a scenic painter named Louis Jacques Mandé Daguerre had the idea of fixing the images of the camera obscura, a tool he used in his scene paintings. Between 1834 and 1839 he perfected and published the process and after unsuccessfully attempting to form a company, he gave to the world the method in return for a pension from the French government.

The camera used by Daguerre was a box with a small opening or lens at the front, a reflecting mirror at a 45-degree angle inside, and a screen below for viewing the scene.

The daguerreotype method is a positive image, in which a highly polished silver plate is submitted to the fumes of iodine until it is coated with a fine layer of silver iodide, and then exposed in the camera. After exposure, the plate is transferred to a box in which it is held over a metal dish of mercury heated from beneath. The mercury fumes ascend and the metal adheres to the parts that were exposed to light, in proportion to the strength of the light. The unaltered iodide is then dissolved away by means of a salt solution—

later known as a hypo—resulting in a brilliant well-defined picture. At the same time, William Henry Fox Talbot, an Englishman, developed a method of forming silver chloride in paper in such a way that an excess of silver nitrate is left. In 1835, he claimed to have achieved negative camera pictures on paper sensitized by alternate washes of solutions of salt and silver nitrate.

Viewers were amazed at the brilliance of the camera images and the details they contained. Within a very short time, production of the daguerreotype camera was begun in both Europe and America.

In 1878, a 24-year-old amateur photographer named George Eastman began making photographic emulsions with material and information gathered from England, then the world's photography center. The early camera signifies an historical turning point in recording visual information and artistic form.

Photography in the Curriculum

Improving communication is a fundamental goal of education. *Photography*, which means "writing with light," is an essential form of communication in our society. We have all heard the saying, "A picture is worth a thousand words." Photographic images and photographic tools can be powerful creative ingredients in our educational programs. Our visual language is as natural as our verbal language; both image and word are essential to life. Together they offer a limitless

13–1 *This is the No. 1 Kodak camera, manufactured in 1888. The basic parts are similar to those used in cameras today. (Courtesy of Eastman Kodak Company.)*

potential for expressing thoughts and ideas. They help us to understand the world around us.

The place to begin inquiring into the uses of cameras and photographic processes is in the elementary school. We are constantly bombarded by television and other mass media. Television is the foremost source of communication today. The television screen brings to us images and facts that are astounding by past standards. Most of us experience it daily and, next to direct experiences, it is becoming the most potent educational instrument, both in and out of the classroom. We are now in a camera conscious age. The teacher has the opportunity to use the camera to teach visual language by including photography in the curriculum. We should teach critical assessment of the television eye, as well as the uses of the camera, its image-making possibilities, and encourage the individual vision and powers of communication of each student.

LOOKING THROUGH THE VIEWFINDER

Practice taking "pretend" pictures. Before loading the film in the camera (as well as with your paper viewfinders) go on a "photography hunt." Practice the following visual awareness

13–2 *For the first time, in 1923, amateur home movie cameras were made available. Subsequent developments have brought the camera into classroom use through still photography, film making, videotape, and television production. (Courtesy of Eastman Kodak Company.)*

skills, and then begin your photography adventure. (See Figure 13–3.)

Procedure
1. Select a subject or object that you feel is important enough to photograph. Be discriminating.
2. Decide what feelings you want your photograph to express. Your photograph will express a small section of reality as you see it; it will be an extension of yourself.
3. What is the best "point of view" for your shot? That is, should it be a close-up, a middle, or a distant shot? Should the camera look up at the subject? Down at the subject?
4. Study what it is that you want to illustrate about the subject—its top, its side, its bottom? Will it benefit from distortion? From unusual perspectives?
5. What kind of light is the most suitable to your idea: sharp darks and strong contrasts or an out-of-focus mist or haze?
6. Turn the camera before you shoot to determine whether it should be held horizontally or vertically.
7. Are the dominant lines in your picture horizontal, vertical, or diagonal? Are there curves to indicate rhythm?
8. Is the composition interesting? Do the parts work well together?
9. Look for the shadows. They can be interesting shapes in themselves or they can cover and hide.
10. Is the camera in focus? Do you have your hair or finger over the lens?
11. Hold the camera still when clicking the shutter. Otherwise, your picture will be blurry.

13–3 *As the student sees parts of her world through the eye of the lens, she learns to be more selective in her visual judgment.*

HOLD STILL! SMILE! SHOOT!

Begin photography experiences early in the curriculum. From the preschool level on, children express decided points of view, learn to be visually selective, perceive details, discover visual relationships, learn how other students see the same subject, and appreciate other students' points of view. Numerous experiences in picture taking and discussion will result in improved skills.

It is fascinating and revealing to have a group of students photograph the same subject. For instance, a visit to a fair, zoo, or museum will illustrate how everyone shooting the same subject will select different images. Even changing distances from a subject will create a different feeling. Sometimes when photographing, hold the viewfinder to your eye and try changing the view by moving closer or farther away from the subject. Or hold your eye to the viewfinder

Photography

and wait for the subject to change and move. Often, by waiting, one can get exactly the idea intended. It's fun to practice shooting. Make yourself and the students a paper viewfinder (a 3 × 4-inch rectangular frame with a 1-inch cutout to look through). Carry this with you and practice selecting objects and points of view.

Discussing photographs taken by professionals helps to understand structure better and develop critical awareness. Evaluate photographs used in posters and as magazine illustrations, as well as original photographs taken by artists. Mount these on a hard board (illustration board or cardboard) with rubber cement and display them. You may want to frame some. Simple acetate sheeting, which is available in local shops, is excellent for photographic displays. Discuss photographs that have been taken by students: How did the student decide on a subject and how could he interpret the idea further to improve on it? After several critical awareness discussions, mount and discuss the photos involved. Because details are sometimes overlooked in a small photograph, place the photographs in an opaque projector for super images.

There will be many opportunities to take photographs that you will want to remember and share. Students are highly enthusiastic about keeping records of their experiences such as field trips expressing attitudes and feelings, and understanding each other's point of view. Through photography, they discover new meanings and relationships, develop their perceptual and visual skills, make discriminating choices in their environment, perform picture-making skills, and enrich many related learning areas.

INTEGRATING PHOTOGRAPHY IN THE CURRICULUM

Use photography with other learning experiences, such as creative writing, plays, poetry, music, dance, language development, and environmental discovery.

1. Use opaque projectors to create super-image compositions; these are also supermotivators.
2. Use photographs as studies for works of art, to study moving subjects such as animals in the zoo, and for nature study.
3. Study the work of professional photographers.
4. Project photographs with other programmed light media in light shows.
5. Project photographs on figures as they dance. (Imagine your own photograph superprojected on you as you move.)

6. Create photographic montages. Select and compose photographic images to express a statement in one picture.
7. Create photographic sculptures (mount photographs on three-dimensional forms such as cardboard boxes, pottery forms, lampshades, toys and dolls, and chairs. Spray them with a plastic coating for a permanent finish.
8. Study a subject such as "lines"; find them in nature and in man-made objects.
9. Photograph the differences and similarities among shapes, textures, patterns, and colors.
10. Create and illustrate stories with a sequence of photographs. (Produce a class newspaper and exchange it with those of other classes or schools.)
11. Illustrate music and poems with photographic images.
12. Photograph selected aspects of life that are important to you—your personal "living book."
13. Develop group projects: books of photographs combined with tapes to describe a learning area, or photographs of a school event amassed on a large mural.
14. Take and make colored slides. Produce your own slide-tape shows for documentaries, instruction, or for fun.
15. Record data. Write down feelings and ideas and illustrate them with photographs; related learning areas are endless and wait for your discovery.

Photography offers one way to better understand the world around us. Everyone can use a camera.

Terms

Before any actual picture taking begins, the student will want to learn the terminology of photography and uses of a camera. At the elementary level, match the types of cameras to the ability of the students. Old box cameras (donated or purchased from thrift shops), Instamatics, Autopak, the Snapshooter, Polaroid, and Autoload are a few cameras available at a comparatively low cost.[1] These cameras are easy to use. With very few instructions, the students can create a compelling and fascinating new world.

Cameras themselves are motivators. They are tools to be used for artistic expression. In the classroom, plan time for the students to experiment with looking through the viewfinder. Discuss the parts of the camera, how to decide when to take a picture, when to click the shutter, and how to adjust and focus a lens. These are important preliminary steps.

[1]Snapshooter Cameras Co., P.O. Box 16225, Philadelphia, Pennsylvania, 19114.

Plan opportunities for handling the camera to discover its parts. Demonstrate how to load and unload film. Teach the following vocabulary in order to be able to discuss photography.

Aperture: The opening in the camera lens where the light enters.

Blueprint Paper: A commercial drafting paper used in this textbook for making images.

Camera: An instrument with a lens and shutter used for taking pictures. An inexpensive camera for classroom use is one with a fixed lens and shutter used for ordinary picture-taking conditions. The lens has been adjusted and fixed for an average focus of about 12 to 15 feet. The lens opening (aperture) is also fixed at an average of F/11, which is for average sunny light. The shutter speed is approximately one thirtieth of a second, so that any moving subject will blur. There are many types of more complex cameras on the market that are designed to provide differences in focus, distance, light conditions, and shutter speeds. Other kinds of cameras are 35 mm, reflex, and either the single-lens or twin lens.

Contrast: The difference in lights and darks found in a negative, print, drawing, or painting.

Diazo Prints: Another inexpensive drafting paper that, when exposed to sunlight, causes the dyes in the paper to change. Where objects obstruct the light, the paper does not fade. It is used in offices for duplicating machines, and is available in several colors.

Diffused Light: Light that scatters in all directions.

Dry Mounting: One way to mount photographs is on a board with heat and *dry mounting tissue.* The tissue is a thin, wax-coated (on both sides) paper that sticks to a surface when heat is applied. The tissue is usually placed in between the photograph and mounting surface, joining all the surfaces.

Emulsion: The shiny side of paper or film that has a light-sensitive coating. The coating is a gelatin containing silver halide crystals.

Exposure: The time when light is applied to light-sensitive material. The time will vary, depending on the light intensity.

F-stop: The aperture size indicated by an F-number. The larger the opening, the smaller the number. In simple cameras, the F-stop is fixed and not adjustable.

Lens: A glass or transparent plastic material made with two opposing surfaces. These surfaces change the direction of the light rays, causing them to meet at a place on the film. The lens is classified as to the way it bends the rays of light.

Montage: A design made of pictures or parts of pictures used to express an idea or impression.

Negative: An exposed image on film, glass, or plastic that is then used to make any number of prints. The lights and darks in the negative are the reverse of those in the subject or finished print.

Positive Print: A print that reproduces the original tones of the subject.

Shutter: A device on the camera for opening and closing the aperture of a lens in order to expose the film.

Slide: A developed film used as a negative. The image slide is used in a projector and projected on a wall, or it can be used as a negative to produce colored prints.

Synchronization: An exact correlation between sounds such as on tape or record, or live sounds to visual images, as in a film. Or when a flash bulb goes off at the exact time that the shutter opens.

Tones or Values: The degrees of light and dark within an image.

Toning: Adding color to prints by using pens, inks, vegetable color, or watercolors, or by placing the print into a toning bath.

Translucent: Semitransparent; light passes through a substance, but is diffused.

Transparent: Anything that is perfectly clear.

Viewfinder: A small, rectangular glass window in the camera that indicates to the viewer the image the camera will photograph.

13–4 *Exposing objects on blueprint paper under a sunlamp.*

THE BLUEPRINT, DIAZO, OR OZALID PRINT

Inexpensive reproducing papers are available from drafting supply houses. The papers have color emulsions of blue, red, brown, pink, green, or black, with blue and black being the most common. Diazo was developed in Germany and was introduced in the United States at about the time of World War II. Diazo is the name of the paper; ozalid is the name of the machine used with it. The paper is available in large sizes and in 50-yard rolls.

Procedure (See Figure 13–4.)
1. Store the paper in the package until you are ready to use it.
2. Place the objects to be printed (or draw designs on transparent acetate paper) on the paper.
3. Expose the paper outside to the sunlight for about 1 minute. The color of the paper will begin to change.
4. Remove the objects and place the exposed paper on a wire screen over a plastic tray that contains 1 cup of household ammonia. (Be careful not to let the ammonia touch the paper. The fumes from the ammonia will rise and react chemically with the emulsion in the paper, causing the

13–5 *A blueprint example using silhouette forms from nature.*

13–6 *Sandwich a variety of transparent materials between acetate papers held together with paper slide mounts or plastic tape. Then project for super dynamic designs and as painting motivations.*

lines to appear in color against a white background.) If the paper is cut in small sizes, place the pieces in a glass or jar that has a little ammonia on bottom. Crinkle up some aluminum foil and place it over the ammonia so that the paper does not come in direct contact with the ammonia. Cover this with a jar lid. (Use with blueprint or diazo paper.)

5. Or cover the tray with a glass plate to hold in the fumes. Developing only takes a few minutes.
6. The print is a positive print. (Engineers and draftsmen use this paper to make reproductions from original drawings on any type of transparent paper. You can make any number of prints in the same way.)
7. Always follow safety precautions when using ammonia.

Note: Blueprint paper can also be exposed in the sunlight for about 1 minute. The paper coating is light-sensitive; where the light hits it, it hardens. The hardened areas will not wash off. After exposing the paper, rinse it in clear water first and then in a preparation that is half diluted bleach and half water. Rinse it again in clear water and dry it. The bleach causes the hardened areas to turn strong colors. The resulting image is a negative one, with light shapes (washed away) against colored backgrounds. Any object can be used during exposure. One teacher has students lie on the paper during exposure to print their silhouettes. Any objects mentioned in the other procedures described can be used as well. The paper is available in sheets or rolls and various colors including fluorescent shades.

Slide Art

Slide art, or creating slides without a camera, is fascinating to all students. Projecting these slide creations on a screen works well for large or small groups. Constructing slides from transparent and opaque "found" materials, turning them into intense, brilliant slides, and projecting them into a superscale color environment can be an exciting art motivation. The viewer interprets these abstract concepts and responds by contributing all sorts of imaginative possibilities into the design meaning and mood. Class discussions of color, mood quality, texture, shape, and composition will be dynamic as a result. Light, and the components of light, such as refraction and reflection, are factors involved in color perception. Moods are forceful and invite such questions as "How does color influence our feelings?" and "Does this remind you of a story? Of a stained glass window?" "Do you see abstract forms in the slides?" "How do we use these colors in our lives?" "How does nature use color?" "How does color change in nature? In seasons? In time of day?" "Do you know any artists who paint from slides?"

When relating art topics to each other—for example, the painting experience—view the slides and share impressions and feelings. Then discuss color, forms, textures, pattern, compositions, space, and light. Next, use the slides to stimulate ideas for watercolor painting. The loose, flowing slide images are easily transposed into watercolor paintings. This project further expands the students' insights into design and composition.

Slide presentations can be combined successfully with the related performing arts. For instances, slides are enhanced by showing them against a background of music—classical, rock, country, or western. After viewing the slides, students can write improvised stories about what they saw and how the slides made them feel. Movement, dance, masks, and costumes offer even more opportunities to relate the arts to each other. Improvisational movements are especially effective when performed in front of these giant images. Try combining media such as using two overlapping slides, or using a slide projector next to an overhead projector. Combine strobe lights and mirrored balls. The possibilities are endless.

Supplies Needed
slide projector
acetate paper or clear food wrap
narrow masking tape
colored cellophane
colored gelatin sheets, cut into strips or shapes (or softened in water for several minutes and fastened to a clear-film backing)
felt-tip pens (permanent)
Pelican acetate inks and pens or brushes
acrylic paints thinned with water
threads, lace, hairs, onion skins, and feathers
clear Con-Tact paper

13–7 *Produce your own slides. Ektagraphics are specially coated slides that can be drawn on with ordinary felt-tip pens. The center eye and the slide to its right are made with a colored photograph lifted with Con-Tact paper. The two slides at bottom left are glass slides painted with Cryst-L-Craze paints in various colors. The slide at bottom right is a slide mount with two pieces of acetate, and sandwiched between the acetate are tissue papers, vegetable coloring, and felt-tip pen designs.*

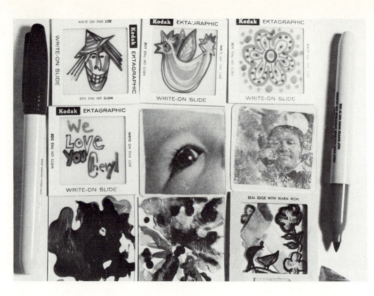

13–8 *Drawing his own face on a T-shirt, this student uses permanent pens and his facial proportions from a slide. Use this method also with slides of designs and lettering, projecting the letters to make banners, posters, and bulletin boards.*

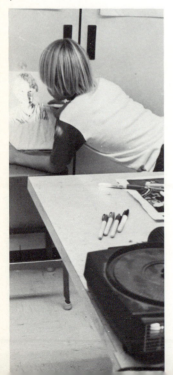

scissors
tape: clear, colored, patterned
floor dust
salt
tissue papers (colors)
Vaseline
rub-on letters and symbols
nylons
slide mounts, or coin mounts (cardboard, glass, or plastic)
single-hole paper punch
vegetable coloring
rubber cement or white glue
old negatives (burn with a match or scratch with a scissors if desired)
bleach, cotton swabs
Cryst-L-Craze paint, glass stain
thin transparent and translucent objects (opaque objects do not project the light)

Procedure (See Figure 13–7.)

1. Decide on the type of slide mounts you will use: masking tape wrapped around two pieces of clear acetate; commercial glass, cardboard, or plastic mounts available in photography shops used with acetate or clear food wrap; or commercial coin holders fitted with cellophane or acetate paper (which lie flat on the surface like an open book).
2. Select two pieces of acetate; they can both be clear, or one can be colored.
3. Tape the pieces of acetate together on one edge to form a hinge effect (to have them open like a book). Use narrow tape to allow more of the slide to be viewed.

4. Paint or draw on the surface of the acetate. (Experiment by combining materials: draw with felt-tip pens and paint, or draw with Pelican inks, glass stain, or drop-on vegetable coloring.)
5. Paint and draw on both inside sides of the acetate. This technique will produce overlays of color when the sides are projected together.
6. Or use colored pens on old negatives. (Bleach will remove any of the film not wanted on the negative.)
7. Or use collage techniques on the slides: use tissue papers, threads, feathers, colored acetates, hairs, lace, rub-on letters and symbols, adhesive-backed transparent colored tapes, screen, netting, found objects, floor dust, or fine grass. Add colored gelatins, Vaseline (which melts and moves when near the lamp heat), salt granules, and vegetable coloring.
8. Rearrange forms, shapes, and textures until they please you. Overlap tissues and acetate papers to get unusual colors. Whenever needed, use a very small amount of glue to glue the materials down.
9. Fold over, sandwich in, and tape together the remaining three edges of the acetate (with narrow strips of masking tape).
10. Your slide is now finished and ready to be projected.

Note: When making a vinyl paper slide place the vinyl paper slide on an acetate sheet and mount it in a slide mount.

Magic with Overhead Light Projectors

Exciting spatial and visual experiences can be created with an overhead projector. Improvisation, invention, and practice will improve the quality and expressiveness of your presentation. All procedures are accomplished with the acetates, drawings, plates, oils, and paints placed on the flat surface of the lighted overhead projector. Try these alone or in combination for some startling visual effects.

Combine these visual effects with humorous comic book stories, a favorite poem, a story, a fantasy dream. These experiences will motivate students to create written or oral stories and paintings.

Also, combine these effects with slides, films, and body movements (dance). Music, whether improvised or planned, always adds to the enjoyment of magic light.

Project images on a wall; a screen; or, for variation, on

13–9 *During a workshop, teachers experiment with assembling visuals to present their own light show. On the overhead projector rests a dish containing water, oils, tissue paper, and vegetable coloring. Under the dish is a felt-tip pen drawing on clear acetate. This image is superimposed on a slide image.*

large, air-filled plastic balloons. Another variation is to present the image on a large hanging sheet of translucent plastic that is hung like a banner. If you project the light from the back of the plastic, the image can be seen on the front. Try inventing large and various forms with the plastic by filling it with air and sealing the shapes with a heated iron. Suspend these plastic shapes on threads from above, and the forms will move in the air while images are projected on them (use plastic garbage bags to form pillows). Create a visual world of your own.

Supplies Needed
projector
2 glass pie plates
mineral oil
food coloring or colored inks
pens and brushes
colored tissue papers and cellophane
overhead projector acetates
glue
straws
liquid soap
plastic wrap
fizzies
rubber cement
floating objects

494

Procedure

1. Place some colored oil or a cup of colored water in the bottom of a glass pie plate.
2. Drop colored inks into the water (if water is used).
3. Place the second pie plate over the first.
4. Move and turn the plates to see the colors mix.
5. If dark oil is placed in the pie plate, scratch through the oil with nails or straws to create designs.
6. Use two projectors and overlap the colors.
7. Or place colored tissues on the bottom of a pie plate and then add water.
8. Or add fizzies, liquid soap, or floating objects to the water in the plate for unusual visual effects.
9. Create transparent flat pictures by cutting shapes out of colored cellophane. Glue these onto clear acetate sheets.
10. Draw abstract forms on the acetate sheets with pens and inks or permanent felt-tip pens. Draw comic strip characters, costumed figures, space creatures, or favorite stories, for example.
11. Glue a transparent straw to the acetate drawing and hold the straw to make the drawing move.

Moving Pictures

If you were to draw a red dot in the corner of every right-hand page in this book, each placed slightly differently from the others, and then flip the corners, you would see the dots dance. That is the principle of moving pictures: the pictures are sequential with just a slight variation in each.

13–10 *Moving pictures are fun. This animated film (Super 8) shows Cheryl Linderman drawing the picture "Don't Smoke in This House."*

13–11 *Drawing on 16 mm film with permanent felt-tip pens is one introductory experience to explain animation. There are two basic approaches. In the first approach, each frame has a drawing on it with the action changing slightly in each frame. In the second; lines, dots, and designs are drawn along the film as shown in the photograph.*

DRAWING ON FILM OR FILMSTRIPS

The same principle is applied to 16 mm film by drawing simple sequential designs in each frame: changing dots, zigzags, straight lines, curving lines, or little figures; or, with felt-tip pens, draw linear designs that move from frame to frame. Norman McLaren is credited with having originated this form of animation in 1948 in a film called *Fiddle De Dee.*

Tape some favorite piano-roll music and play it with your drawn film. View the films after they have been completed and discuss the designs, movement, and patterns created. These first ideas will lead you to explore more film-making adventures.

Supplies Needed
old 16 mm film (from the school movie lab)
household bleach
felt-tip pens or pen and inks
Cryst-L-Craze glass stain, brush
16 mm film projector
splicing machine

Procedure
1. Immerse the 16 mm film or filmstrip into a container of regular household bleach. Let it soak for a few minutes until most of the emulsion is off the film.
2. Rinse the film with cool water and let it dry.

3. Another approach is to use cotton swabs that have been dipped in bleach on selected areas so that some of the original picture and sound remain.
4. Lay the film out on a large table or across several desks in one long strip. If a splicing machine is available, each student can work on a long piece of film—about 3 feet long—and then later the 16 mm strips can be spliced together.
5. Draw on the film or filmstrip with permanent felt-tip pens, dyes, or inks and pens; or, cover the film with a coat of black ink and lightly scratch through a design with a sharp nail or scissors. (Or, scratch through film leader.)
6. For unusual effects in texture, glue floor dust on the design. Or, paint on Cryst-L-Craze glass stain as a finish for a snowflakelike visual effect (available in colors at hobby shops).

Video Camera Workshop

An extension of the still camera, the video camera incorporates movement and sound. This camera is being used more and more as an academic tool as it becomes cheaper. The new cameras can accomplish such things as "manipulation animation," "video-dub," and other capabilities offering many sophisticated production techniques for home and school production.

With the emphasis on electronic equipment today, we find school districts acquiring one-half-inch color video cameras in various ways (professional television uses three-quarter-inch video tape). For instance, the Phoenix Elementary Schools have a studio set up in their classes for gifted students. In Sacaton, Arizona, the middle school has a closed circuit television system and each day the students write and produce a newscast for their schools. Everywhere, video workshops are being held for students and teachers to illustrate how to use the equipment, what it can do for them, and the various possibilities of employing it within the school. In another school, teachers teach music, art, and literature employing the camera. The students do background reading, then write skits and episodes, draw storyboards and graphics to tell the story, and write, perform, and select music for the production. Episodes in American history, agriculture, inventions, literature, space exploration, television commercials, television programming, holidays, pageants, and unusual events are used. These exercises help students learn to become critical of not only their own work but also of their personal television viewing.

The camera can also be used to tape visitors to the classroom, such as artists discussing their own work, teacher demonstrations, and discussion groups. Animation can also be used as a teaching device, such as videotaping drawings on a blackboard of how a plant grows. The shaping of clay figures, taping puppet shows, and showing the creation of a collage are other examples.

VIDEO CAMERA TERMS

Camera Techniques:

Dolly: to move the entire camera toward or away from an object by means of its mobile tripod or base.

Pan: To move the camera left or right without moving the base of the camera.

Pedestal up/down (also known as "booming up or down"): to move the entire camera up or down with an electric or manual boom.

Roll or "rack" focus: to bring an object into focus or take it out of focus by manipulating the focus.

Tilt: to move the camera lens up toward the ceiling (tilt up) or down toward the floor (tilt down).

Truck: to move the entire camera, including the base, left or right, parallel to the plane of action.

Zoom: a change in focussing the lens without moving the camera, which gives the effect of moving either toward or away from an object.

Editing Techniques

Cut: an instantaneous transition from one scene to another.

Dissolve: the overlapping fade-out of one picture and fade-in of another. (Sometimes indicates a lapse of time.)

Fade: to diminish volume of sound or brightness of picture (fade to black).

Camera Set-ups and Special Effects

CU: Close-up shot. Also, "MCU"—medium close-up, "ECU"—Extreme close-up.

Key: electronically inserting one source of video into another (i.e., keying a logo over another background, also called "supering").

LS: long-shot. Full view of set or background.

Two shot: often printed "2-shot." A shot where two persons are seen.

WS: wide shot.

Photography Bibliography

AVEDON, RICHARD. *Observations.* New York: Simon & Schuster, Inc., 1959.

BOURKE, MARGARET. *Portrait of Myself.* New York: Simon & Schuster, Inc., 1963.

BURGNER, JACK W. "Elementary Filmmaking." *School Arts,* **69** (Feb. 1970), 20–23.

———. "Film Production Is Now." *Arts and Activities,* **68** (Jan. 1971), 32–35.

CARTIER-BRESSON, HENRI. *The World of Henri Cartier-Bresson.* New York: The Viking Press, Inc., 1968.

CROY, OTTO R. *Design by Photography.* New York: Focal Press, 1963.

CYR, DON. "Accidental Art: A Photographic Interpretation." *Arts and Activities,* **71** (Feb. 1972).

———. "Photography and the Education of Vision." *School Arts,* **68** (Oct. 1968) 39–41.

EASTMAN KODAK. *Movies and Slides Without a Camera,* Rochester, N.Y.: 1972.

FEININGER, ANDREAS. *The Complete Photographer.* Englewood Cliffs, N.J.: Prentice-Hall, Inc., 1966.

GERNSHEIM, HELMUT. *Creative Photography: Aesthetic Trends 1839–1960.* London: Faber & Faber Ltd., 1962.

HOLTER, PATRA. *Photography Without a Camera.* New York: Van Nostrand Reinhold Company, 1972.

JAMES, PHILIP. "Making Film Strips." *Schools Arts,* **68** (Feb. 1969), 36–37.

MEISELAS, SUSAN. *Learn to See.* Cambridge, Mass.: Polaroid Corporation, 1974.

NEWHALL, BEAUMONT. *The History of Photography from 1839 to the Present Day.* New York: Museum of Modern Art, 1964.

RHODE, ROBERT B., AND FLOYD H. MCCALL. *Introduction to Photography.* 2nd ed. New York: Macmillan Publishing Co., Inc., 1971.

SIMON, MICHAEL, AND DENNIS MOORE. *First Lessons in Black and White Photography.* New York: Holt, Rinehart and Winston, Inc., 1978.

STEICHEN, EDWARD. *The Family of Man.* New York: Simon & Schuster, Inc., 1955.

SZARKOWSKI, JOHN. *The Photographer's Eye.* Garden City, N.Y.: Doubleday & Company, Inc., 1966.

TOWLER, J. *The Silver Sunbeam.* Facsimile edition. Hastings-on-Hudson, N.Y.: Morgan & Morgan, 1969.

WESTON, EDWARD. *My Camera on Point Lobos.* Boston: Houghton Mifflin Company, 1950.

Working cords, for macrame, 300
Wrapping process, for macrame, 305
Wrought metal work, 405–406
WS, for video cameras, 498

Xylophone, 380

Yarn
  baskets woven from, 296–298
  burlap stitching with, 226–228
  crocheting with, 250–251
  dispensing, 255
  dolls from, 177, 238–239
  intermediate grades and, 32
  jewelry from, 414–416, 444
  metallic, 265
  mobiles from, 253–254
  pictures from, 251–253
  pom-poms, 223
  primary grades and, 27
  tassels, 222
  upper intermediate grades and, 36
  see also Needlework; Stitchery; Weaving; Wood

Z-twisted yarn, 267
Zigrosser, Carl, 449
Zoom, for video cameras, 498
Zuni Indians, jewelry of, 402–403, 405